FROMMER'S

COMPREHENSIVE TRAVEL GUIDE

MAUI
1ST EDITION

by Lisa M. Legarde

MACMILLAN • USA

About the Author:

Lisa Legarde was born in New Orleans and graduated from Wellesley College with a B.A. in English. She has traveled extensively in Europe and North America and is author or co-author of 12 Frommer Guides.

Macmillan Travel
A Prentice Hall Macmillan Company
15 Columbus Circle
New York, NY 10023

ISBN 0-671-87152-8
ISSN 1076-2817

Design by Robert Bull Design
Maps by Ortelius Design

SPECIAL SALES

Bulk purchases (10+ copies) of Frommer's Travel Guides are available to corporations at special discounts. The Special Sales Department can produce custom editions to be used as premiums and/or for sales promotion to suit individual needs. Existing editions can be produced with custom cover imprints such as corporate logos. For more information write to: Special Sales, Prentice Hall, 15 Columbus Circle, New York, NY 10023.

Manufactured in the United States of America

CONTENTS

LIST OF MAPS

ACKNOWLEDGMENTS

For the past six months I've been buried under a pile of Maui brochures, hotel press kits, restaurant menus, and hundreds of semi-edited pages. I've finally managed to dig myself out, and I'd like to thank my friends who have all waited patiently (sometimes threateningly) for me to emerge from my office with its eggplant-colored walls and endless piles of papers, books, and empty Diet Coke bottles. Thanks to Marilyn Wood and Leanne Coupe for their support and understanding; Joan and Jim Lonergan who pushed me along, dragged me out of the house on occasion, and generally helped keep me laughing; Rena, Heather, Karestan, Allison, Doug, and Dave, just for being there. Thanks to my family for not holding a grudge when I was grumpy. Thanks especially to Susan (my safety net), and one green and one blue sock (my muse).

In addition, I'd like to thank those Mauians who proved to be indispensable (not to mention incredibly amusing)—Linda, Georja, Michelle, Cynthia, and Bonnie. Thanks also to all the people of Maui whose names I don't have room to list for helping me along with warm Maui aloha during my travels around the island.

Finally, I'd like to thank my cat, Emma, whose incredible displays of patience gave me the daily inspiration to press on.

ABOUT THIS FROMMER GUIDE

What is a Frommer Guide? It's a comprehensive, easy-to-use guide to the best travel values in all price ranges—from very expensive to budget. The one guidebook to take along on any trip.

WHAT THE SYMBOLS MEAN

FROMMER'S FAVORITES—hotels, restaurants, attractions, and entertainments you should not miss

SUPER-SPECIAL VALUES—really exceptional values

FROMMER'S SMART TRAVELER TIPS—hints on how to secure the best value for your money

IN HOTEL AND OTHER LISTINGS

The following symbols refer to the standard amenities available in all rooms:

A/C air conditioning   TEL telephone   TV television

The following abbreviations are used for credit cards:

AE American Express	DISC Discover	MC MasterCard
CB Carte Blanche	ER enRoute	V Visa
DC Diners Club	JCB Card Japan	

TRIP PLANNING WITH THIS GUIDE

Use the following features:

What Things Cost in . . . to help you plan your daily budget
Calendar of Events . . . to plan for or avoid
Suggested Itineraries . . . for seeing the island and towns
What's Special About Checklist . . . a summary of the island's highlights—which lets you check off those that appeal most to you
Easy-to-Read Maps . . . towns, attractions, hotel locations—all referring to or keyed to the text
Fast Facts . . . all the essentials at a glance: embassies, emergencies, information, safety and more

OTHER SPECIAL FROMMER FEATURES

Cool for Kids—hotels, restaurants, and attractions

INTRODUCING MAUI

Maui is at once multicultural, multihued, and multifaceted. A clear, crisp turquoise surrounds the island; deep, fresh greens color the landscapes of Maui's tropical rain forests; parched reds, browns, blacks, and golds are the hues of the island's beaches and "desert" flatlands; and faces of almost every color and ethnicity complete the picture that makes Maui unique among the islands of the world. These are the images that no visitor to Maui is likely to forget.

Kahului (Central Maui), where most people deplane and pick up their rental cars, has been the center of trade and business activity since Maui became an active participant in trade with the Europeans in the late 18th and early 19th centuries. Today, it is still the center of commerce and home to most of the island's shopping malls and fast-food restaurants. Just a few miles west from Kahului you'll find the old historic whaling town of Lahaina, its streets lined with art galleries and T-shirt shops, and the beautiful white-sand beaches of Kaanapali and Kapalua. A trip Upcountry on the slopes of Haleakala Crater (the island's dormant volcano) will bring cooler temperatures, lush tropical greenery, an abundance of herb and vegetable farms, and Maui's paniolos (cowboys).

A bumpy road of switchbacks and one-lane bridges will take you along the Maui coastline and up to Hana, the island's own private paradise. Sparsely populated, Hana is a tropical rain forest where you'll find such natural wonders as Ohe'o Gulch (a series of waterfalls and freshwater pools), the Venus Pool (an unforgettable blue pool), and even black- and red-sand beaches. Haleakala Crater will present you with yet another geographical landscape whose cinder cones give it something of a lunar quality. Until you see them for yourself, it seems almost inconceivable that these varied landscapes exist simultaneously within only 729 square miles.

1. GEOGRAPHY & ECOLOGY

GEOGRAPHY

In the Hawaiian chain, whose volcanic mountain range covers an area of about 1,500 miles under the Pacific, there are 122 islands of which eight are major islands: Niihau, Kauai, Oahu, Molokai, Lanai, Kahoolawe, Maui, and Hawaii. With a land area of 729 square miles, Maui is the second largest of the Hawaiian islands. In addition to the large islands there are scores of other islets and shoals in the Hawaiian

WHAT'S SPECIAL ABOUT MAUI

Beaches

- ☐ Kaanapali (or "Dig Me") Beach, located in front of a strip of resort hotels, is a gorgeous stretch of white sand where locals and tourists alike gather to sun and swim, and see and be seen.
- ☐ Hamoa Beach, located not far from the town of Hana, was Mark Twain's favorite beach.
- ☐ Makena Beach. You'll make your choice between the secluded Big and Little beaches depending on what you're planning, or not planning, to wear.
- ☐ Ho'okipa Beach Park, where the swimming isn't the best but the windsurfing is spectacular.
- ☐ Kapalua Beach (Fleming Beach), lovely for snorkeling and swimming.
- ☐ Red Sand Beach and the beach at Waianapanapa near Hana, two of the island's most beautiful and least populated beaches.

Great Towns and Villages

- ☐ Lahaina, where historic buildings stand side by side with art galleries and some of the island's best restaurants.
- ☐ Makawao, a small, Upcountry cowboy town with quaint shops, excellent eateries, and endless amounts of charm.
- ☐ Paia, one of Maui's last hippie hold-outs; the shops are funky and the restaurants are excellent and inexpensive.

- ☐ Hana, one of Maui's smallest, most remote, and most beautiful towns.

Natural Wonders

- ☐ Humpback whales, frolicking offshore each year from late November to early May.
- ☐ Mount Haleakala, a 10,023-foot dormant volcano that supports a unique population of flora and fauna and offers the most spectacular vista on the island.

Historic Buildings

- ☐ Baldwin House, built in the 1830's and once home to Dr. Dwight Baldwin, Hawaii's first doctor.
- ☐ Wo Hing Temple, built in 1912, was the historic meeting place for the resident Chinese population; it was restored by the Lahaina Restoration Foundation and reopened in 1984.
- ☐ Hale Hoikeike, built between 1833 and 1850 and now one of Maui's most informative museums.

Events and Festivals

- ☐ Halloween, drawing visitors come from all over the world for Lahaina's annual Halloween parade.
- ☐ Run to the Sun, a 37-mile marathon from sea level to the top of Mount Haleakala.
- ☐ Molokai to Oahu Canoe Race, in which men's and women's teams navigate Hawaiian canoes across the treacherous Kaiwi Channel.

---

archipelago. Hawaii enjoys its isolated position in the Pacific at a distance of 2,000 miles southwest of San Francisco and 2,400 miles from Japan.

If you're wondering how the Hawaiian islands came to be so far from any of the major landmasses, given that most islands are pieces of larger landmasses that have broken off as the earth shifted, these islands were formed as a result of volcanic eruptions. This may conjure images of mountains spewing hot molten lava, or islands springing up from the ocean floor in a wild, fiery explosion, but it didn't exactly happen that way. Volcanoes did erupt on the ocean floor, but it took millions of years for the hardened layers of lava to build the enormous mountains and volcanoes we see above the ocean's surface today. Present-day Maui originated as two separate volcanoes, but as Haleakala erupted time and time again lava filled the ocean between the two islands and they became one.

Maui is 48 miles long and 26 miles wide at its widest point; there are 120 linear miles of shoreline and 81 accessible beaches. The island's highest peak, Mount Haleakala, rises to a height of 10,023 feet and is the largest dormant volcano in the world. Haleakala was once higher, but about 3,000 feet have been washed away by the constant erosive action of rainwater. Haleakala has been dormant since the end of the 18th century.

ECOLOGY

Today, as you drive around the island, you'll see any number of tropical flowers, trees, shrubs, grasses, and animals on Maui, but when the Hawaiian island chain emerged from the ocean it was absolutely devoid of plant and animal life. Because of its remote location and unsupportive terrain, it took millions of years for Hawaii to grow into the tropical paradise you see today.

Some of the birds that were able to make the 2,400-mile trip to the islands may have left behind the predators and diseases that populated their homelands, but they were entering a territory that had very little to offer them in the way of food and shelter. Because there were no trees, most of the birds about which ornithologists have been able to gather definitive information adapted as ground-nesting species and had virtually nothing to fear until the arrival of humans. It is interesting to note that scientists have recently discovered that as few as 15 original colonist birds accounted for the approximately 110 endemic species that have been either recorded or discovered in the form of fossils to date. About 40 of those were extinct before the first Westerner, Captain Cook, even arrived.

The Polynesians, the first human colonists, brought dogs, pigs, and rats with them, and the ground-nesting birds had little or no protection against attack by these foreign predators. It is also likely that the Polynesians eradicated some species when they killed the birds for the feathers to make cloaks, leis, and helmets. After the arrival of the Europeans two hundred years ago, it is believed that another 22 species became extinct due to the importation of diseases against which the birds had no protection. Still later, when the rat problem on Maui became unbearable, the mongoose was imported in hopes that it would eradicate the rat population. Unfortunately, the rat and the mongoose live on different schedules—the rat is nocturnal; the mongoose goes about its business during the daylight hours, and never the twain shall meet. Instead of killing rats, the mongoose wreaked havoc on the island's ground-nesting birds. The mongoose, along with feral pigs and dogs, still inhabit the island. It is very likely that you'll see a mongoose or two during your travels around the island, but your chances of coming across a wild dog or pig are very slim unless you're planning on doing some serious hiking.

Many of the birds that landed on the islands, whether they were able to adapt and evolve or not, played a role in the development of Hawaiian plant life because they often carried seeds with them. You might think it impossible for seeds to grow on the barren lava flows—if the wind didn't blow them into the sea, they were likely to be eaten by the very vehicle that carried them to the islands in the first place. Amazingly enough though, some seeds fell into the protective cracks and crevices of the lava, and were able to take root. When the Polynesians arrived they brought other plant life with them. Later, "exotic tropicals" were imported from tropical America, Asia, and Australia. The result has been 960 native and 5,000 imported species. It is on these islands that you will find some of the most interesting plant life on the planet today.

The native flora also has its mammalian enemies, one of which is the feral goat. This vegetarian creature has become such a problem that park services on the slopes of Haleakala have had to fence off certain areas to keep the goats from killing off the vegetation.

FLORA   While visiting Maui you're bound to come across some plants and flowers you've never seen before. Below you'll find descriptions of several different common native species.

Gingers Because of their numbers, one might assume that gingers are native to the islands, but they were imported from Asia or Polynesia. When you first think about ginger you'll probably think of the ginger root you buy at the market, but that form of ginger is actually what's known as a "specialized stem" and it's very different from the beautiful, fragrant blossoms you'll find all over the island.

Ginger blossoms are delicate, like roses or freesias; the "petals" are not petals at all—they are "bracts," which are actually stamens, or the male reproductive part of the flower. The blossoms are protected by the bracts and can only be seen if you look down among them. Red ginger, the bracts of which are spiky and grow in an upward direction (something like an upside-down pine cone), can be seen almost anywhere on Maui. Red ginger blooms can reach up to one foot in length and will last for several weeks after they're cut. My personal favorite, white (or yellow) ginger has the most divine scent and is often used in the making of delicate and extremely fragrant leis. An interesting fact about this particular form of ginger is that the flowers are actually hermaphrodites—that is, the flower is made up of both male and female parts. Each flower has three petal-like stamen and three long, thin petals. The female part of the flower is green and is located on the stamen. You might see white ginger growing wild in Hana or along waterways on other parts of the island. If you can't get to Hana and would rather just sit on the beach at Kaanapali or Wailea, you can always pick up a ginger lei at the florist.

Another variety of ginger that you're likely to spot on your way up to Hana is shell ginger, called 'awapuhi-luheluhe, or "drooping ginger," by the Hawaiians. It hails from Southeast Asia, and looks a bit like a small bunch of grapes. Its stems are tall, and the blossoms curve downward. When shell ginger blossoms, it produces small, bright, yellow and red flowers.

Amidst 15-foot bamboo-like stalks you might be lucky enough to find 3- to 6-foot-tall plants, the tops of which are decorated with large, deep pink torch ginger blooms. The blossoms, whose shape is reminiscent of the fire of a lighted torch, have an almost artificial appearance.

Heliconias There are between 200 and 400 species of heliconia in existence, and they fall into two major categories—erect and pendant. The leaves of all heliconias grow directly up from the ground, rather than from a stem or trunk, and the brightly colored bracts (yellow, red, green, orange, and combinations thereof), which overlap as they climb upward (or downward if it's pendant), hold small flowers that you may not even see if you don't look closely. No doubt you'll notice their waxy forms everywhere you go on Maui. Some of the red ones have been aptly named "lobster claws." The rainbow heliconia is a spectacular sight. The green-edged yellow bracts with a blush of red at the center are quite beautiful.

Heliconias of the pendant variety hang upside-down. The hanging lobster claw is fairly prevalent on Maui, and can be identified by the lowest bracts that look even more like lobster claws than the erect variety. From a distance the hanging lobster claw looks like a hanging caterpillar with a wide red stripe down the center of its back and narrow yellow stripes on either side.

Once you've identified one type of heliconia, you'll have no trouble identifying others. To make it a little easier you might consider purchasing one of the tropical flower books I've mentioned at the end of this chapter.

Birds of Paradise You'll recognize the orange bird of paradise with its tall stalks, purple and red "head," orange crest, and blue "beak." The leaves are paddle shaped and are recognized by their red central veins.

The white bird of paradise is less commonly seen. Its white flowers grow out of a bluish-purple sheath on a small palm-like tree and are often coated in a sticky substance, which makes it somewhat unappealing. If you purchase a white bird of paradise from a florist, the sticky stuff will have been cleaned off.

Other Flora Named for French navigator Louis A. de Bougainville, bougainvillea can be found all over the island. They're often planted in hotel flower boxes, and

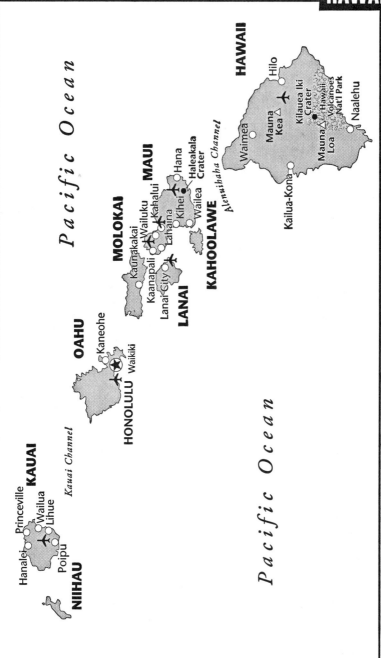

HAWAII

Pacific Ocean

0 ━━━━━ 50 km
31 mi

HAWAII

Hilo
Kilauea Iki
Crater
Waimea
Mauna
Kea △
Hawaii
Volcanoes
Nat'l Park
Naalehu
Mauna △
Loa
Kailua-Kona

Alenuihaha Channel

MAUI
Hana
Haleakala
Crater
Wailuku
Kahalui
Kihei
Wailea
Lahaina
Kaanapali
Kaumakakai
MOLOKAI
Lanai City
LANAI
KAHOOLAWE

Pacific Ocean

OAHU
Kaneohe
Waikiki
HONOLULU

KAUAI
Princeville
Wailua
Lihue
Hanalei
Poipu
NIIHAU

Kauai Channel

Pacific Ocean

Airport ✈

6954

their paper-thin crimson or purple blossoms are sometimes used in the making of leis, although they don't last long off the stem and quickly lose their color.

The 4- to 5-foot-high heart-shaped leaves of the ape (pronounced "ah-pay") hide large, odd-looking white flowers that grow upward and shelter a white spadix (a clublike stalk bearing tiny flowers). They don't have a pleasant smell, but their juices are said to take away the sting of nettles. You can find these flowers in the Iao Valley along the sides of the footpath that leads to the overlook.

If you're Upcountry and take a trip to the Kula Botanical Gardens (see Chapter 7 for more information) you might be lucky enough to get a glimpse of the cup of gold flower on a large bush to the right of the parking area. The cup of gold is a relative of the potato, and can climb to approximately 60 feet in height. Its blossoms reach up to 9 inches in length and last for about four days on the stem. While in bud the flowers are a cream color, and as they mature they change to gold and then finally to apricot just before they fall from their stems. They have a lovely smell, but if you put your nose inside the cup of gold it'll come out covered with pollen.

You'll see orchids just about everywhere on the island. They come in all different shapes, sizes, and varieties, and you're likely to find them dropped in your tropical drink, placed on your pillow at evening turndown service, and used as a garnish at dinner.

On the drive up to Hana you should watch for the red blossoms of the African tulip tree. The flowers, which bloom only a couple at a time, do so around a central core of buds. The bud core releases blooms continually throughout the year.

One of my favorite trees is the angel's trumpet. The Hawaiian name for the tree is *nana honua*, which means "looking to the earth." The flowers, which can be up to 10 inches in length, look like miniature white trumpets and give off a musky scent. Each of the flowers looks as though it's been hung on the tree by human hand. There's an angel's trumpet tree just in front of the Kula Lodge and Restaurant. *Note:* If you've got children in tow, make sure they don't put the flowers in their mouths. They contain a narcotic and are poisonous when eaten.

Another tree you might be lucky enough to see in full bloom (also at the Kula Lodge) is the jacaranda. Its light blue blossoms are a welcome change from the bright, flashy colors of other tropical flowers on the island. The small bell-shaped flowers bloom in clusters at branch ends, and the leaves look like tiny ferns.

As you walk the grounds of your hotel you'll probably be greeted by the fresh, sweet scent that comes from the plumeria blossom (also known as frangipani). The five-petaled flower is the one most commonly used in the making of leis. If you pick one from the rhododendron-like shrub you'll notice the flower's central hole, which makes it perfect for lei making. The white blossoms seem to have a stronger scent than the yellow, pink, and cerise varieties. For a long time Hawaiians refused to make leis with the plumeria flower because the shrubs were frequently planted in Hawaiian cemeteries and superstition was more influential than scent.

Finally, as you drive up to Haleakala Crater you should keep your eyes open for "Haleakala's crown of jewels," the silversword. If you were only to view it from a distance you might be surprised that this odd-looking plant is a member of the daisy family. However, if you take a closer look (between July and September when they're in bloom) you might see that the top part of the plant, which looks like a giant pinecone, is actually made up of scores of red-petaled, daisy-like flowers. One of the truly remarkable things about silversword is that it is able to thrive in extreme conditions. The ground temperature of the otherwise lifeless volcanic cinders often reaches 140°, but silversword is protected by the thick layers of silvery hairs that grow on its leaves and reflect the sun's harmful rays. The plants are also well adapted to retaining water, like a cactus, for long periods of drought. The silversword plant is threatened by feral goats and the boots of hikers who wander off marked trails. The park service has fenced off areas to help keep the goats out and they ask that hikers keep to the trail.

Marijuana *Pakalolo* (Hawaiian for marijuana), literally translated, "crazy tobacco," grows wild throughout the forests of Maui. As in the rest of the country, the growing, selling, and buying of marijuana are absolutely illegal. Still, it is believed that enormous amounts of money are brought into the state every year from marijuana sales. Chances are pretty good that you'll be approached by someone asking if you'd like to buy some "good Maui bud"; more often than not what you'll get is some "good oregano bud," so don't bother.

Incidentally, if you're hiking and happen upon a pakalolo patch, don't be tempted to pick some for yourself. Some local "farmer" has probably declared it his own and you might find yourself in a very uncomfortable situation.

FAUNA Much of Maui's bird life has become extinct; however, there are still some native species to look for when visiting various areas of the island.

Nene Hawaii's state bird, the nene, is coming back from the brink of extinction. Thought to be a relative of the Canadian goose, the nene is approximately 22 to 26 inches long and has a black head and a slightly yellow cheek. The neck is off-white with dark furrows, and the body is grayish-brown. In 1957, in an attempt to curtail the bird's impending extinction, birds bred in captivity at the Wildfowl Trust in England were released on Maui, and to date they seem to be faring rather well. There are approximately 130 nene living on the slopes of Haleakala. The nene's only other island homes are Mauna Loa and Mauna Kea on the Big Island, where they currently number over 500 and are being bred successfully. If you're hiking around Haleakala and you hear what you think is a strange cow, it might be a nene (their primary call is very goose-like).

Pueo A 13- to 17-inch short-eared owl, the pueo is most frequently spotted on the islands of Kauai, Maui, and Hawaii. Active primarily at dawn and dusk, the pueo is brown and white and streaked with dark brown and can be seen hunting in grasslands (perhaps on Kihei-Makena Road or at the crater). With a black bill, yellow eyes, and feathered legs and feet, the pueo is spectacular looking. Ancient Hawaiians held the pueo in highest regard, for it was believed that this owl was a great protector.

Other Birds Sightings of the nene and pueo are somewhat uncommon; some birds that you're more likely to see during your travels on Maui are the 'ua'u (dark-rumped petrel), Maui 'amakihi, i'iwi, apapane, and a'eo (Hawaiian stilt).

The dark-rumped petrel is usually found at Haleakala Crater and is about 16 inches in length. The forehead and underside are white, while the upper parts are charcoal (with a slightly lighter back).

The Maui 'amakihi is a smaller bird (about 4½ inches in length) with a slightly curved bill, and is yellowish-green. By contrast, the 'i'iwi, another small bird, is a bright red color and has a long, curved, salmon-colored bill. The legs of the 'i'iwi are also salmon-colored and black patches on the back are clearly visible. The feathers of the 'i'iwi were often used in Hawaiian featherwork. The 'apapane, often confused with the 'i'iwi, is also red (though slightly duller than the 'i'iwi) with black patches, but is distinguished by its whitish underside.

One of Maui's most whimsical birds is the black-necked stilt (or ae'o). This 16-inch bird, black on the head and down the back with a white underside and white eye ring, is distinguished by its long pink legs and long, thin, black beak. The ae'o can be found on Maui at Kanaha and Kealia ponds.

Humpback Whales Practically every hotel on Maui advertises whale sightings between late November and early May. In fact, these odd-looking playful whales do visit Maui waters every year at the same time. About 600 of them come to Maui and the Big Island from the coastal waters of Alaska to give birth to calves that weigh up to 2,000 pounds. They don't eat during their stay in Hawaiian waters; instead, they live off the blubber they've manufactured while feeding in the Alaskan waters. Humpbacks have an interesting feeding ritual—they blow large underwater bubbles to trap krill and then they swim, mouths open, through the air bubble, and enjoy their meals.

Though the humpback is not the most attractive of whales, its acrobatic performance is spectacular. You can watch these playful whales perform off the southern coast of Maui—Kaanapali Beach in the Lahaina area, Papawai Point on the way from Lahaina to Kihei, and the Kihei beaches are all excellent vantage points.

Some of the antics the whales might perform include a chin slap, tail slap, fluke, and breach (the whale will actually come out of the water and slap its body against the ocean's surface—usually several times in a row). A fluke can be considered the show's finale. After a fluke the whale will stay under water for a long time (perhaps up to 20 minutes) and isn't likely to resurface in the same place.

Whale watching on Maui can be an unforgettable experience. You won't have to ride around on a small, incredibly crowded boat to see them. You might simply be driving along the highway from Kahului to Lahaina, when the traffic suddenly slows and you'll realize that a group of whales is frolicking not far from shore to your left. Sometimes the whales come so close to shore that you'll feel like swimming out to meet them (of course, you shouldn't try it—they're probably farther out than they appear to be and they're not tame).

Game Animals   For information about game animals, see "Hunting" in Chapter 8.

DATELINE

- **2,000,000 B.C.** The first of Maui's volcanos breaks the ocean's surface.
- **1,000,000 B.C.** Mount Haleakala rises to the surface and molten lava flows form the island of Maui.
- **c. A.D. 450** The first Polynesians discover the Hawaiian islands and begin settlement.
- **A.D. 700** Colonists from Tahiti begin arriving on the islands.
- **c. 1550** High chief Pi'ilani rules Maui.
- **c. 1700** Kekaulike establishes a united kingdom on Maui.
- **1778** Captain James Cook of England discovers the island chain of Hawaii. He documents sightings of the

(continues)

2. HISTORY

THE FIRST GREAT NAVIGATORS   Though no one is quite sure of the origins of the Polynesians, they are believed to have come from Southeast Asia and carry some of the features of several different races. It is believed that the Polynesians first migrated to the Indonesian islands and then headed into the South Pacific where they settled on Fiji, Samoa, New Zealand, Tahiti, and the Marquesas. Having developed extraordinary navigational skills, they began exploring northward and crossed vast oceans to reach the Hawaiian islands. The sailing vessels of the first Polynesian explorers were crude, and only a few explorers survived and returned to tell their stories. Chants passed on from one generation of sailors to the next described the Hawaiian islands and how to reach them, but for centuries migrations to the islands ceased and Hawaii became a longed-for, far-off paradise that existed only in the imaginations of most Polynesians.

Historians are unsure about the origin of the name *Maui*, but it is known that throughout Polynesia stories of Maui abound. Many of these tales tell that Maui was a mischievous demigod who, in spite of his love of practical jokes, was charming, well loved, and "blessed" with incredible powers. *Maui-tinihanga* ("Maui-of-a-thousand-tricks") is said to have raised the sky when it was falling, snared the sun when his mother wished for more sunlight, and fished up an island to prove himself to his brothers.

Much of what we know about Polynesian history comes from the ancient chant (or *mele*), known as the Kumulipo—a sacred rendition of the story of Creation. The *kahuna* (Hawaiian priests of sorts) were responsible for singing the chant of the Kumulipo, which tells the story of how the islands of Hawaii, Maui, and Kahoolawe were created from the union of Papa ("earth mother") and Wakea ("sky father"). Later, Wakea joined with a second wife Kaula, and that union produced the island of Lanai. Then, apparently bored with Kaula, Wakea took Hina as his third wife and together they created the island of Molokai. When Papa learned of Wakea's infidelities, jealous and angry, she had an affair with a young god by the name of Lua, and together they produced Oahu. Just to bring the soap opera full circle, Papa and Wakea finally reconciled and gave birth to the last islands—Kauai, Niihau, Kaula, and Nihoa.

Through the Kumulipo, some Hawaiians were able to trace their lineage all the way back to Papa and Wakea, and it was they who had the privileged status of *ali'i* (royalty). Of the ali'i there were two distinct genealogical lines: the Ulu (literally translated: "possessed by a spirit or inspired by a god") were the royalty of Hawaii and Maui, while the Nana'ulu were the royalty of Kauai.

Centuries passed before Polynesian migration really began in force, and the first of those who came to the islands are thought to have been from the Marquesas. They arrived in canoes up to 80 feet in length carrying entire extended families as well as foodstuffs, livestock, and provisions, and they lived a peaceful existence—giving up their traditional practice of cannibalism.

After the migration of the Marquesans, migration continued from Polynesia to Hawaii for several hundred years. However, sometime in the 1100s, war-minded Tahitians arrived in canoes that are reported to have been 100 feet or more in length and able to carry up to 80 people. Their aim was to overthrow the extant Hawaiian chiefs, and with the introduction of their gods and the system of *kapu* they succeeded. Kapu made certain practices, foods, and places either off-limits (taboo) or sacred, or both, and it changed the face of Hawaiian religious worship for many hundreds of years.

After the Tahitians settled the Hawaiian archipelago, travel between Tahiti and Hawaii was maintained for about a century, and then for no reason that is currently evident to historians, the expeditions between the two stopped and the Hawaiian islands remained isolated from the rest of the world for about 500 years until European discovery in the 18th century.

THE MAUI DYNASTIES Though Maui's history is sketchy up until the late 16th century, we do know that each of the islands (or each district on each island) was ruled by a chief of ali'i status. Details about most of the original ruling chiefs have been lost over the years, but historians have been able to trace royal lineage on Maui back to when the ruling chief, Pi'ilani, rose to power. Pi'ilani's rule was peaceful, but upon his death his two sons, Lono and Kiha, quarreled constantly. Kiha was forced to flee to Hana, and there he fell in love with Koleamoku, daughter of the high chief of Hana. Despite Koleamoku's betrothal to Lono, they secretly married, precipitating war. Kiha and his wife fled to the Big Island and the protection of his brother-in-law, Umi. Umi

DATELINE

island of "Mowee," but never actually goes ashore.

• **1779** Cook meets Kalaniopu'u at Kealakekua Bay on the Big Island. The meeting is friendly, but violence later erupts and Cook is killed.

• **1781** Kalaniopu'u dies; his son, Kiawala, takes control of the kingdom. Kamehameha I is appointed keeper of the war god Kukailimoku.

• **1787** French explorer Captain Jean-François de Galoup, Comte de La Pérouse is the first Westerner to land on Maui. He is supposed to claim Maui as French territory, but never does.

• **1790** Kamehameha I unites Maui with the rest of his kingdom. The Olowalu Massacre takes place on Maui's west side.

• **1802** Kamehameha I declares Lahaina capital city of the islands.

• **1819** Kamehameha I dies and his son, Liholiho takes power. Before his death he appoints his widow, Ka'ahumanu, queen regent of the kingdom. The first

(continues)

DATELINE

(continues)

whaling ship, the *Balena*, arrives in Lahaina from New Bedford, Massachusetts.

- **1823** The first missionaries arrive on Maui from New England; Queen Keopuolani dies and is given a Christian burial.
- **1824** Liholiho dies; Queen Ka'ahumanu assumes power because Liholiho's 11-year-old brother isn't old enough to take the throne.
- **1825** Conflicts between the whalers erupt in Lahaina; laws are passed prohibiting prostitution and the sale of alcohol.
- **1828** Operations begin at Maui's first sugar mill.
- **1832** Queen Ka'ahumanu dies; Kamehameha III takes power but refuses to accept his responsibilities and appoints his sister queen regent.
- **1834** Maui's first printing press arrives from Honolulu and the island's first printing house (Hale Pa'i) is built. The first newspaper west of the Rocky Mountains is published.
- **1835** Dr. Dwight Baldwin arrives on Maui.

attacked Maui, defeating Lono and thereby adding Maui to his kingdom.

One of the descendents of the Pi'ilani dynasty was a ruling chief named Kekaulike. Sometime at the beginning of the 18th century, Kekaulike and his men went to war and were able to successfully unite all of the districts of Maui. When he passed his kingdom on to his sons, they fought over who would have more power, but after settling their differences, they ruled in relative harmony for decades.

Things on the Big Island, however, were in flux as the chiefs there and on the other islands battled for power over small kingdoms.

EUROPEAN DISCOVERY OF THE HAWAIIAN ISLANDS In 1776 British explorer Captain James Cook, set out in the HMS *Resolution* (along with another ship, the HMS *Discovery*, whose captain was Charles Clerke) to explore the Pacific for the third time. After sailing around the Cape of Good Hope, and past New Zealand and Tasmania, he came upon the islands of Oahu and Kauai in January 1778. In his diaries he recorded landings on the islands of Kauai and Niihau where he replenished supplies and traded with the natives. He named the archipelago the Sandwich Islands after John Montague, the Earl of Sandwich.

With well-stocked ships and a well-rested crew, Cook continued on in his search for the Northwest Passage (his original goal). He headed toward the North American continent, around which he sailed and continued on into the Atlantic. He headed onward to the Arctic, where he searched, in vain, for the passage. When he realized that his search had proven fruitless, he decided to return to the Sandwich Islands for the winter to repair his badly damaged ships and continue his explorations. Cook and his crew returned to the Sandwich Islands in the dark of night on November 25, 1778. When the sun rose on November 26, Cook made his first sighting of the island of Maui. He was anchored approximately three miles offshore from the city we now know as Kahului, and that very day hundreds of Hawaiians approached his ships by canoe. Cook reported that the Hawaiians "came into the ship, without the least hesitation."

Cook and his crew traded pieces of iron for cuttlefish, potatoes, taro, fruit, and some pigs. Cook was also greeted by Kahekili, the king of Maui, who arrived dressed in full regalia, from his feather-crested helmet to his red-and-yellow-feathered cloak. During his anchorage off Maui, Cook had other visitors, including Kalaniopu'u (ruler of the Hana district of Maui, and arch rival to Kahekili) and a young chief by the name of Kamehameha, who would later become king of the United Hawaiian Kingdom. In his journal Cook recorded the island's name phonetically: "Mowee."

On November 30, 1778, Cook recorded his first sighting of the island of "O'why'he'" (Hawaii). He spent about a month sailing around the Big Island and trading with the natives as he went, and finally, on January 15, 1779, he came upon Kealakekua Bay, where he decided to anchor in order to repair his ships and gather provisions. The Hawaiians were awed by the sight of this foreigner not only because he was very unlike themselves but because he arrived on the day and in the bay that was reserved for Lono, the great fertility god of the land. In his wooden ship Cook bore a striking resemblance to Hawaiian renditions of Lono, and since it was believed that Lono would return to the earth, the Hawaiians mistook Cook for their god. Cook was warmly but formally received and honored with a water procession, fireworks, and, several days later, the presentation of King Kalaniopu'u's own cloak, feather helmet, and kahili.

During Cook's visit to Kealakekua Bay, he and King Kalaniopu'u developed an extremely amicable friendship, but by February 4, 1779, after having clearly worn out their welcome (partially because the natives had come to understand that Cook and his men were mere mortals, and partially because they had eaten the Hawaiians out of house and home), Cook decided that they should press on.

Barely a week had passed when the *Resolution* and the *Discovery* found themselves once again at Kealakekua Bay. The weather had not been favorable and the *Resolution* was in need of repair. While the ships were anchored in the bay there were several incidents of thievery and the British seamen retaliated with force. This only served to increase hostility between the Europeans and the Hawaiians. On February 14, while the ship was under repair, Cook noticed that a small cutter had been stolen and he decided to kidnap the king (some say he went willingly), with whom he was still friendly, and hold him until the cutter was safely returned. Unfortunately, Cook could not have predicted the hostility to which he would fall victim. After the king was taken the natives armed themselves and threatened Cook's life. Cook fired one shot. The natives attacked, and Cook was killed.

After the death of their leader, crew members, including Captain Clerke, continued on with Cook's original plan, exploring the waters surrounding Maui, Molokai, and Lanai. On March 15, Clerke turned his ships northward and made one last attempt to find the Northwest Passage. During the search Clerke took ill and died. The four-year Cook expedition was ended, and after a brief period of trading in China, the ships returned to England.

POST-COOK EUROPEAN EXPLORATION News of Cook's discoveries in the Pacific spread and European trade with the Hawaiians continued, primarily in armaments. Demand for more deadly weapons had grown since Cook first traded iron daggers for provisions as power-hungry Hawaiian chiefs and ali'i sought possession of more land and additional islands. The three major players in Hawaiian rule at the time of Cook's visit were Kalaniopu'u, who ruled over the island of Hawaii and the Hana district of Maui; Kahekili, who controlled all of

DATELINE

- **1850** Lahaina ceases to be the capital of the Hawaiian nation when it is moved to Honolulu.
- **1873** William Lunalilo is elected by popular vote.
- **1875** The Reciprocity Act exempts Hawaiian sugar from import tariffs. Alexander and Baldwin begin building the Hamakua Ditch.
- **1891** David Kalakaua dies and his sister, Lydia Lilikuolani, the last Hawaiian monarch, takes the throne.
- **1893** The Hawaiian monarchy is overthrown by American settlers in Hawaii.
- **1898** President McKinley signs the annexation agreement with Hawaii.
- **1903** The first pineapple is planted on Maui by Dwight Baldwin.
- **1941** Pearl Harbor is bombed and martial law is declared in Hawaii.
- **1946** Maui's tourist trade begins with the opening of the Hotel Hana Maui, the island's first resort property.
- **1959** Hawaii becomes the 50th state of the United States.

(continues)

DATELINE

- **1961** Hawaii's first "master-planned resort," Kaanapali, opens on Maui.
- **1976** A resurgence of interest in Hawaiian culture is sparked by the sailing of the *Hokule'a*, a replica of an ancient Polynesian canoe, and ancestral journeys are re-created.

Maui (with the exception of the Hana district), Kahoolawe, Lanai, and Oahu; and Kaeo, the brother of Kahekili, whose domain was the island of Kauai.

The Hawaiian arms race gathered speed as Europeans, who had become involved in the fur trade, stopped in the Hawaiian islands on their way from North America to China. Among the first European visitors to arrive after the departure of Captain Cook was French explorer Admiral Jean-François de Galoup, Comte de La Pérouse, who was the first to set foot on the island of Maui. His notes and the sketches of the ship's artist were the first written record of Maui's terrain. In La Pérouse's description of the Hana coast he comments that they ". . . beheld water falling in cascades from the mountains and running in streams to the sea. . . . The trees which crowned the mountains and the verdure of the banana plants that surrounded the habitations produced inexpressible charms to our senses." Like Cook, La Pérouse traded pieces of iron for food and provisions. On May 30, 1786, La Pérouse landed in a bay (known today as La Pérouse Bay) just outside Lahaina. He and his crew stayed on Maui for only a short period of time, after which they set sail for the west coast of North America.

THE OLOWALU MASSACRE By the end of the 18th century ship captains en route to China from all over the world were dropping anchor in Hawaii to replenish supplies and repair their vessels. In 1790, the *Eleanora*, an American ship under the command of Captain Simon Metcalfe, arrived. In January, while anchored near Honuaula, off Maui, the ship's boat was stolen and a member of the crew was killed during the night. In retaliation Metcalfe fired shots at a canoe full of Hawaiians. Many were wounded. Metcalfe pretended that the score had been evened and summoned the unsuspecting Hawaiians to his ship, giving them the impression that he was prepared to reestablish trade. Scores of canoes loaded with hundreds of Hawaiians left the shores of Olowalu. They were only a few feet from the *Eleanora* when Metcalfe gave the order for his men to open fire. The result was a bloody massacre, known to the Hawaiians as *Kalolopahu*, or "the spilled brains." About a hundred natives were slain. Metcalfe and his crew set sail for the island of Hawaii.

KAHEKILI During this period of European invasion, a young man by the name of Kamehameha was growing up and entering manhood. He had been instructed in the ways of the Hawaiian military by his uncle Kalaniopu'u (king of the Maui district of Hana and the Big Island of Hawaii), who sought to conquer the entire island of Maui. When Kalaniopu'u died in 1781, his son, Kiwalo, took over the kingship of his father's lands, but before he died Kalaniopu'u granted Kamehameha a great honor and appointed him keeper of the war god Kukailimoku (often referred to simply as Ku).

Kalaniopu'u's enemy, Kahekili, was awaiting his opportunity to seize control of the Hana district, and after the death of his rival he had his chance. It took his forces about a year to conquer Hana, but a final bloody battle wiped out virtually all the defenders of Hana.

Kahekili was not satisfied with simply defeating the Hana chiefs; he also sought to gain control of the Big Island and Oahu. Initial attempts against Kamehameha and his troops on the Big Island were unsuccessful, so Kahekili focused his energies on Oahu and its ruling chief, Kahahana. In January 1783, Kahekili and his wife, Kauwahine, along with scores of warriors, stormed the beaches of Oahu and overpowered the troops of Chief Kahahana. Many died, but many others, along with Kahahana and his wife, fled. Kahahana and the chief of another district on the island of Oahu were both killed by Kahekili. He had successfully defeated the ruling chiefs of Oahu and had, with landholdings that also included Maui, Molokai, and Lanai, become the most powerful king in Hawaii.

KAMEHAMEHA TAKES MAUI Though in 1786 Kahekili was the most powerful force in the islands, he would only hold his position for four short years. The young Kamehameha was becoming a force to be reckoned with. Keeper of the warrior god, Ku; proud owner of Thomas Metcalfe's ship, the *Fair American*, along with all its guns and its cannon; and captor of two seamen, Isaac Davis and John Young, trained in the military ways of the West, Kamehameha was preparing to become king of all the islands. He began by attempting to conquer the island of Hawaii, and for the most part succeeded, although he was unable to defeat one of the island chiefs, Keoua (cousin to Kamehameha, and son of Kamehameha's mentor, Kalaniopu'u). In 1790, frustrated by the situation on Hawaii, Kamehameha turned his attention to Maui. He, Isaac Davis and John Young (Kamehameha's closest advisors), and all of his warriors landed on the beaches at Hana. The battle was easily won. Kahekili realized that Central Maui would be the focus of Kamehameha's next attack. He sent his son, Kalanikupule, along with all of his best warriors, to Wailuku to wait for Kamehameha and his troops. Kamehameha's troops fought hard and forced the Maui warriors to retreat into the Iao Valley. Known as the battle of Kepaniwai ("damming of the waters"), this fight proved to be the turning point for Kahekili. The battle was bloody, and bodies were said to have literally "dammed" the waterway of the Iao Valley. Many of the ali'i were able to escape through the forest and over the mountain, but Kamehameha's message was loud and clear.

Meanwhile, Kamehameha's cousin and rival, Keoua, was burning and pillaging the villages of Kamehameha's newly won districts. Kamehameha rushed back to the Big Island immediately, fought two battles with Keoua, but was still unable to defeat him.

Legend has it that Kamehameha had a dream that told him if he built a *heiau* (temple) to Ku, the war god would aid him in his struggle. He began building the war temple on a hill called Pu'ukohola ("Hill of the Whale") overlooking Kawaihae Bay on the Big Island. Before the job was completed Kahekili dispatched troops from the islands of Oahu, Maui, Molokai, and Kauai. They were headed for Waimea Bay off the Big Island's Hamakua coastline. Kamehameha halted operations at the war heiau so he could meet the warriors off Waimea Bay before they landed. If the battle were to take place at sea Kamehameha would have the advantage: Both sides would be fighting with guns, but Kamehameha's sloop was fitted with two powerful cannons. Yet another bloody battle was fought and Kamehameha again emerged victorious. Kahekili retreated and accepted Kamehameha as king of Maui, though Kahekili remained on the island and served as "chief" until his death in 1794.

With Kahekili stripped of his power, only Keoua remained. Kamehameha and Keoua continued to battle without a final outcome until Keoua and his troops, who were marching near the crater of Kilauea, were enveloped by a cloud of hot ash, issued by the goddess, Pele. Many of his warriors were killed. Keoua was spared, but he knew then that the gods had chosen sides.

After Keoua's retreat Kamehameha returned to building his temple. When it was complete a sacrifice of a high chief was required at its dedication in order to appease the war god. Kamehameha invited Keoua to the dedication. Keoua accepted the invitation knowing his fate. When he arrived he was killed and sacrificed to Ku at the heiau's altar. Kamehameha had risen to the throne of the Big Island.

KAMEHAMEHA'S RISE TO POWER IS COMPLETE Though Kamehameha's island power base was larger than that of any other king, he was still determined to unite all of the islands under one kingdom and made his next move to take Molokai and Maui. The battles were easily won, and the two islands were swiftly added to his kingdom. Kamehameha then turned his attention to Oahu and Kahekili's son Kalanikupule.

Landing at Waikiki, Kamehameha's army was met by defending Oahuans who fought hard, but their efforts were to no avail. Kamehameha's army was strong, and drove the Oahuans to the edge of Nuuanu Pali, a great cliff, from which they were forced by the stronger army to jump or flee for their lives. Their chief Kalanikupule headed for the hills, but it wasn't long before he was captured, killed, and laid at Ku's altar.

After conquering Oahu, Kamehameha had only one island left to add to his kingdom—Kauai. But Kamehameha's attention was turned homeward, to the Big Island, where he was forced to return to put down a revolt.

While he was on the Big Island, Kamehameha decided to set up an interisland system of government. He realized that he needed to install loyal followers in positions of power on the other islands. The system he developed shows that he was not only a fierce warrior but also a brilliant administrative leader. He made every effort to maintain the values and customs of Old Hawaii by continuing to worship the old gods (the Europeans were already trying to convert the Hawaiians to Christianity), but he also instituted systems and policies that would revolutionize this new kingdom. All the high chiefs, even the ones who had given Kamehameha problems in the past, were appointed members of the royal court. He began a system of taxation, gathered around him a group of skilled trades- and craftspeople, and appointed a governor for each of his islands.

With his power consolidated and strengthened, Kamehameha focused on defeating Kaumuali'i, the ruler of Kauai. In 1820, with a new fleet of canoes (800 of them), a handful of newly constructed schooners, and an enormous stockpile of Western arms, Kamehameha set out to conquer Kauai, stopping first at Lahaina on Maui and then on Oahu. Unfortunately, a deadly smallpox epidemic had begun on Oahu, and by mid-1804 Kamehameha's army was devastated by the disease. The king was spared and remained on Oahu for a few more years before he made the decision not to fight Kaumuali'i. Instead, he only asked that the king of Kauai recognize Kamehameha as the most powerful force in the islands. It took until 1810, but finally, after much gift giving, negotiating, and the diplomatic intervention of American Nathan Winship, Kaumuali'i relented; without further bloodshed, Kamehameha's kingdom was complete.

Almost from the moment Kamehameha united the islands of Hawaii he called for peace. There would be no more war under his rule and the islands were to be safe for all Hawaiians. Kamehameha then moved his residence to Lahaina. He inspired his subjects with examples of hard labor, and he exercised tight control over the admittance of foreign merchants to the islands. In order to build the royal lineage, Kamehameha had taken several wives who managed to produce two sons (Liholiho and Kauikeaouli) and a daughter (Nahi'ena'ena).

By the early 19th century, all seemed well in the Hawaiian islands. Trade was excellent and the king was building large storehouses of money as well as goods; his heirs were strong young men; and peace reigned throughout the islands. It appeared as though Old Hawaii was approaching its golden age; however, it was to be short-lived.

QUEEN KA'AHUMANU It is believed that King Kamehameha built the royal palace at Lahaina for his favorite wife (the third of 21), Ka'ahumanu, whose father, Ke'eaumoku, had been appointed by the king to the position of governor of Maui. Born in a cave just outside Hana in 1768, Ka'ahumanu was extraordinarily beautiful by Hawaiian standards (she was very large, which is admired in Hawaiian culture) and also extremely intelligent and charismatic. Kamehameha had such faith in Ka'ahumanu's capabilities as a ruling force that when he died in 1819 (in spite of the fact that his son, Liholiho, was his successor) he granted Ka'ahumanu the title *kuhina nui* (queen regent), which gave her virtually unlimited power as a ruler of the Hawaiian islands.

THE END OF KAPU AND THE LIBERATION OF WOMEN At the time when Liholiho ascended to the throne, there were some old traditions in place that were quickly becoming outdated. The women of Hawaii had to live under certain kapu. Among them was the kapu that forbade women to eat certain foods (like bananas, coconut, pork, and baked dog) and forbade them to eat in the presence of men. Other kapu said that women were not allowed to fish in salt water, nor were they allowed to touch (or even approach) fishing nets. Ka'ahumanu, the woman who unapologetically donned her late husband's feather cloak and carried his spear, believed the kapu to be disgraceful and demeaning to all women, so she conspired with Liholiho's mother, Keopuolani, to abolish them. When the two most powerful women in the land joined forces, they were to be reckoned with.

Since Liholiho was technically the king, he had to give final approval for the abolition of the kapu. Punishment for breaking kapu was, with no exceptions, death, but the women knew that Liholiho would be unwilling to put his own mother and his father's favorite queen to death, so they felt secure in testing him. Ka'ahumanu defied tradition first by peeling and eating a banana right in front of her stepson. By the laws of kapu, he should have had her immediately executed, but legend has it that he simply ignored her, pretending that he didn't notice. Next, his mother, Keopulani, asked him to dine with her. He refused her invitation. But the queen and Keopuolani were not discouraged by his responses—he had made it clear that he was not prepared to follow the laws of kapu if it meant that he would have to put his mother and stepmother to death. They continued eating forbidden foods in front of him, weakening him with every bite. Finally, at a banquet, all three sat down together and participated in the first *ai noa* (free eating). This was a giant step for the liberation of Hawaiian women, but the moment free eating began, the entire traditional religious structure of the islands began to fall. Not long after ai noa and the public breaking of kapu, Ka'ahumanu set forth a decree calling for the complete destruction of all temples and religious idols, making way for Western religions.

THE SACRED WIFE: CHIEFESS KEOPUOLANI
(1778-1823)

The history of Chiefess Keopuolani, known as the "sacred" wife, is an interesting one. Keopuolani's ancestry can be traced through the genealogies of the ali'i, which go all the way back to the god and goddess Wakea and Papa.

Keopuolani was born of what Hawaiians believed to be the most sacred union possible—her mother (Queen Kalola of Maui) and father (King Kalaniopu'u of Hawaii) were brother and sister. Ancient Hawaiians thought that the union of brother and sister would intensify the ali'i bloodline. From birth, the two ere closely guarded in an effort to maintain their virginity until their parents decided they were prepared to participate in the Ho Au ceremony, during which they were to concieve a child together.

On a sacred evening, King Kalaniopu'u and Queen Kalola were taken to the heiau (temple) where they remained through the night under a white kapa tent. All night the villagers stood outside the tent, under the direction of the kahunas, chanting the *mo'okua'auhau*, or genealogical succession, of the king and queen. In the morning, when the couple emerged, the king was free to go, but the queen was held under watch (to ensure the purity of the child) until the child was born. When the queen went into labor the whole town gathered again and chanted and prayed until Keopuolani was born.

King Kamehameha married Keopuolani specifically for her ali'i status. If she bore him sons they would be guaranteed to succeed him to the throne because of their sacred status. The wise Kamehameha knew that if he were to have children with non-ali'i women (which he did), it would not stop others from trying to usurp the throne.

Keopuolani died in 1823 and was given a Christian burial.

THE WHALING INDUSTRY & THE MISSIONARIES The first whaling ships arrived in the islands in 1819, and by 1824, the year of Liholiho's death, over 100 ships were making Hawaii a primary port of call. For the whaling men the islands were a great place to spend the winter. Of the two main whaling ports, Honolulu and Lahaina, Lahaina attracted almost three times as many ships as Honolulu. The bay at what is today's Lahaina Wharf was a natural landing spot, and captains could easily steer their ships to shore.

At Lahaina, fresh produce (bananas, melons, pumpkins, squashes, and potatoes) and meat (goat, beef, turkey) were plentiful, as were women and grog shops. At anchorage, the harbormaster boarded ships and collected $10 in exchange for five barrels of Irish potatoes and "the privilege of purchasing at pleasure in the market for supplies . . . according to the rules of the place." A list of rules was also presented at that time. American sailors preferred Lahaina to Honolulu in part because they could get Irish potatoes (grown primarily in Kula), and in Honolulu they could only get sweet potatoes, but also because fresh water was more plentiful.

Once ashore, the seamen had easy access to alcohol and entertainment. Life in Lahaina in the early to mid-19th century was licentious, and when the missionaries arrived on Maui in 1823 there were clashes between the rowdy seamen and the puritanical New Englanders. Missionaries and government officials were almost constantly in disagreement with the whaling men about what constituted "rest and relaxation." In 1825 laws that prohibited women from visiting the ships were passed. Since the time of Captain Cook's arrival in the 18th century, Hawaiian women had been offering themselves to foreign sailors, and as a result venereal disease was spreading rapidly throughout the islands. The passage of the 1825 law prompted Lahaina's first major riot. Enraged, the crew of the British whaling vessel, *Daniel*, prowled and rioted in the streets of Lahaina for three days. They twice visited the home of the Reverend Richards, founder of Lahaina's first mission, and threatened his life and his home and family because they believed that he was responsible for the passing of the prohibition.

In addition to prostitution, alcohol was another matter of dispute between the seamen and the missionaries. So, a law prohibiting the sale of alcohol was passed. The rowdy grog shops were forced to close their doors and it wasn't until 1843 that the liquor licenses were reissued.

When the missionaries first arrived on the islands, Queen Ka'ahumanu wasn't interested in adopting their religious beliefs; however, as time passed, she saw an increased need for religious direction among Hawaiians. With the abolition of the kapus there were virtually no laws on the islands. Licentiousness reigned, and when Queen Ka'ahumanu came to the realization that outside forces, particularly the whaling men and their tastes for alcohol, were wreaking havoc upon her land, she determined to establish new laws. She collaborated with one of the island reverends, making laws based on the Ten Commandments. She outlawed murder, theft, public brawling, sex outside of marriage, and the desecration of the Sabbath. These laws became known as the *Lua-ehu* laws.

While the Lua-ehu laws helped to stem some of the violence that was occurring throughout the islands, Christianity, the driving force behind them, was a source of great angst for the Hawaiian people, especially the children who grew up torn between the new religion and ancient Hawaiian traditions. Two of the most prominent victims of these bipolar ways of life were the young King Kamehameha III (Kauikeaouli) and his sister, Princess Nahi'ena'ena. Following Hawaiian tradition, the ali'i marriage of this brother and sister was arranged at birth and they were expected to conceive a child together. Christianity forced them to question their intended lifestyle. Kamehameha III became a hopeless drunkard, and Princess Nahi'ena'ena spent her time in a constant internal tug of war, bouncing between her life of dancing, singing, and drinking, and her struggle to examine her soul.

Queen Ka'ahumanu died in 1832 (after having been baptized as a Christian), leaving the throne to the 18-year-old King Kauikeaouli. Initially Kauikeaouli announced that he alone would assume power over the government and would become the primary lawmaker of the land. However, in truth, he was not interested in assuming his responsibilities, and appointed his other half-sister, Kinau, *kuhina-nui* (or premier) of the land. Over the next year, Christian chiefs made a great effort to impose morality on their people, but to no avail. The Hawaiian people were still following the example of their king, who persisted in his drunken revelry.

By 1834 Princess Nahi'ena'ena could no longer resist the impulse to be with her brother and she returned to his side in Honolulu. He begged her to take him back to Maui with her, but she refused out of fear that the missionaries would scold them; desperate, Kauikeaouli tried to kill himself. Later, the two were reunited and news of their union was formally announced. But in 1835 Nahi'ena'ena left her brother again, this time to marry Chief Leleiohoku in a ceremony performed by Reverend Richards in Lahaina. The next year, Kauikeaouli joined her in Lahaina and Nahi'ena'ena again strayed from the ways of the church. The princess and her brother did have a child together, but he died only a few hours after birth. Nahi'ena'ena's physical condition deteriorated after the difficult birth of her son, and in December 1836, she died.

The people of Hawaii were devastated not only for the loss of their princess but because all hope of carrying on the line of ruling chiefs was lost. Christianity would prevail. Kauikeaouli stayed on Maui for eight years, proclaimed his sister's death a public holiday, and saluted her with government cannons every year. Her death so greatly affected him that he even sobered up and became one of the greatest rulers in the history of the Hawaiian islands. He remained in power until his death in 1854.

OUT OF CHAOS COMES EDUCATION   With drunken kings, brawling whaling men, prostitution, and a new religion, one might think that Hawaii, and more specifically Lahaina, was falling completely into a state of disrepair. For the most part, this is true; however, in 1823, when the kingdom's first laws against theft, brawling, murder, and sex outside of marriage were being enacted, another important law was written. It decreed that anyone under the age of 26 who wanted to marry had to be able to read and write. With the enactment of that law came the opening of the first school. Queen Keopuolani was the first pupil on Monday, June 2, 1823. She wanted to learn the *palapala* (writing) and is reported to have been an excellent student who never tired of her studies.

The very next year in Lahaina, Queen Ka'ahumanu called for the establishment of schools throughout the islands so that all Hawaiians would be able to learn the palapala. Most of the original Hawaiian schools, whose pupils were restricted to the ali'i, held classes in grass huts. Seven years later the "first high school west of the Rocky Mountains," Lahainaluna School, was opened in Lahaina. In 1834 the first printing house (Hale Pa'i) in the islands was built by the same missionaries who helped to build the Lahainaluna School. On February 14, 1834, the "first newspaper west of the Rockies," *Kalama Hawaii* ("Torch of Hawaii"), began publication. Today the Lahainaluna School is still operating, and you can visit the Hale Pa'i.

Eight years later schools for native children of all classes opened their doors. In Lahaina on October 10, 1840, King Kamehameha III signed the very first written Hawaiian Constitution, which aside from outlining religious and political development, included previously defined laws regarding Hawaiian education.

THE FALL OF WHALING & THE RISE OF SUGAR   In 1846, the whaling industry reached its peak. Over 600 whaling vessels arrived in Hawaiian ports, two-thirds of them dropping anchor off Maui. Between 1845 and 1860, whaling remained profitable, both for the sailors and for the people of Hawaii, but in the late 1850s, with the discovery of oil, the industry's decline was inevitable. Lahaina's economy suffered and the town ceased to be a bustling center of activity. Honolulu became known as the capital city of the island chain.

The whaling industry virtually nonexistent, Hawaiians were forced to look elsewhere to support their economy. What they discovered had been there all along. Sugar. The Polynesians introduced sugarcane to the islands when they first began settling Hawaii, and since then it had been growing wild on the islands. Hawaii's first sugar plantation was started in Hana in 1849 by a whaler named George Wilfong. He planted about 60 acres of sugarcane and set up a crude sugar refinery. He used whale blubber to heat sugarcane juice until high-quality sugar crystals formed.

Prior to speculation in sugar, Hawaiian land was being sold off systematically by Kamehameha III. Unfortunately, the Hawaiians did not understand the concept of owning parcels of land. They believed that the land belonged to the gods or Mother Earth and could not be possessed. They lived off the land and took from it only what they needed. As a consequence, most of the land being sold was bought up by foreigners and the Hawaiians were finding themselves without homes and without work. Their only alternative was to work for the men who purchased the land. Those who did work on the sugar plantations were nothing more than indentured servants.

In 1850 the Masters and Servants Act allowed the plantation owners to import cheap labor under contract to work their lands. The Chinese were some of the first (c. 1852) to be "imported," followed by the Japanese. Working conditions were so horrendous that few survived the hardships of plantation work, and battles for workers' rights ensued. Eventually, plantation workers were able to gain privileges which, among other things, included access to better living conditions.

In 1846 six of the eleven Hawaiian sugar mills were located on Maui. In 1853 steam power was introduced to Maui, which reduced the need for water and animal power. The next year, Captain Edwards arrived at Lahaina anchorage with a hardier variety of sugarcane which became known as "lahaina cane." For $14,000 Captain James Makee and C. Brewer II purchased Maui's Hailiimaile plantation, and in 1862 C. Brewer and Company, along with one Mr. Edward Bailey, organized the Wailuku Sugar Company, also on Maui. The 1860s marked a distinct period of growth in the number of sugar plantations on Maui.

Demand for Hawaiian sugar increased during the California Gold Rush, but it soared during the Civil War as production of sugar diminished in the American South. Since the United States provided the market, and most plantations were owned by Americans, it became clear that it was in the best interest of the United States and Hawaii for the U.S. government to allow tariff-free sugar imports to the United States. In 1875, the Reciprocity Act exempted sugar from import duties so long as the United States had, among other things, access to Pearl Harbor.

CLAUS SPRECKELS Just as the Reciprocity Act of 1875 was being enacted, an enterprising young Californian was arriving in the islands aboard the steamer, *City of San Francisco*. His name was Claus Spreckels. During his visit to Hawaii he became interested in purchasing land on Maui. He took some time to learn about the sugar business from Henry Baldwin and Sam T. Alexander, who were in the process of setting up their own sugar refinery and were puzzling over an irrigation ditch at the time of Spreckels' visit. The brothers-in-law are credited with having pulled off what was probably the single most difficult undertaking of the Hawaiian sugar industry—the building of the Hamakua Ditch. The men proposed to divert water across the 300-foot-deep, 800-foot-wide Maliko Gulch with 1,100 feet of pipe. The project was arduous, and the men encountered several stumbling blocks along the way, not the least of which was the fact that workers refused to work under such hazardous conditions. Henry Baldwin had lost one of his arms in an unfortunate accident in the sugar mill. Legend has it that the one-armed Baldwin went so far as to lower himself into the 300-foot-deep Maliko Gulch just to prove to his workers that it could be done.

While on Maui in 1876, Spreckels purchased part of the Waihee Plantation, and after seeing what Alexander and Baldwin had gone through to bring water to their cane fields, was concerned about securing water rights to irrigate his own land. He left Maui to puzzle over his purchase and returned two years later with his engineer, Hermann Schussler, who would help him to begin the project. On that visit he also became friendly with King Kalakaua and through him was able to purchase approximately 40,000 acres of land and acquired water rights for the north side of Haleakala. With Schussler's help, Spreckels built a 30-mile ditch made up of thousands of feet of pipe and almost 30 tunnels that would carry approximately 60 million gallons of water per day. In spite of the incredible amount of water carried to Claus' Hawaiian Commercial and Sugar Company, Spreckels found that he needed more, and at a cost of $10,000 per year he rented part of the water supply controlled by another of Maui's sugar companies.

Many resented the way Spreckels made his fortune in the islands. He took advantage of his knowledge of the Reciprocity Act and bought large tracts of land for sugar farming before anyone else knew about it, and he paid off Hawaiian royalty to cut "red tape." However, the positive contributions he made far outweighed the negatives, especially for the island of Maui, its economy, and its people. By the 1880s Spreckels had invested well in excess of $4 million in the Hawaiian economy. Kahului developed as the economic center of the island due to the comings and goings of his steamships as they carried sugar and other products to and from the mainland. He also introduced "controlled irrigation," the use of the steam plow, and the utilization of the railroad for hauling the fruits of his labor. With his building of Spreckelsville and a 30-mile ditch to carry water to the arid land upon which he would cultivate his sugarcane, Spreckels also moved the focus of Maui's economy from Lahaina to Upcountry towns.

The sugar industry proved quite profitable for Spreckels, but in 1898, at the age of 70, he lost control of his sugar plantation when he was bought out by the famed Alexander and Baldwin, who became incorporated in 1900. Since then, Alexander & Baldwin, Inc., has grown consistently, adding to its holdings, among other things, more land, mills, and a shipping company. The interests of Alexander & Baldwin are worldwide, and by the late 1970s, the company owned almost 100,000 acres, most of which were on Maui.

THE DECLINE OF THE HAWAIIAN POPULATION & A REVOLUTION

During the sugar boom not only were the Chinese and Japanese arriving by the boatload, but so were the Portuguese, Filipinos, Koreans, Puerto Ricans, and Germans, all looking for work in the Hawaiian paradise. They brought their religions, their native flora and fauna, and their languages with them, creating an international melting pot. They also brought a variety of diseases to which the Hawaiians had no natural resistance, and as a consequence, the Hawaiian population dramatically decreased. In 1876 89% of the population was either all or part Hawaiian; by 1900 the percentage had dropped to 26%. The initial depopulation that was occurring during the growth of the sugar industry throughout Hawaii is actually one of the reasons sugar plantation operators had to look abroad for their labor forces.

The Kamehameha monarchy survived during the early days of the sugar industry. In 1872, however, Lot Kamehameha (Kamehameha V) died leaving no successor. In 1873, William Lunalilo was elected by popular vote but died childless one year later. David Kalakaua (who was responsible for negotiating the agreement that ended in the Reciprocity Act) took his place. After his death in 1891, his sister, Lydia Liliuokalani, ascended to the throne. She is remembered as the last Hawaiian monarch.

With the native population at an all-time low when the 52-year-old Queen Lilioukalani took office, Hawaii was suffering. The Constitution of 1887, instituted under King Kalakaua, had given Hawaiians and foreigners alike the right to vote provided they met certain property and income restrictions. With the influx of American businessmen and plantation owners, and the decreased native population, it became obvious that the Americans had more control over Hawaii than did its native citizens. Lilioukalani sought to rectify the situation by assuming more political power. At the same time, the McKinley Act went into effect, allowing raw sugar from foreign countries to enter the United States free of tariff, effectively reversing the conditions of the Reciprocity Act of 1875 and devastating the Hawaiian sugar industry. Queen Lilioukalani did not intervene on behalf of the plantation owners, which alienated them. A small group of approximately 30 men, headed by Honolulu publishing giant Lorrin Thurston, set out to overthrow the queen. With little military support on her side, and the military support of the U.S. Congress (who sought annexation) behind the revolutionaries, Lilioukalani was easily ousted. January 17, 1893, marked the end of the Hawaiian monarchy and the beginning of American control.

Lilioukalani surrendered to John Stevens, American ambassador, hoping that the U.S. government would be sympathetic to her predicament and would help to reinstate her as monarch. Unbeknownst to her, the United States actually supported the coup, and when she attempted to orchestrate a counterattack against her enemies in 1895 she was again defeated. Humiliated, Lilioukalani was held prisoner under house arrest and was forced to sign an agreement stating that she would never again attempt to gain control of the Hawaiian throne. She was also required to pledge allegiance to the New Republic. Later she was forced to stand trial in front of a military commission that sentenced her to five years of hard labor and fined her $5,000 for plotting to establish a new cabinet during the counterrevolution.

Although most native Hawaiians remained loyal to the monarchy, they were powerless against the New Republic, primarily because they did not meet the income and property requirements necessary to vote. Annexation was inevitable, despite opposition from the Japanese, and on July 17, 1898, the annexation agreement was signed by President McKinley.

Lilioukalani remained in Hawaii until her death in 1917. During her time in seclusion she wrote *Hawaii's Story* and the famous, familiar hula song, "Aloha O'e."

EARLY 20TH-CENTURY HAWAII For a long time, Maui remained the sleepy island it was prior to the overthrow of Queen Lilioukalani, but early in the 20th century, widespread changes revealed increasing Western influence. Throughout the islands Hawaiian culture had been all but eradicated. The native religion and traditions were gone, and the Hawaiian language, which had previously served as the historical record for Hawaiians, had become virtually nonexistent as the number of missionary-educated Hawaiians increased. Also, interracial marriages were increasing in numbers.

Foreign military leaders had also begun to develop more than a passing interest in the Hawaiian islands. The United States, in particular, recognized their strategic importance and proceeded to install troops at Camp McKinley on Oahu. Two years later another base, the Schofield Barracks (named in honor of General Schofield, who was the first to survey Pearl Harbor in 1872), was established, and Pearl Harbor was officially opened in 1911.

WAR AND STATEHOOD Save for shortages on commodities, World War I had little effect on the Hawaiian Islands. The dramatic bombing of Pearl Harbor on December 7, 1941, however, brought Hawaii and the United States into World War II.

Mauians were stunned by the Japanese attack on Pearl Harbor, and they immediately set about protecting their beaches with whatever military equipment they had. Islanders awaited the expected Japanese invasion, but it never happened. Kahului Harbor was bombed by a submarine, and one ship was sunk off Maui's coastline, but other than that Maui saw very little military action. A military outpost, known as Camp Maui, was established at Kokomo and for several years it served as a training ground and recreational center for the Fourth Marine Division. Some native Mauians also served in World War II. Directed by Americans of Japanese ancestry known as *Nisei*, Hawaiian military units won a total of 18,143 decorations, winning the honor of being the most decorated battalion in World War II.

World War II only served to solidify Hawaii's alignment with the United States. In fact, after the war, most Hawaiians considered themselves to be Americans, especially the Japanese. From the time Lilioukalani was removed from the throne, American government officials had been talking about making Hawaii the nation's 50th state, but it wasn't until March 12, 1959, that Congress passed the Hawaii State Bill.

MAUI: POSTSTATEHOOD DEVELOPMENT   After Hawaii was admitted to the Union as America's 50th state, the islands remained relatively quiet for a period of time. The violence of the Korean and Vietnam wars had little effect on the Hawaiian way of life. However, Maui did see its share of hippies (known as *das hipas*, or "lost sheep," to the Hawaiians) who migrated en masse. They settled in the Upcountry towns of Paia and Haiku, opening craft shops and health-food stores. Today, Paia still reflects the hippie influence with offbeat shops and health-food restaurants. Artists were drawn to the island with its next-to-perfect climate, its brilliance of color, and its clarity of light.

It wasn't long before a more monied class of people discovered Maui and began visiting the island and building vacation homes. The price of real estate soared, and it soon became clear that Maui's economic success would depend on developing tourism. A company known as Amfac (American Factors) owned the land in Kaanapali, just 4 miles west of Lahaina, and they quickly realized the economic potential of their near-perfect, beachfront location. They built one of the most successful resort properties on the island. Restoration of the town of Lahaina was also beginning, and with it came a colony of artists who showed their work every Saturday under the banyan tree in the center of town. The Lahaina that had become a virtual ghost town after the whaling fleet abandoned its shores once again became a bustling center of activity.

Though the tourist industry was rapidly developing, much of Maui remained pristine and untouched as late as 1970. But, alas, progress marches on, and it wasn't long before private developers began constructing high-rise condominiums along the shore from Maalaea to Kihei. Farther inland, along the Kihei hills, wealthy Americans began building million-dollar homes, and the once unsupportive scrub land was transformed as homeowners cultivated a tropical landscape. Because tracts of land in the Kihei area were independently owned, there was no general management system in place to control the types of businesses and restaurants that would open their doors to island visitors. The way was paved for the building of fast-food restaurants and shopping centers. The whole of Wailea (the stretch from Kihei to Makena), on the other hand, was owned by Alexander & Baldwin and the Matson Navigation Company. Its 1,500 acres of lava fields, dotted with kiawe, and laced with yet another coastline of white-sand beaches, was another perfect location for the development of a full-service resort. Architects planned and designed the Wailea landscape with a new understanding of the necessity of preserving the area's historic sites. They unearthed the remains of an old Hawaiian village, a heiau, and the foundations of a chief's house, all of which were restored and can be visited today.

On Maui's west side, beyond Kaanapali, was a parcel of land that since 1911 had been used by Maui Pineapple Company (started by Henry P. Baldwin) as a pineapple plantation. Under the direction of company president Colin Cameron, the company's name was changed to Maui Land & Pineapple Company and development of another major resort, Kapalua, began. By the late 1970s, the Kapalua resort began selling its yet unbuilt condominiums for in excess of $100,000. (Much of the Kapalua Resort area is still a working pineapple plantation.)

Today, though sugarcane and pineapple are still grown on Maui, and smaller interests focus on the raising of cattle and diversified agriculture, the island's major economic interest is tourism.

3. ART & ARCHITECTURE

ART

Art has always been integral to Hawaiian life. The art of early Hawaii often took forms that were useful in everyday life. Kapa cloth was used as bedding and clothing. Beautiful featherwork capes, cloaks, helmets, and leis were worn by the Hawaiian ali'i to indicate rank; and beautifully carved wood bowls were designed specifically to hold poi, a staple of daily Hawaiian life. Ancient Hawaiians took great pride in their work and elevated its execution to an art form. Unfortunately, some of the traditional arts and crafts of Hawaii have died out. This is due, in part, to the commercialization of the islands, but also because the natural supply of craft materials has diminished.

Today, native Hawaiian art is highly prized and every effort is being made to revitalize traditional arts and crafts. Most hotels on Maui sponsor lei-making classes and some even hold quilt-making lectures and demonstrations. There are also arts and crafts shows every year that celebrate local artisans.

Below you will find descriptions of a variety of traditional Hawaiian arts and crafts, that will, I hope, lead you to a greater understanding of Hawaiian culture.

KAPA (TAPA) CLOTH Before woven fabrics made their way from Europe and the U.S. Mainland to Hawaii, the women of Hawaii made cloth from the bark of a variety of trees and plants. The kapa-making process was long and somewhat tedious and it was so much a part of daily life that many households reserved a separate hut in which to work. Each day, village men would go out searching for wauke, mamake, ma'aloa, or poulu plants, the branches of which they would cut and take back to their wives. The women would peel the bark from the branches (not in strips, but whole), and then set the inner bark in a stream to soak until it reached the desired softness. After the bark had soaked long enough, the women would beat it on a log (*kua*) with a round club (*hohoa*) until it was flat and paper thin. The soaking and flattening process might take up to four days. The last step was to set the kapa in the sun to dry. Mamake bark was preferred above all others because its cloth was the most durable, but rather than being soaked first, mamake was steamed in an oven with a *pala'a* (a fern that gave out a dark red dye in the cooking process). After the steaming process was finished, mamake was soaked and beaten just like the other types of bark.

Most Hawaiian women dyed their kapa using the color of a variety of different plants. The mao plant would stain the cloth green, while the hoolei gave it a yellow tint. It was also customary for women to print patterns on the cloth. Almost every design was different and as individual as the artists who created them.

So old is the art of making kapa that it is even mentioned in the mythology of the demigod Maui. It is said that his mother complained that the sun moved too quickly across the sky and her kapa didn't have enough time to dry in the afternoon. Maui, sensitive to the needs of his mother, snared the sun by lassoing his legs (all 16 of them) and threatened to hold him there forever if he didn't slow his pace through the sky. The sun, like the rest of us, enjoyed a good night's sleep, so he agreed to slow down.

HAWAIIAN QUILTS Not so ancient as the art of kapa, but equally as beautiful, the art of quilting has been in existence in Hawaii since the mid-19th century. In fact, the first quilting bee held in the Hawaiian islands took place on April 3, 1820. The basic techniques were introduced to the women of the islands by missionary women from New England; however, the appliqués and stitch patterns you'll see on original Hawaiian quilts are authentically Hawaiian. Early quilt patterns were similar to designs found on kapa cloth, and very often women were inspired to create original designs by dreams or major events in their lives.

Usually the quilt consisted of a single-colored appliqué on a white background. The material to be used for the appliqué could be cut freehand, or with a paper pattern. Interestingly, the paper pattern was often made of kapa. Usually the appliqué material would be folded four or eight times before it was cut so the pattern would be uniform in all sections of the quilt. Most often the designs were inspired by the leaves of various trees and plants, like the fig or breadfruit trees and ferns. Outlines of pineapples, the octopus, and the sea turtle were also popular design elements.

Many of the patterns were unique to a particular artist, and most of the women knew the designs of their fellow quilters. If a woman invented a particular design it would forever be associated with her. Other women were not allowed to copy her design without crediting her. However, if a pattern were not carefully guarded before a quilt was completed it could be (and was often) stolen by someone else who might try to claim it as her own.

While the patterns and design elements of the appliqué were important, so were the stitches around the appliqué, because the stitching is actually what makes a quilt a quilt. Traditional New England–style stitch patterns used parallel lines and diagonals; Hawaiian women incorporated these patterns into their early work, but later they began inventing their own freehand stitch patterns that are much more elaborate and, in many ways, more beautiful than what we recognize as traditional stitching. This technique is referred to as "quilting following the pattern." The stitches flowed in free-form lines around the appliqué, in most cases following the pattern of the appliqué, but I've seen quilts with free-form stitching around the appliqué and cross-hatching superimposed on the appliqué. You can view antique quilts like the ones described above at some of the island's hotels.

FEATHERWORK   Unfortunately, little is known about the origins of Hawaiian featherwork because over the years its history has been lost, but David Malo recorded in his writings that "the feathers of birds were the most valued possessions of the ancient Hawaiians," and around 1778, Captain Cook, along with members of his crew, reported and marveled at Hawaiian featherwork in their writings. Some of the ali'i of Kauai who greeted Cook and his shipmates went aboard the ship wearing feather cloaks, leis, and helmets and presented Cook with half a dozen feather cloaks. He was awed by the brilliant colors and the intricacies of the work.

Because feathers were so sacred, a guild of professional bird catchers was established on the islands. They caught the birds by enticing them onto a branch or stick covered with a sticky substance, trapping them, or throwing stones at them until they fell to the ground. The most valued feathers were yellow, particularly those found under the tail and wings of the mamo. Red feathers, especially those of the i'iwi, were next in order of importance, and black feathers were the least well liked. Today many of the birds with the most prized plumage have fallen into extinction.

Lei Hulu   Adornments known as lei hulu were worn on the heads of Hawaiian women, as well as around the neck, and were constructed in several ways. Some are completely cylindrical (or *pauku*), like the more common flower leis you'll see today. Some pauku might have been made from the light yellow feathers of the o'o while others were made of green, red, black, and yellow feathers (some in a spiral pattern, others in blocks of color). Another style lei was known as *kamoe*. The feathers on these leis were laid flat and attached directly to the lei backing. Leis made solely of yellow feathers were the most highly prized, and any other leis made only of one color were more valuable than those made of two or more. The lei hulu *manu* was worn by women of the ali'i class to distinguish them from the Hawaiian commoners, and later, men wore the leis as hatbands.

Kahili   These plumed staffs of state resemble giant bottle brushes. Everywhere the king went the kahili (and kahili bearer) followed. In the evenings when the king slept the kahili were used to keep flies from settling on his highness's face. One report insists that rather than flies, the kahili were used to chase off bad *mana* (the Hawaiian equivalent of karma). No Hawaiians other than the ali'i could carry kahili. Because of their association with Hawaiian royalty, kahili were made with great care and came in an endless variety of shapes and sizes. The feathers from which they were formed were usually the tail and wing feathers of larger birds, such as the nene, the frigate bird, and even ducks and chickens. Handles were frequently made of tortoise shell or whale bone and the staffs might reach 10 to 25 feet in height.

Head Gear   *Manihole*, or feathered head gear, were also mentioned in the journals of Captain Cook, who described these ornate head coverings as ". . . caps . . . made so as to fit very close to the head with a semicircular protuberance on the crown exactly like the helmets of old." He also comments that "the Ground-work of the Cap is Basket Work, made in a form to fit the Head, to which the Feathers are secured." It seems that Hawaiians believed the head to be the most important part of the body, and feathers were thought to have the power to ward off evil, so the helmet was as much a physical adornment as it was a form of protection for the wearer.

There were several different types of manihole, including the crescent-crested, low-crested, wide-crested, hair helmets, and ornamented helmets. No one really knows the significance of each style because these things were never documented, but it is safe to assume that all who wore them had some connection to Hawaiian royalty. Most of the helmets that survive today have lost the majority of their feathers and what you'll see is the "basket work" described by Captain Cook. There are a few, however, that have been well preserved over the years—for example, the helmet of Kaumuali'i, the last king of Kauai, covered with red feathers and trimmed (on the crest) with feathers of an exquisite gold, which can be seen at the Bishop Museum on Oahu.

If you have the good fortune to see a manihole helmet you'll no doubt be struck by the number of feathers used in its creation. It is unfortunate that there is no written record of the people who assembled these wonderful creations. I, for one, wonder just who would have the patience to sit for what must have been an endless number of hours, painstakingly weaving each feather into the underlying basketwork.

Capes Perhaps the most spectacular and beautiful pieces of Hawaiian featherwork are the capes and cloaks once worn by Hawaiian royalty. They are said to have been worn as a means of identification in battle. Each high chief or king had his own design. We do know, however, from Cook's writings that wartime was not the only time these capes were worn.

The majority of the capes (which reached to the feet of the wearer) were made with a background coloring of red or yellow, and design elements, like circles, triangles, or crescent shapes were most frequently made of the opposite color (if the background were red, the design elements would be yellow, and vice versa). Sometimes black feathers were introduced into the pattern as well. Some people believe that the geometrical designs were representational of gods or birds, but in truth, not much is known about the patterns. Unless you visit the Bishop Museum on Oahu, you probably won't get a look at a feather cape, but many bookstores carry books about Hawaiian featherwork.

LEIS Of all ancient Hawaiian art forms, traditional lei making is the only one that has survived intact throughout the ages and is still being practiced island-wide today. Past and present, leis of all shapes and sorts have special significance. They are presented at comings and goings of all varieties—births, deaths, weddings, graduations, departures to another land, as well as homecomings, and they represent and encompass the true spirit of aloha. During your trip you'll have no trouble finding flower and ti leaf leis, and if you're lucky you'll come across an even rarer lei to take home and share with your friends.

Perishable Leis There are all sorts of perishable leis being made in the islands today, the most common of which is the flower lei. Leis made with fragrant plumeria blossoms are particularly popular with tourists. Easily strung, these flowers can be found almost everywhere on the island. My personal favorite flower lei is made with white ginger, which has a light but distinctive fragrance. The white ginger blossoms are typically gathered in the evening when they are about to open so they'll last longer, and if someone presents you with a white ginger lei you should be deeply flattered, for it is one of Hawaii's most special leis. Gardenia leis are also very fragrant, but are less common. Experienced Hawaiian lei makers can construct a lei with virtually any flower of any shape or size. I've even heard that some people have made leis of the very delicate bougainvillea blossom. The manner in which the flowers are strung depends entirely on the shape and size of the flowers being used.

Leis can also be made of ferns and garlands of almost any variety. Primitive-looking ti leaf leis can be extraordinarily beautiful because the ti leaf is pliable and easily manipulated. Primitive Hawaiians believed that the ti plant had special healing powers, and the kahuna of ancient Hawaii often used it to ward off evil spirits. If you buy a ti leaf lei to wear home, don't throw it out or hang it to dry when you get there—put it in the freezer where it will keep its shape and color until you feel like wearing it again.

Nonperishable Leis While flower and ti leaf leis are most often purchased by visitors to the islands, there are several other types of nonperishable leis that you can take home and keep forever. Some of the most popular are *lei pupu* (shell leis) and *lei hua* (seed leis).

Shell leis can be both simple and extremely intricate. Early Hawaiians gathered shells from the beaches of Kauai and Niihau, and either filed them down to make holes for stringing or strung them using the shells' natural holes. The first lei pupu were typically made up of several separate strands, each holding up to 200 shells. Other lei pupu were fashioned out of shells that are flat, like buttons, after having been worn down by the constant wave action of the ocean. Ancient Hawaiians collected the shell fragments that had washed ashore, punched holes in them, and strung them together. Many of today's shell leis are made much the same way as they were in ancient Hawaii. Lei pupu might be sold for a few dollars or a few hundred dollars, depending on the quality and rarity of the shells. If you're interested in purchasing a really fine shell lei, try to find one that was made on Kauai.

The most common seed lei is the kukui nut lei. I say common, but even as I write, these leis are becoming less and less common. This is largely because the process of polishing the kukui nuts is so difficult and time-consuming that it is simply not cost-effective. The fruit of the candlenut tree, the kukui nut might be "blond," brown, or black. In Old Hawaii, the leis made of black kukui nuts were the most coveted. The nuts would be gathered by lei makers after they'd fallen from the tree, and then sorted according to shape and size. The difficulty comes in polishing the nuts. In old Hawaii, all the polishing was done by hand. The outer layer of the shells in their raw form has a cloudy, whitish layer that must be removed. Then the grooves, which give the nut a walnut-like quality, have to be filed down, and finally, the shell is polished to a high shine. Ancient Hawaiians utilized natural files, such as sea urchin spines, and natural sandpapers like shark skin. The final polish was done with a pumice stone. Old-time kukui nut lei makers had an interesting way of extracting the nutmeat from the shell—they would make a hole in the top and bottom of the nut and then they would bury it until the nutmeat was eaten out by insects. Today there are polishing machines available, but most kukui nut lei makers believe it's best to polish the shells by hand. Kukui leis are moderately expensive, depending on where you buy them, but they are uniquely Hawaiian, and they're quite beautiful.

Currently, other seeds in a variety of shapes and sizes are being used in lei making, but they're more difficult to find. On my last trip to Maui I also visited Molokai, where I found a rare kukui nut and ekoa seed lei.

WOOD CARVING For ancient Hawaiians wood carving was a way of life. Primitive wood sculptures have been found all over the islands, and it seems that they were used for religious as well as practical purposes. Many religious figures were sculpted for the dedication of a heiau, or for a religious ceremony, and are thought to have been representational of particular Hawaiian gods. Ancient Hawaiians also carved food vessels (such as poi bowls), canoes, and furnishings out of wood. Some of the woods used by ancient woodcraftsmen included koa and ohi'a, both of which can be found on Maui today.

Koa wood is especially favored by current-day artists, but due to its extensive use in Hawaiian culture (both past and present), it is becoming more and more difficult to find. As a result, koa pieces you find in gift shops, from bracelets to bowls, are fairly costly. You'll probably end up buying a koa piece anyway—the wood is so rich and light that you'll have a difficult time passing it by. A word of advice: Be wary of carved figurines. Though they might appear to be Hawaiian, chances are they aren't even made in Hawaii.

SCRIMSHAW   This art form deserves mention particularly in regard to the island of Maui because of its history as the whaling capital of the islands. You'll find a number of shops that specialize in scrimshaw on Lahaina's Front Street. The primary sources for scrimshaw ivory used to be whalebone and elephant tusk, but today gathering of ivory from those sources is strictly forbidden, so most of the new scrimshaw is done on walrus tusk, which can be legally hunted by Eskimos. Typically, scrimshaw pieces are used in the construction of jewelry, including earrings, rings, bracelets, belt buckles, and brooches, and the etchings are usually of seascapes, whales, and ships. Prices on fine pieces of scrimshaw might run into thousands of dollars.

ARCHITECTURE

When the Polynesians arrived in Hawaii they knew how to build shelters with walls and thatched roofs, but it is generally believed that the first Hawaiians, like Papa and Wakea of Hawaiian mythology, lived in caves. The first man-made freestanding structures are thought to have been built of wood and tree bark. It wasn't until much later that the Polynesians introduced their "thatching" architecture to the islands.

Historical accounts tell us that houses of varying sizes and of differing construction materials were built according to class standards. The homes of chiefs, or the ali'i, were large and might consist of a number of different buildings, each serving a different purpose in the life of the chief. The homes of commoners (or the *maka'ainana*) were much smaller. Some maka'ainana didn't even have homes and were said to have sponged off their generous friends for shelter during inclement weather. Most of the early Hawaiian homes took the shape of a thatched tent. Some of the thatched gabled roofs were supported by four wood or stone walls, while others had only two or three.

Ancient Hawaiians typically slept on woven mats under kapa cloth sheets. Homes were usually lighted by the oil produced from the kukui nut. In order to remove the shells, the nuts were baked until the shells cracked. The oil-laden kernels were strung together on the hard, central rib of a palm leaf, creating a sort of jointed candle. A typical kukui nut candle was about 12 kernels in length, and each kernel burned for approximately 3 minutes. As the life of each candle was short, scores of them could be found hanging in Hawaiian homes at any one time. Kukui oil was also used in stone lamps with wicks made of tapa cloth strips.

When the missionaries began settling on the islands, they brought other architectural styles with them. After living in a grass hut in Lahaina for four years, Reverend William Richards, a New England missionary, built the first coral-stone house in Hawaii in 1823. Next door to the Richards' home, a man by the name of Ephriam Spaulding built another coral-stone house. It was later occupied by Dr. Dwight Baldwin. Known today as the Baldwin Home, it has been fully restored by the Lahaina Restoration Foundation.

Today you won't find any grass huts on the island, but you'll see just about everything else—from ramshackle ranch-style homes, to stately, two-story New England–style buildings.

4. RELIGION & FOLKLORE

Before the missionaries arrived in the 19th century, the Hawaiians had their own mythology and religion. It grew out of a deep respect for nature—the plants and animals that gave them food, the earth that gave them the materials to build shelters, the sun that gave them warmth and light, and the rain that quenched their thirst and watered their taro patches. Ancient Hawaiians believed that all human life evolved out of animal life, and therefore, everything in nature was sacred. The religion, Huna, taught that everything in the world had a partner, or an opposite, a polarity similar to the principal of the yin and yang.

Huna literally means "secret," and the kahuna, or priests, were the "keepers of the secrets." The kahuna were drawn from the members of the ruling class, or the ali'i, as children. To be chosen as kahuna, the ali'i children had to demonstrate an interest in learning and a high level of intelligence, for they were not only being trained as priests who could recite the mele of ancient Hawaiians, but they would be schooled as doctors, lawyers, teachers, astronomers/navigators, agriculturalists, artists, and sorcerers. In addition to worshiping the highest gods—Kane, Ku, Lono, Kanaloa, and Hina—the kahuna could transfer mana (a force similar to karma) to a subgroup of gods. Many times, this transference of mana (known as ho'omanana) was done on the bones of dead chiefs so their remaining family and its descendants would be protected.

Ancient Hawaiians believed that when a person died, his or her soul would go to *po* ("place of night") to be eaten by the gods, but they didn't believe this was the end for the human soul. They believed that all human souls would be reincarnated (*hou-ola*, "new life") so that eventually they might also become gods.

In Old Hawaii, much of the organized worship took place in the heiau, or temple, where the kahuna presided over the ceremonies. Most heiaus were constructed with stone foundations (many of which can be found throughout the islands today), but the actual shelters were built of straw or wood and have long since disappeared. Though human sacrifices were known to have been made at certain temples, most were simply places of idol worship. When Queen Ka'ahumanu abolished the tabu that had previously restricted women, who were considered less well developed than men, from eating certain foods or participating in ceremonies or events, she also ordered the destruction of the heiau and all religious idols, which left the Hawaiian people vulnerable to the Christian missionaries who were already setlling in Hawaii.

Though it all but eradicated the Huna, Christianity filled a spiritual void in the lives of Hawaiians; it also brought education to the islands. Today you'll find churches and temples of all religious denominations throughout the islands, including a smattering of Buddhist temples, and one synagogue (on Oahu).

5. PEOPLES & LANGUAGE

Maui's population of 92,000 reflects a multiculturalism found virtually nowhere else in the world. Its people represent a unique ethnic mix of Hawaiian, Filipino, Portuguese, Japanese, Korean, Irish, German, Chinese, and *haole* (or Caucasian) people, most of whom immigrated to Hawaii in search of a better life. They brought with them their languages, cuisines, modes of dress, art forms, and cultural entertainments, all of which have impacted Maui's social structure. Cultural influences can be experienced today on Maui simply by taking a walk along the beach where you might hear a surprising number of different languages. A walk down Front Street will dazzle you with art galleries that hold the works of Asians, Hawaiians, and haoles alike. Island restaurants represent a cross-section of cultural tastes and the blending of the spices of East and West.

PEOPLES

HAWAIIANS The story of the native Hawaiian people is one of disaster. Today, the number of full-blooded Hawaiians is a mere fraction of the 300,000 living in the islands at the time of Captain Cook's arrival in 1778. The early introduction of venereal diseases by Cook's shipmates proved devastating for the Hawaiians whose women displayed little or no inhibition when it came to sexual contact with the European sailors. By 1820, the Hawaiian population was estimated at less than half of what it was in 1778. The influx of foreign visitors also brought other diseases, both major and minor, against which the Hawaiians had no natural resistance, and wars between ruling chiefs obliterated another portion of the Hawaiian population. It is also believed that one-quarter of all Hawaiian men simply shipped out, never to return as they pursued careers in the whaling industry and found their livelihoods elsewhere. The final blow to the Hawaiian race came, simply, with the increase in interracial marriages. Today, most of those people claiming Hawaiian heritage are not full-blooded Hawaiian; in fact, the current portion of the population that is 100% Hawaiian is probably somewhere in the neighborhood of 1,500.

CHINESE   It is believed that the first Chinese to arrive on the Hawaiian archipelago came aboard an American ship skippered by Captain John Meares. They were a group of carpenters who built Meares a ship he called the *North West American*. None of the Chinese carpenters remained on the islands after their trip with Meares; however, in 1789 when Captain Simon Metcalfe visited Hawaii it is believed that several Chinese went ashore with John Young during the Olowalu Massacre. No one is sure if any of them survived.

The first real migration of Chinese to the Hawaiian islands began in 1852 when the first contract field laborers arrived from Hong Kong. Their passage was paid, and their five-year contracts granted them a salary of $3 a month plus room and board. They worked long, hard days on the sugar plantations and looked forward to the ends of their contracts when they would begin setting themselves up in business, leaving plantation work to the next wave of immigrants. Some of the first interracial marriages that took place in Hawaii were among the Chinese and the native Hawaiians. Today the Chinese population on Maui remains strong, although it makes up only a small percentage of the general population.

JAPANESE   Some historians believe that the Japanese arrived in Hawaii long before Captain Cook dropped anchor; however, the first documented Japanese arrivals (who intended to stay) took place in 1868. Originally, over 300 Japanese intended to migrate to Hawaii in search of plantation work, but only about one-third of that group actually left Japan because the Japanese government disapproved of their departure. Japanese immigration halted until 1885 when huge numbers of Japanese workers began immigrating to Hawaii. Only 15 years later, the Japanese population in Hawaii was figured to be just over 60,000. Japanese workers were as industrious as the Chinese labor force, but they found themselves the victims of cruel discrimination and were not given the same opportunities as their Chinese and Hawaiian co-workers.

Eventually, in spite of the discrimination, the Japanese were able to rise through the ranks from plantation worker to a professional career–oriented group of people. The children and grandchildren of the first large group of immigrants were educated in American schools and felt a strong alliance with the United States—so much so that many of them fought valiantly in World War II. After the war, these Japanese men who emerged as heroes were able to take advantage of the G.I. Bill, which allowed them to pursue college educations. Many of them became doctors, dentists, lawyers, teachers, and businessmen. The first Japanese-American governor, George Ariyoshi, was elected in Hawaii in 1974. Currently, the Japanese make up about 25% of Hawaii's total population and 23% of Maui's population.

HAOLES   Today the word *haole* refers to any person of Caucasian descent. Basically, to Hawaiians, it really doesn't matter where you're from—if your skin is white, you're a haole.

The haole history of Hawaii goes all the way back to John Young and Isaac Davis, members of Captain Simon Metcalfe's crew who were held as prisoners by King Kamehameha during the Olowalu Massacre in 1790. More significant, though, were the numbers of haole immigrants who came as missionaries from New England. They established themselves permanently on the islands long before the Chinese and Japanese, and have since been the most powerful economic force ever to settle in Hawaii, adopting a "colonist" attitude toward the natives, whom they looked down upon and whose customs and cultural activities they considered primitive and, oftentimes, disgusting. Most of the New England missionaries did not mingle with the Hawaiians, and so dilution of pure haole bloodlines among the missionaries was rare.

Another group of haoles living on the islands is the Portuguese. Between 1878 and 1887 approximately 12,000 Portuguese immigrants arrived in Hawaii, and another 6,000 came in the early 1900s. The olive-skinned Portuguese immigrants were welcomed with traditional Hawaiian aloha, mainly because they were dark enough not to be considered haole. Many Portuguese men and women worked on sugar plantations and rose into the top ranks of plantation laborers. They weren't, however, well educated, which is probably the reason that some Hawaiians constantly crack jokes about the Portuguese. Here again, as with the other ethnic groups, there was some interracial marriage among the Portuguese and the Hawaiians. When any member of the white population marries a Hawaiian, their offspring is referred to as *hapa-haole*, or "half-white, half-Hawaiian."

Much later, with the development of the resort properties, more haoles arrived; this time they came primarily from the U. S. mainland, and they have upheld the haole tradition of having a controlling interest in Hawaii's economy, sometimes at the expense of Hawaii's native people. Today, haoles make up approximately 33% of Hawaii's general population, while they number close to 36% on Maui.

FILIPINOS American nationals since the Spanish-American War in 1898, Filipinos did not have as much difficulty immigrating to Hawaii as the Chinese or Japanese did, mainly because they were not restricted by the same kinds of immigration laws that stopped many Asians. Hailing from the northern Philippines, 120,000 Filipinos were imported to Hawaii as plantation laborers between 1907 and 1931. Japanese workers in Hawaii had gone on strike in 1909, and plantation owners looked elsewhere for workers. They couldn't believe their luck when they discovered that the Filipinos would take the lowest-paying jobs and work under conditions that no other group would.

Like the Chinese, most of the Filipinos who immigrated to Hawaii were men (between 1924 and 1930 the ratio of Filipino men to Filipino women in Hawaii was approximately 19 to 1) who planned to return to their families and homeland after they saved a bit of money. By 1950 the Filipino population was about one-eighth of Hawaii's general population. Today the Filipino population is 14% of Hawaii's general population, but the percentage of Filipinos living on Maui is considerably less.

OTHER PEOPLES The rest of the Hawaiian population is made up of Koreans (who immigrated between 1903 and 1905), Puerto Ricans (who arrived at approximately the same time as the Koreans), African Americans, Vietnamese, and a small but fast-growing group of Samoans.

LANGUAGE

With such a diverse population, it should come as no surprise that Maui is a multitongued island. Of course, English is the dominant language spoken here, so you won't have any trouble communicating. Occasionally you'll hear some Chinese, Japanese, Portuguese, and Spanish, but there are two other Hawaiian languages that are the key to understanding the Hawaiian spirit and culture.

PIDGIN In early Hawaii, when migrant plantation workers came to the islands from all over the world, all speaking different languages, communications were difficult. Over time they all learned to communicate with each other in a language now known as pidgin. Pidgin is a true reflection of Hawaii's ethnic mix and it is quite literally a combination of several different languages. Its base is Hawaiian, but it also has English, Japanese,

Filipino, Chinese, and Samoan elements. The Portuguese had their own influence on pidgin—not in terms of vocabulary but intonation and musicality.

Some people consider pidgin low-class, nonsensical, and illiterate, and many have even tried to wipe it out, but to no avail. *Brah* (brother), *cockaroach* (steal), *geev um* (sock it to them), *hele on* ("right on" or "hip"), *lesgo* (let's go), and *tita* (short for sister, but used only with friendly, earthy types) are just a few of the words you might pick up during your trip. Today, pidgin is such a part of daily Hawaiian life that the Hawaiian House of Representatives has declared it one of Hawaii's official languages. If you'd like to learn more, try reading the very funny *Pidgin to Da Max* and *Fax to Da Max* (Bess Press, Honolulu), both of which are humorous "studies" of the language.

HAWAIIAN   The Hawaiian language has its roots in the languages of the Polynesians; however, the Hawaiian spoken today is probably very different from the Hawaiian of old. Over the years, as the oral tradition was changed to a written one, translations and transcriptions inadvertently changed the spellings and meanings of certain words and phrases. For a long while, after the introduction of English, and pidgin, Hawaiian was a dying language. Fortunately, today it is experiencing a rebirth through courses of study and the Hawaiian people's general interest in their roots.

Two of the most commonly used Hawaiian words are *aloha* (hello or goodbye; an expression of love) and *mahalo* (thank you). I've put together a short list of words and phrases for you in the appendix of this book. If you're interested in learning more, virtually every bookstore stocks a Hawaiian dictionary or two.

6. SPORTS & RECREATION

The outdoor sports enthusiast will not be disappointed on a trip to Maui. A wide array of water sports (that usually include lessons from an instructor and any equipment you might need) is available to people with all levels of experience. Perhaps you'd like to head out on a deep-sea fishing expedition, or stay closer to shore while snorkeling near a coral reef. Boating, windsurfing, surfing, and scuba diving are also offered island-wide. If, after a while, you're beginning to feel like one of the sea creatures you've been studying through your snorkel mask, you can also take advantage of your hotel's freshwater pool.

If you start to become water-logged there are plenty of activities that will get you out of the water and onto dry land. Tennis facilities abound all over the island, as do golf courses. Every major resort area, like Kaanapali, Kapalua, and Wailea, have challenging courses of their own, and in most cases the views are spectacular. If golf and tennis aren't your cup of tea, island hiking is unsurpassed. You can head out on your own, or sign up with one of the agencies that put together organized hikes. Biking is also fairly popular. If you get tired of exercising, try one of the downhill biking tours that takes you to the summit of Haleakala and requires only about 40 yards of actual pedaling; or, see the island on horseback.

For more information on the various sports activities offered on Maui, see Chapter 8, "Maui Sports & Recreation."

7. FOOD & DRINK

FOOD

Maui's diversity in cuisine reflects its multicultural roots. You'll find everything from local Hawaiian cuisine to the fine Eastern cuisines of Japan and Thailand.

Consult the Appendix of this book for a list of food terms you'll find used on the island.

LUAUS   You'll no doubt treat yourself to a luau sometime during your visit to Maui, and it might be your only taste of traditional Hawaiian cuisine. No luau is complete without *poi* and *kalua* pig (pig baked in an underground oven called an *imu*), but you'll probably also find chicken luau, *pipikaula*, and *laulau* (see below for definitions) on the main menu. Sweet potatoes and macaroni salad are typical accompaniments. Dessert will likely include *haupia* (coconut pudding) and fresh fruit. For information about choosing a luau, see Chapter 7, "What to See and Do on Maui."

LOCAL FOOD   Not really traditional Hawaiian cuisine, "local food" gets its name as a result of its popularity with the local population. It's basically of the plate lunch variety, consisting of deep-fried foods, teriyaki beef, chicken, or pork, and a side dish of the ever-present macaroni salad.

HAWAIIAN REGIONAL CUISINE   In a word: spectacular. You simply can't visit Maui without having a taste of the island's best cuisine. A delightful combination of Eastern and Western spices along with local produce and fishes, Hawaiian regional cuisine is also known as Pacific Rim cuisine. You'll find it prepared in the island's best restaurants, including the Plantation House Restaurant, Avalon, David Paul's Lahaina Grill, and Roy's Kahana Bar and Grill, to name a few.

ASIAN CUISINES   Japanese restaurants can be found all over the island, and most have excellent sushi bars. You'll also find a smattering of Thai and Chinese restaurants. Noodle shops are also popular among the local population.

DRINK

Soft drinks in Hawaii are much the same as the ones you'll find on the mainland; however, you will find some unusual juices, including orange/guava/passion fruit juice, which is absolutely delicious.

Tropical fruit drinks are the most popular alcoholic beverages for island visitors—try a mai tai or a lava flow. You should also give Maui blanc a try. It's a pineapple wine that is made at the island's Tedeschi Vineyards. Early versions of the wine were almost sickeningly sweet, but recent years have seen a surprisingly light wine that leaves only a slight pineapple taste on your palate at the finish. They also make an interesting passion-fruit wine, a couple of champagnes, a blush, and a red. Give them all a try, and as they say in Hawaiian, *okole maluna* (oh-ko-lay mah-loo-nah), or "Bottoms up!" (For more information on Tedeschi Vineyards, see Chapter 7.)

8. DANCE

If you know anything about Hawaii, you know that the *hula* is the dance of the Hawaiian people. There are no other people in the world who perform this unique dance that is as beautiful to watch as it is difficult to perform.

Earliest accounts of Hawaiian dancing reported that there were two forms practiced in the islands. The *ha'a* was performed only in the heiau (temple), and the hula was performed as a form of entertainment in public. The ha'a was a sacred dance performed only by men and taught, choreographed, and directed by the kahuna. Hawaiian royalty or high-ranking chiefs were its primary audience. The ha'a often had religious overtones (as it was frequently performed in conjunction with certain religious ceremonies, rituals, and chants) and was often shadowed in secrecy. The dances are also reported to have been extremely masculine and sexual. Men who wished to join the ranks of the ha'a dancers had to go through a rigorous selection process. Some even believe that the dances were used as a sort of training program for the military because it was from the groups of ha'a dancers that the members of the Hawaiian 'olohe (secret military society) were chosen.

Just before the missionaries arrived on Maui, the face of Hawaiian culture was changing due to political and religious unrest. Queen Ka'ahumanu ordered the destruction of all temples and religious idols, which effectively destroyed Hawaiian religion, and with it, the ha'a. The arrival of the missionaries in 1823 only ensured its end.

However, the hula, which had previously served as a form of entertainment for the Hawaiian maka'ainana (common people), managed to survive. This form of Hawaiian dance was less sexual, less religious in overtone, and more likely to be performed by female dancers. The hula required that the dancer (who often developed large hip and thigh muscles called *hula ku* as a result of the hip-rotating action that is the basis for the hula) have poise, grace, strength, and balance. What makes the hula unique is its costumery and its obvious representations of environmental events. Hula is a dance that requires the dancer to have complete control over every part of his or her body, and performed well, the hula should appear to be completely fluid and effortless. Every movement has a specific meaning, and every expression of the dancer's hands has great significance. The movements of a dancer's body might represent certain plants, animals, and even war. Chants accompany the movements and aid in telling the dancer's story.

Between 1832 and 1873 hula dancers adopted and adapted some European dance steps, and as the Hawaiians became increasingly sterile due to the introduction of venereal diseases by the Europeans, fertility dances (*mele ma'i*) in a public forum became much more popular. In many ways, Hawaiian dance wasn't dying out—it was growing in popularity among the islanders. At this time there were hula schools, or *halau*, throughout the islands, but it wasn't until the mid-1870s that the hula experienced a real growth spurt.

The people most responsible for the resurgence in the popularity of the hula were King Kalakaua and his family, who ascended to the Hawaiian throne in 1873. They became ardent supporters of traditional Hawaiian customs and culture and documented in writing the history of the hula by studying oral chants and traditions associated with early Hawaiian dance. They declared the hula a traditional symbol and expression of Hawaiian identity, promoted the use of grass skirts as costumery, and encouraged women to take major roles in dance performances. Not only did they preserve the past and promote hula, but they gave it a future by organizing more halau throughout the islands and by introducing stringed instruments (including the violin, guitar, and ukulele) as musical accompaniment.

Shortly after the turn of the century with the advent of war, Hawaiian dance became well known around the world, as it had become popular with military servicemen. In fact, during both world wars hula troupes were transported from Hawaii to the mainland and around the islands for the amusement of the U.S. servicemen. As radio introduced Hawaiian music to the world, people began to fantasize about the dance of the island paradise of the Pacific. It wasn't long before the civilian peoples of the world would get their first glimpse of the hula at the movie theater.

Not long after hula's celluloid introduction to the world, certain elements of the dance began to change. It became a more commercial enterprise with the addition of hapa-haole (half Anglo) dances and dancers. Hula was cheapened with the addition of plastic "grass skirts" and plastic flower leis. The instrumental accompaniment, rather than the dance, became the primary focus of a performance. The dancers, almost always female, took an ornamental role. Less experienced dancers were accepted into hula troupes as the demand for performers increased. Traditions of the ancient hula were being forgotten, and hula chanting even began to disappear.

Around the middle of the 20th century, after World War II, the popularity of hula took a downward turn. Demand for live performances dwindled, becoming confined primarily to tourist luaus. As the continuing migration of Asians and Europeans brought new music and dance to the islands, Hawaiians lost interest in their native dance and developed a preference for rock and roll. Due to the growth of the tourist industry, the government no longer saw the need to promote Hawaiian culture. With all of these factors working against the hula, one might think the dance would have died out completely, but the general public's reduced interest in the dance actually served to aid in its preservation. Those involved in the preservation of Hawaiian culture were free to revitalize the traditions of old Hawaii without interference by non-Hawaiian interests. During that time, the University of Hawaii maintained an interest in the dance, and an all-male dance group was formed at the Church College of Hawaii in 1958.

After 1960 there was a resurgence of interest in Hawaiian culture. The Hawaiian school system was restructured and hula was given a more prominent role in students' lives; the government took a renewed interest in the dance by celebrating it with special festivals and events and by granting honors to individuals who made lifetime contributions to the hula.

Today there is a return to the hula of old. Plastic grass skirts and flowers have thankfully been replaced by ti leaf skirts and fresh flower leis. Children all over the state compete for the few highly coveted spots in hula troupes just as they did in old Hawaii. The numbers of men and boys involved have increased dramatically, and competition among the troupes is fierce. Today's best hula troupes often travel the world demonstrating their skills and spreading interest in traditional Hawaiian culture.

9. RECOMMENDED BOOKS & RECORDINGS

BOOKS

HISTORY, POLITICS & SOCIOLOGY

Allen, Helena G., *The Betrayal of Liliuokalani: Last Queen of Hawaii 1838–1917* (Mutual Publishing, 1982).

Beaglehole, J. C., *The Life of Captain James Cook* (Stanford University Press, CA 1974).

Beckwith, M., ed., *The Kumulipo* (University of Hawaii Press, 1981).

Bird, Isabella L., *Six Months in the Sandwich Islands* (University of Hawaii Press, 1964). Original edition 1873.

Bradley, H., *American Frontier in Hawaii: The Pioneers, 1789–1843* (Stanford University Press, 1942).

Breitha, Olivia Robello, *Olivia: My Life of Exile in Kalaupapa* (Arizona Memorial Museum Association, 1988).

Buck, Sir Peter H., *Explorers of the Pacific* (Bishop Museum Press, 1953).

Burns, Irma Gerner, *Maui's Mitee and the General: A Glimpse into the Lives of Mr. and Mrs. Frank Fowler Baldwin* (Ku Pa'a Inc., 1991).

Daws, Gavan, *Shoal of Time: A History of the Hawaiian Islands* (University of Hawaii Press, 1968).

Day, A. Grove, ed. *Mark Twain's Letters from Hawaii* (University of Hawaii Press, 1975).

Dole, Richard and Elizabeth Dole Porteus, *The Story of James Dole* (Island Heritage Publishing, 1990).

Dudley, Michael Kioni, and Keoni Kealoha Agard, *A Call for Hawaiian Sovereignty* (Na Kane O Ka Malo Press, 1993).

Fornander, Abraham, *An Account of the Polynesian Race: Its Origins and Migrations and the Ancient History of the Hawaiian People to the Times of Kamehameha I* (Charles E. Tuttle Company, 1969).

Holt, John Dominis, *Monarchy in Hawaii*, 2nd ed. (Topgallant Publishing Co., 1971).
Joesting, Edward, *Hawaii: An Uncommon History* (W. W. Norton & Company, Inc., 1972).
Lee, W. Storrs, ed., *Hawaii: A Literary Chronicle* (Funk & Wagnalls, 1967).
Malo, David (translated by Dr. Nathaniel B. Emerson), *Hawaiian Antiquities* (Bishop Museum Press, 1951).
Maui Historical Society, *Lahaina Historical Guide* (Charles E. Tuttle Company, 1961).
Mellen, Kathleen Dickenson, *The Magnificent Matriarch* (Hastings House, 1952).
Mirantz, Maxine, *Women of Old Hawaii* (Aloha Publishing Co., Ltd., 1975).
Nickerson, Roy, *Lahaina: Royal Capital of Hawaii* (Hawaiian Service, 1978).
Speakman, Cummins E. Jr., *Mowee: An Informal History of the Hawaiian Islands* (Pueo Press, 1978).
Stewart, Charles, *Journal of a Residence in the Sandwich Islands, 1823–1825* (University of Hawaii Press, 1970).

NATURE

Canham, Rod, *Hawai'i Below: Favorites, Tips, and Secrets of the Diving Pros* (Watersport Publishing Inc., 1991).
Hargreaves, Dorothy and Bob Hargreaves, *Hawaii Blossoms* (Ross-Hargreaves, 1958); *Tropical Trees of Hawaii* (Ross-Hargreaves, 1964).
Hawai'i Audubon Society, *Hawaii's Birds* (Hawai'i Audubon Society, 1989).
Kepler, Angela K., *Exotic Tropicals of Hawaii: Heliconias, Gingers, Anthuriums & Decorative Foliage* (Mutual Publishing, 1989).
Kepler, Cameron B., and Angela Kay, *Haleakala: A Guide to the Mountain* (Mutual Publishing, 1988).

ART, MUSIC & DANCE

Buck, Peter H. (Te Rangi Hiroa), *Arts and Crafts of Hawaii*, vols. 1–14 (Bishop Museum Press, 1957).
Cox, J. Halley, and William H. Davenport, *Hawaiian Sculpture* (rev. ed.) (University of Hawaii Press, 1988).
Holt, John Dominis. *The Art of Featherwork in Old Hawai'i* (Topgallant Publishing Co., 1985).
Jones, Stella M., *Hawaiian Quilts* (Daughters of Hawaii and the Honolulu Academy of Arts and Mission Houses Museum, 1973).
Kanahele, George S., ed., *Hawaiian Music and Musicians: An Illustrated History* (University Press of Hawaii, 1979).
McDonald, Marie A., *Ka Lei: The Leis of Hawaii* (Ku Pa'a Inc. and Press Pacifica, 1989).
Stagner, Ishmael, *Hula* (The Institute for Polynesian Studies, Bringham Young University, 1985).

MYTHOLOGY & FOLKLORE

Lyons, Barbara, *Maui Mischievous Hero* (The Petroglyph Press, 1969).
McBride, L. R., *The Kahuna: Versatile Mystics of Old Hawaii* (The Petroglyph Press, 1972).

REFERENCE

Pukui, Mary Kawena, and Samuel H. Elbert, *New Pocket Hawaiian Dictionary* (University of Hawaii Press, Honolulu, HI, 1975).

FICTION

Bushnell, O. A., *Ka'a'awa: A Novel about Hawaii in the 1850s* (University of Hawaii Press, 1980); *The Return of Lono* (University of Hawaii Press, 1971); *The Stone of Kannon* (University of Hawaii Press, 1979); *The Water of Kane* (University of Hawaii Press, 1980).
Jones, James, *From Here to Eternity* (Dell, 1985).
London, Jack, *Tales of Hawaii* (Press Pacifica, 1964).

RECORDINGS

Through the centuries, Hawaiian music, which originally took the form of chanting with the accompaniment of a shark-skin drum, has gone through many changes. European classical composers were the first to leave their mark, next came jazz musicians, and finally, rock and roll artists. Each musical genre contributed to a change in Hawaiian music, from intonation to instrumentation. This is why today there is no such thing as true Hawaiian music.

If you're interested in a more traditional sound, something you're not likely to hear much of today, try a recording from Emma Veary or Palani Vaughan. Aunty Edith Kanakaole is well known for her emotional renditions of classic Hawaiian chants. The Brothers Cazimero, the Sons of Niihau, and Aunty Genoa Keawe are also popular traditionalists.

Well-known modern male musicians include Frank Hewett, Jerry Santos, and Alfred Apaka; female artists include Karen Keawehawaii, Nohelani Cypriano, and Melveen Leed. "Gabby" Charles Philip Pahinui is a wonderful slack key guitarist who, in his youth, was heavily influenced by jazz. Pahinui has three musician sons, Cyril, Martin, and Bla. In addition to performing on their own, Cyril and Martin recorded with the Peter Moon Band.

CHAPTER 2

PLANNING A TRIP TO MAUI

This chapter is devoted to the when, where, and how of your trip—the advance-planning issues required to get it together and take it on the road.

After deciding where to go, most people have two fundamental questions: "What will it cost?" and "How do I get there?" This chapter will answer both questions and provide other essential facts, such as when to go and where to obtain more information about Maui.

---

1. INFORMATION & ENTRY REQUIREMENTS

SOURCES OF INFORMATION No matter what your point of origin, you should contact the **Maui Visitors Bureau** (1727 Wili Pa Loop, P.O. Box 580, Wailuku, HI 96793; tel. 808/244-3530, or toll free 800/525-MAUI), a branch of the Hawaii Visit Bureau, either before you go or once you get to ntors Bureau, either before you go or once you get to formation ranging from activities to accommodations.

The state body responsible for tourism is the **Hawaii Visitors Bureau.** For those who live in the United States, there are several U.S. mainland offices. The Chicago office is located at 180 N. Michigan Ave., Suite 2210, Chicago, IL 60601 (tel. 312/236-0632). In New York, 350 Fifth Ave., Suite 808, New York, NY 10118 (tel. 212/947-0717). In Los Angeles, 3440 Wilshire Blvd., Room 610, Central Plaza, Los Angeles, CA 90010 (tel. 213/385-5301). In San Francisco, 50 California St., Suite 450, San Francisco, CA 94111 (tel. 415/392-8173).

In Canada try the office at 205-1624 56th St., Delta, B.C. V4L 2B1 (tel. 604/943-8555).

If you're coming from Australia, you can contact the Hawaii Visitors Bureau, c/o Walshes World, 92 Pitt St., 8th Floor, Sydney, N.S.W. 2000, or G.P.O. Box 51, Sydney, N.S.W. 2001 (tel. 61-2-235-0194).

From New Zealand, write c/o Walshes World, 87 Queen St., 2nd Floor, Dingwall Bldg., Auckland, or Private Bag 92136, Auckland 1, New Zealand (tel. 64-9-379-3708).

The office in the United Kingdom is at 14, The Green, Richmond, TW9 1PX, England (tel. 44-81-332-6969).

ENTRY REQUIREMENTS Documents Canadians only need proof of Canadian residence to enter the United States. Those from the United Kingdom need only a valid passport. Australians and New Zealanders must have both a passport and a tourist visa to enter the country. (See Chapter 3, "For Foreign Visitors," for further details.)

Customs/Agricultural Regulations In addition to the regulations below, there are regular U.S. Customs regulations for foreign visitors. They are outlined in Chapter 3.

No one traveling to Maui is allowed to carry foodstuffs, plants, or seeds onto the island without previous permission. Anything you do carry onto the plane (even if it's simply a banana) will have to be declared and inspected by the U.S. agricultural inspectors at the airport. Fido won't have any fun on this trip because pets entering Hawaii must be quarantined for three months to ensure that they don't have rabies.

Please respect the regulations placed on the import of foods, plants, and animals because not doing so could have a devastating effect on the island's plant and animal life. Small insects and bacteria could hitch a ride with you. Rules are strict because Hawaii has already lost an enormous number of indigenous species, and the state is trying to protect the ones that still remain.

WHAT THINGS COST ON MAUI	U.S. $
Taxi from Kahului Airport to West Maui	42.00–45.00
Airport shuttle from Kahului Airport to South Maui	12.00
Local telephone call	.25
Double room at the Grand Wailea (deluxe ocean view)	425.00
Double room at the Royal Lahaina (moderate)	180.00
Double mountain-view room at the Maui Sun (inexpensive)	84.00
Lunch for one at Avalon (expensive)	25.00
Lunch for one at Scaroles Ristorante (moderate)	18.00
Dinner for one without wine at Roy's Kahana Bar & Grill (expensive)	35.00
Dinner for one without wine at Ming Yuen (moderate)	18.00–20.00
Bottle of beer	3.00
Cup of coffee	1.00
Coca-cola	1.50
Roll of ASA 100 Kodacolor film, 36 exposures	6.50
Movie ticket	5.00–7.00

2. WHEN TO GO—CLIMATE, HOLIDAYS & EVENTS

CLIMATE Maui's climate is tropical; however, its intensity varies depending on where you are on the island. If you choose to stay in the Kapalua area of West Maui, you will be treated to warm sunny weather during the day with infrequent rain showers and refreshing trade winds in the evenings. Only a few miles up the road in Lahaina (meaning "Merciless Sun"), rain showers are less frequent, and the sun is much more intense. Still hotter and much more arid are the towns of Kihei, Maalea, Wailea, and Makena. If you go Upcountry to Kula, Paia, and Makawao, you'll feel a drop in temperature and an increase in humidity—especially in the evening. Finally, the top of Haleakala Crater experiences the most extreme variations in temperature. In the evening and early hours of the morning it's usually cold, and during the day temperatures are approximately 20 degrees lower than those of the rest of the island.

Island temperatures average between 70 and 77 degrees, but I've seen the mercury rise to over 90 in places like Kihei and Lahaina. September and October are characteristically Maui's hottest months, but it is also low season, so hotel rates are cheaper.

Annual rainfall ranges from zero to 10 inches on average, so while you may get caught in a shower, it won't last long, and it certainly won't be enough to drive most sunbathers off the beach. You will also find that while it may be raining in Kapalua, it might be sunny in Lahaina.

MAUI'S AVERAGE ISLAND-WIDE TEMPERATURES

	Jan	Mar	May	June	Sept	Nov
Low °F	62	62	64	62	64	60
High °F	80	83	86	85	90	82

MAUI
CALENDAR OF EVENTS

JANUARY

☐ **Celebration of Whales** Three days of discussions, whale-watch excursions, entertainment, and an art exhibition at the end of January. Contact the Four Seasons Resort, 3900 Wailea Alanui, Wailea, Maui, HI 96753 (tel. 808/874-8000) for details.

☐ **Lahaina Whale Festival** The town of Lahaina celebrates the coming of the whales. For the last week of January and the first week of February, a series of ongoing special events is held throughout Lahaina. Call or write the Lahaina Town Action Committee, P.O. Box 1271, Lahaina, Maui, HI 96767, tel. 808/667-9175, for more information.

FEBRUARY

☐ **Hawaiian Cultural Arts Expo** Held at the Coast Gallery at the Hyatt Regency Maui, the Hawaiian Cultural Arts Expo is a multimedia exhibition of contemporary and classical works by Hawaiian artists. Call the Coast Gallery at 808/661-2777 for information.

MARCH

☐ **Na Mele O Maui** Festival celebrating island arts, crafts, dances, and music. Contact the Kaanapali Beach Resorts Association, 2530 Kekaa Dr., Suite B1, Kaanapali, Maui, HI 96761 (tel. 808/661-3271).

☐ **Art Maui** Hui No'eau Visual Arts Center in Makawao sponsors an annual juried show from March 19 to April 16 featuring works by island artists. Admission is free and all are welcome. Call or write the Hui No'eau Visual Arts Center, 2841 Baldwin Ave., Makawao, Maui, HI 96790 (tel. 808/572-6560).

MAY

☐ **Lei Day** An island-wide celebration with lei-making competitions, and Lei Day Pageants in the local schools. Write or call the Maui Visitors Bureau, P.O. Box 580, Wailuku, Maui, HI 96793 (tel. 808/244-3530) for information on the locations of specific events.

☐ **Hula Pakahi and Lei Festival** Held at the Maui Inter-Continental Resort, the Hula Pakahi is a hula competition featuring individual male and female dancers from all over Hawaii. Contact the Maui Inter-Continental, 3700 Wailea Alanui, Wailea, Maui, HI 96753 (tel. 808/879-1922), for more information.

JUNE

☐ **Kamehameha Day Celebration** Every year, Lahaina sponsors a parade to celebrate Hawaii's great king, Kamehameha. Call or write the Lahaina Town Action Committee at P.O. Box 1271, Lahaina, Maui, HI 96767 (tel. 808/667-9175) for more information.

☐ **Annual Upcountry Fair** Held at the Eddie Tam Center in Makawao, the Annual Upcountry Fair is an old-fashioned farm fair that features 4-H products and live entertainment. Admission is free; call 808/572-8883 for details.

☐ **Kapalua Music Festival** For two weeks in June, the Kapalua Bay Hotel sponsors a chamber-music festival featuring world-renowned musicians. There is an admission fee per concert. Call the Maui Philharmonic Society at 808/244-3771 for details.

☐ **Makawao Parade & Rodeo** A grand-scale Fourth of July celebration, complete with paniolo. Admission is free. Call 808/572-9928 for more information.

☐ **Maui Onion Festival** The Maui Onion Festival, held every year in the Kaanapali Resort area, features food, live entertainment, and the Maui Onion cook-off. Call or write the Kaanapali Beach Resort Association, 2530 Kekaa Dr., Suite B1, Kaanapali, Maui, HI 96761 (tel. 808/667-3271) for more information.

☐ **Kapalua Wine Symposium** Food and wine lovers will enjoy themselves at the Kapalua Wine Symposium. For one weekend in July, an international delegation of experts come together for gourmet meals, wine tastings, and panel discussions. For more information write or call the Kapalua Wine Society, 500 Bay Dr., Lahaina, Maui, HI 96761 (tel. 808/669-0244 or toll free 800/KAPALUA).

☐ **Lantern Boat Ceremony/Bon Dance** An interesting Buddhist ceremony to honor the souls of the dead. Call the Lahaina Jodo Mission at 808/661-4304 for details.

SEPTEMBER

☐ **Taste of Lahaina** Scores of Maui chefs participate in this fund-raising food tasting. There is live entertainment, wine tasting, and cooking demonstrations. You buy scrip tickets when you arrive and use them to buy the specialties offered by various Maui restaurants. Call or write the Lahaina Town Action Committee, P.O. Box 1271, Lahaina, Maui, HI 96767, tel. 808/667-9175, for more information.

☐ **Bud Light Maui Triathlon Championship & World Cup at Kaanapali** Triathletes compete in a combination 1,500-meter swim, 40-kilometer bike ride, and 10-kilometer run. Call 800/254-9299 for details.

☐ **Maui Channel Relay Swim** An annual 9-mile, six-person relay race from Lanai to Kaanapali. Call 808/522-7619 for more information.

OCTOBER

☐ **Maui County Fair** Located at the War Memorial Complex in Wailuku, the Maui County Fair features a parade, arts and crafts, ethnic foods, amusements, and a grand orchid festival. Call 808/244-7643 for details.

☐ **Hula O Na Keiki** Kaanapali Beach Hotel sponsors a children's hula competition. *Keikis* compete solo in ancient and contemporary dance. There is an admission fee. Contact the Kaanapali Beach Hotel, Kaanapali Beach, Kaanapali, Maui, HI 96761 (tel. 808/661-0011).

☐ **Aloha Classic** This is the final event in the Pro Boardsailing Association's World Tour. Participants from all over the world compete. The Aloha Classic is held at Ho'okipa Beach Park near Paia, and admission is free. Call 808/575-9151 for more information.

☐ **Halloween in Lahaina** Halloween in Lahaina is indeed a special event. People come from all over the world to take part in the parade that takes place on Front Street. Call or write the Lahaina Town Action Committee at P.O. Box 1271, Lahaina, Maui, HI 96767, tel. 808/667-9175, for more information.

NOVEMBER

☐ **Maui County Rodeo Finals** This major rodeo event, featuring Maui's best, takes place every year at Oskie Rice Arena in Makawao. Call 808/572-9928 for information.

☐ **Hawaii International Film Festival** Films from Asia, the Pacific, and North America are screened at various locations throughout Maui. Seminars and workshops are available. Call 808/944-7007 for information.

DECEMBER

☐ **Gala Tree-Lighting Ceremony** A month-long holiday celebration is sponsored annually by the Ritz-Carlton, Kapalua. It includes brunches, dinners, a life-size gingerbread house, and keiki hula. For more information, contact the Ritz-Carlton Kapalua, 1 Ritz-Carlton Dr., Kapalua, Maui, HI 96761 (tel. 808/669-6200).

☐ **Santa Comes to Wailea** On Maui Santa arrives not in a sleigh with reindeer but in an outrigger canoe. He lands at Wailea Beach near the Inter-Continental Hotel. Contact the Inter-Continental Hotel, 3700 Wailea Alanui Dr., Wailea, Maui, HI 96753 (tel. 808/879-1922) for information.

☐ **Christmas House** Every year at the Hui No'eau Visual Arts Center in Makawao there's a Christmas craft show featuring handcrafted items. There's a nominal admission fee. For information, contact the Hui No'eau Visual Arts Center, 2841 Baldwin Ave., Makawao, Maui, HI 96790 (tel. 808/572-6560).

3. HEALTH & INSURANCE

HEALTH Fortunately for travelers to Maui, there are few health concerns. You'll need no vaccinations, and as a matter of fact, people living in this island paradise live an average of 5.5 years longer than men and women who live on the mainland. Tap water on the island is clean, so you needn't worry about picking up water-borne bacteria in a restaurant or hotel room. However, some of Maui's streams and waterways are polluted, so don't drink the water while you're out hiking. It's a good idea to always carry fresh water when you hike. One liter per person should be adequate, and even though you might not feel like you need to, drink steadily as you hike because you can easily become dehydrated.

Sun Safety Many people who travel to Maui are interested in one thing—a deep, dark, tropical tan. If you're careful, you can certainly leave with the darkest tan you've ever had. However, Maui sun is strong, and you can burn in less than 10 minutes if you're fair-skinned. At the beginning of your trip stay in the sun for short periods of time and use sunscreen with a high SPF. As you tan you'll be able to spend more and more time in the sun (with less and less SPF) without fear of getting burned to a crisp.

Some people complain that they develop white dots, bumps, or spots on their skin that won't tan no matter how long they spend in the sun. I've been told that the spots are harmless and you shouldn't worry if you get them as long as you're not experiencing discomfort. If for some reason they should become painful or itchy, you should see a doctor.

Ocean Safety Maui's beautiful beaches and clear waters are enticing, but you should approach the water with caution, regardless of what it looks like on the surface. Most beaches don't have lifeguards, so it's up to you to protect yourself and your family. Don't ever swim alone, and always locate rocks, strange currents, and coral reefs before you enter the water. Wherever you decide to swim, don't just dive right in—you could be in for a nasty shock. Sometimes the water looks deeper than it actually is, and if you dive head-first, you may get pulled out feet-first.

If you see warning signs posted on the beach, take them seriously. Respect the ocean. If you ever get caught in a riptide (a scary but temporary event), don't panic, and don't try to swim directly against it. Don't waste your energy flailing about and yelling for help; just swim on a diagonal across the riptide and you'll be back in safer waters in no time. If you get tired and need to rest, float on your back.

When surfing or body surfing, never ride the waves straight in to the beach—surf to shore at an angle. If you're an inexperienced surfer, stay out of the water when the surf is very high because it's probably stronger than it looks, and it's likely that you're weaker than you think you are.

Finally, never, ever turn your back on the ocean.

Sea Creatures For the most part you're not in danger of being attacked by much in Maui waters. If you're swimming, the most you'll probably encounter is a jellyfish or man-of-war. Pay attention to where you're swimming, and if you run into one, give it a wide berth and swim carefully around it. They have a nasty sting, and if you are stung you should seek medical attention. If you go further out in the water (surfing or windsurfing) there's always a chance that you'll encounter a shark. If you do, I've been told that you should try to stay calm (I'm not sure how) and yell for help. Swimming frantically will only attract the animal's attention.

Look out for sea urchins if you're walking on the ocean floor—they have spines, and if you get one in your foot, it will be extremely painful. Another thing you should be careful of before you put your foot down is coral. If you step on coral not only are you going to scratch up your feet (which is much more painful than it sounds) but you'll also be destroying some very fragile marine life.

INSURANCE Before setting out on your trip, check your medical insurance policy to be sure it covers you away from home. If it doesn't, it's wise to purchase a relatively inexpensive traveler's policy, widely available at banks, travel agencies, and automobile clubs. In addition to medical assistance, including hospitalization and surgery, it should include the cost of an accident or death, loss or theft of baggage, costs of trip cancellation, and guaranteed bail in the event of an arrest or other legal difficulties.

4. WHAT TO PACK

To make travel easier on yourself you should pack only what you need. Ideally, you should only be carrying one medium-sized suitcase and one bag that can be stowed under the seat or in the overhead compartment of the airplane. Obviously, a bathing suit is a must (you might want to bring two so that when one is wet you can wear the dry one). Underwear and socks take up little room, so carry at least a week's worth of each. Maui is very casual, so men will very rarely be required to wear a jacket and women can get by with a light dress or nice pants. Other than that, you should take only a few changes of clothing. Shorts and T-shirts for the beach, a pair of nicer shorts for dining out or sightseeing, and a pair of jeans for the sunrise at Haleakala or an Upcountry hike. You also might consider carrying a light jacket because the higher elevations can get rather nippy early in the morning or after dark in the evening.

If you plan on doing more than sunbathing, a variety of footwear might be necessary. A pair of flip-flops, or as the locals call them, slippers, is ideal for the beach. If you plan on doing a lot of snorkeling you might consider investing in a pair of beach shoes to protect your feet from sea urchins and coral scratches. Hiking boots (or at least good sneakers) are essential if you plan on walking any of the trails covered later in this book. Finally, you should pack at least one pair of nice shoes for going out to dinner.

Some other small items you might consider carrying are a travel alarm clock; a Swiss Army knife, an indispensable item for impromptu picnics; a small first-aid kit (especially if you plan on doing any hiking); travel-size packets of laundry detergent for laundry emergencies; and, of course, your camera.

You're best off not to carry items like travel irons, hairdryers, curling irons, or too many toiletries. Irons and hairdryers are provided in most hotels, and you can buy travel-size toiletries once you get to Maui.

5. TIPS FOR THE DISABLED, SENIORS, FAMILIES & STUDENTS

FOR THE DISABLED   There are a couple of agencies you might want to contact for information before you leave home. **Over the Rainbow Disabled Travel Services,** at 186 Mehani Circle, Kihei, Maui, HI 96753 (tel. 808/879-5521), specializes in assisting disabled travelers to Maui. **The Commission on Persons with Disabilities,** State Office Building, 54 High St., Wailuku, HI 96793 (tel. 808/244-4441) will send you an *Aloha Guide to Accessibility* if you call ahead for an order form. It will cost $3, and it covers all the major islands in the state of Hawaii.

When making hotel reservations you should let the hotel know in advance if you have any special needs—that way they and your room will be ready for you when you arrive.

Several car-rental companies on the island offer rental cars with hand controls. Among them are Avis, Budget, and National. All of them require confirmation of the hand controls 48 hours in advance of pickup and a deposit of $50 for the use of the hand controls. The deposit will be refunded when you return the car. It is most likely that the hand controls will be placed in a full-size luxury vehicle, but you should check in advance.

FOR SENIORS   Travelers over the age of 65—and in some cases even 55—might qualify for a variety of discounts that aren't available to the average adult traveler.

Check with hotels for senior-citizen discounts when you make your reservations because they might offer 10% to 20% discounts. Some attractions offer discounts of up to 50% off the regular adult admission price. In most cases these discounts are listed in this book, but you should get in the habit of asking just in case they don't advertise senior discounts.

If you are retired and are not already a member of the **American Association of Retired Persons (AARP),** consider joining. The AARP card is valuable throughout the United States in your search for travel bargains.

FOR FAMILIES   Discounts for children abound. For instance, most hotels will allow children to stay free if they're in their parents' room. Children are also eligible for extremely discounted admission prices at most attractions—children aged 5 to 12 (sometimes even as high as 18) might only have to pay half of what an adult pays, and in many cases children 5 and under are admitted free.

In spite of the fact that Maui is a wonderful place to travel with children (mainly because of its abundance of outdoor activities), sometimes Mom and Dad need a break, and the best way to assure yourself that you're going to have time alone is to stay in a hotel that has a good children's day-care program (see "Frommer's Cool for Kids: Hotels" in Chapter 5). Many of Maui's hotels pride themselves on their children's programs, which generally take the children for the whole day and expose them to a variety of outdoor and indoor activities, feed them lunch, and keep them entertained until you return for them in the late afternoon or early evening. If you're in need of a romantic dinner for two, most of the hotels either offer babysitting services or can refer you to the island's most reliable.

FOR STUDENTS   It's a good idea to carry your student identification because you never know when you might be able to get a discount with the appropriate proof.

6. GETTING THERE

Your options for getting to Maui are limited. You're not going to make it by train, bus, or even by boat (unless you're on a cruise). Your only option is to travel by plane, and that can be quite an adventure depending on your point of origin. In most cases you'll have to fly to Honolulu first and then switch to a smaller airline for the short hop to Maui.

AIRPORTS   There are three airports on Maui, but most likely you'll arrive at Maui's **Kahului Airport** (tel. 872-3893), which was recently renovated and has just gotten approval for the building of a longer runway. That means international flights will one day be landing directly on Maui. The project is scheduled to take several years, though, so for now you'll just have to make changes in Honolulu.

Kapalua–West Maui Airport (tel. 669-0228) is Maui's newest airport, and it's very convenient if you're planning to stay at any of the hotels in Kapalua or the Kaanapali resorts. You can rent a car and drive to your hotel from the airport, or check with your hotel before you arrive to see if they offer a shuttle service. If you're staying in Kapalua the drive will only be about 10 or 15 minutes, and if your hotel is in Kaanapali it will take you about 20 or 25 minutes instead of the 35 or 40 minutes it would take you to get there from Kahului Airport.

Hana Airport (tel. 248-8208) is a tiny airport that services Aloha Island Air commuter flights from Kahului airport several times daily.

FLIGHTS FROM THE U.S. MAINLAND TO MAUI   There are only three airlines that fly direct from the mainland to Maui. If you're traveling to Maui from the East Coast, these direct flights might make a big difference in your flight schedule. You will only have to change planes once, and you won't have a layover in Honolulu, which could cut a significant amount of time off your travel schedule (and

FROMMER'S SMART TRAVELER: AIRFARES
VALUE-CONSCIOUS TRAVELERS SHOULD TAKE
ADVANTAGE OF THE FOLLOWING:

1. Shop all the airlines that fly to Honolulu and Maui.
2. Always ask for the lowest-priced fare, not just a discount fare.
3. Begin your hunt for low fares early—keep calling the airlines to check rates. Availability of inexpensive seats often changes daily, and as the departure date draws nearer, more seats might be sold at lower prices.
4. Ask about senior-citizen discounts.
5. Ask for air/land packages. This allows you to get your hotel at a discounted rate—just keep in mind that your choices for accommodations will then be limited.

you'll be able to get to bed sooner). All three airlines fly into Maui's Kahului Airport.

United Airlines (tel. 808/242-7911, or toll free 800/241-6522) offers one nonstop flight daily from Los Angeles to Maui, and one from San Francisco to Maui. Each flight departs mid- to late morning, so if your point of origin is on the East Coast you'll have to get a very early flight out to make the connection. United Airline flights originating from other major cities make stops in San Francisco or Los Angeles.

Hawaiian Airlines (tel. 808/871-6132, or toll free 800/367-5320) has several daily nonstop flights from San Francisco or Los Angeles to Maui.

Delta Airlines (tel. toll free 800/221-1212) also offers a nonstop flight from the mainland to Maui.

Many more airlines fly a less direct route from the mainland to Honolulu where you can hop one of the interisland carriers. They include **Continental Airlines** (tel. 808/523-0000, or toll free 800/525-0280), **American Airlines** (tel. 244-5522, or toll free 800/433-7300); **Canadian Airlines International** (tel. toll free 800/426-7000); **China Airlines** (tel. 808/955-0088); **Japan Air** (tel. toll free 800/231-1052); **Lufthansa German Airlines** (tel. toll free 800/645-3880); **Northwest Airlines** (tel. toll free 800/225-2525); **Philippine Airlines** (tel. toll free 800/435-9725); **TWA** (tel. toll free 800/221-2000); and **USAir** (tel. toll free 800/428-4322).

FLIGHTS FROM HONOLULU TO MAUI There are only a few interisland carriers, the largest of which are **Hawaiian Airlines** (tel. 808/871-6132, or toll free 800/367-5320) and **Aloha Airlines Inc.** (tel. 808/244-9071). Both airlines fly regularly from Honolulu to Maui. Hawaiian Airlines offers the Hawaiian Airpass, which allows you to make unlimited interisland flights in a given period of time for a flat rate. A 5-day pass costs $169; a 7-day pass goes for $189; a 10-day pass will run you $229; and a 2-week pass costs $269.

Air Molokai (tel. 808/877-0026) and **Aloha Islandair, Inc.** (tel. 808/244-9071, or toll free 800/652-6541) are smaller companies, but they're just as reliable, and you'll probably be able to get cheaper fares. Both airlines offer regular flights from around 6am to 7pm. If you're afraid of small planes, you're better off going on Hawaiian or Aloha Airlines.

In 1993 a new airline, **Mahalo Air** (tel. 808/833-5555), charged onto the scene offering $25 round-trip fares to Honolulu. There's no telling how long this small airline is going to last, but if you're lucky enough to get one of their cheap flights you'll save a bundle—interisland flights on the other airlines can go all the way up to $170 round-trip.

SUPER APEX/APEX FARES   Advance Purchase Excursion fares vary depending on how many days in advance you make your booking. A reservation must be made 14 or 21 days in advance, and you must stay in your travel destination for a certain number of days to get the reduced fare. If you're flying from New York to Los Angeles or San Francisco, and then on to Honolulu, you're probably looking at spending anywhere from $625 to $1,250 round-trip, depending on when you're planning to travel. First-class tickets are considerably more—well in excess of $2,000 round-trip in most cases.

There are always cheaper alternatives, however. Be on the lookout for special promotional fares. In many cases you'll find them advertised in the newspaper or even on television. There will probably be restrictions placed on your dates of travel, but it can't hurt to try.

Finally, call a discount travel agency that has booked blocks of tickets and sells them at a severely discounted rate. You may get up to 40% off a regular economy (or first-class) fare, but once you've paid for them, you won't be able to make any changes at all, so be sure about your departure and return dates before you hand over any money.

CHAPTER 3

FOR FOREIGN VISITORS

1. **PREPARING FOR YOUR TRIP**
2. **GETTING TO & AROUND THE U.S.**
- **FAST FACTS: FOR THE FOREIGN TRAVELER**

Although American fads and fashions have spread across Europe and other parts of the world so that the United States may seem like familiar territory before your arrival, there are still many peculiarities and uniquely American situations that any foreign visitor will encounter. The following information will help make your trip run more smoothly.

1. PREPARING FOR YOUR TRIP

ENTRY REQUIREMENTS

DOCUMENT REGULATIONS Canadian citizens may enter the U.S. without visas; they need only proof of residence.

Citizens of the United Kingdom, New Zealand, Japan, and most western European countries traveling on valid passports may not need a visa for fewer than 90 days of holiday or business travel to the United States, providing that they hold a round-trip or return ticket and enter this country on an airline or cruise line participating in the visa waiver program. (Note that citizens of these visa-exempt countries who first enter the United States may then visit Mexico, Canada, Bermuda, and/or the Caribbean islands and then reenter this country, by any mode of transportation, without needing a visa. Further information is available from any U.S. embassy or consulate.)

Citizens of countries other than those stipulated above, including citizens of Australia, must have two documents: a valid **passport,** with an expiration date at least six months later than the scheduled end of their visit to the United States; and a **tourist visa,** available without charge from the nearest U.S. consulate. To obtain a visa, the traveler must submit a completed application form (either in person or by mail) with a 1½-inch square photo and must demonstrate binding ties to a residence abroad.

Usually you can obtain a visa at once or within 24 hours, but it may take longer during the summer rush from June to August. If you cannot go in person, contact the nearest U.S. embassy or consulate for directions on applying by mail. Your travel agent or airline office may also be able to provide you with visa applications and instructions. The U.S. consulate or embassy that issues your visa will determine whether you will be issued a multiple- or single-entry visa and any restrictions regarding the length of your stay.

MEDICAL REQUIREMENTS   No inoculations are needed to enter the United States unless you are coming from, or have stopped over in, areas known to be suffering from epidemics, particularly cholera or yellow fever.

If you have a disease requiring treatment with medications containing narcotics or drugs requiring a syringe, carry a valid signed prescription from your physician to allay any suspicions that you are smuggling drugs.

CUSTOMS REQUIREMENTS   Every adult visitor may bring in free of duty: one liter of wine or hard liquor; 200 cigarettes or 100 cigars (but no cigars from Cuba) or three pounds of smoking tobacco; $100 worth of gifts. These exemptions are offered to travelers who spend at least 72 hours in the United States and who have not claimed them within the preceding six months. It is altogether forbidden to bring into the country foodstuffs (particularly cheese, fruit, cooked meats, and canned goods) and plants (vegetables, seeds, tropical plants, and so on). Foreign tourists may bring in or take out up to $10,000 in U.S. or foreign currency with no formalities; larger sums must be declared to Customs on entering or leaving.

INSURANCE

There is no national health system in the United States. Because the cost of medical care is extremely high, we strongly advise every traveler to secure health coverage before setting out.

You may want to take out a comprehensive travel policy that covers (for a relatively low premium) sickness or injury costs (medical, surgical, and hospital); loss or theft of your baggage; trip-cancellation costs; guarantee of bail in case you are arrested; costs of an accident, repatriation, or death. Such packages (for example, "Europe Assistance" in Europe) are sold by automobile clubs at attractive rates, as well as by insurance companies and travel agencies.

MONEY

CURRENCY & EXCHANGE   The U.S. monetary system has a decimal base: one American **dollar** ($1) = 100 **cents** (100¢)

Dollar bills commonly come in $1 ("a buck"), $5, $10, $20, $50, and $100 denominations (the last two are not welcome when paying for small purchases and are not accepted in taxis or at subway ticket booths). There are also $2 bills (seldom encountered).

There are six denominations of coins: 1¢ (one cent or "penny"), 5¢ (five cents or "nickel"), 10¢ (ten cents or "dime"), 25¢ (twenty-five cents or "quarter"), 50¢ (fifty cents or "half dollar"), and the rare $1 piece.

TRAVELER'S CHECKS   Traveler's checks denominated in U.S. dollars are readily accepted at most hotels, motels, restaurants, and large stores. But the best place to change traveler's checks is at a bank. Do not bring traveler's checks denominated in other currencies.

CREDIT CARDS   The method of payment most widely used is the credit card: VISA (BarclayCard in Britain), MasterCard (EuroCard in Europe, Access in Britain, Chargex in Canada), American Express, Diners Club, Discover, and Carte Blanche. You can save yourself trouble by using "plastic money" rather than cash or traveler's checks in most hotels, motels, restaurants, and retail stores (a growing number of food and liquor stores now accept credit cards). You must have a credit card to rent a car. It can also be used as proof of identity (often carrying more weight than a passport), or as a "cash card," enabling you to draw money from banks that accept them.

Note: The "foreign-exchange bureaus" so common in Europe are rare even at airports in the United States, and nonexistent outside major cities. Try to avoid having to change foreign money, or traveler's checks denominated other than in U.S. dollars, at a small-town bank, or even a branch in a big city; in fact, leave any currency other than U.S. dollars at home—it may prove more nuisance to you than it's worth.

SAFETY

GENERAL   While tourist areas are generally safe, crime is on the increase everywhere, and U.S. urban areas tend to be less safe than those in Europe or Japan. Visitors should always stay alert. This is particularly true of large U.S. cities. It is wise to ask the city's or area's tourist office if you're in doubt about which neighborhoods are safe. Avoid deserted areas, especially at night. Don't go into any city park at night unless there is an event that attracts crowds—for example, New York City's concerts in the parks. Generally speaking, you can feel safe in areas where there are many people and many open establishments.

Avoid carrying valuables with you on the street, and don't display expensive cameras or electronic equipment. Hold on to your pocketbook, and place your billfold in an inside pocket. In theaters, restaurants, and other public places, keep your possessions in sight.

Remember also that hotels are open to the public, and in a large hotel, security may not be able to screen everyone entering. Always lock your room door—don't assume that once inside your hotel you are automatically safe and no longer need to be aware of your surroundings.

DRIVING   Safety while driving is particularly important. Question your rental agency about personal safety, or ask for a brochure of traveler safety tips when you pick up your car. Obtain written directions, or a map with the route marked in red, from the agency showing you how to get to your destination. And, if possible, arrive and depart during daylight hours.

Recently more and more crime has involved cars and drivers. If you drive off a highway into a doubtful neighborhood, leave the area as quickly as possible. If you have an accident, even on the highway, stay in your car with the doors locked until you assess the situation or until the police arrive. If you are bumped from behind on the street or are involved in a minor accident with no injuries and the situation appears to be suspicious, motion to the other driver to follow you. *Never* get out of your car in such situations. You can also keep a pre-made sign in your car that reads: PLEASE FOLLOW THIS VEHICLE TO REPORT THE ACCIDENT. Show the sign to the other driver and go directly to the nearest police precinct, well-lighted service station, or all-night store.

If you see someone on the road who indicates a need for help, do *not* stop. Take note of the location, drive to a well-lighted area, and telephone the police by dialing 911.

Park in well-lighted, well-traveled areas if possible. Always keep your car doors locked, whether attended or unattended. Look around you before you get out of your car, and never leave any packages or valuables in sight. If someone attempts to rob you or steal your car, do *not* try to resist the thief/carjacker—report the incident to the police department immediately.

You may wish to contact the local tourist information bureau at your destination before you arrive. They may be able to provide you with a safety brochure.

2. GETTING TO & AROUND THE U.S.

Travelers from overseas can take advantage of the **APEX (Advance Purchase Excursion) fares** offered by all the major U.S. and European carriers. Aside from these, attractive values are offered by **Icelandair** on flights from Luxembourg to New York and by **Virgin Atlantic Airways** from London to New York/Newark.

Some large American airlines (for example, TWA, American Airlines, Northwest, United, and Delta) offer travelers on their transatlantic or transpacific flights special discount tickets under the name **Visit USA**, allowing travel between any U.S. destinations at minimum rates. They are not on sale in the United States, and must, therefore, be purchased before you leave your foreign point of departure. This system is the best, easiest, and fastest way to see the United States at low cost. You should obtain information well in advance from your travel agent or the office of the airline concerned, since the conditions attached to these discount tickets can be changed without advance notice.

The visitor arriving by air, no matter what the port of entry, should cultivate patience and resignation before setting foot on U.S. soil. Getting through Immigration control may take as long as two hours on some days, especially summer weekends. Add the time it takes to clear Customs and you'll see that you should make very generous allowance for delay in planning connections between international and domestic flights—an average of two or three hours at least.

In contrast, travelers arriving by car or by rail from Canada will find border-crossing formalities streamlined to the vanishing point. And air travelers from Canada, Bermuda, and some places in the Caribbean can sometimes go through Customs and Immigration at the point of departure, which is much quicker and less painful.

For further information see "Getting There" in Chapter **2**.

 FOR THE FOREIGN TRAVELER

Automobile Organizations Auto clubs will supply maps, suggested routes, guidebooks, accident and bail-bond insurance, and emergency road service. The major auto club in the United States, with 955 offices nationwide, is the American Automobile Association (AAA). Members of some foreign auto clubs have reciprocal arrangements with the AAA and enjoy its services at no charge. If you belong to an auto club, inquire about AAA reciprocity before you leave. The AAA can provide you with an international driving permit validating your foreign license. You may be able to join the AAA even if you are not a member of a reciprocal club. To inquire, call toll free 800/336-4357. In addition, some automobile rental agencies now provide these services, so you should inquire about their availability when you rent your car.

Automobile Rentals To rent a car you need a major credit card. A valid driver's license is required, and you usually need to be at least 25. Some companies do rent to younger people but add a daily surcharge. Be sure to return your car with the same amount of gas you started out with; rental companies charge excessive prices for gasoline. See "Getting Around" in Chapter 4 for more information on rentals and driving.

Business Hours Banks are open weekdays from 9am to 3 or 4pm, although there's 24-hour access to the automatic tellers (ATMs) at most banks and other outlets. Generally, offices are open weekdays from 9am to 5pm. Stores are open six days a week, with many open on Sunday, too; department stores usually stay open until 9pm at least one day a week.

Climate See "When to Go" in Chapter 2.

Currency See "Money" in "Preparing for Your Trip," earlier in this chapter.

Currency Exchange You will find currency exchange services in major airports with international service. Elsewhere, they may be quite difficult to come by. In New York, a very reliable choice is **Thomas Cook Currency Services, Inc.,**

which has been in business since 1841 and offers a wide range of services. They also sell commission-free foreign and U.S. traveler's checks, drafts, and wire transfers; they also do check collections (including Eurochecks). Their rates are competitive and service is excellent.

Drinking Laws   See "Liquor Laws" in "Fast Facts: Maui," Chapter 4.

Electricity   The United States uses 110–120 volts, 60 cycles, compared to 220–240 volts, 50 cycles, as in most of Europe. In addition to a 100-volt converter, small appliances of non-American manufacture, such as hairdryers or shavers, will require a plug adapter, with two flat, parallel pins.

Embassies and Consulates   All embassies are located in the national capital, Washington, D.C.; some consulates are located in major cities, and most nations have a mission to the United Nations in New York City. Foreign visitors can obtain telephone numbers for their embassies and consulates by calling "Information" in Washington D.C. (tel. 202/555-1212). Listed here are some major consulates located in Hawaii or on the West Coast of the United States.

The **Australian** consulate in Hawaii is at 1000 Bishop St., Penthouse, Honolulu, HI 96813 (tel. 808/524-5050); the consulate in Los Angeles is at 611 N. Larchmont Blvd., Los Angeles, CA 90004 (tel. 213/469-4300). Also on the West Coast in San Francisco is the consulate at 1 Bush St., San Francisco, CA 94109 (tel. 415/362-6160).

The **Canadian** consulate in Los Angeles is located at 300 Santa Grand Ave., Suite 1000, Los Angeles, CA 90071 (tel. 213/687-7432).

The **Irish** consulate in San Francisco is located at 655 Montgomery St., Suite 930, San Francisco, CA 94111 (tel. 415/392-4214).

The **New Zealand** consulate in Los Angeles is located at 10960 Wilshire Blvd., Los Angeles, CA 90024 (tel. 213/477-8241).

The **British** consulate in Los Angeles is located at 1766 Wilshire Blvd., Suite 400, Los Angeles, CA 90025 (tel. 310/477-3322).

The **Japanese** consulate in Hawaii is located at 1742 Nuuanu Ave., Honolulu, HI 96817 (tel. 808/536-2226).

Emergencies   Call 911 to report a fire, call the police, or get an ambulance. If you encounter traveler's problems, check the local directory to find an office of the Traveler's Aid Society, a nationwide, nonprofit, social-service organization geared to helping travelers in difficult straits. Their services might include reuniting families separated while traveling, providing food and/or shelter to people stranded without cash, or even emotional counseling. If you're in trouble, seek them out.

Gasoline [Petrol]   One U.S. gallon equals 3.75 liters, while 1.2 U.S. gallons equals one Imperial gallon. You'll notice there are several grades (and price levels) of gasoline available at most gas stations. And you'll notice that their names change from company to company. The unleaded ones with the highest octane are the most expensive (most rental cars take the least expensive "regular" unleaded), and leaded gas is the least expensive, but only older cars can take this, so check if you're not sure.

Holidays   On the following legal national holidays, banks, government offices, post offices, and many stores, restaurants, and museums are closed: January 1 (New Year's Day);   Third Monday in January (Martin Luther King Day);   Third Monday in February (Presidents Day, Washington's Birthday);   Last Monday in May (Memorial Day);   July 4 (Independence Day);   First Monday in September (Labor Day);   Second Monday in October (Columbus Day);   November 11 (Veteran's Day/Armistice Day);   Last Thursday in November (Thanksgiving Day); and   December 25 (Christmas).

Finally, the Tuesday following the first Monday in November is Election Day, and is a legal holiday in presidential-election years.

Languages   Major hotels may have multilingual employees. Unless your language is very obscure, they can usually supply a translator on request.

Legal Aid The foreign tourist, unless positively identified as a member of the Mafia or of a drug ring, will probably never become involved with the American legal system. If you are pulled up for a minor infraction (for example, of the highway code, such as speeding), never attempt to pay the fine directly to a police officer; you may wind up arrested on the much more serious charge of attempted bribery. Pay fines by mail, or directly into the hands of the clerk of the court. If accused of a more serious offense, it's wise to say and do nothing before consulting a lawyer. Under U.S. law, an arrested person is allowed one telephone call to a party of his or her choice. Call your embassy or consulate.

Mail If you want your mail to follow you on your vacation and you aren't sure of your address, your mail can be sent to you, in your name, c/o General Delivery at the main post office of the city or region where you expect to be. The addressee must pick it up in person and produce proof of identity (driver's license, credit card, passport, etc.).

Generally to be found at intersections, mailboxes are blue with a red-and-white stripe and carry the inscription U.S. MAIL. If your mail is addressed to a U.S. destination, don't forget to add the five-figure postal code, or ZIP (Zone Improvement Plan) code, after the two-letter abbreviation of the state to which the mail is addressed (CA for California, FL for Florida, NY for New York, and so on).

Newspapers/Magazines National newspapers include the *New York Times*, *USA Today*, and the *Wall Street Journal*. National news weeklies include *Newsweek*, *Time*, and *U.S. News & World Report*. European newspapers and magazines are difficult to come by in Hawaii.

Radio and Television Audiovisual media, with four coast-to-coast networks—ABC, CBS, NBC, and Fox—joined in recent years by the Public Broadcasting System (PBS) and the cable network CNN, play a major part in American life. In big cities, televiewers have a choice of about a dozen channels (including the UHF channels), most of them transmitting 24 hours a day, without counting the pay-TV channels showing recent movies or sports events. All options are usually indicated on your hotel TV set. You'll also find a wide choice of local radio stations, each broadcasting particular kinds of talk shows and/or music—classical, country, jazz, pop, gospel—punctuated by news broadcasts and frequent commercials.

Safety See "Safety" in "Preparing for Your Trip," earlier in this chapter.

Taxes In the United States, there is no VAT (Value-Added Tax) or other indirect tax at a national level. Every state, and each city in it, has the right to levy its own local tax on purchases, including hotel and restaurant checks, airline tickets, and so on. In Hawaii, state sales tax is 4.17% and lodging tax is 9.17%.

Telephone, Telegraph, Telex The telephone system in the U.S. is run by private corporations, so rates, especially for long-distance service, can vary widely—even on calls made from public telephones. Local calls in the U.S. usually cost 25¢.

Generally, hotel surcharges on long-distance and local calls are astronomical. You are usually better off using a public pay telephone, which you will find clearly marked in most public buildings and private establishments as well as on the street. Outside metropolitan areas, public telephones are more difficult to find. Stores and gas stations are your best bet.

Most long-distance and international calls can be dialed directly from any phone. For calls to Canada and other parts of the U.S., dial 1 followed by the area code and the seven-digit number. For international calls, dial 011 followed by the country code, city code, and the telephone number of the person you wish to call.

For reversed-charge or collect calls, and for person-to-person calls, dial 0 (zero, *not* the letter "O") followed by the area code and number you want; an operator will then come on the line, and you should specify that you are calling collect, or person-to-person, or both. If your operator-assisted call is international, ask for the overseas operator.

For local directory assistance ("information"), dial 411; for long-distance information, dial 1, then the appropriate area code and 555-1212.

Like the telephone system, **telegraph** and **telex** services are provided by private corporations like ITT, MCI, and above all Western Union, the most important. You can bring your telegram into the nearest Western Union office (there are hundreds across the country), or dictate it over the phone (a toll-free call, 800/325-6000). You can also telegraph money, or have it telegraphed to you, very quickly over the Western Union system.

Telephone Directory There are two kinds of telephone directories available to you. The general directory is the so-called **White Pages,** in which private and business subscribers are listed in alphabetical order. The inside front cover lists the emergency numbers for police, fire, and ambulance, and other vital numbers (like the Coast Guard, poison-control center, crime victims hotline, and so on). The first few pages are devoted to community-service numbers, including a guide to long-distance and international calling, complete with country codes and area codes.

The second directory, printed on yellow paper (hence its name, **Yellow Pages)**, lists all local services, businesses, and industries by type of activity, with an index at the back. The listings cover not only such obvious items as automobile repairs by make of car, or drugstores (pharmacies), often by geographical location, but also restaurants by type of cuisine and geographical location, bookstores by special subject and/or language, places of worship by religious denomination, and other information that the tourist might otherwise not readily find. The *Yellow Pages* also include city plans or detailed area maps, often showing postal ZIP Codes and public transportation routes.

Time The United States is divided into six time zones. From east to west, these are: eastern standard time (EST), central standard time (CST), mountain standard time (MST), Pacific standard time (PST), Alaska standard time (AST), and Hawaii standard time (HST). Always keep changing time zones in mind if you are traveling (or even telephoning) long distances in the United States. For example, noon in New York City (EST) is 11am in Chicago (CST), 10am in Denver (MST), 9am in Los Angeles (PST), 8am in Anchorage (AST), and 7am in Honolulu (HST).

Daylight saving time is in effect from the last Sunday in April through the last Saturday in October (actually, the change is made at 2am on Sunday) except in Arizona, Hawaii, part of Indiana, and Puerto Rico. Daylight saving time moves the clock one hour ahead of standard time.

Tipping This is part of the American way of life, on the principle that you must expect to pay for any service you get. Here are some rules of thumb:

Bartenders: 10%–15%.
Bellhops: at least 50¢ per piece; $2–$3 for a lot of baggage.
Cab drivers: 15% of the fare.
Cafeterias, fast-food restaurants: no tip.
Chambermaids: $1 a day.
Checkroom attendants (restaurants, theaters): $1 per garment.
Cinemas, movies, theaters: no tip.
Doormen (hotels or restaurants): not obligatory.
Gas-station attendants: no tip.
Hairdressers: 15%–20%.
Redcaps (airport and railroad station): at least 50¢ per piece, $2–$3 for a lot of baggage.
Restaurants, nightclubs: 15%–20% of the check.
Sleeping-car porters: $2–$3 per night to your attendant.
Valet parking attendants: $1.

Toilets Foreign visitors often complain that public toilets are hard to find in most U.S. cities. True, there are none on the streets, but the visitor can usually find one in a bar, restaurant, hotel, museum, department store, or service station—and it will probably be clean (although the last-mentioned sometimes leaves much to be desired). Note, however, a growing practice in some restaurants and bars of display-ing a notice that "toilets are for the use of patrons only." You can ignore this sign, or better yet, avoid arguments by paying for a cup of coffee or soft drink, which will qualify you as a patron. The cleanliness of toilets at railroad stations and bus depots may be more open to question, and some public places are equipped with pay toilets, which require you to insert one or more coins into a slot on the door before it will open.

CHAPTER 4

GETTING TO KNOW MAUI

1. **ORIENTATION**
- **NEIGHBORHOODS IN BRIEF**
2. **GETTING AROUND**
- **FAST FACTS: MAUI**

If you look at a map of the island of Maui, you'll notice that the shape of the island resembles the head and torso of a man. The island is 25 miles wide and 40 miles long, and though driving can be rough and time-consuming, you'll have no trouble finding your way around. If you're even the slightest bit adventurous, you'll come to know Maui quite well by the time you leave, even if you've only got a week on the island. The people of Maui are generally friendly and helpful, but if you need some extra assistance, you'll find just about everything you'll need to know listed in this chapter.

1. ORIENTATION

ARRIVING

Most flights arrive at **Kahului Airport,** which is located in Central Maui, or at what would be the nape of the man's neck. The airport is small and easy to get around, and all the car-rental booths are located directly outside the baggage claim area.

If you're not renting a car at the airport, most hotels have shuttles that will pick you up at the airport and transport you to your hotel, but you should check in advance to see if you need reservations or if they have a regular shuttle schedule.

Akina Bus Service runs an independent airport shuttle that begins service from hotels in the Wailea-Kihei area at around 8 or 8:15am and continues until about 7pm. The first shuttle leaving the airport is at 8:45 or 8:50am; the last is at 7:45pm. The ride is about 45 minutes to the Kihei area from Kahului. The fare is $12 per adult, $6 for children 3 to 11 years old, and $3 for children under 3.

The Trans Hawaiian Airporter shuttles travelers from Kahului to the Lahaina/Kaanapali Resort area. They begin shuttle service at 7am and continue until 6pm. The fare is $13 per person. For reservations call 877-7308.

If you're staying in the Kapalua resort area and you've decided to fly directly into **Kapalua–West Maui Airport** to save time, you can rent cars there also, or you can call your hotel for an airport transfer shuttle.

TOURIST INFORMATION

The **Maui Visitors Bureau** is located at 1727 Wili Pa Loop (P.O. Box 580, Wailuku, HI 96793, tel. 808/244-3530) in the industrial area of Wailuku in Central Maui. To get there from the airport, follow the sign to the airport exit, go right on Route 36 (the Hana Highway) to Kaahumanu Avenue. Go left on Kaahumanu

Avenue (Route 32). Follow it past Maui Community College (on the right) and the Wailuku War Memorial Park (also on the right) onto East Main Street in Wailuku. Go right when you get to North Market Street and right again onto Mill Street. Go left on Kala Street and then left again onto Wili Pa Loop.

ISLAND LAYOUT
MAIN STREETS AND ARTERIES

There are main highways, or pi'ilani, that will take you to each town, community, or resort area. The highway you'll take from Kahului to Lahaina, Kaanapali, Kahana, Napili, and Kapalua is the Honoapiilani Highway, or Route 30. To get to most of the condos in Kahana and Napili, you'll want to take the Lower Honoapiilani Highway, which can be reached via virtually all of the streets that head off *makai* (toward the water) of the Honoapiilani Highway.

Lahaina's main street is Front Street, on (or just off of) which you'll find all major establishments and places of business.

From Kahului Airport to Kihei, Wailea, or Makena (the south side), you'll take the Mokulele Highway (Route 350) to the Piilani Highway (Route 31), which runs from Maalaea (pronounced "Ma-lye-ya") all the way to Makena (currently the end of the line on this side of the island). All the hotel and condominium properties are located *makai* (toward the water), off the Piilani Highway. The main road through Kihei is Kihei Road, which runs north to south along the coastline through Kihei and right up to Wailea. The main road through Wailea is Wailea Alanui Drive, which runs all the way through the resort area and connects to Makena Road.

You should also know that you can get from Lahaina to the south coast via the Honoapiilani Highway and the Piilani Highway, which connect near Maalaea.

The main road from Kahului to Wailuku is Kaahumanu Avenue (Route 32), which will take you right onto Wailuku's Main Street. The other main artery in Wailuku, where you'll find restaurants and shops, is North Market Street.

To get Upcountry to Paia you can take the Hana Highway (Route 36) from Kahului. This portion of the Hana Highway is not the one of "switchback" fame. That will come later as you continue along past Haiku, and it will take you all the way up to Hana on the island's east coast.

Further Upcountry from Paia is Makawao, which can be reached in one of two ways. You can drive to Paia as described above and then take a right on Baldwin Avenue (Paia's main drag) and follow it to Makawao; or you can take the Haleakala Highway (Route 37) to Makawao Highway (Route 400), where you'll take a left. It will take you right into Makawao. The first route will get you there a little more quickly.

Instead of going left off Haleakala Highway, continue along, and Haleakala Highway will turn into Kula Highway, which will lead you directly into the town of Kula.

If you go left off the Kula Highway, another Haleakala Highway will take you up to the summit of Haleakala Crater and Haleakala National Park.

FINDING AN ADDRESS

Finding an address on Maui is fairly simple, especially if you're looking for a shop, restaurant, or hotel. In almost all cases, commercial establishments are located off one of the main roads mentioned above.

The notable exception to this rule is Kahului. You should note that Papa Street runs in a half circle around the city of Kahului, and just about every street you'll need to find intersects with Papa Street at one time or another. Block numbers are posted on the street signs, so you can tell if you are in the general area of the address you're looking for without having to squint at building numbers. If you still can't find what you're looking for, stop and ask someone—most people are more than happy to help.

Islanders often use the Hawaiian words *mauka*, meaning inland, and *makai*, meaning toward the water, when giving directions.

NEIGHBORHOODS IN BRIEF

Central Maui   The small strip of land that connects the head and shoulders of Maui is known as Central Maui. Major roads that connect the east side to the west side go through this area. The two major towns here are Kahului and Wailuku. Kahului is home to Maui's airport as well as many of Maui's malls and department stores. There are only a couple of choices for accommodations in the Kahului area, and they're not the nicest places on the island. Only a couple of miles from Kahului is Wailuku, which has an eclectic mix of shops, restaurants, and accommodations. You'll find art galleries and antique shops on Main Street in Wailuku, as well as a less attractive industrial area.

West Maui   The resort areas of Kaanapali and Kapalua, as well as the towns of Lahaina, Napili, and Kahana, lie in West Maui. Lahaina is where most of the action takes place. Tourists and locals alike mingle in historic Lahaina because it's where you can find some of the island's finest restaurants, as well as the Baldwin House Museum, the famous banyan tree, art galleries, jewelry stores, antique shops, T-shirt shops, and a couple of bars. Further along the island's west coast you'll come to the resort area of Kaanapali, which includes the Marriott Hotel, the Westin, the Hyatt, the Royal Lahaina, the Sheraton, and many others. The Kaanapali resort is the largest and most active (especially in terms of nightlife) of all the island's resorts. It also has some incredible white-sand beaches. As you continue along the coast, you'll pass Napili and Kahana, which are much more subdued and hold most of the area's condominiums. Beyond Napili is the Kapalua Resort, where you'll find some of the island's most beautiful golf courses. Kapalua is home to the Kapalua Bay Hotel, several condominiums, and the newest addition to the hotel scene, the Ritz-Carlton Hotel.

South Maui   South Maui is the area that falls along the strip of coastline from Maalaea to Makena. The quaint fishing town of Maalaea is worth taking a quick drive through, although there are no tourist-oriented shops and only one restaurant worth noting. The next town along the coast is Kihei, and it's loaded with condominiums, fast-food restaurants, strip malls, and, in spite of it all, some of the island's best beaches. Kihei is where you'll find some less-expensive lodging and dining options, and it's very popular with the locals who gather to picnic on the beaches or do a little windsurfing. Being a resort area, Wailea is much quieter than Kihei. There are many major hotels in the Wailea resort, including the Grand Wailea (which is worth a sightseeing trip in and of itself), and a couple of golf courses. Like Kaanapali, Wailea also has some beautiful beaches, and many of them aren't heavily populated. Just beyond the Wailea resort is Makena. With a handful of historic sites and only a couple of hotels, Makena's main attraction is its beaches. Makena has Little Beach, Maui's only nude beach.

Upcountry   Upcountry Maui is a completely different experience than any other you'll have on the island. First of all, there are no beaches. Second, the temperature is often 10 to 20 degrees cooler, and at night you might even need a jacket. Technically, the Upcountry region begins in Paia, where you'll find Ho'okipa Beach Park and some of the best windsurfing on the island. As you continue Upcountry to Makawao, you'll leave the beaches behind, and instead you'll see farmland and even a log cabin or two. In Kula look for Tedeschi Vineyards, the island's only winery. In the same area you'll find the farms where the famous sweet Maui onions are grown and herbs for many of the area's restaurants are raised. If you're there on July 4th you'll be treated to a very unique rodeo.

East Maui   Basically what you'll find in East Maui is Hana. Hana, the tropical forest where waterfalls dot the countryside amidst guava and African tulip trees. The road to Hana takes a series of switchbacks and is narrow and bumpy—a challenge to the skill, patience, and stomach of even the best driver and least queasy passenger.

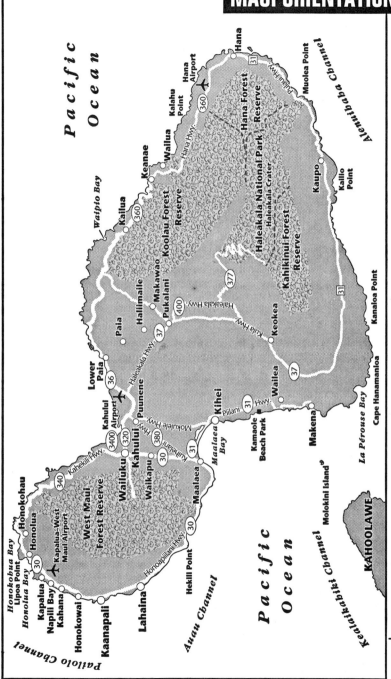

N

0   5 mi
     8 km

Pacific Ocean

Hana

Muolea Point

Hana Airport

Kalahu Point

360

Hana Forest Reserve

31

Alenuihaha Channel

Waipio Bay

Kailua

Keanae

Wailua

360

Koolau Forest Reserve

Kaupo

Kailio Point

Makawao

Halilmaile

Pukalani

377

Haleakala National Park

Haleakala Crater

Kahikinui Forest Reserve

Kanaloa Point

Paia

400

31

Haleakala Hwy.

Kula Hwy.

Keokea

37

37

Lower Paia

36

Kahului Airport

Puunene

Kihei

Piilani

31 Hwy.

Wailea

Makena

La Pérouse Bay

Cape Hanamanioa

3400

320

Kahului

380

Mokulele Hwy.

Kamaole Beach Park

Molokini Island

Kahului Hwy.

Waikapu

30

Kuihelani Hwy.

31

Maalaea Bay

340

West Maui Forest Reserve

Wailuku

Maalaea

Hekili Point

Honokohau Bay

Lipoa Point

Honokohau

Honolua

Honolua Bay

Kapalua-West Maui Airport

30

Honoapiilani Hwy.

Kapalua

Napili Bay

Kahana

Honokowai

Kaanapali

Lahaina

Auau Channel

Pacific Ocean

Pailolo Channel

Kealaikahiki Channel

KAHOOLAWE

Airport

6955

There is a small airport for those who don't wish to make the three-hour drive, and there are a few hotels, and even fewer restaurants. Before you get to Hana you can make a stop at the Hana Gardenland Cafe where Hillary Clinton breakfasted three mornings in a row during her recent trip to Maui. If you follow the Hana Highway through the town of Hana you'll arrive at Mark Twain's favorite beach, Hamoa Beach. There's also a black-sand beach and a red-sand beach, as well as several blue pools that can be found by only the most intrepid tourist. Beyond all of that, you'll come to the famous Seven Sacred Pools, or Ohe'o Gulch.

STREET & ROAD MAPS

Street maps of the various towns of Maui are difficult to come by. There are some decent ones in the front of the local phone book, and I found a book titled *Maui Road Maps* in several of the island's bookstores that proved to be very helpful. It is locally produced, and it shows most of the local streets in all the major towns on Maui.

Good road maps for Maui are also difficult to find; however, you can get one or two from the Maui Visitor's Bureau (see "Tourist Information," above for address and telephone number). You might also ask your rental-car agency if they have the map published by the University of Hawaii Press—it's a full-color topographic map with details of Lahaina, Wailuku, and Kahului. I know that Dollar Rent-A-Car distributes it at a charge of $2.95. If you can't get this map at your rental-car agency, check at one of the Waldenbooks stores around the island. Even if they don't have it, they usually have several others from which to choose. There's a Waldenbooks in Whalers Village and Lahaina Cannery Mall, both in Lahaina; Kaahumanu Center and Maui Mall Shopping Center in Kahului; and in the Kukui Mall in Kihei.

2. GETTING AROUND

BY PUBLIC TRANSPORTATION   Basically, there is no public transportation on Maui. I've heard that there used to be a public bus, and from what I've been told, it was very hit or miss. If you were in a rush, you would have been better off to ride your bike. Passengers apparently carried all sorts of things aboard—from babies to small farm animals—and the bus driver was apt to stop for lunch (at his own house) if the passengers agreed that they weren't in any sort of a hurry. I'm not sure whether I should be relieved or outraged that the old bus system is no more.

Because there is no public transportation system on Maui, several of the resorts have started their own shuttle services that will transport visitors all over the resort, and in the case of the Kaanapali Trolley, into Lahaina several times a day. The Wailea Shuttle runs all around the resort as well, transporting people from hotels to condos to golf courses to tennis courts all day long.

BY TAXI   There are many taxi companies on Maui, including **Yellow Cab of Maui** (tel. 877-7000) and **Ali'i Cab Co**. (tel. 661-3688). However, I wouldn't recommend trying to get around the island by cab. A ride from the airport to Lahaina will cost you between $42 and $45, and it's only about 20 miles.

BY CAR   Rentals   The only way to get around Maui is by car. All of the major car rental agencies have offices on Maui, including **Dollar Rent-A-Car,** which has branches at Kahului Airport (tel. 877-2731), Kaanapali (tel. 667-2651), and Hana (tel. 248-8237); **Alamo** at Kahului (tel. 871-6235) and Kaanapali (tel. 661-7181); **Avis** at Kahului (tel. 871-7575) and Kaanapali (tel. 661-4588, or toll free 800/831-8000); **Budget Rent-A-Car** at Kahului (tel. toll free 800/527-0700); and **Thrifty** at Kahului (tel. 871-7596) and Kaanapali (tel. 667-9541).

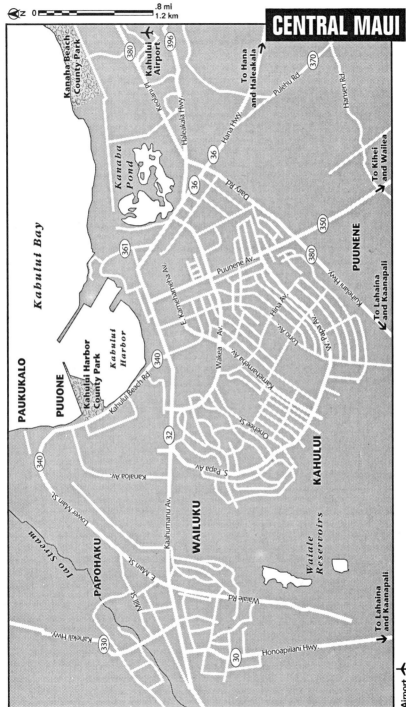

CENTRAL MAUI

0 ·8 mi
1.2 km

Kanaha Beach
County Park

Kahului
Airport

To Hana
and Haleakala

Hansen Rd.

Kojani Pl.

Haleakala Hwy.

Pulehu Rd.

Kanaha
Pond

Hana Hwy.

To Kihei
and Wailea

Kahului Bay

Dairy Rd.

PUUNENE

Puunene Av.

E. Kamehameha Av.

Kuihelani Hwy.

To Lahaina
and Kaanapali

PAUKUKALO

Kahului Harbor
County Park

PUUONE

Kahului
Harbor

Kahului Beach Rd.

Wakea   Av.

Hina Av.

Lono Av.

W. Papa Av.

KAHULUI

Kamehameha Av.

Onehee St.

S. Papa Av.

Kanaloa Av.

Lower Main St.

Kaahumanu Av.

WAILUKU

Waiale Reservoirs

Iao Stream

PAPOHAKU

E. Main St.

Mill St.

Waiale Rd.

To Lahaina
and Kaanapali

Kahekili Hwy.

Honoapiilani Hwy.

Airport

9569

Each of these agencies offers unlimited mileage and most have convertibles for rent. The one drawback to these rental companies is that their prices are fairly high. Cars can range from $50 a day to $90 a day—without coverage, and without the recently instituted mandatory $2-a-day Hawaiian surcharge. Check with your credit-card companies before you leave home to make sure that they do in fact guarantee insurance coverage on a rental car, so you can decline that extra cost when you pick up your car.

Some other, less well-known rental agencies offer lower rates because their cars are not in the greatest shape. **V.I.P. Car Rentals** at Kaahumanu Avenue (tel. 877-2054, or toll free 800/367-6080) offers "clean used cars," airport pickup, and unlimited miles. There's also **Word of Mouth Rent-A-Used-Car** located at 607 Haleakala Hwy. (tel. 877-2436, or toll free 800/533-5929) from which you'll also get unlimited miles and airport pickup. You won't feel out of place driving around in a beat-up old car—that's what most of the locals drive. You'll probably escape the attention of Maui's petty thieves as well.

Most of the car companies rent some kind of four-wheel-drive car, but only **Adventures Rent-A-Jeep** at 571 Haleakala Hwy. (tel. 877-6626) specializes in off-road vehicles.

Note: Most of the rental companies will ask you to sign a piece of paper stating that you'll downshift your car when descending Haleakala Crater. This is to protect the brakes on the car as much as it is to protect you. If you don't downshift you'll have to use the brake all the way down and you'll suddenly find yourself the center of attention as you coast down the crater with clouds of smoke billowing behind you. If that goes on long enough, your brakes might fail. Also, if your rental car is not meant to be used off-road, don't use it off-road. If anything should happen to the car while you are driving it off-road, the car company will make you pay for damages and towing charges. They won't go easy on you either.

Some money-saving advice: Before you make a reservation directly with the rental agency, check to see if your hotel offers a room/car package (most do)—it could save you a bundle.

Parking Parking places in Maui are fairly easy to come by. In most towns you can park on the street, and where there are time limitations, a parking lot that allows you unlimited time is available. The only town where parking might be difficult is Lahaina. You probably won't be able to get a space on the street, but if you're lucky you'll get one in the lots that don't charge a fee. If you have to pay to park, it won't break the bank—you could park for an entire day and only pay $10.

Driving Rules For the most part, driving rules are the same on Maui as the rest of the United States. Drive the speed limit, observe all traffic signals and signs, and make a right turn on a red light only after coming to a complete stop. Hawaii has a mandatory seat-belt law, so don't forget to buckle up. Sometimes the speed limit changes three or four times on the same stretch of road, so pay careful attention to road signs. Most of the time the line of cars on a given road is so long that you don't have any choice but to go the speed limit (much of the time you'll find that you're driving well below the speed limit because someone at the front of the line is putting along).

Gas stations on Maui can be scarce, and driving is often rough, causing you to use more gas than you might anticipate, so be sure to keep your tank fairly full at all times. Those of you who are traveling to Maui from the mainland are in for a shock over gas prices—at the time of publication regular unleaded gas was approximately $1.65 per gallon.

BY FERRY You won't be taking a ferry to get around the island, but if you want to go to Molokai or Lanai and you don't feel like flying, you can go by ferry. **Expeditions** (tel. 661-3756) will take you to Lanai from the public loading dock adjacent to the *Brig Carthaginian* at the Lahaina Wharf. You should make reservations in advance because the boat is fairly small. The ride to Lanai will take about an hour and is very pleasant, especially if you can get a seat on the upper deck. There are four or five departures daily, and round-trip fare is $50. Plan to get there 15 minutes in advance of the scheduled departure.

The *Maui Princess* (tel. 244-7799), operated by Island Marine Activities (505 Front St., Rm. 225) ferries passengers to Molokai twice a day. You should arrive at *Maui Princess's* slip at the Lahaina Wharf 15 minutes prior to your departure time, and you can purchase your tickets there. The round-trip fare is $50 plus tax. At press time passengers didn't have to make a reservation in advance, but call ahead to be sure. **Island Marine Activities** offers several different package trips to Molokai, which may save you some money, so you should inquire when you call to confirm departure times.

BY MOPED   If you don't feel like spending a bundle on a rental car, and also don't have the energy to ride a bicycle all over the island, renting a moped might be the best alternative. Try **A & B Moped Rental** at 3481 Lower Honoapiilani Rd. (tel. 669-0027) or the **Kukui Activity Center** at 1819 S. Kihei Rd., Bldg. E (tel. 875-1151).

BY BICYCLE   It is possible to get around Maui on bicycle (although you'll have to be in excellent shape), and there are even designated bike lanes in some areas. Many people rent bikes so they can do some off-road exploration—places where the car won't go (or the rental agency won't allow the car to go). **Cruiser Bob's Rent-A-Bike,** located at 99 Hana Hwy. (tel. 579-8444) and 155 Dickenson St. (tel. 667-7717), **Maui Mountain Bike Adventures** at Honokowai (tel. 669-1169), and **South Maui Bicycles** at 1913C S. Kihei Rd. (tel. 874-0068) are three reputable bicycle rental agencies.

HITCHHIKING   Though hitchhiking is never recommended as the safest way to get around, many island locals use hitchhiking as their means of transportation (which you can probably understand given the lack of public transportation). As in most states, hitchhiking on Maui is illegal, and if you've got your thumb in the wind, you might just be arrested. Locals don't solicit a ride—they just hang around on the side of the road hoping someone will take pity on them and ask them if they'd like a ride. So, if you're going to hitchhike, which, for the record, I don't recommend (especially for women traveling alone), don't be obvious about it or you might get a ride to the local police station.

 MAUI

Airports   See "Orientation" earlier in this chapter.

American Express   The main American Express office is located at 2805 Honoapiilani Hwy., Suite 116 (tel. 661-4456). Branch offices are located in several of the island's hotels, including the Grand Wailea (tel. 875-4526), Hyatt Regency Maui (tel. 667-7451), Kaanapali Beach Hotel (tel. 661-4908), Maui Marriott (tel. 667-7991), Ritz-Carlton Kapalua (tel. 669-6016), Sheraton Maui (tel. 661-5556), and Westin Maui (tel. 661-7155). If you need to report lost or stolen traveler's checks call toll free 800/221-7282.

Area Code   The area code for all the Hawaiian islands is 808.

Babysitters   Most hotels will help you make arrangements with a babysitting service if they don't offer their own, but if you're staying in a condominium where you don't have access to this service, try calling Babysit Service of Maui at 661-0558 or Nanny Connection at 875-4777. Both services will send babysitters to hotels or condos. Before you leave your child with any babysitter, do some checking to make sure that the person is reliable.

Bookstores   If you're looking for rare books, you're not going to find them on Maui. However, there are several Waldenbooks stores on the island, and in addition to their usual selection, they stock lots of Hawaiiana. You'll find Waldenbooks at Kaahumanu Center (tel. 871-6112) and Maui Mall (tel. 877-0181); Kukui Mall in Kihei (tel. 874-3688); Lahaina Cannery Mall (tel. 667-6172) and Whalers Village (tel. 661-8638) in Lahaina.

The Whalers Book Shoppe at 658 Front St. in the Wharf Cinema Center (tel. 667-9544) has a good selection of art, history, Hawaiiana, and fiction. After you browse and/or buy, you can sit and have a cup of coffee or tea in the bookstore's cafe.

The Bailey House Museum at 2375A Main St. in Wailuku (tel. 244-3326) has a good selection of Hawaiiana.

If you're looking for a paperback book that you can take to the beach and leave in your hotel room when you head home, try Paperbacks Plus at 1977 Main St. in Wailuku (tel. 242-7135). They have an enormous selection of used paperbacks from which to choose. Here you'll find everything from romance novels to fiction to art books to history to New Age and self-help.

Miracles Bookery Too, 3682 Baldwin Ave. in Makawao (tel. 572-2317), has a great selection of New Age books, as well as music, symbolic jewelry, and incense.

Business Hours Everything in Maui will be open by 9am—in fact, most places open their doors sometime between 8 and 8:30am because Mauians like to get an early start so they can quit early and get to the beach before the sun goes down. They also get an early start because of the time difference between the islands and the mainland. *Pau hana* (or "end work") is between 4 and 5pm. Most banks open at 8:30am and close at 3pm daily except on Friday when they close at 5 or 6pm. Malls and department stores stay open until about 9pm during the week.

Car Rentals See "Getting Around" earlier in this chapter.

Climate See "When to Go" in Chapter 2.

Currency Exchange You can get money changed at most banks, but it's often easier just to carry traveler's checks in U.S. currency to avoid the hassle of standing in lines at the bank or being caught with no cash after banks close.

Dentist The dentists on Maui are innumerable, so if you need to find a good one in an emergency, call the Dental Referral Service at 661-9023.

Doctor If you're staying in Lahaina, Kaanapali, or Kapalua and become ill, but it isn't an emergency, call Doctors on Call at 667-7676. They'll come to your hotel any day of the week on the same day you make the call. The Kihei Clinic at 1993 S. Kihei Rd., Suite 19 (tel. 879-1440), welcomes visitors, and they also make "hotel" calls. Upcountry Medical Center at 81 Makawao Ave. (tel. 572-9888) is open daily.

Driving Rules See "Getting Around" earlier in this chapter.

Drugstores Your best bet for a drugstore or pharmacy is Longs Drug Store. There are several located all over the island. In Kahului there's one in the Maui Mall (tel. 877-0041, or 877-0068 for prescriptions). In Kihei there's one at 1215 S. Kihei Rd. (tel. 879-2259, or 879-2033 for prescriptions). In Lahaina you'll find one in the Lahaina Cannery Mall (tel. 667-4384 or 667-4390). In addition to getting your prescriptions filled, you can get everything from aspirin to coffee to suntan lotion at Longs. If you're Upcountry, try Paradise Pharmacy, 81-21 Makawao Ave. (tel. 572-1266).

Embassies/Consulates See Chapter 3, "For Foreign Visitors."

Emergencies For police, fire, or ambulance, dial **911**.

Eyeglasses If you need your glasses repaired or need an entirely new pair, the Eye Gallery at 1325 S. Kihei Rd. in Kihei Professional Plaza (tel. 879-8544) specializes in same-day service for most jobs. The Aloha Eye Clinic Ltd Optical Department at 239 Wakea Ave. in Kahului (tel. 871-7485) also offers same-day service for most prescriptions. Sun Opticals at 1826 Wili Pa Loop Millyard in Wailuku (tel. 242-1803 or 877-3011) can make you a pair of glasses in about an hour.

Holidays See "Fast Facts: For the Foreign Traveler" in Chapter 3.

Hospitals The island's major hospitals are Maui Memorial Hospital at 221 Mahalani in Wailuku (tel. 244-9056, or 242-2343 for emergencies); Kula Hospital at 204 Kula Hwy. (tel. 878-1221); and Hana Medical Center in Hana (tel. 248-8294).

Hotlines HELPLINE, crisis counseling (tel. 244-7407); Women Helping Women, abuse counseling (tel. 579-9581); Maui AIDS Foundation (tel. 871-2437); Sexual Assault Crisis Center (tel. 242-4357).

Information See "Information & Entry Requirements" and "When to Go," in Chapter 2.

Laundry/Dry Cleaning Just about every hotel has laundry and dry-cleaning services, but if you don't want to pay the inflated prices of the hotel laundry service, there are a couple of options. W & F Washerette Inc. at 125 S. Wakea Ave. in Kahului (tel. 877-0353) is open daily until 9pm. You can drop your laundry off, or you can do it yourself. In Kihei, there's Kihei's Kukui Laundromat at 1819 S. Kihei Rd., Unit D104 (tel. 879-7211). Cabanilla Kwik 'n Kleen (tel. 667-5182) is located in the Lahaina Shopping Center. Upcountry at Pukalani Terrace Center is the Washtub, Inc. (tel. 572-1654).

For dry cleaning, Fabritek Cleaners is located at 325 Hukilike, Suite 10 (tel. 877-4444), in Kahului, and Lahaina Shopping Center (tel. 661-5660) in Lahaina. Also in Kahului is Valley Isle Dry Cleaners (tel. 877-4111) at 180-F Wakea Ave; they also have a branch in West Maui at Napili Plaza (tel. 665-0076).

Legal Aid If you're in need of legal assistance, call the Legal Aid Society of Hawaii at 244-3731.

Libraries There are branches of the Hawaii State Public Library System in Wailuku (tel. 244-3945), Hana (tel. 248-7714), Kahului (tel. 877-5048), Kihei (tel. 879-1141), Lahaina (tel. 661-0566), and Makawao (572-8094).

Liquor Laws The legal drinking age in Hawaii is 21. There are heavy penalties for anyone caught driving under the influence of alcohol.

Mail Many people wonder if it costs more to send a letter or postcard from Maui to the mainland than it does within the 48 contiguous states. It doesn't. Postage for a regular letter is 29¢. There are **post offices** in Haiku (tel. 575-2773), Hana (tel. 248-8258), Kahului (tel. 871-4710), Kihei (tel. 879-2403), Kula (tel. 878-1765), Lahaina (tel. 661-0550 or 667-6611), Makawao (tel. 572-8895), Paia (tel. 579-9205), Pukalani (tel. 572-8235), Puunene (tel. 871-4744), and Wailuku (tel. 244-4815). The main post office is on Oahu, so most mail originating on Maui is sent to Oahu to be postmarked.

If you want to send something novel home to your friends and family, write them a coconut postcard—you literally write on a coconut and the post office will mail it for you.

Newspapers/Magazines The main daily newspaper is the *Maui News*, but many of the towns put out their own papers as well. The island's magazine, *Maui Inc.*, is a bimonthly business publication.

Photographic Needs Many of the hotels have photo processing centers where you can buy film, throw-away cameras, and get film developed in an hour. You can also have film processed for a reasonable price at any of the Longs Drug Stores on the island, as well as in ABC Discount Stores. If your photographic needs are more extensive, try Roy's Photo Video Hi Fi Center in the Maui Mall (tel. 871-4311) or the Kahului Camera Image Center at 180 Wakea Ave. Bay G (tel. 871-6848).

Religious Services Among the many churches and temples on the island are Baptist, Buddhist, Catholic, Church of Christ, Congregational, Episcopal, Evangelical, Korean, and Lutheran houses of worship. Ask at your hotel or consult the telephone directory for locations.

Safety All in all, Maui is a safe place to visit, but when traveling, you should always exercise caution. No matter what you do, as a tourist you'll probably stand out. One of the biggest problems in Maui is car theft. Tourists' cars are easy to spot because they're generally in much better shape than the cars the locals drive. Don't leave money or valuables in the car, and keep all doors and windows locked when you're parked at the beach or at a major tourist destination.

Shoe Repair Try Lahaina Shoe & Luggage Repair at 761 Wainee St. (tel. 661-3114), or Tester's Shoe Repair at 55 Kaahumanu Ave. (tel. 877-7140).

Television   Most hotels have full cable television service, and many of them now offer a channel specifically for tourists. Check your hotel television directory for details.

Time   Maui is 5 hours behind eastern standard time, 4 hours behind Central, and 2 hours behind Pacific. Remember, however, that Maui does not observe daylight savings time, so add an hour when this is in effect on the mainland.

Weather   Call 244-8934, ext. 1520.

CHAPTER 5

MAUI ACCOMMODATIONS

1. **WEST MAUI**
- **FROMMER'S SMART TRAVELER: HOTELS**
- **FROMMER'S COOL FOR KIDS: HOTELS**
2. **CENTRAL & SOUTH MAUI**
3. **UPCOUNTRY & HANA**

Maui has always welcomed visitors with the warmest aloha, and today, islanders carry on the tradition by providing visitors to the island with a wide variety of accommodations, available in any number of styles and price categories. There are high-rise hotels, cottages, condominiums, and bed-and-breakfast inns from which to choose.

Choosing where you want to stay on Maui will depend largely on how much you want to spend and what kind of atmosphere best suits your personality. If you're looking to be at the center of the action, enjoy a good round of tennis or golf, and can afford to spend a fair amount on accommodations, Kaanapali is probably a best bet for you. It's right near Lahaina, and there's always something happening in Kaanapali. If you've got less money to spend, but still want to be in a lively location, try Kihei, where you can rent a condominium on or off the beach for slightly more reasonable rates. You can do the same in Napili or Kahana, but it's a bit of a drive to get to Kaanapali or Lahaina. If you're looking for peace and quiet in addition to good golf and tennis, you should try to stay in either Kapalua or Wailea resorts. Kapalua is smaller than Wailea and has only a couple of hotels and condominiums. Wailea has several hotels and condos, isn't as large as Kaanapali, but might be a bit more expensive than Kaanapali, depending on the hotel you choose. You can really save a bundle if you opt to stay Upcountry in a bed-and-breakfast inn, but it will probably take you an hour or more (unless you're in Hana) to get to the beach. Upcountry accommodations are typically frequented by locals who want to get away from the tourists and cool off a little.

Rates for hotels will usually include full resort privileges. Unless you have a golf package, you will always have to pay more for golf, and you'll often have to pay for tennis. Water-sports equipment like snorkels and boogie boards can be rented through the hotel for a nominal fee, and beach towels are typically provided free of charge to hotel guests.

Condominiums within a resort usually offer access to golf and tennis; however, your general expenses are likely to be lower because you'll have a kitchen where you can prepare breakfast and pack a lunch for the beach, and you won't be at the mercy of the hotel for all your meals. Some condos, but not all, provide a grocery start-up package of milk, juice, and coffee (some provide other items as well), but don't assume that you'll have milk for your morning coffee—ask before you arrive. Many will also offer to do your grocery shopping for you, but the service is costly.

The accommodations listed in this chapter have been carefully chosen to reflect a range of prices, and I have attempted to supply you with rates that will be accurate for the life of this book, but you might find slight discrepancies when you call to make reservations. Hotels listed under the category **expensive** are $165 and up; **moderate** hotels range from $100 to $165; the **inexpensive** category covers everything from $80 to $100; and the hotels in the **budget** range are under $80.

All accommodations are subject to 4.17% Hawaii state tax and a 5% Hotel Tax, so before you make a reservation be sure to figure in the tax.

1. WEST MAUI

West Maui includes the Kaanapali and Kapalua resort areas, Lahaina, and the area between Kaanapali and Kapalua. A youngish crowd is typically drawn to Kaanapali where there's always something going on. For those on a budget who can't afford to stay in Kaanapali, but still want to be at the center of activity, some of the hotels in Lahaina, or just off the highway between Kaanapali and Kapalua, would be a better option. Kapalua, on the other hand, is a good choice for those looking for a quiet, relaxing golf or tennis vacation.

KAANAPALI

EXPENSIVE

HYATT REGENCY MAUI, 200 Nohea Kai Dr., Lahaina, Maui, HI 96761. Tel. 808/661-1234, or toll free 800/233-1234. Fax 808/667-4498. Telex 743-1331. 813 rms, 32 suites. A/C MINIBAR TV TEL

$ Rates: $240–$260 terrace view; $295–$320 golf/mountain view; $325–$350 ocean view; $355–$380 deluxe ocean view; $390–$420 Regency Club mountain view; $430–$450 Regency Club ocean view. Extra person on standard floors $25, on Regency Club floors $45. Children 18 and under stay free in parents' room. Special packages are available. AE, DC, JCB Card, MC, V. **Parking:** Complimentary validation for hotel guests.

When the Hyatt opened in 1980 it was one of only a handful of hotel properties in the Kaanapali Resort area, and at that time was one of the island's most opulent. Today it is still a first-class establishment surpassed perhaps by only one of the newer properties on the island. Enter through the beautifully landscaped, open-air atrium dotted with palm trees, tropical birds, and pieces from the hotel's extensive Asian and Pacific art collection. In the lobby garden alone you'll find a large pair of Chinese cloisonné vases, some Japanese dragon pots, and Thai elephant bells. This is only the beginning—the hotel holds a veritable treasure trove of art. All public spaces are decorated with original pieces of artwork, including specially commissioned Hawaiian quilts, Burmese and Cambodian buddhas, Ming Dynasty wine pots, Chinese stone animals, and a breathtaking 17-foot-high cast-bronze sculpture titled, *The Acrobats*. Even the elevators here are spectacular: Teak-paneled interiors are accented with brass fixtures and luxurious Chinese carpets cover the floors.

The hotel consists of three connected wings, the tallest of which is only nine stories. The only things standing between the beach and the hotel are the pool, a row of palm trees, and a small strip of grass. All the guest rooms were renovated in 1990 and have views of the ocean, the West Maui mountains, Kaanapali golf courses, or the hotel's gardens, and they are pleasantly decorated with rich floral bedspreads, teal and peach color schemes, wood furnishings, and Asian lamps—a welcome change from the beige or sandy-colored interiors that many of the other hotels have incorporated into their guest rooms. Accommodations here have either king or double beds, separate sitting areas, and private lanais. Amenities include in-room safes and hairdryers. In addition to the standard rooms, there are private-access Regency Club rooms located on the top two floors in the Atrium Tower. Each of the Regency Club floors has a private concierge who handles all special requests, the complimentary breakfast service, and sunset cocktails and hors d'oeuvres. The hotel's suites range from the Ocean Suite, a one-bedroom unit with two lanais and two televisions, to the Deluxe Suite with a living room, dining area, three lanais, two televisions, and a wet bar. If you've got money to burn, consider the Presidential Suite, which has seven lanais, a full dining room, library, dressing room, sauna, Jacuzzi, and two full baths.

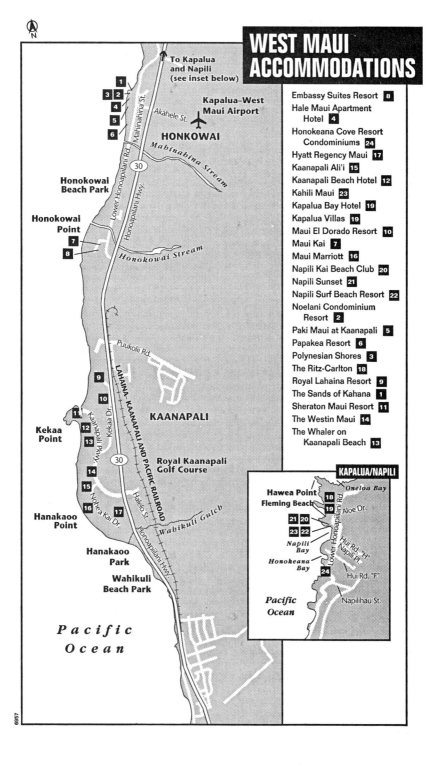

WEST MAUI ACCOMMODATIONS

Embassy Suites Resort **8**

Hale Maui Apartment Hotel **4**

Honokeana Cove Resort Condominiums **24**

Hyatt Regency Maui **17**

Kaanapali Ali'i **15**

Kaanapali Beach Hotel **12**

Kahili Maui **23**

Kapalua Bay Hotel **19**

Kapalua Villas **19**

Maui El Dorado Resort **10**

Maui Kai **7**

Maui Marriott **16**

Napili Kai Beach Club **20**

Napili Sunset **21**

Napili Surf Beach Resort **22**

Noelani Condominium Resort **2**

Paki Maui at Kaanapali **5**

Papakea Resort **6**

Polynesian Shores **3**

The Ritz-Carlton **18**

Royal Lahaina Resort **9**

The Sands of Kahana **1**

Sheraton Maui Resort **11**

The Westin Maui **14**

The Whaler on Kaanapali Beach **13**

KAPALUA/NAPILI

The Hyatt offers some special programs, one of which is the rooftop astronomy program, Tour of the Stars. In January 1991 the Hyatt announced that a "revolutionary new telescope system" for "public, educational, and recreational astronomy" had been developed and the prototype had been installed on the hotel's rooftop. Developed by Bill Leighty of Juneau, Alaska, this incredible telescope is outfitted with a computer that has the capacity to identify and locate 1,000 different stars, planets, clusters, nebulae, and galaxies. While the viewer observes various star formations, he or she can listen to a prerecorded message about the stars being viewed. Reservations for this program are a must, and there is an admission fee. Garden, art, and wildlife tours are also available, as are hula and Hawaiian arts and crafts lessons.

Dining/Entertainment: The Hyatt has several restaurants and bars. One of the hotel's fine dining establishments, Swan Court, serves a buffet breakfast on Monday through Saturday from 7 to 11:30am (Sunday from 7am to 12:30pm), and a continental dinner is served from 6 to 10pm (see Chapter 6 for complete listing). Spats, an Italian restaurant featuring Northern Italian cuisine, is the hotel's other fine dining venue (see Chapter 6 for complete listing). A more casual approach would take you to the Lahaina Provision Company, an open-air surf-and-turf garden restaurant. The Provision Company offers two unique specialties—the Tropical Salad Bar at lunch and the Chocoholic Bar at dinner. Another option for a casual dinner would be Mozzarella's Tiki Cafe, open from 6 to 10pm seasonally. Here you can dine poolside on pasta, pizza, and submarine sandwiches. The Pavillion is the hotel's other poolside dining spot, where diners enjoy breakfast (indoors or out) from 6 to 11:30am and lunch and snacks from 11:30am to 6pm. The Pavillion serves everything from fruit plates to pancakes to bagels for breakfast, and burgers, sandwiches, and salads at lunch. The Hyatt offers its own luau on the Sunset Terrace on Monday, Wednesday, Friday, and Saturday nights (see Chapter 7 for a full listing). For tropical drinks and smoothies, try the Grotto Bar, which is tucked away under the dual waterfalls. The Lahaina Provision Company's lounge is open from 11am to 11pm daily, and the Weeping Banyan (in the lobby, floating on the koi pond) is open from 6 to 10pm and offers contemporary Hawaiian music nightly.

Services: Concierge service offers all sorts of information about the resort and the island. Room service; babysitting service available on request. An American Express travel desk is available to help guests plan island sightseeing, as well as arrange cruises and airline reservations, and Budget and Avis car rental desks are also located in the lobby.

Camp Hyatt is the hotel's children's program that sponsors daily supervised activities for 3- to 12-year-olds. Rock Hyatt is an activity program for teens between the ages of 13 and 17. The teen program offers sports and social activities as well as off-property day trips. Nondenominational church services are offered every Sunday.

Facilities: The hotel's Great Pool is one of the main attractions. It holds 750,000 gallons of water and spans a half-acre. In the pool there's a swim-up cocktail bar and a swinging rope bridge for guests to enjoy. The Regency Health Club has a weight and exercise room, Jacuzzi, sauna, massage studio (both Eastern and Western techniques are practiced by the masseurs), and a billiard room. Aerobics classes are offered daily. Six hard-surface tennis courts are available for guest use. The Kaanapali Golf Courses are available for guest use (see Chapter 8, for detailed golf course listings). There is a game room on premises, as well as a small lending library. Rental equipment for snorkeling is available through the hotel, and *Kiele V*, the Hyatt's 55-foot catamaran, sponsors snorkel trips as well as whale-watching excursions and evening cruises. In addition, hotel guests may rent bicycles, kayaks, boogie boards, video cameras, and underwater cameras. Several floors have been set aside for nonsmokers.

KAANAPALI ALI'I, 50 Nohea Kai Dr., Lahaina, Maui, HI 96761. Tel. 808/ 667-1400, or toll free 800/642-MAUI. Fax 808/661-0147 264 units. A/C TV TEL

$ Rates: High season (Jan 5–Mar 31 and July 1–Aug 31): one-bedroom $235 garden view, $260 deluxe garden view, $305 ocean view; two-bedroom $290 garden view,

$310 deluxe garden view, $385 ocean view, $460 ocean front; $650 Club Ali'i Suite.
Low season (Apr 1–June 30 and Sept 1–Dec 15): one-bedroom $200 garden view,
$215 deluxe garden view, $255 ocean view; two-bedroom $260 garden view, $280 deluxe garden view, $320 ocean view, $420 ocean front; $650 Club Ali'i Suite. AE, MC,
V. **Parking:** Free.

All of the condominium units at the Kaanapali Ali'i are spacious—the ocean-front
accommodations range in size from 1,500 to 1,900 square feet and each is developer
or individually owned and decorated. One-bedroom units will accommodate up to
four, and two-bedroom units are large enough for six. There is no charge for an extra person if existing bedding is used. Each unit comes equipped with a washer and
dryer, dishwasher, whirlpool bathtub, and private lanai. Guests have use of the on-
site exercise room, pool, wading pool, Jacuzzi, saunas, barbecue grills, and beach activities desk. Three tennis courts are available for guest use. No fee is charged for
court time; however, if you wish to have lessons there is a nominal charge. There
are no restaurants on the property, but guests of the Kaanapali Ali'i have charge-
back privileges at the Westin and may order room service from the Maui Marriott
(located next door).

If you choose to have Club Ali'i Service, additional amenities include a full-size
rental car, fully stocked bar, plush terrycloth robes, and the "Maui Morning" grocery package (including champagne). Daily maid service is included in the rates for
all guests.

**MAUI MARRIOTT, 100 Nohea Kai Dr., Lahaina, Maui, HI 96761. Tel.
808/667-1200,** or toll free 800/228-9290. Fax 808/667-0692. Telex 397301
MAUMR UD. 720 rms, 19 suites. A/C TV TEL

$ Rates: $195 mountain golf; $225 mountain ocean; $255 ocean view; $275 deluxe
ocean; $440–$1,100 suite. Room & car, honeymoon, and golf packages are available.
AE, DC, JCB Card, MC, V. **Parking:** $8 per day valet or self-parking.

One of my favorite resort hotels on the island, the Maui Marriott offers its
guests a casual, comfortable atmosphere, a well-trained and friendly staff, and
all the amenities you'd find in any luxury hotel in the area. The most significant difference between the Marriott and some of the other hotels in this category is
the way you feel when you enter the hotel. Instead of worrying about your appearance, you'll want to let your hair down, change into your favorite T-shirt and a pair
of shorts, and head for the beach. The staff is efficient and extremely friendly—not
stuffy or overtrained like some of the staffs at other island properties.

The open-air lobby is tastefully furnished and landscaped with waterfalls, palm
trees, and scores of varieties of tropical plants. The hotel's two nine-story wings are
named for the island each one faces (Molokai and Lanai) and they flank the lobby
area. Each room in the hotel is entered via the open-air, bougainvillea-lined promenades that look down into the superbly landscaped lower lobby.

All of the hotel's spacious rooms have been recently refurbished with light-wood
furnishings, and a bright, airy color scheme. Each contains a king-size or two double
beds as well as a queen-size sofa sleeper, and features such amenities as a
minirefrigerator, in-room safe ($3 a day charge), ironing board and iron, hairdryer,
daily newspaper, daily complimentary Kona coffee, and direct-dial telephones with
voice mail. It's difficult to imagine that anyone could want for anything in one of
the Marriott's rooms. Each of the rooms also has a private lanai, and although
many of the rooms don't have ocean views, the rooms facing *mauka* "inland" have
beautiful mountain views.

The hotel has a full guest activities desk where you can arrange to attend exercise classes, scuba lessons, windsurfing and sailing demonstrations, tennis clinics,
classes in Hawaiiana (including lei making, hula lessons, regional foods, quilt making, and Hawaiian legends). They will also arrange helicopter rides, horseback riding,
deep-sea fishing, and whale-watching tours at your request.

Dining/Entertainment: There are three bars available to guests on the property.
The Lobby Bar is located directly across from the check-in desk and features

karaoke as well as live stand-up comedy. The Makai Bar is a popular spot with hotel guests and locals alike. If you arrive early enough, you'll be able to watch the sun set while enjoying tropical drinks, pupus, and live local entertainment. The Kau Kau Grill & Bar serves poolside cocktails as well as breakfast and salads, burgers, and sandwiches throughout the day. The Moana Terrace restaurant serves a buffet breakfast as well as a dinner buffet or à la carte menu. The Lokelani Room (see Chapter 6 for full listing), a more formal restaurant (although the dress code is fairly casual—resort wear is acceptable), serves dinner only and specializes in fresh fish and regional cuisine. Nikko Steak House (see Chapter 6 for full listing) is the hotel's Japanese restaurant, and it features the ancient technique of teppan-yaki cooking for dinner only. The Marriott also offers a sunset luau on Kaanapali Beach that features Hawaiian/Polynesian music and a show (see Chapter 7 for information).

Services: Room service from 6am to 10pm daily; 24-hour babysitting service; tour and car-rental desks.

Facilities: Two swimming pools, two whirlpools, separate children's pool, tennis courts (three lighted for night play), pro shop, exercise room with Universal Weights, exercise bikes, Stairmasters, a nine-hole putting green, and a video game room. There are 14 retail shops and a beauty salon on the lobby level of the hotel that offer everything from T-shirts to film to beach wear, to jewelry and fine arts.

SHERATON MAUI RESORT, 2605 Kaanapali Pkwy., Lahaina, Maui, HI 96761-1991. Tel. 808/661-0031, or toll free 800/325-3535. 494 rms. A/C TV TEL

$ Rates: $139 Molokai wing; $159 standard room; $180 mountain cottage; $215 garden view; $250 partial ocean view; $270 ocean view; $320 ocean-front cottage or Molokai wing suite; $570 garden suite; $630 cliff suites. Extra person $25. Children 17 and under stay free when using existing bedding in parents' room. Special packages are available. AE, CB, DC, DISC, ER, JCB Card, MC, V. **Parking:** $3.50 per day.

Built atop Black Rock Promontory in 1963, the Sheraton Maui was the first in a long line of resort hotels that would line the beautiful stretch of white sand known today as Kaanapali Beach. Because it was the first, it is also one of the most spread out. Covering 23 acres, the buildings that make up the Sheraton Maui are low-rise and have been constructed in a melange of architectural styles. There is one large eight-story building, but the rest of the rooms are housed in the 26 separate cottages, each of which has four units on the first floor and two on the second. The rates on all the rooms, whether they're in the main building or the cottages, are the same (varying only according to view as listed above).

Currently the Sheraton is undergoing a massive renovation effort, so it is impossible for me to describe here what the rooms will look like or what the new amenities will be. If you're interested in staying at the Sheraton, I would recommend first calling ahead to make sure they are open (they were planning to close the hotel down during renovations) and to find out what their rates are (they expected no major price increase).

One of the Sheraton's major attractions is the cliff-diving and torchlighting ceremony every evening at sunset. In ancient times, Mauians designated Black Rock as one of three *uhane-lele* (or "soul leaping") spots in all of the Hawaiian islands. It was believed that the souls of the dead would leap into the ocean from Black Rock just as the sun was setting and would follow the sun to the sea of Kai'lalo (Eternal Paradise). Much later, Kahekili, the last king of Maui, was trying to keep his life (and rouse a weary army) as he fought against Kalaniopu'u, the high chief of the island of Hawaii; in a show of inspiration to his warriors he leapt from Black Rock into the ocean. Today the tradition continues as a scantily clad young man lights the evening torches as he runs to make his leap from Black Rock.

The beach in front of the Sheraton also attracts a large green sea turtle in the early mornings, and guests who rise early enough and are quiet enough might be able to catch a glimpse of this wonderful creature.

Dining/Entertainment: The Sheraton's Discovery Room Restaurant gives guests a panoramic view of Black Rock Promontory, Kaanapali Beach, and the islands of

Molokai and Lanai. The Discovery Room features breakfast and dinner buffets, as well as à la carte dining. On the Rocks Bar serves lunch daily and cocktails every evening. The Snack Shop is open for continental breakfast and quick lunches. The Sundowner Bar is open from 10am to 8pm daily, and there is a karaoke bar on the eighth floor that is open nightly from 9pm to midnight. The Sheraton Maui also has an evening luau (except on Sunday).

Services: Valet laundry service; babysitting service; room service; Avis Rent-A-Car direct line; nondenominational poolside religious services on Sunday.

Facilities: 24-hour coin-op laundry facilities; two outdoor pools; three outdoor tennis courts; activities desk to help arrange sightseeing tours, boat cruises, fishing excursions, and more; access to nearby Kaanapali Golf Courses.

THE WESTIN MAUI, 2365 Kaanapali Pkwy., Lahaina, Maui, HI 96761.
Tel. 808/667-2525, or toll free 800/228-3000. Fax 808/661-5764 . Telex 7431212. 761 rms, 28 suites. A/C MINIBAR TV TEL
$ Rates: $230 terrace; $265 garden view; $295 golf/mountain view; $335 ocean view; $365 deluxe ocean view; $395–$405 Royal Beach Club; $500–$2,000 suite. Additional person in standard rooms $25, Royal Beach Club Room $45. Children 17 and under stay free in parents' room. 25% discount on additional rooms occupied by children.
Parking: Complimentary valet and self-parking available.

⭐ Located on some of Kaanapali's prime oceanfront property, next door to the Whalers Village Shopping Complex, The Westin Maui is something of a beachfront fantasy land. The moment you enter the spacious open-air lobby you will feel relaxed. At check-in you're greeted with warm hospitality and an equally warm hand towel with which to refresh yourself while waiting for your room key. The resort's five swimming pools are located just outside the lobby area, and they are surrounded by lush gardens and a variety of tropical birds sitting atop their own personal perches or swimming in the small outdoor ponds. In addition, the hotel has a $2 million art collection scattered throughout many of the public spaces.

Guest rooms are located in the Ocean Tower or Beach Tower and either have views of the ocean or the Kaanapali Golf Course and the West Maui Mountains. Each room is freshly decorated in light, crisp colors and has a king-size or double beds. In addition to all the standard amenities, you'll also find in-room safes, an iron and ironing board, coffee makers, and private lanais.

The Royal Beach Club is located on the top two floors of the Beach Tower and is comprised of 37 guest rooms. A private staff is available between 6:30am and 10pm, and those staying on the Royal Beach Club floors receive a complimentary lei and champagne greeting on arrival. Extra services and amenities include a complimentary Japanese robe, daily newspaper, upgraded bath amenities, and hairdryers. In the Beach Club Lounge guests may enjoy a continental breakfast buffet, afternoon tea, and early evening cocktail service.

Dining/Entertainment: Sound of the Falls is the hotel's most romantic evening dining spot. Pacific Bistro Cuisine is offered in the open-air dining room that is surrounded by cascading waterfalls. A pianist tickles the ivories nightly. Reservations are recommended. (For full listing see Chapter 6.) The Villa Restaurant serves fresh island seafood nightly amidst the beautifully landscaped lagoons and waterfalls. (For full listing see Chapter 6.) The Villa Terrace is a casual spot that offers a full all-you-can-eat seafood buffet (served seasonally in a 21-foot outrigger canoe). The poolside Cook's at the Beach serves breakfast, lunch, and dinner daily, and six nights a week you'll be treated to Hawaiian music and a hula show. The Garden Bar with a 25-inch television is open from 11am to 6pm and serves the breakfast, lunch, and dinner menus from Cook's at the Beach. In the morning the Colonnade Lounge offers take-out coffee and danish, and in the evening it serves as a meeting place where hotel guests may gather for cocktails.

Services: Guest Services will help plan activities, tours of the hotel, and will give information about various points of interest on the island. American Express and Hertz Rent-a-Car have desks in the hotel lobby. Japanese Guest Services provides translations of hotel information, as well as reservations and assistance with any activities that might be planned. Secretarial services are available to all guests upon request. Nondenominational church services are held every Sunday.

Facilities: The Stylists is the hotel's beauty salon and it's located on the mezzanine level of the Beach Tower. There are also eight retail shops on the hotel's lobby level.

Keiki Camp is the Westin's children's program. Counselors supervise children up to 12 years old from Monday through Friday on and off property. Activities might include movies, a ride on the Sugar Cane Train (see Chapter 7 for full listing), or a trip to the Omni Theatre to view *The Hawaii Experience* (see Chapter 7 for full listing).

There are five swimming pools available for guest use, three of which are joined together by a series of water slides and a swim-through grotto. There is also an outdoor swim-up Jacuzzi, organized water games, and aquacise classes. Scuba lessons for beginners (or refresher courses) are offered in the hotel's pool. After your first dive in the pool, you'll probably be ready and able to take a guided ocean beach dive, or attend a scuba certification course.

The Westin's health club has weight training, aerobic, and exercise rooms, men's and women's locker rooms, a Jacuzzi, massage therapy by appointment, and several classes offered daily. Hotel guests have access to the Kaanapali Golf Course.

THE WHALER ON KAANAPALI BEACH, 2481 Kaanapali Pkwy., Lahaina, Maui, HI 96761. Tel. 808/661-4861, or toll free 800/367-7052. Fax 415/283-3129. Telex 414506. 340 units, 161 managed by Village Resorts. A/C TV TEL

$ Rates: High season (Dec 16–Dec 31 and Feb 1–Mar 31) $175 garden-view studio, $195 ocean-view studio, $210 garden-view one-bedroom/one-bath, $245 ocean-view one-bedroom/one-bath; $255 ocean-view one-bedroom/two-bath, $310 oceanfront one-bedroom/two-bath, $300 garden-view two-bedroom/two-bath, $355 ocean-view two-bedroom/two-bath, $425 oceanfront two-bedroom/two-bath. Oceanfront Presidential Suite $565. Low season (Jan 1–Jan 31 and Apr 1–Dec 20), $10 to $15 lower. Rollaway $15. Crib $5. AE, MC, V. **Parking:** Free underground parking.

Not only does The Whaler on Kaanapali Beach have one of the best locations of any condominium on Maui, but it has some of the most spacious rooms as well. It's located right on the beach, nestled between the Kaanapali Beach Hotel and Whalers Village Shopping Center and just across Kaanapali Parkway from the Kaanapali Golf Courses. All of the individually owned units are tastefully decorated and come equipped with a full kitchen, marble-tiled bathrooms, VCRs, safes ($2.50 a day), and daily coffee setups. Units range from studios (for up to two people) to two-bedroom units (up to six people), and all have private lanais. There are laundry facilities on each floor (however, there is a laundry service available) and there's an exercise room and sauna on the property (open 7am to 9pm daily). Guests may also use the large pool or spa, barbecue grills, and video game room. There are no restaurants on the property, but guests have charge-back privileges to several restaurants in the Whalers Village Shopping Center. Court fees for tennis are $7 a day, and guests of The Whaler receive discounts at the Kaanapali Resort Golf Courses. The lobby area houses a minimarket for last-minute grocery shopping. There is a 24-hour front desk with 24-hour phone service.

MODERATE

KAANAPALI BEACH HOTEL, 2525 Kaanapali Pkwy, Lahaina, Maui, HI 96761-1987. Tel. 808/661-0011, or toll free 800/262-8450. Fax 808/667-5978. 422 rms, 8 suites. A/C TV TEL

$ Rates: Double room $140 standard, $150 courtyard view, $160 partial ocean view, $170 ocean view, $180 oceanfront; suites $185 Junior Courtyard View, $200 Junior Ocean View, $220 Oceanfront Family Suite, $550 Kaanapali Suite Oceanfront. Extra person $20. Rollaway $15. Special packages are available. AE, CB, DC, MC, V. **Parking:** Free.

Built in 1964 and most recently renovated in 1991, the Kaanapali Beach Hotel is one of the least expensive hotels in the Kaanapali Beach Resort, but it doesn't scrimp on guest activities and aloha spirit. Rooms here are spacious, and all feature minirefrigerators and a shower or tub/shower combination. Rooms also have lanais, and all face inward toward the courtyard and the beach. The gardens in the courtyard are beautifully landscaped with plumeria and palm trees, and the lawn is well manicured. The central feature of the gardens is the whale-shaped swimming pool. Chaise longues are placed invitingly around the pool and are scattered throughout the gardens for those who would rather sit in the shade of a palm tree. The hotel property borders a great rock formation, affording guests excellent snorkeling opportunities. One of the most unique features of this hotel is the giant checkerboard in the courtyard.

The Kaanapali Beach Hotel is known for its Hawaiian activities program in which guests can learn to cut pineapple, make ti leaf skirts and leis, weave lauhala (pandanus leaf), and participate in lau printing. Guests may also take advantage of some of the island's most authentic hula lessons. Every evening there is a complimentary hula show and other Hawaiian entertainment, including a nightly torchlighting ceremony. Each day brings a host of other activities, and on Fridays there's a craft fair and lobby show. The hotel employees are extensively educated in Hawaiiana and show great pride in their hotel.

Dining/Entertainment: The hotel's Koffee Shop serves an all-you-can-eat breakfast, lunch, and dinner buffet daily. Prices range from $5.95 for breakfast and lunch to $11.95 for dinner. The Tiki Terrace is open daily for breakfast and dinner and serves a Sunday champagne brunch. The Tiki Grill is the hotel's poolside grill where guests can order sandwiches and hot dogs. The Tiki Bar, also poolside, specializes in tropical cocktails.

Services: United Airlines desk; babysitting service; daily maid service; activities desk; free scuba and snorkeling lessons.

Facilities: Swimming pool; children's programs offered seasonally ($15 per child, including lunch); coin-op laundry facilities; beauty salon; beach equipment rentals (boogie boards, snorkeling and scuba equipment, sailboats, windsurfers, and catamarans); access to 10 tennis courts (6 lit for night play) and Kaanapali Golf Courses; Deli and Gift Shoppe; Kaanapali Beach Shop (featuring resort and active wear); Island Image (sundries).

MAUI EL DORADO RESORT, 2661 Kekaa Dr., Kaanapali, Maui, HI 96761. **Tel. 808/661-0021,** or toll free 800/535-0085. 204 units (106 for rent through resort). A/C TV TEL

$ Rates: High season (Dec 23–Dec 31 and Feb 1–Mar 31) $159 studio garden, $175 studio ocean; $195 one-bedroom garden, $215 one-bedroom ocean; $255 two-bedroom garden, $290 two-bedroom ocean. Low season (Jan 1–Jan 31 and Apr 1–Dec 22) $140 studio garden, $155 studio ocean; $170 one-bedroom garden, $190 one-bedroom ocean; $220 two-bedroom garden, $250 two-bedroom ocean. Rollaway or crib $15. Special packages and weekly and monthly discounts are available. AE, MC, V. **Parking:** Free.

You might not think about staying at the El Dorado because it's located inland from the hotels that line Kaanapali Beach, and the exterior is a bit dated, but if you're trying to save some money, you shouldn't pass it by. The condominiums were some of the first accommodations built in the Kaanapali Beach Resort (in the early 1970s). Back then, larger parcels of land were easier for developers to come by, so rather than the high rises that are so typical today, architects were free to design sprawling hotels and condominiums that blended with the landscape. The El Dorado is comprised of 12 separate buildings covering 10 acres, which gives visitors a greater sense of privacy. The studio and one- and two-bedroom units are larger than average, and furnishings are adequate. A typical studio is somewhat like a hotel room with small living and dining areas and a kitchenette. Washer/dryer combinations are standard to each unit, and all condos have private lanais with outdoor furniture. One- and two-bedroom units have the same amenities but are larger and have more than one bathroom. The maximum number of guests allowed in a studio is two, a one-bedroom could take four, and a two-bedroom could take six. Most of the units look out over the Kaanapali Golf Course. The ocean is a fair distance away, so when you book your condo, keep in mind that an "ocean-view" unit is in the same general area as a garden-view unit, the only difference is that it will be located on the second floor where you'll be able to get a glimpse of the water. All of the condos have beautiful views of the golf course, however.

There is a shuttle service that will transport guests to the El Dorado's private Beach Club located on the beach right near Black Rock, a lava formation where snorkelers and scuba divers can amuse themselves for hours in a wildlife preserve. Every Friday night there is a complimentary Manager's Cocktail Party at the Beach Club. There are three swimming pools on the property as well as a small gourmet grocery store.

MAUI KAI, 106 Kaanapali Shores Place, Lahaina, Maui, HI 96761. Tel. 808/667-3500, or toll free 800/367-5635. Fax 808/667-3660. 80 units, 60 in rental pool. A/C TV TEL

$ **Rates:** High season (Dec 18–Mar 31) $135 studio; $155 one-bedroom, $165 one-bedroom corner; $205 two-bedroom. Low season (Apr 1–Dec 18) $115 studio; $135 one-bedroom, $145 one-bedroom corner; $185 two-bedroom. Extra person $10. Minimum stay of one week during Christmas. MC, V. **Parking:** Free.

The Maui Kai is small and set off the main road, so many people don't even know it's there. All the studio, one-, and two-bedroom units at the Maui Kai are oceanfront, but they're a little smaller than some of the units at other properties (don't let that scare you off, though—the views are worth it). Each of the condos is individually decorated in light color schemes, making the units pleasant and cheerful. Kitchens are fully equipped, and private lanais are either enclosed or open-air. Included in the rates listed above is twice weekly maid service, but daily maid service can be requested at an additional cost. A pool and Jacuzzi are located on the property and guests have the use of an outdoor cabana with a kitchen (to prepare a quick lunch if you'd rather not go back up to the room). Other facilities include gas barbecues, laundry facilities, a Guest Activity Service, Ping-Pong table, and a lending library. You can't go wrong here.

PAKI MAUI AT KAANAPALI, 3615 L. Honoapiilani Hwy., Lahaina, Maui, HI 96761. Tel. 808/922-9700, or toll free 800/535-0085. Fax 808/922-2421. 110 units, 77 in rental pool. TV TEL

$ **Rates:** $129–$149 studio; $129–$169 one-bedroom; $189–$229 two-bedroom. Extra person $15. Children under 18 stay free. Weekly discounts and special packages available. AE, DC, DISC, MC, V. **Parking:** Free.

The Paki Maui is located right on the water, and while the beach isn't sandy, a rolling strip of lawn runs down to the water's edge. Sunbathing is a favorite activity of the guests of Paki Maui, but swimming, sandcastle building, and snorkeling are best saved for the nearby sandy beaches located just a few minutes away. Studios, and one- and two-bedroom apartments offer mountain, garden, ocean, or oceanfront views and rates vary according to what you'll see from your private, fully furnished lanai. Naturally, ocean and oceanfront rooms are excellent, but if you want to save a little money, go for the mountain- or garden-view suites. If you opt for the garden view, you'll feel like you're living in Old Hawaii as you look out into the courtyard with its lagoon falls and koi pond. Each unit is fully furnished and individually decorated. All have microwaves and most have VCRs. Daily maid service is included in the rates, and so is the daily continental breakfast. Relax in the outdoor pool or jet spa, and have a cookout using the barbecue facilities on the property. The manager hosts a weekly Mai Tai party for guests of the Paki Maui, and the activity and travel desk will help you plan your day.

FROMMER'S SMART TRAVELER: HOTELS

1. Hotel rates skyrocket during the high season and during major festivals and events, so try to make your trip during the off-season. This shouldn't be a hardship since the weather is almost perfect year-round.
2. Always ask if the hotel has a special package rate, particularly if you're a golfer. Many offer golf packages that slash regular greens fees.
3. Most people who travel to Maui want to stay in a hotel that fronts the beach, but you can save a lot of money if you're willing to stay in a hotel that's farther inland.
4. Explore the possibilities of staying in a condominium. You can save a lot of money if you cook your own meals once or twice a day.

ROYAL LAHAINA RESORT, 2780 Kekaa Dr., Lahaina, Maui, HI 96761. Tel. 808/661-3611, or toll free 800/44-ROYAL. Fax 808/661-6150, or toll free 800/432-9752 for reservations. 540 rms, 26 suites. A/C TV TEL

$ Rates: $140 standard; $180 superior; $205 deluxe; $250 deluxe oceanfront; $240 garden resort cottage; $300 oceanfront cottage; $615 one-bedroom suite; $615–$1,550 two-bedroom suite. Extra person $20. AE, CB, DC, DISC, JCB Card, MC, V. **Parking:** Valet and self-parking available.

The newly redecorated Royal Lahaina Resort is said to be located on a site "chosen by the monarchs of the Islands" because it was the "best location on the beach." Though there are over 500 rooms here, the accommodations are spread over 27 acres in moderately sized buildings or cottages, giving guests a greater feeling of privacy than a high-rise hotel with the same number of rooms. The low-rise cottages that dot the carefully landscaped grounds lend an air of serenity, and as you wander along the pathways between palm trees bent by trade winds, you'll be treated to a potpourri of scents from saltwater and sun to plumeria blossoms and coconut oil. One of the best buys in the Kaanapali Beach Resort, the Royal Lahaina offers tastefully decorated rooms with traditional Hawaiian appointments, like bedspreads with Hawaiian quilt appliqués. The furnishings are wicker and rattan with floral, solid, or striped cushions, and color schemes are neutral with touches of teal, peach, green, and light blue. All rooms have minirefrigerators, private lanais, and in-room safes, as well as ironing boards (housekeeping will supply the iron). Some rooms and all cottage suites have ceiling fans. Specialty suites are oceanfront, have two bedrooms, three baths, a living room, kitchen, private garden, pool, whirlpool, and waterfall (the price tag is high though).

Guests may rent beach and water-sports equipment, including Hobie Cats, windsurfers, ocean kayaks, paddleboats, and snorkel gear. The traditional hula and lei-making classes are also offered here, and you might also have an opportunity to participate in Hawaiian quilt-making classes and ukulele lessons. There is a shopping arcade on the property where you can get everything from film to fine jewelry.

Dining/Entertainment: The Royal Ocean Terrace Restaurant is an open-air restaurant featuring Hawaiian and American cuisines. At breakfast there is a buffet as well as an à la carte menu, and the restaurant serves lunch and dinner as well. Sunday brunch and the Friday seafood buffet are specialties of the restaurant. Chopsticks Restaurant features Asian cuisine (Chinese, Thai, Japanese, and Micronesian). Moby Dick's, overlooking the Kaanapali Golf Course, serves up fresh seafood and continental cuisine. The Royal Ocean Terrace Lounge offers Hawaiian specialty drinks, poolside service, and Hawaiian-style entertainment daily. The Chopsticks lounge features a large imported beer selection as well as exotic drinks. The Royal Scoop Ice Cream Parlor serves pastries and sandwiches in addition to a large selection of ice creams. The Royal Lahaina Luau (see Chapter 7 for more information) takes place nightly at 5:30pm from September 1 to April 30 and at 6pm from May 1 to August 31.

Services: Room service, valet laundry and dry cleaning, babysitting referral service; daily complimentary introductory scuba lessons; Dollar Rent A Car; Pleasant Hawaiian Holidays Travel Desk.

Facilities: Three swimming pools; Jacuzzi; a world-class tennis facility featuring 10 courts, 6 lit for night play, Tennis Stadium that seats up to 3,500, pro shop, snack shop, and three resident pros; two golf courses are adjacent to the property— the Kaanapali North Course and the Kaanapali South Course, pro shop, and driving range; beach and boating center; shuffleboard court; volleyball facility; croquet setup. There's also a beauty salon and a guest laundromat.

LAHAINA

EXPENSIVE

EMBASSY SUITES RESORT, 104 Kaanapali Shores Pl., Lahaina, Maui, HI 96761. Tel. 808/661-2000, or toll free 800/462-6284. Fax 808/667-5821. 413 suites. A/C MINIBAR TV TEL

$ Rates: One-bedroom suite $220 terrace view, $250 mountain view, $280 ocean view, $300 deluxe ocean view, $335 oceanfront; two-bedroom suite $450; Presidential Suite $1,200. Extra person $20. AE, CB, DC, DISC, JCB Card, MC, V. **Parking:** $4 per day.

⭐ With its pink exterior and stepped-back architecture, this all-suite 12-story hotel is difficult to miss as you drive along the Honoapiilani Highway. It's one of the last hotels built on Kaanapali Beach before you get to Honokowai. If you take advantage of the room capacities (four people for the one-bedroom and six people for the two-bedroom), the rates are extremely reasonable. The large rooms are attractively furnished. Neutral color schemes set the backdrop for blue and white wide-striped pull-out couches in the living rooms and blue and white floral print bedspreads with shell-shaped, fabric-covered, padded headboards. The living room features a 35-inch color television, VCR, AM/FM radio and cassette stereo system, kitchenette (with microwave, minirefrigerator with automatic ice-maker), wet bar, and coffee maker. Complimentary Kona coffee is replenished daily. All bedrooms have a second 20-inch TV and private lanais. Spacious white-tiled bathrooms have double vanities, soaking tubs, and separate showers. Complimentary breakfast buffet with omelets made to order, and a daily two-hour cocktail reception are included in the room rate. Snorkeling, windsurfing, and scuba lessons are also available to guests.

Dining/Entertainment: The North Beach Grill, the hotel's oceanfront restaurant, features local seafood as well as steak, pasta, and a large salad bar. Poolside you'll find the Ohana Grill, which serves pizza and light meals. The Deli Planet in the lobby makes sandwiches and picnic baskets to go. Moonbeams Bar serves mixed drinks, wine, beer, and sodas.

Services: Room service, year-round children's program.

Facilities: One-acre swimming pool with 24-foot water slide; exercise room with sauna and steam rooms, video arcade, retail shops, self-service laundry facilities.

PUUNOA BEACH ESTATES, 45 Kai Pali Place (write 50 Nohea Kai Dr. for reservations), Lahaina, Maui, HI 96761. Tel. 808/667-5972, or toll free 800/642-MAUI. 10 units. A/C TV TEL

$ Rates (including full-size rental car): High season (Jan 5–Mar 31) $590 standard two-bedroom unit, $700 two-bedroom unit with loft; $750 standard three-bedroom unit, $820 three-bedroom unit with loft. Low season (Apr 1–Dec 15) $560 standard two-bedroom unit, $590 two-bedroom unit with loft; $625 standard three-bedroom unit, $685 three-bedroom unit with loft. Minimum stay of three nights. AE, MC, V. **Parking:** Free.

The exclusive Puunoa Beach Estates is perhaps one of the island's most unexpected and delightful properties. In spite of Puunoa's central location, it is amazingly

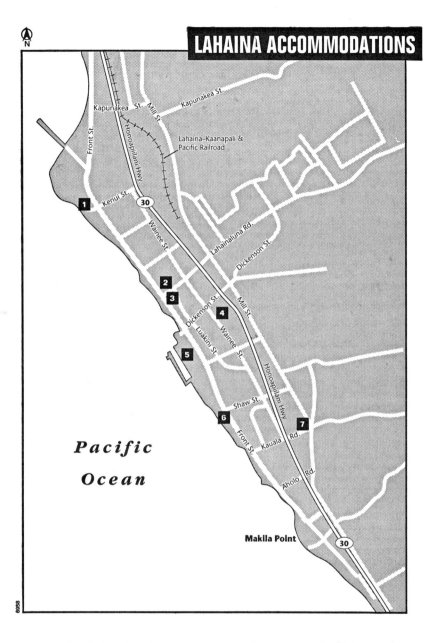

N

Kapunakea St. Mill St.

Kapunakea St.

Front St.

Honoapiilani Hwy.

Lahaina–Kaanapali &
Pacific Railroad

Kenui St.

30

1

Wainee St.

Lahainaluna Rd.

Dickenson St.

2

3

Dickenson St.

Mill St.

4

Wainee St.

Luakini St.

5

Honoapiilani Hwy.

Shaw St.

6

Front St.

Kauala Rd.

7

Pacific

Ocean

Aholo Rd.

Makila Point

30

6056

The Lahaina Hotel **2**

Lahaina Shores
 Beach Resort **6**

Maui Islander **4**

Pioneer Inn **5**

The Plantation Inn **3**

Puunoa Beach
 Estates **1**

Tony's Place **7**

private. The five two-story buildings are situated on three lovely acres of oceanfront property, and each building houses two condominium units. The units range in size from 1,700 to 2,100 square feet and are appointed with modern but elegant furnishings. Special touches like fine Oriental carpets and beautiful ceramic pieces make each of the "estates" unique. Kitchens are fully equipped, and all master bathrooms have oversized Roman Jacuzzi tubs. Every unit also has a wet bar, full-sized washer and dryer, two TVs, and a VCR. Upstairs apartments have vaulted ceilings and appear to be even more spacious.

The property is bordered by a lovely strip of white-sand beach, and the pool is much more private than most. There is a sauna available for guest use, and if you feel like exploring the rest of the island the concierge will arrange your activity schedule. When you arrive you'll find a "Maui Mornings" grocery package waiting for you, and the *Wall Street Journal* and a local newspaper will be delivered daily to your home away from home. If you can afford it, Puunoa Estates is unbeatable.

THE SANDS OF KAHANA, 4299 L. Honoapiilani Hwy., Lahaina, Maui, HI 96761. Tel. 808/669-0400, or toll free 800/367-7052. Fax 510/283-3129. 196 units, 129 in rental pool. TV TEL

$ Rates: High season (Dec 22–Jan 3 and Feb 1–Apr 19) mountain view $195 one-bedroom, $250 two-bedroom, $320 three-bedroom; ocean view $220 one-bedroom, $270 two-bedroom, $330 three-bedroom; oceanfront $255 one-bedroom, $320 two-bedroom, $365 three-bedroom. Low season (Jan 4–Jan 31 and Apr 19–Dec 20) mountain view $165 one-bedroom, $210 two-bedroom, $290 three-bedroom; ocean view $185 one-bedroom, $245 two-bedroom, $300 three-bedroom; oceanfront $215 one-bedroom, $290 two-bedroom, $335 three-bedroom. Rollaway $15. Crib $5. AE, MC, V. **Parking:** Free.

There are scores of condominium complexes between Kaanapali and Kapalua, but there aren't many that offer spacious accommodations, ample recreational activities, and a beach perfect for swimming, sunning, and snorkeling. The Sands of Kahana has all of that and much more. The characteristic blue-tiled roofs are easy to spot from the road, and the sand-colored stucco exteriors blend nicely with the landscape in spite of their height. Near the entrance there's a well-stocked koi pond, and palm trees line the pathways leading to each of the condominium buildings. Pineapple-cutting and lei-making demonstrations are held in the courtyard just outside the lobby area, and there's a lovely beachfront pool and spa. Barbecue grills are centrally located for guest use, and there's even a separate pool, playground, and activities program for children. Three lighted tennis courts are available for guest use, as is a putting green. There's an open-air poolside restaurant on the property.

One-, two-, or three-bedroom condo units have large living rooms, many of which open directly into a bedroom (they can be closed off any time with accordian doors). Washers and dryers are standard, and kitchens are roomy with more than enough storage space for those who plan on staying a while. Private lanais feature bougainvillea-filled window boxes and functional outdoor furniture (usually enough for outdoor dining). Rates are higher here than at other properties, but so are the standards.

MODERATE

HONOKEANA COVE RESORT CONDOMINIUMS, 5255 L. Honoapiilani Hwy., Lahaina, Maui, HI 96761. Tel. 808/669-6441, or toll free 800/237-4948. 38 units, 31 in rental pool. TV TEL

$ Rates: $105 one-bedroom unit; $115–$125 one-bedroom loft unit; $155 two-bedroom unit; $175 three-bedroom unit; $170 two-bedroom townhouse. Extra person in loft unit $15, lower units $10. Weekly and monthly discounts available. Minimum stay of three nights. No credit cards. **Parking:** Free.

Love to snorkel? Well, at Honokeana Cove you'll find great snorkeling in the condominium's own private cove. All the one-, two-, and three-bedroom units are just steps away from the ocean, and even though the shoreline is rocky, a sandy strip of beach is only a five-minute walk away on a shoreline path. Each apartment is individually owned and decorated—some are a little better than others. All units are outfitted with dishwashers and fully equipped kitchens. Laundry facilities and barbecue grills are available for guest use. Near the ocean's edge across a beautifully manicured lawn is the swimming pool where pupu parties are held weekly.

THE LAHAINA HOTEL, 127 Lahainaluna Rd., Lahaina, Maui, HI 96761. Tel. 808/661-0577 or toll free 800/669-3444. Fax 808/667-9480. 13 rms. A/C TEL

$ Rates: $89 mountain view; $99 harbor view; $129 Makai Room; $129 Mauka Room; $129 Lahainaluna Room. Wedding packages available. AE, MC, V. **Parking:** $8 per day.

The Lahaina Hotel comes as something of a surprise in the middle of one of Maui's busiest and most commercial towns. It's a haven that takes you away from tourist traps, fast-food restaurants, and the busy wharf. In 1938 what is now the Lahaina Hotel was opened as a general store. After several different owners, and a stint as the Lahainaluna Hotel, Rick Ralston (current owner and also the owner of Crazy Shirts, Inc.) bought the structure and began an extensive restoration project.

Plush Oriental rugs, a Victorian camelback couch, and a rich walnut staircase welcome you into the hotel's lobby. At the top of the stairs you'll find the guest rooms, all of which are individually decorated with antiques from Ralston's own collection. Each room has a private lanai with either an ocean or mountain view. Antique leaded glass lamps, fine fabrics, hand-done needlework pillows, floral wallpapers, intricately carved wood furnishings, lace curtains, and period paintings are just some of the lovely details that are scattered throughout the small hotel. Ralston thought of everything, down to the antique lock sets on guest-room doors, and no expense was too great—when the wooden floors didn't creak authentically Ralston had the carpenters rip them up and lay them again so they would whine and squeak as guests walked around the hotel. There's a room here to suit anyone's taste. All accommodations are air-conditioned, and continental breakfast is included in the room rate.

Adjoining the lobby is David Paul's Lahaina Grill (see Chapter 6 for full listing) serving New American/Hawaiian regional cuisine.

LAHAINA SHORES BEACH RESORT, 475 Front St. (reservations office 50 Nohea Kai Dr.), Lahaina, Maui, HI 96761. Tel. 808/661-4835, or toll free 800/628-6699. 199 units, 154 in rental pool. A/C TV TEL

$ Rates: $100–$147 studio; $132–$182 one-bedroom; $172–$237 penthouse oceanfront unit. Rollaway or crib $10. AE, MC, V. **Parking:** Free.

This resort hotel bills itself as "Right on the Beach. Right in the Town. Right on the Money," and it's exactly that. In fact, it is the only hotel in Lahaina town that is located directly on the beach. The individually owned studios and one-bedroom units are comfortable. One-bedroom units sleep up to five (most have queen-size or two twin beds, and some have Murphy beds, depending on what the owners chose to install), and all have fully equipped kitchens. About one-third have microwaves. Laundry facilities for studios and one-bedroom units are located in the hall, but irons and ironing boards are standard to each condo. The six penthouse units have washers and dryers, king-size beds, and sofa sleepers. For the money, penthouse condos are probably your best bet. In general, bathrooms are small but serviceable. Just off the hotel's newly renovated lobby you can relax in the whirlpool spa or the hotel's swimming pool. There are no restaurants on the property, but complimentary breakfast is offered at the daily island orientation, and poolside lunch service is provided by Hecocks restaurant next door.

NAPILI SUNSET, 46 Hui Dr., Lahaina, Maui, HI 96761. Tel. 808/669-8083 or toll free 800/447-9229 (8am–7pm Hawaiian time). Fax 808/669-2730. 42 condo units. TV TEL

$ Rates: $90 garden-view studio for two; $169 one-bedroom beachfront apartment for two; $269 two-bedroom beachfront apartment for four. Minimum stay of three nights. MC, V. **Parking:** Free.

Built in the 1970s, the Napili Sunset enjoys a great beachfront location where the swimming is excellent and the views from oceanfront studios, one-, and two-bedroom units are spectacular. One of the great things about the units is that they are some of the most spacious on the island in this price category. The fully equipped kitchens are additionally outfitted with microwaves. Ceiling fans, complimentary in-room safes, and irons and ironing boards are standard. Local calls are free, and so is the use of beach towels. Some studios have a view of the small kidney-shaped swimming pool. Maid service is provided daily, and there is a coin-op laundry facility for guest use. There is also a small convenience store on the property where guests can pick up groceries for a picnic or a beachside barbecue.

NAPILI SURF BEACH RESORT, 50 Napili Place, Lahaina, Maui, HI 96761. Tel. 808/669-8002, or toll free 800/541-0638. Fax 808/669-8004. 53 units. TV TEL

$ Rates (based on double occupancy): Apr 15–Dec 15: $99 garden-view studio, $120 ocean-view studio, $159 one-bedroom condo. Dec 15–Apr 15: $105 garden-view studio, $125 ocean-view studio, $165 one-bedroom condo. Room/car packages and monthly discounts available. Extra person $15. Children 6 and under free in parents' room. No credit cards. **Parking:** Free.

Of all the condominium complexes in the area and this price range, the Napili Surf is probably the best place to stay for those seeking a quiet Hawaiian vacation. Its beautiful, sandy crescent beach is great for sunbathing and ocean swimming. There's also a snorkeling reef just offshore. Even the least expensive unit is nicely furnished, comes with a fully equipped kitchen (including a microwave and dishwasher), has ceiling fans, and is serviced daily by the housekeeping staff. Laundry facilities are available to guests, as are barbecues. There are two swimming pools, and the beautifully manicured grounds with winding pathways are dotted with plumeria trees and other tropical flora.

PAPAKEA RESORT, 3543 L. Honoapiilani Hwy., Lahaina, Maui, HI 96761. Tel. 808/669-4848, or toll free 800/367-7052. Fax 510/283-3129. Telex 414506. 364 units, 114 in rental pool. A/C TV TEL

$ Rates: High season (Dec 21–Jan 3 and Feb 1–Apr 19) $145 partial ocean-view studio, $155 oceanfront studio; $155 partial ocean-view one-bedroom suite, $185 oceanfront one-bedroom suite; $220 partial ocean-view two-bedroom suite, $260 oceanfront two-bedroom suite. Low season (Jan 4–Jan 31 and Apr 19–Dec 20) $130 partial ocean-view studio, $140 oceanfront studio; $140 partial ocean-view one-bedroom suite, $170 oceanfront one-bedroom suite; $195 partial ocean-view two-bedroom suite, $235 oceanfront two-bedroom suite. Minimum stay of two nights. Rollaway $15. Crib $10. AE, MC, V. **Parking:** Free.

Papakea is a wonderful resort condominium property. Several four-story buildings are spread out over 13 acres and are surrounded by beautifully landscaped gardens, freshwater lagoons, and impeccably manicured lawns. There are even two Japanese fish ponds. Oceanfront units offer gorgeous views—you'll feel as though you can jump right off your lanai into the water. Don't, however, because the only drawback to this property is the fact that there is no sandy beach here. Never fear, if you can't live without it, you won't have to go far to find one. Chances are that you'll be completely content at Papakea, especially if you enjoy sports. There are two oceanfront pools and spas, two 18-hole putting greens, three lighted tennis courts (complimentary), and shuffleboard courts. Through the guest activities service you can find out about aquacise classes and tennis clinics, and if you want to relax head for the cabana and hop in the sauna.

Large studio, one-, and two-bedroom condo units offer standard features like fully equipped kitchens with additional amenities such as microwaves, washer/dryer combinations, and full daily maid service. Papakea offers just about everything you could possibly need on your long-awaited Hawaiian vacation.

POLYNESIAN SHORES, 3975 L. Honoapiilani Hwy., Lahaina, Maui, HI 96761. Tel. 808/669-6065, or toll free 800/433-MAUI on the U.S. mainland, 800/488-2179 in Canada. Fax 808/669-0909. 52 units, 35 in rental pool. TV TEL
$ Rates: $115 one-bedroom unit; $140 two-bedroom loft; $155 two-bedroom end unit; $165 three-bedroom unit. Extra person $10. Minimum stay of three nights. MC, V. **Parking:** Free.

If you're looking for a small, private condominium property with a guaranteed ocean view, Polynesian Shores fits the bill. A rolling lawn leads to the swimming pool, and guests will find excellent snorkeling right at the edge of the property. Swimming is better a short walk down along the shoreline, but if all you want to do is sunbathe, the pool deck and the shoreline tiki lanai (outfitted with barbecues) are good bets. The one-, two-, and three-bedroom units are handsomely furnished, and have fully equipped kitchens. Coin-op laundry facilities are available. The hotel's well-maintained tropical gardens are a delight.

THE PLANTATION INN, 174 Lahainaluna Rd., Lahaina, Maui, HI 96761. Tel. 808/667-9225, or toll free 800/433-6815. Fax 808/667-9293. 18 rms and suites. A/C TV TEL
$ Rates: $99–$129 deluxe; $149 superior; $179 suites. AE, DISC, MC, V. **Parking:** Free.

Just about a block from the waterfront you'll find another surprise—The Plantation Inn. As soon as you pass through its doors you'll forget that you're right in the heart of one of Maui's busiest towns. One reason is that all the rooms have been soundproofed. Each of the guest rooms has been individually decorated and is outfitted with amenities that will suit even the pickiest of travelers. Your room might have a canopy or four-poster bed, floral prints or stripes, Oriental rugs, wall-to-wall carpeting, or hardwood floors. Color schemes might be pastel or of deeper, richer tones. For instance, Suite 8 has a separate living room with a roomy couch, an armchair, dividing doors with stained-glass art featuring humpback whales, a beautiful rice four-poster bed, lace-covered lampshades, and floral fabrics. Room 10, on the other hand, has an Asian theme—the walls are a deep Chinese red, a lacquered four-poster bed is the room's centerpiece, and Oriental rugs cover hardwood floors. Many of the furnishings in other rooms were handcrafted in Thailand, and beautiful stained-glass creations are scattered throughout. All rooms have VCRs, refrigerators, private bathrooms, and verandas. Suites have extra amenities, including full cooking facilities.

Water-sports equipment and a tiled swimming pool are also available for guest use. Gerard's Restaurant (see Chapter 6 for full listing), which features fine French cooking by a chef who was voted "Best Chef on Maui" two years in a row, is located on the ground floor.

INEXPENSIVE

HALE MAUI APARTMENT HOTEL, 3711 L. Honoapiilani Hwy. (P.O. Box 516), Lahaina, Maui, HI 96767. Tel. 808/669-6312. Fax 808/669-1302. 12 units. TV
$ Rates: $70–$100 apartment for two. Minimum stay of three nights. Extra person $10. MC, V. **Parking:** Free.

This tiny apartment building almost gets lost amidst the larger condominium complexes that line the beach in this area, but if you're looking for a bargain, you shouldn't miss it. There's no swimming pool, but the building is just steps from the beach, and all the units have private lanais. Even though there's no air conditioning, the trade winds that blow through the apartments keep them amazingly cool (one side is cooler than the other, but you won't suffer no matter where you are). All the rooms have been refurbished and kitchens are fully equipped.

MAUI ISLANDER, 660 Wainee St., Lahaina, Maui, HI 96761. Tel. 808/667-9766, or toll free 800/367-5226. Fax 808/661-3733. 372 rms and condo units. A/C TV TEL

$ Rates: $72 standard double; $87 studio with kitchen; $99 one-bedroom suite with kitchen; $154 two-bedroom suite with kitchen. Dec 20–Mar 31 add $8 to all rates. Room-and-car packages available. AE, DC, DISC, MC, V. **Parking:** Free.

Located just a couple of blocks away from Lahaina's busy Front Street, the Islander affords the budget-minded traveler the opportunity to stay near some of Maui's most beautiful beaches—which are all public, by the way—in clean, comfortable accommodations without the high price of one of the resort hotels. At the Islander you'll have a choice of a standard hotel room with a minirefrigerator, a studio, or a one- or two-bedroom suite with a full kitchen. The hotel is currently undergoing a two-year renovation that should be completed shortly after publication of this book. Room decors are not yet known, but all accommodations will be upgraded and freshly decorated. All the rooms have daily maid service, cable TV, in-room safes ($2.50 a day), air conditioning, and ceiling fans. The one-bedroom suites are large enough to accommodate four, and the two-bedroom suites are large enough for six.

The hotel's kidney-shaped outdoor swimming pool, lighted tennis court, and barbecue area are available for guest use, and there's an activities center available to help you plan your day. The activities center also sponsors free hula and lei-making lessons, scuba and snorkel lessons, as well as a Maui orientation with complimentary coffee and rolls each morning at 8am. There is a coin-operated laundry facility available for guest use.

NOELANI CONDOMINIUM RESORT, 4095 L. Honoapiilani Rd., Lahaina, HI 96761. Tel. 808/669-8374, or toll free 800/367-6030. Fax 808/669-7904. 50 units, 41 in rental pool. TV TEL

$ Rates: $87 studio; $107 one-bedroom; $150 two-bedroom; $180 three-bedroom. Extra person $7.50. Special room/car packages and weekly or monthly discounts available. Minimum stay of three nights. AE, MC, V. **Parking:** Free.

You won't get stuck in a condo with a bad view at Noelani because all units are oceanfront. A sandy beach is adjacent to the property, but if you don't feel like getting sand in your shoes, you can relax by one of the two oceanfront swimming pools where Mai Tai parties are held a few times monthly. Orientation continental breakfasts are included in the rates. Studios have full kitchens, queen-size beds, and the added bonus of a dressing area off the bathroom, so you're getting a good deal more space than you would in the average hotel room. The kitchens in all the units are furnished with microwaves and dishwashers. One-, two-, and three-bedroom units have the added benefit of washers and dryers (there are laundry facilities on the property for those staying in studio units), and the three-bedroom condos are bilevel with one bedroom downstairs and the other two on the upper floor. Decor in most of the units is bright and airy, with floral or Hawaiian print fabrics. You'll be well entertained here, but if you feel like getting out, there's full concierge service, and if you'd rather stay in, many of the units have VCRs. There are also barbecue grills and a picnic area. Maid service is once weekly.

BUDGET

PIONEER INN, 658 Wharf St., Lahaina, Maui, HI 96761. Tel. 808/661-3636, or toll free 800/457-5457. Fax 808/667-5708. 48 rms.

$ Rates: Original building $30 single or double without bath, $35–$42 single or double with bath; Mauka Building $60 superior, $80 deluxe. Extra person $10; Children under 10 $5. AE, CB, DC, JCB Card, MC, V. **Parking:** None available on-site. Free on street or for about $8 to $10 a day in a nearby lot.

The Pioneer Inn is a Lahaina landmark, and has been the center of action in town since its opening as a hotel and wholesale and retail liquor business in 1901. Back then it offered sailors clean but spartan accommodations, and it does the same today. As a result, room rates here are the lowest you'll find in Lahaina. In recent years though, while critics have praised the hotel's low prices and historic atmosphere, they've complained about noise levels from the downstairs saloon. Well, change may be coming. The inn is currently undergoing renovation, which includes a change in the downstairs restaurant and an upgrade in room amenities. Renovations should be completed by the time you read this, but you should call ahead to see if the project has been finished.

TONY'S PLACE, 13 Kauaula Rd., Lahaina, Maui, HI 96761. Tel. 808/661-8040. 3 rms (none with bath).
$ Rates: $50 single; $60 double. MC, V. **Parking:** Free.

If you're looking for really inexpensive accommodations right in Lahaina, and just steps away from the beach, give Tony Mamo a call. He rents clean, comfortable rooms right in his own home. Two of the bedrooms share a bath and one shares a bath with Tony's room. The public spaces are communal, and guests may make use of the refrigerator, telephone, television, and rather extensive library. Tony spent 17 long, cold years in Alaska, and he moved to Maui to warm up and relax—he expects his guests to do the same.

KAPALUA

EXPENSIVE

KAPALUA BAY HOTEL, One Bay Drive, Kapalua, Maui, HI 96761. Tel. 808/669-5656, or toll free 800/367-8000. Fax 808/669-4694. Telex 7431249. 194 rms, 3 suites, 125 villas. A/C MINIBAR TV TEL
$ Rates: Hotel $230 garden view; $280 garden-view prime; $330 ocean view; $375 ocean-view prime; $435 oceanfront; $650–$1,350 suite. Extra person $35. AE, DC, DISC, JCB Card, MC, V. **Parking:** Free valet parking.

Before the Ritz-Carlton appeared on the scene a couple of years ago, the 15-year-old Kapalua Bay Hotel and Villas (see also below) was the only hotel in the Kapalua Resort, and it was considered to be one of the island's best. In recent years, the hotel has gone through some ups and downs due to frequent changes in ownership, but today the Kapalua Bay Hotel appears to be making a comeback.

If you're looking for peace, quiet, a little tennis, and a lot of golf, the Kapalua Bay Hotel and Villas are for you (see Chapter 7 for full descriptions of golf courses). The Kapalua resort is comprised of 1,500 landscaped acres on a 23,000-acre pineapple plantation. When you check in, a member of the hotel's efficient staff will escort you to the skylighted lobby where you can relax with a cold glass of juice while they check to see that your room is ready.

Most of the rooms at the Bay Hotel have ocean views, but there are some with golf course or gardens views. Rooms that fall under the prime garden-view category typically afford guests a view of the ocean as well, but it's not a full ocean view. Each room has a long, narrow bathroom with a separate bathtub and shower, and two sinks (one at each end of the room). Closets are located in the bathroom as well. At the time of publication, guest rooms were undergoing renovation to lighten outdated color schemes and repair wear and tear. Each room has a private, spacious lanai with patio furniture for outdoor dining.

Dining/Entertainment: The Bay Club Restaurant is one of the jewels of the Kapalua resort. Set on a promontory overlooking the bay, the Bay Club Restaurant is open for lunch and dinner daily and serves fresh island seafood (see Chapter 6 for a full listing) in a romantic setting with a quiet piano soloist playing in the background from 6:30 to 10:30pm. Hotel guests may also dine alfresco in The Garden at breakfast daily and dinner every day except Sunday and Monday. There is live entertainment in The Garden from 7 to 11pm on Tuesday through Saturday. The Pool Terrace is the hotel's poolside, casual restaurant where continental breakfast is served, and salads, sandwiches, burgers, and entrees complete the bill of fare at lunch. The Bay Lounge is where a pianist entertains hotel guests who gather for drinks in the evening.

Services: Room service is available from 6:30am to 10:30pm in the hotel, and 6:30am to 10pm in the villas; twice-daily maid service; ice service (ice is delivered to your room late every afternoon, and also on request); resort shuttle service;

complimentary airport transfer to the Kapalua West Maui Airport; car rental office on property; church services; daily tea service; secretarial services; babysitting services on request; resort and garden tours are also offered.

Facilities: Two swimming pools on hotel grounds, nine others throughout the Kapalua villa and condo complexes (see below for descriptions of Kapalua condos), exercise facility with one-on-one fitness training (for a fee) and aerobics and aquacise classes. The Kapalua resort also has three fine golf courses (each with its own pro shop) and 10 plexi-pave tennis courts for day and night play. Villa guests have access to two additional tennis courts. Children between the ages of 5 and 12 might want to take advantage of Kamp Kapalua where they can enjoy snorkeling, surfing, tide pool exploration, lei making, and cookie baking among other activities. Adults can make plans for similar activities (excluding the cookie baking) through the hotel's Beach Activity Center. The Kapalua Shops (see Chapter 7 for more details) are located within easy walking distance from the hotel. Also in the Kapalua shopping area is the Market Cafe (see Chapter 6 for full listing), a perfect spot for a quick lunch.

KAPALUA VILLAS, 500 Office Rd., Kapalua, Maui, HI 96761. Tel. 808/ 669-8088, or toll free 800/545-0018. Fax 808/669-5234. A/C TV TEL

$ Rates: One-bedroom $155–$185 fairway view, $200–$250 ocean view, $255–$285 oceanfront; two-bedroom $205–$235 fairway view, $255–$305 ocean view, $325–$385 oceanfront. **Parking:** Free.

The Kapalua Bay, Ridge, or Golf Villas are an excellent choice for travelers who want the independence and economy of a condominium, but who want to take advantage of the serenity of Kapalua and its beautiful golf courses and excellent tennis facilities. The villas are arranged in three private clusters: bay, golf, and ridge. All of the condominiums are privately owned, and therefore individually decorated, but are managed by the Kapalua Land Company, developer of the Kapalua resort. Villa guests have access to all of the resort's amenities and enjoy the privilege of special golf rates, advance tee times, and complimentary tennis. Each cluster of villas has private swimming pools and outdoor barbecues. A resort shuttle is available to transport guests to and from resort beaches and facilities, and those staying at the villas have charge-back privileges at some of the facilities located in the nearby Ritz-Carlton Hotel. Maid service is twice weekly. When you call to make your reservation be sure to ask about the villa special packages.

THE RITZ-CARLTON, One Ritz-Carlton Dr., Kapalua, Maui, HI 96761. Tel. 808/669-6200, or toll free 800/241-3333. Fax 808/669-3908. 550 rms, 58 suites. A/C MINIBAR TV TEL.

$ Rates: $295 golf view; $335 partial ocean view; $410 ocean view; $465 oceanfront; $505 Club Level; $635–$1,200 suites. Extra person $35. Children under 18 stay free in parents' room. AE, DC, JCB Card, MC, V. **Parking:** Free valet parking.

Located only 10 miles from historic Lahaina amidst ancient cook pines and ironwood trees, The Ritz-Carlton is the most recent jewel in the crown that is the 1,500-acre Kapalua resort community. Original architectural plans called for building the hotel closer to the beach than it is today, but during preliminary construction it was discovered that the projected building site was over an ancient Hawaiian burial ground, so plans had to be changed. The Ritz-Carlton has been appointed the caretaker of the burial site, which is now on the State Register of Historic Places.

In keeping with the Ritz-Carlton's dedication to the preservation of culture and art, the walls display 18th- and 19th-century European paintings as well as work by local artists. There are some beautiful landscapes of Haleakala Crater, Hana, and Upcountry. George Allan, Joyce Clark, Betty Hay Freeland, and Fred Ken Knight are among the local talent whose work graces the walls of the Ritz. The enormous ceramic vases and pots you'll see as you walk through hallways and other public spaces are the work of local artist Tom Faught.

The guest rooms further illustrate the Ritz's dedication to excellence with features such as full marble bathrooms with separate showers, double vanities, and an extra telephone. All rooms have complimentary in-room safes, AM/FM clock radios, hair-dryers, and incredibly plush terrycloth robes. All of the rooms have private lanais outfitted with a table and chairs, and most of the rooms have ocean views. Ritz-Carlton Club Level rooms, located on the top three floors of the Napili wing, offer guests extra amenities, personal attention, and more privacy. Access to the Club Level floors is by elevator key. A concierge can be found in the Club Level lounge, which is set with food and beverage presentations throughout the day.

You can easily walk to the beach from the hotel, but for those who'd rather not expend the energy, a complimentary golf cart shuttle service is available to and from the strip of white sand at the end of the path.

During your stay here you might choose to lie on the beach or by the pool working on your tan, or you can take advantage of the hotel's jogging and walking trails, complimentary scuba lesson, snorkeling, sunset sails, windsurfing, or deep-sea fishing. Whatever your desire, it will be fulfilled by the hotel's impeccable and efficient staff.

If you're traveling with young children, I can't think of a better place for them. The children's program, Ritz Kids, will entertain children between the ages of 4 and 12 with scores of fully supervised activities. They'll learn about Hawaiian culture through story-telling and Hawaiian arts and crafts, such as lei making, hula lessons, and coconut leaf weaving. Counselors will lead shoreline shell safaris and help the children build sandcastles on the beach. There's even a Ritz Kids Theater where kids can catch a movie and snack on popcorn. Soccer, volleyball, croquet, and baseball will get them up and running, and best of all, Mom and Dad can relax on their own for a day or two. The full-day program costs $40 per child and includes lunch. The half-day program is $25. If you'd like to spend Saturday night in a Lahaina restaurant and don't want to leave the kids stranded in the hotel room with a babysitter, sign them up for the Saturday evening program. For $30 they'll have dinner at the Terrace Restaurant and be treated to a feature movie.

Dining/Entertainment: The Grill Restaurant serves contemporary American cuisine with an oceanfront view at lunch and dinner (see Chapter 6 for full listing). In the evening a pianist sets the mood for a fine dining experience. The Terrace Restaurant serves breakfast, Sunday brunch, and dinner daily either indoors or alfresco, and features traditional Hawaiian music nightly. The Banyan Tree specializes in Mediterranean cuisine for lunch and serves pupus and cocktails in the early evening. The Beach House is the Ritz's beachside snack shop where guests can have a quick sandwich amidst palm trees right on the sand. In the early evening you might choose to have a cocktail in the Lobby Lounge and Library while enjoying solo Hawaiian guitar music, or perhaps you would prefer the Sunset Lounge where classical entertainment is featured nightly. Whichever you choose, you won't be far from Maui's dramatic sunset.

Services: 24-hour room service; transportation to and from the airport; secretarial services; babysitting services; shuttle to and from golf courses; same-day laundry service; car rental agency on property.

Facilities: 10,000-square-foot swimming pool; 10 tennis courts with 5 lit for night play; full health center with outdoor aerobics classes, exercise and weight equipment, as well as spa treatments and massage.

MODERATE

KAHILI MAUI, 5500 L. Honoapiilani Hwy., Kapalua, Maui, HI 96761. Tel. 808/669-5635, or toll free 800/786-7387. 34 units, 30 in rental pool. A/C TV TEL
$ Rates High season (Dec 21–Mar 31): $109 studio suite; $140 one-bedroom suite. Low season (Apr 1–Dec 20): $89 studio suite; $120 one-bedroom suite. Rollaway $15.

Ⓕ FROMMER'S COOL FOR KIDS: HOTELS

Four Seasons Resort *(see p. 95)* The Four Seasons Resort has one of the island's best children's programs. Kids 5 to 12 can participate in Hawaiian arts and crafts classes, marine life demonstrations, and sand sculpting, among other things. There's even a special facility for older children that features a big-screen TV and billiards. Scuba and windsurfing lessons for children over 12 are complimentary.

Grand Wailea *(see p. 97)* Camp Grande, the Grand Wailea's children's program, features a children's restaurant, pool, arts and crafts room, game room, computer learning center, and theater. In addition to the Grand's comprehensive children's program, kids will love the hotel's 2,000-foot-long action pool with mountains, grottos, waterfalls, slides, rapids, and even a rope swing.

The Ritz-Carlton *(see p. 84)* The children's program at the Ritz entertains children between 4 and 12 with scores of supervised activities. Lei making, hula lessons, and coconut leaf weaving are all popular with the kids. Children can also watch movies in the Ritz Kids Theater.

Crib $10. Children under 18 stay free in parents' room if existing bedding is used. AE, MC, V. **Parking:** Free.

 A recent renovation makes the Kahili one of the best properties in the Napili Bay area. Only a five-minute walk from Napili and Kapalua Beach, the Kahili is surrounded by mango, papaya, and banana trees, which make up for the lack of ocean views. The studio and one-bedroom units are small, but absolutely spotless, attractively and individually furnished. Each unit has two bathrooms, queen-size sofa beds in the living room, a washer and dryer, and fully equipped kitchens. Guests also have full use of the condo's pool and Jacuzzi.

NAPILI

EXPENSIVE

NAPILI KAI BEACH CLUB, 5900 Honoapiilani Rd., Napili Bay, Maui, HI 96761. Tel. 808/669-6271, or toll free 800/367-5030 (line is open Mon–Fri, 6:30am–4:30pm Hawaii time). Fax 808/669-5740. 163 units. TV TEL

$ Rates (based on double occupancy): $165–$185 luxury garden-view studio; $195–$215 luxury ocean-view studio; $200 deluxe ocean-view studio; $205 deluxe beachfront studio; $240–$260 luxury oceanfront studio; $220–$420 deluxe ocean-view suite; $250–$285 deluxe beachfront suite; $300–$445 luxury garden-view suite; $370–$540 luxury ocean-view suite; $295–$480 luxury oceanfront suite. Crib, rollaway, or extra person $5. No credit cards. Traveler's checks, personal checks, and cash are accepted. **Parking:** Free.

Located right on a beach between Lahaina and Kapalua, the Napili Kai Beach Club bills itself as "Maui's Most Hawaiian Resort." As a guest you will be granted a guest membership in the Beach Club, which includes morning coffee or tea, a weekly putting party on the property's 18-hole putting green with 50¢ cocktails (except during high season), a weekly Mai Tai party, lei-making and hula lessons, and afternoon tea, and access to beach towels, beach chairs, snorkels and masks, tennis rackets, and putters.

Room sizes vary according to location. A studio is a large hotel-like room with the added bonus of a fully equipped kitchenette. The two-room suites accommodate up to four people, and have one or two baths and a fully equipped kitchenette. The three-room suites offer two bedrooms and an additional bed in the living room and they sleep up to six. Each of the units has a private lanai. Most amenities and the decor are slightly outmoded, but if you'd rather not stay in one of the high-rises in Kaanapali and are dead set on being on the beach on the island's west side, the Napili Kai could be what you're looking for.

Dining/Entertainment: The Beach Pagoda serves fast food, including burgers, hot dogs, fries, shakes, beer, and various tropical drinks. The Sea House and Sea Breeze Terrace Restaurants serve breakfast, lunch, and dinner daily and often feature Hawaiian entertainment and dancing. The unfortunately named Bikini Watchers' Bar is also available to guests.

Services: Daily maid service; activities desk.

Facilities: The Hankipanki Whirlpool (the Beach Club boasts that it's "Hawaii's largest heated whirlpool"); four swimming pools; barbecue facilities; shuffleboard; gift shop and boutique; nearby tennis courts with pro on duty ($10 fee to use the courts).

2. CENTRAL & SOUTH MAUI

Central Maui's main draw is its inexpensive accommodations, most of which are youth hostels and aren't located on or near a beach. South Maui, Kihei, Wailea, and Makena offer a variety of hostelries in a wide range of prices. Maui's south shore is attractive to visitors because the weather is almost always sunny—Kihei has the lowest average rainfall on the island. Kihei's shoreline is lined primarily with affordable condominiums, but there are also a few full-service hotels. More upscale hostelries can be found in Wailea, another of the island's planned resorts. Guests who stay in the Wailea resort will have access to all resort facilities, including world-famous golf courses. Makena remains undeveloped, save for the existence of the Maui Prince, and it has some of the island's most beautiful coastline.

CENTRAL MAUI

BUDGET

MAUI BANANA BUNGALOW, 310 N. Market St., Wailuku, Maui, HI 96783. Tel. 808/244-5090, or toll free 800/846-7835. Fax 808/242-9324. 27 rms (none with bath).

$ Rates: $15 per person in shared accommodations; $31.95 single; $38.95 double. Weekly and monthly discounts available. MC, V. **Parking:** Free on street.

One of several Wailuku youth hostels/hotels, the Maui Banana Bungalow is a favorite with windsurfers and European travelers. Shared accommodations house three or four beds (twins or bunk beds), single rooms have double beds, and double rooms either have twins or one queen-size bed. There is a common lounge area where hostel guests gather around the television. There are communal refrigerators, a pay phone, and a laundry room. Guests may play volleyball and Ping-Pong or toss some horseshoes. A barbecue grill is available for guest use, as are picnic tables and hammocks. There is a guest kitchen, and free videos are screened every night. Airport and beach transfer are complimentary services, and group trips are frequently arranged. Rental cars can be arranged for $10 a day when guests stay for three or more days. There is also a windsurfer storage shed.

MAUI SEASIDE HOTEL, 100 Kaahumanu Ave., Kahului, Maui, HI 96732. Tel. 808/877-3311, or toll free 800/367-7000. Fax 808/922-0052. 190 rooms. A/C TV TEL

$ Rates: Apr 1–Dec 14: $59–$94 single or double; Dec 15–Mar 31: $69–$104 single or double. Extra person $12. AE, MC, V. **Parking:** Free.

If you've got to stay in Kahului because you have an early flight and want to be near the airport, your choices are limited, and none of them compare to the island's other hostelries. The best you'll be able to do is the Maui Seaside Hotel. The rooms are small, and a bit outdated, but clean, and the prices are good. The least expensive rooms face the garden. The next level up face the pool, and the most expensive rooms are located in the Towers and are slightly larger. Some of the rooms have kitchenettes. The hotel's restaurant, Vi's, serves a variety of cuisines, including Asian, American, and Italian. Entrees are in the inexpensive range.

All in all, the Maui Seaside is a bargain, but it's not a first choice for spending more than a night or two.

MAUI VINEYARD INN, 2102 Vineyard St., Wailuku, Maui, HI 96783. Tel. 808/242-0007. 20 rms (none with bath).
$ Rates: $20–$30 single or double. No credit cards. **Parking:** Free.

Operated by the same people who own Maui Boy Restaurant, the Maui Vineyard Inn is a good alternative for people on a budget. Rooms are tiny and bathrooms are shared, but the Maui Vineyard is clean, quiet, and safe. The owner lives in one of the rooms, so you can be sure house rules will be enforced. There are refrigerators in all rooms, and the more expensive ones also have a TV. Towels are supplied, and there is maid service. There are no in-room telephones, but there is a pay phone downstairs. All rooms have ceiling fans. Like its neighbor, the Northshore Inn, the Maui Vineyard Inn is popular with windsurfers and Europeans.

NORTHSHORE INN, 2080 Vineyard St., Wailuku, Maui, HI 96793. Tel. 808/242-8999. Fax 808/244-5004.
$ Rates: $14.95 per night shared accommodations; $29.95 single; $39.95 double. Weekly discounts are available. AE, MC, V. **Parking:** Free.

This is one of the best hostels I've ever seen. It's clean and comfortable; there's a lounge area with a TV and VCR, laundry facilities, a communal kitchen, and a porch overlooking Vineyard Street. Owner Katie Moore spent a lot of time traveling and experienced accommodations of all types and varieties. She strives to make the Northshore Inn a "home away from home" for all her guests, many of whom are windsurfers and Europeans. She's so in tune with the needs of her guests that she decorated some rooms specifically for men and some for women. There is a nominal one-time charge for a towel, top sheet, and blanket. The rooms that fall under "shared accommodations" have five or six beds each, but there are also single and double rooms for those who would like more privacy. Van pickups at the airport can be arranged, and the Northshore Inn also sponsors some bus tours around the island (frequency varies according to the number of people interested in going, and charges vary according to the distance to be traveled). There is no curfew, but the gate is locked at 9pm for safety reasons (guests are given keys to the gate). There is no smoking indoors, but it's allowed on the outdoor porch.

KIHEI/MAKENA

EXPENSIVE

MAUI HILL, 2881 S. Kihei Rd., Kihei, Maui, HI 96753. Tel. 808/879-6321, or toll free 800/922-7866 from the U.S. mainland or 800/445-6633 from Canada. 36 units. A/C TV TEL
$ Rates: High season (Dec 22–Apr 1): $175 one-bedroom unit; $195 two-bedroom unit; $285 three-bedroom unit. Low season (Apr 1–Dec 22): $145 one-bedroom unit; $165 two-bedroom unit; $255 three-bedroom unit. Extra person $12. AE, CB, DC, JCB Card, MC, V. **Parking:** Free.

As you might have guessed from its name, the Maui Hill is not an oceanfront property—on the contrary, its buildings are nestled into a hillside. When it was built almost 15 years ago it was one of the only properties constructed away from the oceanfront and some wondered if it would survive. Well, it has, in spades. In fact,

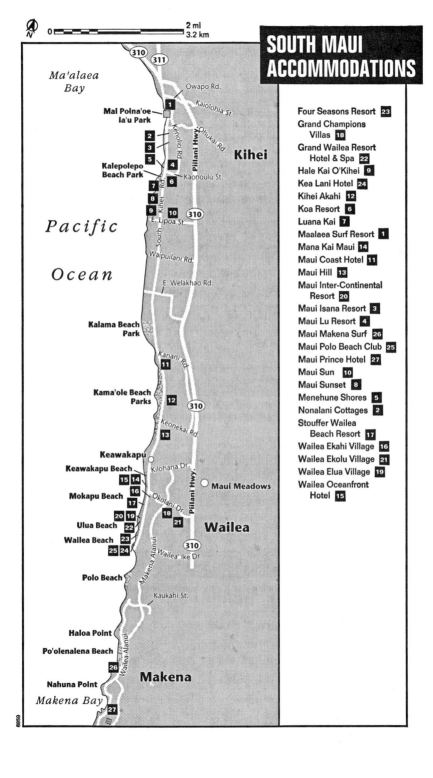

Four Seasons Resort **23**
Grand Champions
   Villas **18**
Grand Wailea Resort
   Hotel & Spa **22**
Hale Kai O'Kihei **9**
Kea Lani Hotel **24**
Kihei Akahi **12**
Koa Resort **6**
Luana Kai **7**
Maalaea Surf Resort **1**
Mana Kai Maui **14**
Maui Coast Hotel **11**
Maui Hill **13**
Maui Inter-Continental
   Resort **20**
Maui Isana Resort **3**
Maui Lu Resort **4**
Maui Makena Surf **26**
Maui Polo Beach Club **25**
Maui Prince Hotel **27**
Maui Sun **10**
Maui Sunset **8**
Menehune Shores **5**
Nonalani Cottages **2**
Stouffer Wailea
   Beach Resort **17**
Wailea Ekahi Village **16**
Wailea Ekolu Village **21**
Wailea Elua Village **19**
Wailea Oceanfront
   Hotel **15**

Ma'alaea
Bay

Owapo Rd.

Kaiolohia St.

Mal Polna'oe
la'u Park

1

Kenolio Rd.

Ohukai Rd.

Piilani Hwy.

Kihei

2
3
5
4

Kalepolepo
Beach Park

Kihei Rd.

6

Kaonoulu St.

7

8

9 **10** 310

E. Lipoa St.

Pacific

Ocean

Waipuilani Rd.

E. Welakhao Rd.

South Kihei Rd.

Kalama Beach
Park

Kanani Rd.

11

Kama'ole Beach
Parks

12 310

Keonekai Rd.

13

Keawakapu

Keawakapu Beach

Kilohana Dr.

15 14

16

Mokapu Beach

17

Okolani Dr.

Piilani Hwy.

Maui Meadows

20 19

22

Ulua Beach

18

21

Wailea

Wailea Beach

23

25 24

Makena Alanui

Wailea Ike Dr.

310

Polo Beach

Kaukahi St.

Haloa Point

Po'olenalena Beach

Wailea Alanui

26

Makena

Nahuna Point

Makena Bay

27

2 mi
3.2 km
0

N

it's probably the best deal you'll find on South Kihei Road, its only drawback being its distance from the beach.

There are 12 three-story buildings constructed in a Spanish architectural style with red-tile roofs and stucco exteriors. The suites, or apartments, are all spacious, and though the owners' tastes in decorating vary greatly, each is pleasantly appointed. Upstairs units all have lofts, and all the lodgings have ocean views. Gourmet kitchens are an added extra for people who'd rather cook than go out to eat, and there's a barbecue area on the property for those who'd rather not be tied to the stove. Guests have access to the Maui Hill tennis court, shuffleboard, putting green, and freshwater pool and jet spa. There is daily maid service, and concierge service is available for those who need help with reservations or activities. Each week the manager hosts a cocktail party for guests.

MAUI ISANA RESORT, 515 S. Kihei Rd., Kihei, Maui, HI 96753. Tel. 808/879-7800, or toll free 800/633-3833. Fax 808/874-5321. 50 units. A/C TV TEL

$ Rates: $130 one-bedroom unit; $170 two-bedroom unit. Extra person $15. Room/car packages available. Weekly and monthly discounts available. AE, MC, V. **Parking:** Free.

Many of the hotels, especially those in the resort areas, are geared toward the Japanese traveler, but that isn't usually the case with condominium complexes. The condominiums in the Maui Isana Resort complex have definitely been designed and outfitted with the Japanese traveler in mind. In many of the individually owned units you're likely to find sleek wood furnishings and little fanfare—no extra decorative appointments. Some are, however, outfitted in much the same way as other condos in the area. Bedrooms in the one- and two-bedroom units are spacious, and all apartments have ceiling fans. All accommodations have washer/dryer combinations, dishwashers (none have microwaves, although there are many with crockpots), and ocean-view lanais; however, maid service is limited. Since this condominium building is also on the *mauka* side of South Kihei Road, you'll have to walk across the street to the beach, but there is a pool and a Jacuzzi on the property. The Isana sponsors windsurfing and scuba-diving lessons, and there is an activities and travel desk available for guests.

MAUI PRINCE HOTEL, 5400 Makena Alanui, Kihei, Maui, HI 96753-9986. Tel. 808/874-1111, or toll free 800/321-MAUI. Fax 800/338-8763. Telex 5106006992. 310 rms, 20 suites. A/C TV TEL

$ Rates: $240 partial ocean view; $280 ocean view; $330 prime ocean view; $380 oceanfront; $440–$880 suite. Special packages, including golf packages, are available. No extra charge for third person provided existing bedding is used. $25 for rollaway or crib. AE, CB, DC, JCB Card, MC, V. **Parking:** Free.

The Maui Prince is the only hotel in the Makena resort, and it couldn't have a better location. Somewhat removed from the hustle and bustle of Kihei and Wailea, the Prince offers its guests beaches and amenities as magnificent as many of the other full-service hotels in the area, but with a lot less hoopla. At check-in all guests are greeted by friendly staff members expressing their warmest aloha with a floral lei and *oshibori* (refreshing, warm towels). Guest rooms are reached via open-air promenades that overlook the lobby. Each of the rooms has an ocean view, private lanai, and a large bathroom with a hairdryer and telephone. In your room you'll also find a complimentary sampling of Hawaiian treats, and your minirefrigerator will be stocked with fruit juices and bottled water (restocked daily). In addition, all rooms have VCRs and videos can be rented in-house. The hotel gardens are immaculately maintained, and if you wander the grounds you'll find waterfalls that lead into carp-stocked ponds dotted with yellow and white water lilies. Every evening brings light to the Japanese lanterns that line the walkways and a halt to the waterfalls in the courtyard so classical musicians may set the mood for dining under the stars.

Dining/Entertainment: The hotel's main dining room, the Prince Court, offers

Hawaiian regional cuisine, and Cafe Kiowai serves light meals in an open-air setting. Both restaurants have spectacular views of the ocean and neighboring islands.

Services: Room service from 6am to 10pm daily.

Facilities: Pool; 36 holes of golf; six plexi-pave tennis courts; pro shop.

MODERATE

KOA RESORT, 811 S. Kihei Rd., Kihei, Maui, HI 96753. Tel. 808/879-1161, or toll free 800/877-1314. Fax 808/879-4001. 54 units, 30 in rental pool. TV TEL

$ Rates: High season (Dec 1–Mar 31): $120 one-bedroom unit; $135–$145 two-bedroom unit; $170–$195 three-bedroom unit. Low season (Apr 1–Nov 30): $100 one-bedroom unit; $115–$125 two-bedroom unit; $150–$175 three-bedroom unit. Extra person $10. Minimum stay of five nights. Monthly discounts are available. MC, V. **Parking:** Free.

Koa Resort bills its accommodations as "Deluxe Townhouse Condominiums," and they are. In fact, this is one of my favorite Kihei condominium properties. It's not on the beach like many of the other properties, but that's actually to its benefit. Because the buildings are set across the street from the beach, they're likely to be quieter than some of the other condominiums in the area. In addition, the grounds have been landscaped so beautifully that you probably won't even notice the lack of sand.

Furnishings and decor vary from unit to unit, but whatever you find you won't be disappointed, because the management maintains certain standards to which all apartment owners must adhere. There are several sizes from which to choose—from one-bedroom units with one bath to three-bedroom units with three baths. Fully equipped kitchens with dishwashers and microwaves are sizeable, and each unit is outfitted with laundry facilities. Most of the accommodations don't have air conditioning, but all have ceiling fans. The upstairs units have cathedral ceilings, and all have private lanais that look out over the gardens.

On-site facilities include two tennis courts, an extra-large 18-hole putting green, shuffleboard, three gas barbecues, an enormous, uniquely shaped pool (crossed by a bridge), and a Jacuzzi. The patio around the pool is very conducive to private sunbathing because the chaise longues are "partitioned" off from each other by cleverly placed trees and shrubbery.

LUANA KAI, 940 S. Kihei Rd., Kihei, Maui, HI 96753. Tel. 808/879-1268, or toll free 800/669-1127. Fax 808/879-1455. 113 units, 70 in rental pool. TV TEL

$ Rates (including car): High season (Dec 20–Mar 31): $130 one-bedroom garden view, $145 one-bedroom ocean view; $150 two-bedroom garden view, $175 two-bedroom ocean view; $225 three-bedroom garden view. Low season (Apr 1–Dec 19): $105 one-bedroom garden view, $120 one-bedroom ocean view; $125 two-bedroom garden view, $150 two-bedroom ocean view; $175 three-bedroom garden view. AE, DC, MC, V. **Parking:** Free.

Luana Kai has a great location and some exceptional facilities. The beach is just a short walk across the lawn from the condominium units; there are four tennis courts, an impressive putting green, a sauna, and a fenced-off private pool and whirlpool area. One-, two-, and three-bedroom units come fully furnished and all have ceiling fans in lieu of air-conditioning units. The upstairs units have loft bedrooms, and most are equipped with VCRs. Furnishings are generally contemporary and color schemes are neutral or a combination of pastel and neutral tones. The only drawback here is that some of the condos haven't been redecorated recently and they're beginning to show their age, but you really can't go wrong (especially with an economy car included in the rates).

MAALAEA SURF RESORT, 12 S. Kihei Rd., Kihei, Maui, HI 96753. Tel. 808/879-1267, or toll free 800/423-7953. Fax 808/874-2884. 33 units in rental pool. A/C TV TEL

$ Rates: High season: $170 one-bedroom unit; $240 two-bedroom unit. Low season: $150 one-bedroom unit; $210 two-bedroom unit. No credit cards. **Parking:** Free.

Located just off the "beaten path" in Kihei, the Maalaea Surf Resort is a nice surprise. All the one- and two-bedroom units in a series of low-rise buildings are individually owned, but most of them have been upgraded, so your chances of getting stuck in a less-than-perfect unit are slim. Well-equipped kitchens have the added luxury of a microwave and dishwasher. Air conditioning is standard and so are ceiling fans and VCRs. Most of the two-bedroom apartments have one room with twin beds for those traveling with children. There are laundry facilities in each building, and a housekeeping staff services the condos daily (except Sunday and holidays). Each unit has a full ocean view, and five miles of beach begin almost right outside your door.

There are two swimming pools and two tennis courts on the property in addition to shuffleboard and basketball courts. The five acres on which the Maalaea Surf is situated are beautifully landscaped, and as you wander around the property you're likely to find various fruits ripening on the trees, including kumquats (which taste like a cross between a lemon and an orange—you can eat the whole thing, including the peel) and avocados.

MANA KAI MAUI, 2960 S. Kihei Rd., Kihei, Maui, HI 96753. Tel. 808/879-1561, or toll free 800/525-2025 (Mon–Fri 5:30am–3pm Hawaiian time). Fax 808/874-5042. 98 units, 67 in rental pool. TV TEL

$ Rates (including rental car): High season (Dec 17–Apr 16): $100 hotel unit with breakfast; $185 one-bedroom apartment; $205 two-bedroom apartment. Low season (Apr 17–Dec 16): $95 hotel unit with breakfast; $165 one-bedroom apartment; $185 two-bedroom apartment. Extra person $10. Children 6 and under stay free. AE, CB, MC, V. **Parking:** Free.

If you're traveling on a tight budget, the Mana Kai Maui might be just the thing. Your rental car will be included in the rate, and if you rent one of the hotel units (with a divider for separating the sleeping area from the living area at night) you get breakfast in the deal as well. The one- and two-bedroom units are a little more pricey and have full kitchens. A two-bedroom apartment will sleep up to six. There are laundry facilities on every floor, and daily maid service is standard for all accommodations. Nestled in among the pine trees is a large swimming pool, and the mile-long stretch of beach that borders the property is great for swimming. The Ocean Terrace is the on-property beachside restaurant, and on the ground floor of the six-story apartment building is a shopping area that includes a beauty salon, a gift shop, an apparel shop, and a general store. Ocean Activities Center (see Chapter 7 for full listing) also has an office on the property. All things considered, the Mana Kai Maui is one of the best deals on the island.

MAUI COAST HOTEL, 2259 S. Kihei Rd., Kihei, Maui, HI 96753. Tel. 808/874-6284, or toll free 800/426-0670. Fax 808/875-4731. 260 rms. A/C TV TEL

$ Rates: Terrace $109 standard, $139 alcove suite; ocean view $120 standard, $149 alcove suite; $165 standard one-bedroom suite, $180 deluxe one-bedroom suite; $225 standard two-bedroom suite, $250 deluxe two-bedroom suite. Room/car packages available. AE, MC, V. **Parking:** Free.

Opened in February 1993, the Maui Coast is one of Kihei's newest properties. The rates at the Maui Coast are slightly lower than some of the other hotels in the area because it's located across South Kihei Road from the beach, and none of the rooms have the spectacular views that rooms in a beachfront property might have. However, you won't be disappointed with the accommodations.

The spacious and graciously designed lobby is representative of what you'll find in your room after you've enjoyed a refreshing glass of "welcome juice" at check-in. All the rooms are large and pleasantly decorated in pastel green, purple, and pink color schemes, and no matter which room type you choose, you'll be more than comfortable. If you stay in a standard room you'll have a choice of twin, two double, or one king-size bed. The Junior Suites are alcove suites with king-size or two double beds as well as a pull-out couch. Additionally, in the Junior Suites you'll have a wet bar and an oversized whirlpool tub. The one-bedroom suite has a king-size bed and an extra TV. Two-bedroom suites are also available and sleep up to six adults. All deluxe suites have whirlpool tubs, and all rooms have sitting areas with modern furnishings, minirefrigerators, clock radios, coffee makers with complimentary coffee each morning, scales, hairdryers, complimentary in-room safes, individually controlled air conditioning, and ceiling fans. In each room sliding glass doors open onto a private lanai outfitted with patio furniture.

Dining/Entertainment: The hotel's Kamaole Bar & Grill Restaurant serves three meals daily in a casual setting.

Services: Room service; activities desk.

Facilities: Complimentary laundry facilities (you only have to supply detergents); heated swimming pool; children's wading pool; two outdoor Jacuzzis; two tennis courts—both lit for night play; gift shop.

MAUI LU RESORT, 575 S. Kihei Rd., Kihei, Maui, HI 96753. Tel. 808/ 879-5881, or toll free 800/922-7866 from U.S. mainland or 800/445-6633 from Canada. 120 rms. A/C TV TEL

$ Rates: High season (Dec 22–Mar 31): $95 standard garden view, $100 superior garden view, $135 deluxe ocean view, $160 oceanfront. Low season (Apr 1–Dec 22): $85 standard garden view, $95 superior garden view, $125 deluxe ocean view, $150 oceanfront. AE, CB, CD, JCB Card, MC, V. Extra person $12. Room/car packages available. Minimum stay of four nights during Christmas season. **Parking:** Free.

With four categories of rooms and several cottages available for rent, the Maui Lu Resort has something to suit almost every taste and every wallet. Most of the rooms are located on the *mauka* side of South Kihei Road and face the garden, so you won't get a sweeping panoramic view of the ocean, but the hotel also has several oceanfront rooms across the street. Whatever the view, your lodging will be a standard hotel room with two double beds (rooms with "superior" status are slightly larger), a minirefrigerator, coffee maker, and in-room safe ($1.50 a day). Color schemes are light and refreshing, and furnishings are contemporary. There are two tennis courts on the property (you can rent balls and rackets), as well as an activities desk to help you plan your itinerary. One of the most interesting features of the hotel is its swimming pool—it was built in the shape of the island of Maui. The Longhouse restaurant and lounge offers American cuisine with a Pacific influence.

MENEHUNE SHORES, 760 S. Kihei Rd. (P.O. Box 1327), Kihei, Maui, HI 96753. Tel. 808/879-3428 and 808/879-5828, or toll free 800/558-9117. Fax 808/879-5218. 89 units. AC TV TEL

$ Rates: High season (Dec 15–Apr 15): $100 one-bedroom unit; $120–$130 two-bedroom unit; $140–$160 three-bedroom unit. Low season (Apr 16–Dec 14): $85 one-bedroom unit; $98.50–$110 two-bedroom unit; $130–$150 three-bedroom unit. Extra person $7.50. Minimum stay of five nights. Monthly discounts available. No credit cards. **Parking:** Free.

The stuccoed exterior of the horseshoe-shaped building that houses Menehune Shores is decorated by whimsical modern petroglyphs. Because of the condominium's unique shape, all of the units face the ocean (some more directly than others). Inside you'll find agreeably decorated one-, two-, and three-bedroom units with full kitchens and private lanais. The two- and three-bedroom condos have two full bathrooms, and all apartments are outfitted with washers and dryers. Menehune Shores is situated adjacent to the 16th-century Ali'i (Royal) Fish Pond of Kalepolipo, which is a great "swimming hole" for whose who'd rather stay out of the heavier surf that usually beats the shores of this side of the island. The swimming hole is protected by a coral reef and is an excellent place for children to get their feet wet. If you'd rather swim in a freshwater pool, however, the condominium complex has a large oval-shaped pool surrounded by a large patio. There are also barbecue areas, and a shuffleboard is available for guest use. If you get tired of cooking for yourself and your family, you can always give the Menehune Shores' oceanfront cocktail lounge and restaurant a try.

INEXPENSIVE

HALE KAI O'KIHEI, 1310 Uluniu Rd. (P.O. Box 809), Kihei, Maui, HI 96753-0809. Tel. 808/879-2757, or toll free 800/457-7014. 40 units. TV TEL

$ Rates (based on double occupancy for one-week minimum stay): High season (Dec 16–Apr 15): $660 one-bedroom unit; $835 two-bedroom unit. Low season (Apr 16–Dec 15): $455 one-bedroom unit; $625 two-bedroom unit. Extra person $10 per day. Monthly discounts available. **Parking:** Free.

From the outside the Hale Kai O'Kihei looks like your average cement-block apartment building, but don't be fooled. The interiors are actually rather charming and the building manager is welcoming and extremely friendly. You can't book an apartment here for less than a week, so you'll really begin to feel at home with your neighbors and other guests, who you'll see sunning themselves by the pool or practicing on the putting green. By the time you leave you'll probably be gathering a group together for an evening barbecue and a game of shuffleboard. The beach out front is great for swimming, snorkeling, and surfing, and since the weather on this side of the island is almost always sunny, you'll get more than your money's worth.

All units feature full kitchens (most with microwaves) and private lanais with outdoor furniture. Bathrooms are large, and the decor in all the apartments is bright and fresh. There's no air conditioning, but the ceiling fans are adequate. Coin-op laundry facilities are centrally located.

KIHEI AKAHI, 2531 S. Kihei Rd., Kihei, Maui, HI 96753. Tel. 808/879-2778, or toll free 800/367-5242 on the U.S. mainland, 800/663-2101 in Canada. Fax 808/879-7825. 70 units. TV TEL

$ Rates (per night for 4–6 nights): High season (Dec 15–Mar 31): $90 studio; $110 one-bedroom; $145 two-bedroom. Low season (Apr 1–Dec 14): $70 studio; $85 one-bedroom; $115 two-bedroom. Extra person $12. Special air/car/condo packages and weekly and monthly discounts are available. Minimum stay of four nights. No credit cards. **Parking:** Free.

Not to be confused with Kihei Ekahi, located in the Wailea Resort, Kihei Akahi is located directly across the street from one of Kihei's best beaches—Kamaole Beach Park II. A small grouping of low-rise buildings is complemented by nicely landscaped grounds. There are also two eight-story buildings in the complex. Most of the apartments have rattan furnishings with modern light fixtures, silk flower arrangements, and floral print fabrics. Each is also outfitted with a full kitchen, washer and dryer, ceiling fans, and a private lanai. You have to cross the street to get to the beach, but you'll be happy to know there are two pools on the property for guest use. Other facilities include barbecues and a tennis court.

MAUI SUN, 175 E. Lipoa St., Kihei, Maui, HI 96753. Tel. 808/875-9000, or toll free 800/762-5348. Fax 808/874-8446. 229 rms and suites. A/C TV TEL

$ Rates: Standard rooms $84 mountain view, $94 deluxe garden view, $104 partial ocean view. Suites $115 one-bedroom mountain view; $130 two-bedroom deluxe garden view; $160 two-bedroom partial ocean view; $350 presidential. Hotel/golf and room/car packages available. AE, DC, DISC, MC, V. **Parking:** Free.

The Maui Sun is a relatively new addition to the Kihei/Wailea hotel scene, but it's different than anything else you'll find in the area. For one thing, the prices for this luxury hotel are unmatched. You'd even be hard-pressed to find a condominium offering lower rates. One of the reasons it is less expensive than some of the resort hotels that offer the same amenities is that it's not in a resort area, and relatively speaking, it's not close to the beach (it won't take more than five minutes to get to the shoreline, though). I wouldn't consider either of those to be negative features. In fact, it has one more plus that most of the condominium and hotel properties on South Kihei Road don't have—it's not on South Kihei Road, which can be terribly busy and traffic-jammed, especially at night. The moment you enter the vast marble-tiled lobby with etched glass ceilings and original sculpture, you'll know you've just gotten one of the best deals in the Kihei area. The Maui Sun is located right across the street from the Silversword Golf Course, and shuttle bus service to other golf courses, shops, and nearby beaches is offered. Two six-story buildings house freshly appointed guest rooms. All rooms have one king-size or two queen-size beds and a private lanai. Suites have pull-out couches, a minirefrigerator, and two televisions. The oversized pool (and I mean *oversized*) is definitely a plus, and the meticulously manicured grounds also feature koi ponds, waterfalls, and a whirlpool spa. The hotel features ground-floor gardens that are open to the outside by a six-story shaft, around which many of the rooms are built. Frangipani, the hotel's restaurant and lounge, is definitely worth trying out. Room service features "Meals to Go," such as pizza and hamburgers.

MAUI SUNSET, 1032 S. Kihei Rd., Kihei, Maui, HI 96753. Tel. 808/879-0674, or toll free 800/843-5880. 225 units. TV TEL
$ Rates: High season: $105–$125 one-bedroom; $145–$155 two-bedroom; $185–$225 three-bedroom. Low season: $85–$105 one-bedroom; $110–$130 two-bedroom; $155–$185 three-bedroom. AE, MC, V. **Parking:** Free.

The condominiums at the Maui Sunset were refurbished in 1989, so most of the furnishings are modern and color schemes are of current fashion—neutral tones and rattan furnishings with pastel floral and striped accents. Many of the units have sporting gear, like boogie boards, stored in closets for guest use. The Maui Sunset is one of the area's most popular condominiums, and that has largely to do with the fact that it's situated on a good-size piece of property and offers a beachfront location. Guests enjoy an abundance of on-property activities, including the swimming pool and hot tub, croquet, the putting green, shuffleboard, and the tennis courts. There are barbecue areas as well. All the units have ocean or garden views, and there is ample parking.

NONALANI COTTAGES, 455 S. Kihei Rd., Kihei, Maui, HI 96753. Tel. 808/879-2497, or toll free 800/733-2688. 8 cottages.
$ Rates: High season (Apr 16–Dec 1): $85 cottage for two. Low season (Dec 2–Apr 15): $80 cottage for two. Extra person $7. Minimum stay of four nights during high season. Weekly and monthly rates available. No credit cards. **Parking:** Free.

You're not interested in staying in a youth hostel, and you can't afford to stay in a condominium, let alone one of the luxury hotels in Wailea. Well, how about one of eight one-bedroom cottages equipped with a full kitchen, set on a small but lushly landscaped piece of property? The cottage interiors are somewhat outdated and oddly furnished, but they're still a step up from a youth hostel. Hammocks are strung from tree to tree, and a beautiful white-sand beach is only a short walk across the street. Each of the cottages has an outdoor deck where you can watch the sun set between plumeria, palm, and citrus trees. For reservations call one of the two numbers listed above, or write to Dave and Nona Kong, P.O. Box 655, Kihei, Maui, HI 96753.

WAILEA
EXPENSIVE

FOUR SEASONS RESORT, 3900 Wailea Alanui, Wailea, Maui, HI 96753. Tel. 808/874-8000, or toll free 800/334-MAUI. Fax 808/874-2222. 380 rms, 83 suites. A/C MINIBAR TV TEL
$ Rates: $345 partial ocean view, $430 ocean view, $550 ocean view on Club Floor; $660 Four Seasons Executive Suite, $770 Four Seasons Executive Suite on Club Floor, $690–$5,000 Deluxe Suite. Children's Room (excluding those on Club Floor) $225. AE, DC, JCB Card, MC, V. **Parking:** Free valet or self parking.

The moment you enter the lobby of the Four Seasons you'll be swept into a world of elegance, opulence, and decadence. In addition to a virtually unobstructed view of the ocean, the lobby holds an abundance of tropical flowers, oversized wicker furnishings, and an extensive art collection. From the custom commission Art Screen behind the registration desk to the antique Chinese wedding baskets at the coffee table near the fountain to the ceiling murals, the Four Seasons is a virtual museum.

Just on the other side of the open-air lobby are all the things that brought you to Hawaii in the first place—the blue waters of the resort's fountained swimming pool, bright white cabanas, lanky palm trees, a strip of the most exquisite white-sand beach, and the brilliant turquoise Pacific Ocean. That's only the beginning.

Your room here will be equally luxurious. Although color schemes (neutral with peach and green highlights) vary from room to room, the basic amenities (including private lanais and slightly whimsical seashell-patterned bedspreads) remain the same, no matter what the view. All rooms are outfitted with ceiling fans, rattan and wicker furniture, and wooden shutters. In addition, you'll find a fully stocked minibar, a most ingenious ice bucket with a drip hole to keep ice and water separate, VCR (the hotel has a movie library for guest rentals), clock radio, in-room safe, terry robes, and teak patio furniture on the lanai. The marble-tiled bathrooms are elegantly appointed with enormous framed mirrors, separate showers, oversized bathtubs, and separate makeup areas with vanity mirrors. The attention to detail here is unsurpassed. The management is so concerned with the comfort of the guests that it instituted a unique housekeeping policy. This is the only hotel in which you will never ever see a housekeeping cart in the hallways. The cleaning staff works in teams—some clean, some run for supplies, and some restock minibars. They move swiftly (in 15 minutes) through each room, leaving not a speck of dust behind—all of this so you won't be disturbed by staff members more than once a day. If you plan on staying for 10 nights or more, the hotel will also inquire in advance by mail about any special needs that you might have. And, if you just can't stand looking at those suitcases the entire time you're on vacation, unpack them and have them stored. The utmost in decadence is the poolside service that consists of an Evian spritz and cold oshibori towels for those who get too warm while soaking up the rays.

If you want even more privacy and some special privileges (like free movie rentals, complimentary continental breakfast, afternoon tea, sunset cocktails and hors d'oeuvres, and after-dinner liqueurs and desserts) you should book a room on the Four Seasons Club Floor.

Traveling with children? Well, the Four Seasons takes great pride in its children's facilities, which are open year-round from 9am to 5pm. Activities available to kids 5 to 12 years old include lei-making lessons, hula classes, Hawaiian arts, crafts, and games, beach games, marine life demonstrations, sand sculpting, and tennis. The indoor facility is chock-full of toys, games, and books, and the best thing about the children's program is that it's complimentary. For older children there's Teens for All Seasons, a teen recreation center that features billiards, shuffleboard, and a big-screen TV. All children over 12 are also entitled to complimentary scuba and windsurfing lessons. There's a children's pool and Jacuzzi, and there's even a kids' rate for laundry service.

Dining/Entertainment: Seasons (see Chapter 6 for full listing), open for dinner only, is the hotel's formal dining room specializing in Mediterranean cuisine. Dine at candlelit tables indoors or out while enjoying the sounds of a jazz trio. The Pacific Grill serves breakfast, lunch, and dinner daily. The Cabana Cafe is open daily for lunch and dinner and it serves pupus, sandwiches, burgers, and salads (most of which are prepared with local ingredients), and has all-day beverage service. For cocktails, head for the Games Bar (which doubles as the Teens for All Seasons recreation center during the day), where you can play pool and watch sports on the big screen TV. The Games Bar also serves pupus, sandwiches, and specialties from the Pacific Grill.

Services: 24-hour room service; afternoon ice service; complimentary evening shoe-shine service.

Facilities: Full health facility with separate men's and women's locker rooms, exercise and weight equipment; two on-site tennis courts, both lit for night play, as well as access to the 14-court Wailea Tennis Center; access to Wailea resort golf courses; complimentary Ping-Pong, volleyball, croquet, badminton, and biking equipment and facilities; the beach pavilion provides guests with scuba and snorkeling gear, boogie boards, kayaks, and paddleboats.

GRAND CHAMPIONS VILLAS, 3750 Wailea Alanui, Wailea, Maui, HI 96753. Tel. 808/874-3554, or toll free 800/367-5246. Fax 808/874-3554. 188 units, 28 in rental pool. A/C TV TEL

$ Rates: High season (Dec 15–Mar 31): $150 one-bedroom golf, garden, or tennis view, $170 ocean view; $190 two-bedroom golf, garden, or tennis view, $210 two-bedroom ocean view; $235 three-bedroom ocean view. Special honeymoon, golf, and car packages available. Minimum stay of three nights. AE, MC, V. **Parking:** Free.

Set on 11 acres between the Wailea Tennis Court and the Wailea Blue Golf Course, Grand Champions Villas is one of many properties managed by Destination Resorts. Mostly residential, Grand Champions is a great place for couples who want a quiet apartment not far from the beach and away from the hubbub of the luxury resort hotels. All of the one- and two-bedroom units are air-conditioned and have large, fully outfitted kitchens. Washers and dryers are standard, and a housekeeping service is offered daily. All guests have access to the property's two pools, barbecue area, and two whirlpool spas. There is a private guard at the entrance; however, I only saw him there once during my stay at the Grand Champions property. The condominiums were built in 1989, so they are still new and freshly decorated, but unless you're a tennis or golf fanatic, you'd probably rather stay at one of the other resort properties located closer to the beach.

GRAND WAILEA RESORT HOTEL & SPA, 3850 Wailea Alanui, Wailea, Maui, HI 96753. Tel. 808/875-1234, or toll free 800/888-6100. Fax 808/874-5143. 767 rms, 53 suites. A/C MINIBAR TV TEL

$ Rates: Standard $375 terrace, $425 ocean view, $450 oceanfront, $500 deluxe ocean, $975–$2,200 suite; $550 Napua Tower Suite, $1,400–$8,000 Napua Club Suite. AE, DC, JCB Card, MC, V. **Parking:** Complimentary valet- and self-parking available.

Whether you're a hotel guest or simply visiting for the day, the moment you pass the Grand Wailea's grand waterfall at the hotel's entrance you'll be transported to another world. The secrets of the Grand Wailea's success are its six themes of genuine Hawaii feeling: flowers, water, trees, sound, light, and art. There are more flowers on this property than on any other on the island. In addition to the ocean, you'll find waterfalls, pools, a lagoon, and smaller waterways throughout the property. The only sounds you'll hear evoke serenity. And the light is the best nature can provide. The $30-million collection of commissioned artwork by notables such as Fernard Leger, Fernando Botero, Zou Ling, Satoru Abe, Herb Kane, and Jan Fisher is testimony to the hotel's dedication to the preservation of classical elegance. All things considered, the Grand Wailea is the grandest of them all.

Even the most basic of guest rooms here is elegantly furnished. Beautifully polished wood furnishings are standard, as are Oriental-style area rugs, and fine artwork is scattered throughout the guest rooms. Basic amenities include in-room safes, ironing boards and irons, three telephones, and a basket of fresh fruit that is replenished daily. All rooms have private lanais with teak outdoor furniture. Bathrooms have oversized marble tubs and separate showers, and hairdryers. The exclusive Napua Club is comprised of 100 rooms and suites on floors accessible only by elevator key. Some of the special features offered to guests on these floors are complimentary breakfast, hors d'oeuvres, and butler-style VIP service.

Spa Grande, at 50,000 square feet, is Hawaii's largest spa, and one of the Grand Wailea's most luxurious features. Treat yourself to a massage in one of the spa's oceanfront rooms, get a facial, take a Japanese bath, or relax under a waterfall massage. The choices are legion: aromatherapy, parafango (mud and seaweed), saunas, cold dips, shiatsu massage, herbal wraps, lomi lomi massage. Better yet, go for the Terme Wailea Circuit. The Circuit begins with a choice of exfoliating and cleansing treatments—a loofa scrub by a spa technician or a Japanese bath including a "sitting shower" and a Japanese furo tub with a cool dip. The next phase might be a limu bath for detoxification or a Maui mud bath for balancing hormones and remineralizing the body. Phase three might be the tropical enzyme bath for toning and softening the skin. The cascading waterfall massage is next followed by the jet shower. From there guests can either head upstairs to the private treatment rooms where they'll receive a massage or facial, or indulge in the Hawaiian Salt Glo treatment that uses rock salt and kukui nut oil to exfoliate and soften skin. Finally, head to the Sonic Relaxation Room where you'll sit on a lounge chair wrapped in blankets listening to calming music (which comes from the "hood" of the lounge chair and vibrates through the chair) while watching nature videos. If you're not relaxed after all of that, you probably never will be. In the event that you'd rather work up a sweat using your muscles, the spa also features weight training, aerobics, and raquetball.

The New England–style floating Seaside Chapel, with its stained-glass windows depicting a traditional Hawaiian wedding, and bell and clock tower, is one of the island's favorite places for wedding ceremonies. Even if you aren't getting married, you'll appreciate its quaintness as you sit in one of the gazebos enjoying the surrounding gardens.

Dining/Entertainment: The Grand Dining Room Maui is the hotel's classical dining establishment (see Chapter 6 for full listing) with an international menu, where guests can enjoy breakfast, Sunday brunch, and dinner. There is live entertainment in the evenings and during brunch. Kincha is one of the country's most authentic Japanese restaurants (see Chapter 6 for full listing). In the center of the restaurant there's a stage where authentic tea ceremonies and flower arranging are often performed. There's also a sushi bar, tempura bar, and three private tatami rooms. Cafe Kula serves country spa cuisine, low in fat, salt, and cholesterol, but packed full of flavor (see Chapter 6 for full listing). Humuhumunukunukuapua'a (it'll take you a while to learn to pronounce this one), named for the official fish of the State of Hawaii, is made up of a series of thatched-roof huts all "floating" on a stocked, saltwater lagoon. Appropriately, Humuhumunukunukuapua'a serves seafood. Bistro Molokini, named for the crescent-shaped sliver of an island located just in front of Kaho'olawe, is an open-air bistro serving Italian specialties, many of which are cooked in a woodburning oven. The Volcano Snack Bar is a convenient poolside spot for a quick breakfast, sandwich or salad, and the occasional tropical drink. There are 12 bars scattered around the property, but Tsunami is the hotel's nightclub that features laser light shows, a hydraulic dance floor, and 20 video monitors—it's also a favorite with locals.

Services: Room service; babysitting service; concierge.

Facilities: The 2,000-foot-long Action Pool sweeps swimmers through mountains and grottos, drops them about 35 feet (gradually, of course), and takes them through waterfalls, slides, and rapids. There's even a rope swing bordered by authentic-looking rubber "rocks" in case you chicken out and don't drop into the water as you swing out. The 15,000-square-foot formal pool is inlaid with glass and mosaic tile and bordered by 60-foot royal palms. The section of pool closest to the beach is inlaid with a floral design and is for adults only. Guests are granted access to five golf courses, and the tennis courts at the Wailea Resort Tennis Club.

The children's program, Camp Grande, is unsurpassed. Facilities include a children's restaurant, pool, arts and crafts room, game room, computer learning center, and a children's theater. The program is fully supervised.

There is also an elegant shopping arcade for those who simply cannot survive without a little window shopping.

KEA LANI HOTEL, 4100 Wailea Alanui, Wailea, Maui, HI 96753. Tel. 808/ 875-4100, or toll free 800/882-4100. Fax 808/882-4100. 413 suites, 37 villas. A/C MINIBAR TV TEL

$ Rates: One-bedroom suite $250 garden view, $300 partial ocean view, $355 ocean view, $425 deluxe ocean view; ocean-view villa $730 two-bedroom, $945 three-bedroom. Oceanfront villas are $100 more. Rollaway $25. AE, CB, DC, DISC, JCB Card, MC, V. **Parking:** Complimentary valet parking.

You can't miss the Kea Lani Hotel. Architecturally it looks like it belongs somewhere in the Middle East. With its spotlessly white exterior, the Kea Lani ("white heaven") paints itself unique among all the hotels on the island. As you pass the small fountain in the entryway you'll enter the marble-floored lobby, to the left of which is a small bamboo "forest." You'll know as soon as you walk in that you've made the right choice.

The suites, decorated in various shades of white, all have 27-inch televisions, VCRs, laser disc/compact disc players, full stereos, microwaves, coffee makers, complimentary Kona coffee, and fully stocked minibars. Bathrooms are appointed with elegant freestanding sinks, Roman bathtubs, telephones, and hairdryers. Ironing boards and irons are standard amenities in all suites.

To get to the more private Kea Lani Villas you'll pass through the pool area where guests are relaxing in cabanas or on chaise longues around the 20,000-square-foot lagoon-style swimming pool with a water slide. The grounds are spacious and white plumeria trees abound. Tropical plant life is clearly labeled.

Though the villas are located at the back of the hotel in front of the beach, they are low to the ground and don't intrude on guest suite ocean views. They have all the same amenities as standard suites; however, they also have private swimming pools (a bit larger than a large Jacuzzi), teak outdoor furniture, and full kitchens (with dishwashers, microwaves, and coffee makers). Cooks can be hired through the hotel if you feel like being really pampered, and washers and dryers are standard. All are oceanfront or offer ocean views. The two- or three-bedroom villas also have daily maid service and complimentary daily newspaper. Yellow-and-white-striped kimonos are available for guest use.

Dining/Entertainment: The Kea Lani Restaurant features Pacific Rim cuisine in addition to daily specials. Caffe Ciao is a great little spot (see Chapter 6 for full listing) that offers fresh pastries, breads, and deli specials. The Polo Beach Grille & Bar serves lunch and snacks from 11am to 7pm. The Lobby Bar features Hawaiian entertainment.

Services: Daily maid service; concierge; Keiki Lani (children's camp) is available 9am to 3pm daily.

Facilities: Fitness center; separate adult and children's pools; florist; Jacuzzi; video library; activities desk; rental equipment includes snorkel equipment, air mattresses, boogie boards, and beach towels.

MAUI INTER-CONTINENTAL RESORT, 3700 Wailea Alanui, Wailea, Maui, HI 96753. Tel. 808/879-1922, or toll free 800/367-2960. Fax 808/874-8331. 516 rms and suites. A/C MINIBAR TV TEL

$ Rates: $175 garden view, $195 mountain view, $215 ocean view, $245 oceanfront; $385 quad; $405 Junior Suite; $565 deluxe quad; $705 Honeymoon or Ocean Suite; $765 one-bedroom Executive Suite; $945 two-bedroom Executive Suite; $1,200 one-bedroom Presidential Suite; $1,439 two-bedroom Presidential Suite. AE, CB, DC, JCB Card, MC, V. **Parking:** Complimentary valet and self-parking available.

Opened in 1976 as the first hotel in the Wailea Resort, the Maui Inter-Continental Resort is a first-class choice for any traveler. A series of seven low-rise buildings and one, seven-story tower surrounded by 22 acres of painstakingly maintained lawns and gardens is designed to provide as many guest rooms as possible with ocean views. A few years ago, the hotel's public spaces were renovated to the tune of $40 million, and it shows. Large, comfortable sitting areas in the open-air lobby afford guests beautiful views of the ocean and neighboring islands. Artifacts from the hotel's Pacific Rim art collection are scattered throughout. In the lobby alone there's a wooden Tahitian outrigger canoe, Thai spirit houses, wooden Japanese chests, calabashes, raku ceramic sculptures, original oil paintings, and a plumeria design quilt. All of the hotel's spacious rooms have recently been renovated and upgraded.

Each features separate dressing and bath areas with marble-topped sinks, and all rooms have private lanais with sliding glass doors. Complimentary guest activities include hula, scuba, snorkel, and windsurfing lessons. There are also lei-making and exercise classes, and you can arrange to go deep-sea fishing or take a trip on a catamaran. The children's program, Keiki's Club Gecko, is a supervised activities program for children 5 and older. In addition to taking swimming lessons and participating in arts and crafts classes, kids will learn about Hawaiian culture and the environment. There are also off-property field trips, including whale watching in the winter.

Dining/Entertainment: Hula Moons, located poolside, offers fresh seafood and meat specialties, as well as a great salad bar. It's open 5:30 to 10pm. Lanai Terrace, open daily for breakfast and dinner, allows visitors gorgeous ocean views. Lanai Terrace offers a pasta bar on Wednesdays, and there is a prime rib special on Saturdays. The menu at the casual Hula Terrace offers a good selection of sandwiches, salads, pizza, and ice cream. Inu Inu Lounge features live entertainment on Friday to Sunday from 8pm to 2am. The Inter-Continental also has its own luau on Tuesday, Thursday, and Friday (see Chapter 7 for more details).

Services: 24-hour room service; same-day laundry and valet service; multilingual concierge; poolside beverage service; babysitting service.

Facilities: Three swimming pools; gift shops, sundry shops, and a newsstand; beauty salon and barber shop; licensed massage therapist available by appointment.

MAUI MAKENA SURF, 3750 Wailea Alanui, Wailea, Maui, HI 96753. Tel. 808/879-1595, or toll free 800/367-5246. Fax 808/874-3554. 100 units, 50 in rental pool. A/C TV TEL

$ **Rates:** High season (Dec 15–Mar 31): $260 one-bedroom ocean view, $315 one-bedroom oceanfront, $335 two-bedroom oceanfront ground floor; $315 two-bedroom ocean view, $360 two-bedroom oceanfront, $385 two-bedroom oceanfront ground floor; $395–$460 three-bedroom oceanfront. Low season (Apr 1–Dec 20): $210 one-bedroom ocean view, $260 one-bedroom oceanfront, $295 one-bedroom oceanfront ground floor; $250 two-bedroom ocean view, $300 two-bedroom oceanfront, $335 two-bedroom oceanfront ground floor; $345–$415 three-bedroom oceanfront. Extra person $20. Honeymoon, golf, and car/condo packages available. Minimum stay of three nights. AE, MC, V. **Parking:** Free.

Probably one of the most luxurious condominiums on Maui, the Makena Surf is also one of the most isolated properties on the island. Located between the Wailea and Makena resorts, the Makena Surf offers centrally air-conditioned units with spacious interiors. All apartments are individually (and in most cases exquisitely) decorated and have full kitchen facilities, wet bars, washers and dryers, and a Jacuzzi tub in the master bathroom. All of the apartments have at least an ocean view and large, private lanais. Because of the way the low-rise buildings were constructed (some in 1983, the new ones in 1992), the ground-floor units are more spacious and therefore more expensive. Besides an incredible white-sand beach, facilities for guest relaxation and exercise include two pools, two whirlpool spas, four tennis courts, barbecue areas, and a tropical garden. Daily maid service is standard, and there is a concierge on duty to help you plan activities ranging from snorkel/sails to biking down Haleakala. In addition to a resident manager, there is a rental manager to assist you with any problems or questions you might have with your apartment (though it's unlikely that you will have any). If you're looking for a condominium that offers great facilities, access to resort golf courses and tennis courts, privacy, and elegance, you're looking for the Maui Makena Surf.

MAUI POLO BEACH CLUB, 3750 Wailea Alanui, Wailea, Maui, HI 96753. Tel. 808/879-1595, or toll free 800/367-5246. Fax 808/874-3554. 71 units, 34 in rental pool. A/C TV TEL

$ **Rates:** High season (Dec 15–Mar 31): $235 one-bedroom oceanfront, $295 one-bedroom prime oceanfront; $285 two-bedroom oceanfront, $335 two-bedroom prime oceanfront. Low season (Apr 1–Dec 20): $215 one-bedroom oceanfront, $255 one-bedroom prime oceanfront; $235 two-bedroom oceanfront, $285 two-bedroom prime oceanfront. AE, MC, V. **Parking:** Free underground parking.

You can't tell it from the outside, but the Maui Polo Beach Club has some of the most spacious, exquisitely appointed, privately owned condominium apartments on the island. Situated on only about 2¹/₂ acres, the Polo Beach Club borders the Wailea Resort and has nothing but oceanfront and prime oceanfront condominiums for rent. Each apartment has koa wood and marble accents, elegant furnishings, and vast windows and glass doors that look out over the neatly trimmed lawn and perfectly smooth, white-sand beach. Private lanais are so spacious that you might never want to leave. Of course, you'll have go out to do some grocery shopping to stock the fully equipped kitchen (there's even a microwave), and you should take advantage of the pool and whirlpool spa, but other than that, there really is no reason to leave. Daily maid and concierge services are included in the rates.

STOUFFER WAILEA BEACH RESORT, 3550 Wailea Alanui, Wailea, Maui, HI 96753. Tel. 808/879-4900, or toll free 800/992-4532. Fax 808/874-5370. 347 rms, 12 suites. A/C MINIBAR TV TEL

$ Rates: $225 mountainside; $255 mountain view; $295 oceanside; $315 ocean view; $420 Mokapu Beach Club; $595 one-bedroom Makai Suite. Extra person $35. Children 18 and under stay free in parents' room. AE, CB, DC, DISC, ER, JCB Card, MC, V. **Parking:** Free valet or self-parking.

From the moment you walk into the lobby of the Stouffer Wailea Beach Resort you'll know that you've discovered pure gold. Indeed, shafts of golden light bathe the open-air lobby, and brass accents are polished to a high shine. You'll be greeted by gracious employees carrying fresh leis. Though room views vary, the quality of your room will be consistent no matter what rate you pay—mostly due to the fact that the hotel has just completed a massive $43-million renovation. Decor is neutral in tone and light in feeling. Wicker and rattan furnishings might include a loveseat, glass-topped coffee table, and armchair and ottoman. Each room is outfitted with a VCR and movies are complimentary. Two of the three telephones in guest rooms have modem capability. Minibars are fully stocked with beverages and snacks, and the use of in-room safes is complimentary. Light sources are more than adequate, and louvered doors, which lead to private lanais, are easily opened to allow sunlight. Lanai furniture is sturdy and stylish. All bathrooms are well-lit, and feature a marble-topped double vanity, telephone, hairdryer, lighted makeup mirror, vanity stool, and recessed glass shelves housing bathroom amenities. "Hapi" coats (robes) are also provided for guest use. Request a wake-up call and you'll receive complimentary coffee and newspaper. If you want extra-special service, stay in a room that's part of the Mokapu Beach Club. You'll have the exclusive services of the club manager, VIP check-in, complimentary continental breakfast served on your lanai or in your personal blue cabana, and terry robes (in addition to Hapi robes). The best part about the Beach Club rooms is their location. You couldn't get much closer to the beach, and nothing could be better than relaxing just outside your room in a hammock strung between palm trees.

The property on which the resort is situated is split by a lava formation, creating two very separate crescent-shaped beaches, giving all guests the added air of privacy and seclusion. The lava formation is an excellent place to snorkel, and there are endless nooks and crannies in which to capture a private moment.

Dining/Entertainment: For fine dining, Raffles is open Tuesday through Saturday and serves Pacific Rim cuisine. The Palm Court Restaurant, offering American specialties and an international buffet, features ponds and waterfalls and a spectacular ocean view. Hana Gion is the hotel's Japanese restaurant, and the Maui Onion is located poolside and offers light meals daily. Monday and Thursday evenings bring the hotel's luau, and the Sunset Terrace offers Hawaiian entertainment nightly.

Services: 24-hour room service; multilingual concierge and hotel staff; Avis car rental desk; Ocean Activities Center service desk; complimentary hula and lei-making lessons, garden tours, and pineapple-cutting demonstrations; Camp Wailea, a supervised children's program, is available for a nominal fee; complimentary shuttle service within the Wailea Resort; babysitting service; massage therapy clinic; check-cashing service; complimentary incoming fax service (small charge for outgoing fax service).

Facilities: Two swimming pools; four whirlpool spas; complimentary health club and fitness center; two on-property complimentary tennis courts with access to the 14 courts at the Wailea Tennis Club; access to Wailea Resort Golf Courses with special guest rates; jogging paths; complimentary scuba lessons daily; beauty salon; self-operating laundry facilities; shopping boutique; nonsmoking floors.

WAILEA ELUA VILLAGE, 3750 Wailea Alanui, Wailea, Maui, HI 96753. Tel. 808/879-1595, or toll free 800/367-5246. Fax 808/874-3554. 152 units, 63 in rental pool. A/C TV TEL

$ Rates: High season (Dec 15–Mar 31) $205 one-bedroom garden view, $240 one-bedroom ocean view, $320 one-bedroom oceanfront; $285 two-bedroom garden view, $330 two-bedroom ocean view, $420 two-bedroom oceanfront; $385 three-bedroom garden view, $525 three-bedroom oceanfront. Low season (Apr 1–Dec 20) $175 one-bedroom garden view, $210 one-bedroom ocean view, $260 one-bedroom oceanfront; $235 two-bedroom garden view, $280 two-bedroom ocean view, $350 two-bedroom oceanfront; $320 three-bedroom garden view, $460 three-bedroom oceanfront. Special honeymoon, golf, and car packages available. Minimum stay of three nights. AE, MC, V. **Parking:** Free.

Located on Ulua Beach between the Maui Inter-Continental and the Stouffer Resort, Wailea Elua Village is unsurpassed among condominium properties. As you drive up to the Elua, you'll pass through the security gate and by the guard house into the 18 acres of landscaped grounds that surround the condominiums. With purchase prices of $500,000 or more, you can be sure that the privately owned units are superbly decorated and strikingly appointed. The one-, two-, and three-bedroom apartments will be oceanfront or have ocean or garden views. However, it doesn't matter what the view—you'll be just steps away from an excellent snorkeling reef, two pools (one with whirlpool spa), a paddle tennis court, putting green, and beachfront promenade to the major hotels in the area (and some of the island's finest restaurants). All of the condos are centrally air-conditioned and come equipped with a washer and dryer, VCR, full kitchen, and a gas barbecue on the lanai.

MODERATE

WAILEA EKAHI VILLAGE, 3750 Wailea Alanui, Wailea, Maui, HI 96753. Tel. 808/879-1595, or toll free 800/367-5246. Fax 808/874-3554. 294 units, 59 in rental pool. TV TEL

$ Rates: High season (Dec 15–Mar 31): $150 garden-view studio; $180–$200 one-bedroom garden view; $285 two-bedroom garden view. Low season (Apr 1–Dec 20): $130 garden-view studio; $150–$170 one-bedroom garden view; $235 two-bedroom garden view. Special honeymoon, golf, and car packages available. Minimum stay of three nights. AE, MC, V. **Parking:** Free.

In the late 1970s when the Wailea Resort was emerging out of infancy, three luxury condominiums were built and named for the Hawaiian words for one, two, and three—Ekahi, Elua, and Ekolu. The Wailea Ekahi Village was the first built, and as a result, it is situated on an enormous, prime piece of property within the Wailea Resort. The 34 acres upon which the Ekahi is built used to be scrubland, but it has since been transformed into lush tropical gardens surpassed maybe only by a few other island properties. The condominiums, which include individually owned studio, one-, and two-bedroom apartments, are set back from the Keawakapu Beach, but the walk through the gardens to get there is so pleasant that you hardly notice. From the beach you can walk 1½ uninterrupted miles to the Kihei area. Most of the units have window air-conditioning units, but even the ones that don't stay fairly cool. The apartments are privately owned, so the decorating tastes vary from unit to unit, but you probably won't find anything that's unacceptable. The second-floor units have high ceilings, and all have private lanais (many of which are shaded by a canopy of bougainvillea). Amenities such as washer and dryer and fully equipped kitchen are standard, as is daily maid service. Outdoor facilities include four swimming pools, two paddle tennis courts, shuffleboard, and a beach pavilion with a barbecue area.

WAILEA EKOLU VILLAGE, 3750 Wailea Alanui, Wailea, Maui, HI 96753. **Tel. 808/879-1595,** or toll free 800/367-5246. Fax 808/874-3554. 148 units, 33 in rental pool. TV TEL

$ Rates: High season (Dec 15–Mar 31): $170 one-bedroom golf/ocean view; $220 two-bedroom golf/ocean view. Low season (Apr 1–Dec 20): $145 one-bedroom golf/ocean view; $170 two-bedroom golf/ocean view. Special honeymoon, golf, and car packages available. Minimum stay of three nights. AE, MC, V. **Parking:** Free.

The Wailea Ekolu (meaning "three") is the least expensive of the group. One of the reasons is that it's not located right on the beach. The other is that the accommodations aren't as spacious or as elegant as some of the others in the Wailea Resort. Some of the units do have ocean views, but keep in mind that you'll be a good distance from the beach. Most of the apartments don't have air conditioning, but all have ceiling fans, washers and dryers, and fully equipped kitchens. The decor in some of the units is a bit out of date, but all are spotlessly clean and well kept. Among the apartments for rent are one- and two-bedroom units. The two-bedroom condos only have bathtubs in the master bathroom (showers are in the second bath). In addition to the recreation pavilion, there are two solar-heated swimming pools and several barbecue areas.

INEXPENSIVE

WAILEA OCEANFRONT HOTEL, 2980 S. Kihei Rd., Kihei, Maui, HI 96753. **Tel. 808/879-7744,** or toll free 800/367-5004. Fax 808/874-0145. 86 rms. A/C TV TEL

$ Rates: $90 standard; $95 superior; $105 deluxe; $110 ocean view; $165 one-bedroom family unit. AE, MC, V. **Parking:** Free.

The rooms here are very small, but some are practically on the beach—in fact, Carelli's On the Beach, one of the island's best Italian restaurants, is located right next door. You'll be hard-pressed to find an oceanfront property this close to the Wailea Resort for less money. All rooms have been recently renovated and come equipped with alarm clocks and a minirefrigerator. The tropical floral bedspreads give the rooms a bright, fresh look. Coin-operated laundry facilities are available for guest use. Complimentary coffee and doughnuts are served daily in the lobby. As long as you don't plan to spend too much time in your room (I can't imagine why you would on Maui!), Wailea Oceanfront Hotel is a good choice.

3. UPCOUNTRY & HANA

Most visitors to Maui don't think about booking accommodations Upcountry because of its distance from the beach, but you might want to spend a couple of days and nights living like a true Maui native (most Mauians actually live Upcountry because rents are less expensive). There are no major hotels (except the Hotel Hana Maui) in Upcountry Maui, but there are scores of small bed-and-breakfasts hidden away among the trees on the slopes of Haleakala. Most of them are rooms in residents' homes, or guest cottages on residents' properties. They were too small to be written up here, but if you're considering staying Upcountry for a night or two, try booking a room in one of the places listed below, or call or write **AA Paradise Network Maui**, P.O. Box 171, Paia, Hawaii 96779, tel. 579-8500, or toll free 800/ 942-2242. **Bed and Breakfast Hawaii** (P.O. Box 449, Kapaa, Kauai, Hawaii 96746, tel. 808/822-7771, or toll free 800/733-1632) is also an excellent reservation service.

UPCOUNTRY

MODERATE

KELLEY'S COTTAGE, 137 W. Kuiaha Rd., Haiku, Maui HI 96708. Tel. 808/575-9032. 1 cottage. TV TEL
$ Rates: $100–$125 per night depending on the number of people. Minimum stay of six nights. No credit cards. **Parking:** Free.
For five years the Kelleys have been accommodating people in their lovely guest cottage. Located on 2½ acres, this tropical paradise holds a host of surprises—including some cows, orange trees, avocado trees, banana trees, and macadamia nut trees. The Kelleys supply everything you might need during your stay—all they tell their guests is, "Just bring your toothbrush." In this two-bedroom cottage with cathedral ceilings in the living room, you'll not want for anything. There's a television, VCR and stereo, full kitchen, washer and dryer, and private telephone line.

KULA LODGE, R.R. 1 (Box 475) Kula, Maui, HI 96790. Tel. 808/878-2517, or toll free 800/233-1535. Fax 808/878-2518. 5 chalets.
$ Rates: $125 Chalet 3, 4, and 5; $155 Chalet 1 and 2. Extra person $30. AE, MC, V. **Parking:** Free.

⭐ So, you've spent some time on the beach, which, after all, is what you came here to do, but you're feeling like you need to escape the crowds and spend time amidst some pine trees and eucalyptus. You want to hear birds (other than the ever-sociable mynah and the smart-alecky parrot) singing, and you long to see some flora other than plumeria and birds of paradise. Kula Lodge is just the place you're looking for. At 3,200 feet above sea level, nestled on the slopes of Haleakala, Kula Lodge is surrounded by flower farms that cultivate carnations and the intriguing protea. You'll probably have an incredible view from your chalet, and after the sun drops below the horizon and a chill is in the air, you'll be able to retreat to your rustic home and bask in the light of the fire (note: not all rooms have fireplaces). Chalets 1 and 2 have queen-size beds, a fireplace, private lanai, and loft area with two twin beds. Chalets 3 and 4 also have queen-size beds and a sleeping loft, but the beds in the loft are futons. Chalet 5 is one story with a double bed, studio couch, and private lanai.
As you've probably guessed, Kula Lodge is very popular with locals, so if you're considering a stay here you should book well in advance—just because it's not on the beach doesn't mean rooms are easy to come by.
Adjacent to the chalets is the hotel's restaurant (see Chapter 6 for full listing), which is a popular spot for locals and tourists alike.

INEXPENSIVE

HAIKULEANA BED AND BREAKFAST, 555 Haiku Rd., Haiku, Maui, HI 96708. Tel. 808/575-2890. 4 rms. **Directions:** From Kahului Airport follow the signs to Hana Highway, Route 36. Pass through the town of Paia along the coast past Hookipa Beach Park. At mile marker 11 turn right onto Haiku Road, continue about **1** mile to 555 Haiku Rd. on the left. You won't see a sign because they're not allowed on Maui, so look for the number on the mailbox.
$ Rates: $70 single; $85 double. Discounts for stays longer than five days. **Parking:** Free.
One of my personal favorites, Haikuleana Bed and Breakfast is set on 1½ acres of Upcountry land. Built in 1870, the home's main purpose was to attract a doctor to the Haiku pineapple plantation. Since then it has been home to one doctor after

another—in fact, patients used to wait on what is now the screened porch. In 1947 Dole bought out the Haiku Pineapple Company. Miss Lindsay (said by some to have been an old maid) then took up residence here along with her servants. It later became a pig or chicken farm (no one remembers which) and fell into disrepair. Denise and Clark Champion began the renovations, and Fred Fox finished the job.

When you walk in the front door the common area is off to your right, and straight ahead is where guests gather in the mornings for breakfast. There's a television in the living room, and it's tastefully appointed with Oriental rugs and floral-patterned fabrics. The first room (to the left), decorated with blue and white stripe accents, was the original doctor's office. It's a twin-bedded room, but the beds can be pushed together to form a king-size bed. Another room is paneled in cedar. All have showers, and some of the original woodwork and wood floors have been redone. Antiques are scattered throughout the inn, and some of the bathroom sinks came from the old Lake Placid Inn. All the rooms have ceiling fans and electric blankets for when the evening chill sets in. The fourth room has a separate entrance and painted wood furnishings. In the breakfast area guests will find a small guest refrigerator stocked with juices and sodas. Full breakfast includes a hot dish that might be pancakes with macadamia nuts and coconut, topped with coconut syrup, and there are always homemade breads, coffee, tea, and juices available. Every evening guests are treated to complimentary pupus.

A GAY B&B

CAMP KULA-MAUI B&B, P.O. Box 111, Kula, Maui, HI 96790. Tel. and fax 808/878-2528. 2 rms.
$ Rates: $42–$52 single; $65–$78 double.
Camp Kula is "where happy campers play." Proprietors D.E. and Ray say there's no need to pitch a tent at this camp. They've opened the doors of their home and the cabinets of their kitchen to gay and lesbian visitors to Maui. Located in Upcountry Kula on the slopes of Haleakala, Camp Kula is a slice of paradise, and because it's not on the beach, a stay here will make you feel like a real local. You can relax in one of the hammocks or on the koa swing while dozing to the tinkling sound of wind chimes. D.E. and Ray will help you find popular local beaches, waterfalls, hiking trails, and snorkeling spots. If you're traveling alone, the Prince Kuhio Jr. Suite, with its own entrance, is perfect. Queen Emma's room is larger and is "suitable for a king or two queens." There's a king-size bed, TV, and separate sitting area. All rooms have shared baths. Rates include a "help yourself" continental breakfast, including fruit, fresh-baked breads, coffee, tea, and juice. Camp Kula is a member of the International Gay Traveler Association.

HANA

EXPENSIVE

HOTEL HANA MAUI, Hana Hwy., Hana, Maui, HI 96713-0008. Tel. 808/248-8211. Fax 808/248-7202. 96 rms and cottages. MINIBAR TEL
$ Rates: $335 standard garden room; $395 garden Junior Suite; $550 Garden Suite; $450 Sea Ranch Cottage; $815 Sea Ranch Cottage Suites. Honeymoon, wellness, family, and extended stay packages available. AE, DC, MC, V. **Parking:** Free.
The Hotel Hana Maui is the best hotel in town—certainly, it is the only hotel in its price category in Hana. When you check in you will receive a lei greeting, fresh fruit, and a glass of juice before you're driven to your room in a golf cart by a staff member. Currently managed by ITT Sheraton, the Hotel Hana Maui was originally opened in 1946 by Paul Fagan, a major player in the sugar trade who decided to turn his sugar plantation into a cattle ranch with a small hotel to attract visitors to Hana. Paul Fagan also owned a baseball team, which he brought to the Kauiki Inn (now the Hotel Hana Maui) for spring training. Sports writers wrote home about the new luxury resort in Hana and it wasn't long before wealthy tourists began

arriving at an airstrip in Hamoa for their stay at the 10-room Kauiki Inn. These days the Hotel Hana Maui, which underwent major renovation in 1989, is a haven for many celebrities who head to Hana seeking privacy. Privacy is exactly what you'll get if you decide to stay at the Hotel Hana Maui. There's no TV to distract you from enjoying your time in Hana—no reminders of the outside world.

Guest rooms are located in cottage-style buildings and are spread out over the hotel's 66 acres. All rooms feature bleached hardwood floors, oversized furnishings, traditional Hawaiian quilt bedspreads, ceiling fans, and fully stocked minibars with built-in automatic ice makers. The tiled bathrooms are spacious and all have large soaking tubs with views of private gardens. Each room is supplied with terry robes for guest use and a variety of tropically scented soaps, shampoos, and body lotions. Along with fresh coffee beans, each room is equipped with coffee makers and grinders for complimentary guest use. All units have sliding glass doors that open onto landscaped patios. The very private Sea Ranch Cottages are a new addition to the hotel, and they feature sun decks (most with hot tubs) and huge picture windows. They are located on a coastal bluff.

The hotel's new Wellness Center is a major part of the Hana Health and Fitness Retreat, which sponsors a daily schedule of activities including nature walks, aquacise, and low-impact aerobics. The 25-meter heated pool and Jacuzzi are available to all guests, and so are the stair-climbers, stationary bikes, and multistation weight-training machine. The program is designed to slow guests down and teach them to acknowledge the connection between mind, body, and spirit. There's even a modified yoga class called Inner Rhythmns that works on breathing techniques to calm the mind and tune into the body.

Although the hotel does have a restaurant (for which you must make reservations), room service is not available to guests. In addition to a beauty salon for men and women, there are several shops located within the hotel. Your room rate includes transportation to and from Hana Airport, tennis, practice golf (as of yet there is no golf course in Hana), use of bicycles, snorkeling, and beach equipment. Car rentals can be arranged by the hotel.

MODERATE

HANA KAI-MAUI RESORT, 1533 Uakea Rd. (P.O. Box 38), Hana, Maui, HI 96713. Tel. 808/248-8426 or 808/248-7346, or toll free 800/346-2772. Fax 808/248-7482. 20 units.

$ Rates: $120 studio for two; $135–$155 one-bedroom apartment. Children 8 and under stay free with parents. Weekly and monthly discounts available. AE, MC, V. **Parking:** Free.

So, you survived the switchbacks on the way to Hana and you want a comfortable studio or one-bedroom apartment to call home while you explore this beautiful area. The Hana Kai-Maui, tucked away in a cove on Hana Bay, is the perfect choice. There aren't too many restaurants in Hana, so if you're planning to spend more than a couple of days in town you'll need the comfort of your own fully equipped kitchen, which you'll get at the Hana Kai-Maui. No matter which apartment you choose, you're unlikely to have a bad view. In most cases, private lanais look out over Popolana Beach. All units are decorated with neutral tones and pastel tropical floral print fabrics and rattan furnishings. Wall-to-wall carpeting is standard. There is a barbecue area outside for guest use.

HANA PLANTATION HOUSES, P.O. Box 489, Hana, Maui, HI 96713. Tel. toll free 800/657-7723. 12 units. TV TEL **Directions:** The Hana Plantation Houses office is located off Hana Highway. behind the Hana Gardenland Botanical Gardens. You'll see a sign on your right at the Kalo Road intersection.

$ Rates: $85 Lani Makaalae Studio, $115 Lani Makaalae Too; $105 Hale Kipa Downstairs, $140 Hale Kipa Upstairs; $130 Keolulani; $140 Hamoa Cottage; $155 Ainahau Cottage; $165 Waikaloa Beach House (Waikaloa Beach Annex $35 extra); $190 Hale Kilohana. CB, DC, MC, V (with 4% service charge). **Parking:** Free.

If you're looking for a true home away from home where you can rest and enjoy complete privacy, you should call the folks who run Hana Plantation Houses. They manage a group of houses and studios that are scattered around the town of Hana, and they'll do everything in their power to make your stay as relaxing and rejuvenating as it can be. You might choose to stay in Hamoa Cottage, a Hawaiian-style cottage located only a short distance from Hamoa and Koki Beach. You'll have a living/dining room (with queen-size pull-out couch), fully equipped kitchen, and bedroom with a queen-size bed. A barbecue grill is available for guest use. Another option would be the Hale Kilohana, a private home with three bedrooms and a loft area. Hale Kilohana sleeps up to 10 comfortably. There are three bathrooms, a fully equipped kitchen, Jacuzzi, covered lanai, and barbecue grill. If you choose to stay here, you'll be within walking distance from Hamoa Beach and you'll have a view of an ancient Hawaiian fish pond. If there are just two of you, ask about the beautiful Ainahau Cottage. Built in 1992, it is located on Waikoloa Point and is surrounded by four acres of tropical landscaping. Papaya and banana trees dot the property (you can pick the bananas and papaya), and you'll find a duck pond, hiking trails, and views of Hana Bay. The cottage is powered by solar energy and there's a satellite dish for the utmost in television viewing. The floor plan in Ainahau is open and is a perfect romantic retreat for a vacationing couple. Other options include the Lani Makaalae Studio and Lani Makaalae Too, a Japanese-style studio and a Japanese-Balinese-style cottage, respectively. There are too many choices to be listed here, but take my word for it, there's something for everyone at Hana Plantation Houses.

BUDGET

ALOHA COTTAGES, 73 Keawa Place (P.O. Box 205), Hana, Maui, HI 96713. Tel. 808/248-8420. 5 cottage units.
$ Rates: $55–$90 double. Extra person $10–$20. No credit cards. **Parking:** Free.

If you're watching your wallet, your choices in Hana are somewhat limited. However, Mrs. F. Nakamura, proprietress of the Aloha Cottages, offers two-bedroom cottage units for a fraction of the cost of some of the other accommodations in town. Each cottage will easily accommodate up to four people; there are two units that will accommodate larger groups. If you're looking for the current rage in decorator fashions, the Aloha Cottages aren't for you. However, they are perfect if you want clean, comfortable lodgings with a fully equipped kitchen, sizeable living room, and bathroom with a full tub/shower combination. Also available is a studio with a two-burner hot plate, toaster, refrigerator, adequate kitchen supplies, and a bathroom with a shower. Three of the units have TVs, but there are no telephones in the rooms (messages will be taken for you). There are barbecue grills. Aloha Cottages are centrally located near the grocery store and town restaurants. Beaches are nearby.

CABINS

WAIANAPANAPA STATE PARK, off Hana Hwy. (write the Department of Land and Natural Resources, Division of State Parks, 54 S. High St., Wailuku, Maui, HI 96793). Tel. 808/243-5354. 12 cabins. **Directions:** Before you get to the town of Hana, the entrance to Waianapanapa State Park will be on your left.
$ Rates: $14 for two in a two-room cabin; tent camping free. Maximum stay of five nights in cabins. No credit cards. **Parking:** Free.

The cabins at Waianapanapa State Park are so popular with locals and tourists alike that reservations should be made up to six months in advance. You can't just stop by and hope to get one, but if you call ahead for a reservation, you can camp all year-round for free. The two-room cabins that can accommodate up to six are located not far from a black-sand beach and some even overlook the ocean. From here you can also pick up several different hiking trails that will take you along the coastline. Towels, bedding, kitchen equipment and cooking utensils, and electricity are provided (although several of my friends who have spent time in the cabins say you should bring your own sheets and towels if you can, and bug spray is probably a good idea in the summer also). Not only is this the least expensive way to see Hana, it's also one of the most interesting.

MAUI DINING

The first time I visited Maui, over ten years ago, the dining scene really left something to be desired. I'm happy to report that today exciting things are going on with food on Maui. Most chefs are taking advantage of the island's natural resources, especially the Hawaiian fishes like *opakapaka* (pink snapper), *ahi* (yellowfin tuna), *ono* (another mackerel or tuna-like fish), *lehi* (orange snapper), and *onaga* (long-tail red snapper). They're also using island-grown fruits, vegetables, and herbs. Many of Maui's chefs are health conscious, but not in a way that sacrifices taste. Virtually every cuisine is represented somewhere on the island, and there's something to suit everyone's taste.

For help with food terms that may be unfamiliar to you, see "Glossary of Island Foods" in the Appendix of this book.

Most restaurants on Maui are informal. Only a handful of restaurants require men to wear jackets, and only a couple insist on jackets and ties. In upscale restaurants, you'll see diners in resort wear (a nice shirt and pants for men, and nice pants or a dress for women), and in shorts in more casual eateries. Even though the dining scene is generally informal, you should check to see if reservations are necessary.

To help you choose where to eat, restaurants below are divided by area, then by price. **Expensive** refers to a restaurant at which most main courses are $20 or higher; **moderate,** from $15 to $19; **inexpensive,** from $10 to $14; and **budget,** less than $10.

1. WEST MAUI

West Maui is home to most of the island's best restaurants. You'll find some of them on or just off Front Street in Lahaina. Many more are in the major hotels in the Kaanapali Resort area, and you'll find a few scattered between Kaanapali and Kapalua. Finally, even though Kapalua is home to only two hotels, you'll find still more in that resort area. If you're staying anywhere on the west side, you won't have to go very far for good food.

LAHAINA

EXPENSIVE

CHEZ PAUL, Honoapiilani Hwy., Olowalu Village. Tel. 661-3843.
   Cuisine: FRENCH. **Reservations:** Necessary. **Directions:** From Central Maui,

follow Honoapiilani Highway until you come to Olowalu Village, where the speed limit drops and you'll see a small grouping of businesses on your right—Chez Paul is among them.

$ Prices: Appetizers $5–$13; main courses $21–$32. AE, DC, MC, V.
Open: Two seatings nightly at 6:30pm and 8:30pm.

I love Chez Paul. Perhaps it's because it's both quaint and elegant, or perhaps it's because it's reminiscent of French restaurants I've frequented in the past. Whatever the reason, I do know that Chez Paul (open since 1968, a rarity on the Maui food scene) serves some of the island's best French cuisine. Chez Paul offers two seatings only, so reservations are absolutely necessary.

Traditional appetizers such as *bloc de foie gras* (goose-liver pâté) with toast points and escargots bourguignons, and entrees like *canard lapernousse* (boneless roast duck with dijon mustard and a breaded Swiss-cheese crust over a cream-sherry sauce) are common menu offerings. You might also find a *fond d'arichaud à la framboise* (sliced artichoke with raspberry vinaigrette) to start or *poisson et hommard à façon* (fresh island fish served over a duxelle of mushrooms and sliced Maine lobster served in a sorrell sauce. The *noisette d'agneau des pre's sale's* (sautéed sliced lamb flank with a thyme-raspberry sauce topped with a garlic cream) is excellent, as are the *medallions de veau normande* (thin slices of white veal over a duxelle of mushrooms in a Madeira wine sauce). Naturally, the desserts are spectacular, and the wine list is extensive. Chez Paul is a local favorite, so if you're planning to dine there, call a couple of days in advance for reservations.

GERARD'S, 174 Lahainaluna Rd. Tel. 661-8939.
Cuisine: FRENCH. **Reservations:** Recommended.
$ Prices: Appetizers $6.50–$16.50; main courses $24–$29. AE, MC, V.
Open: Dinner Mon–Sat 6–10pm.

For truly authentic French cuisine in a lovely, Hawaiian plantation-style setting (indoors, on the patio, or in the garden), Gerard's can't be beat. In business on Maui for over a decade, Chef Gerard Reversade hails from the Gascony region of France where he learned to cook at the tender age of 10 (by 12 he was baking croissants from scratch—no small feat for a person of any age, I assure you). Still a true lover of food and cooking, Chef Gerard can almost always be found in the kitchen whipping up incredible dishes.

You simply must have a full three-course meal when you dine here. Don't deprive yourself of anything. Begin your meal with a nice salad of Kula field greens with a lemon vinaigrette or the marinated fish with lemon, Hawaiian peppers, ginger, and olive oil served with a cucumber salad and coriander. Follow that with the confit of duck with cabbage and lentils or the daube of veal shank simmered with pinot noir and carrots served with a potato gnocchi. Also offered are regional specialties, like opakapaka roasted in a crust of Hawaiian salt served with ginger-orange butter, and Ulupalakua lamb curry with brown rice and mango chutney. A fresh island fish of the day is always on the menu, and desserts (many of which feature Hawaiian chocolate from the Big Island) are simply not to be believed. Try the unique mango tarte tatin with coconut ice cream or the macadamia-nut chocolate cake with a raspberry coulis. The frozen vacherin with white chocolate and Kona coffee ice cream is wonderful.

MODERATE

AVALON RESTAURANT & BAR, 844 Front St. Tel. 667-5559.
Cuisine: HAWAII REGIONAL. **Reservations:** Recommended.
$ Prices: Appetizers $4.95–$16.95; main courses $9.95–$27.95. AE, MC, V.
Open: Daily 11:30am–midnight.

Located right in the center of Lahaina on Front Street, Avalon is one of the island's most popular eateries. A friend aptly describes the decor here as "tropical madness," and personally, I wouldn't expect anything but tropical madness from a self-taught chef/restaurateur who once owned a catering company called "Can't Rock and Roll,

But Sure Can Cook." In both the indoor and outdoor dining areas, you'll find tables laid with tropical print cloths. Walls are hung with the works of local artists.

The menu is exotic, innovative, and healthful. To start, try Chef Mark Ellman's Avalon seared sashimi, fresh Hawaiian ahi (yellowfin tuna) that's quickly seared, sliced thin, and served with a shiitake mushroom and ginger sauce. Also excellent are the Avalon summer rolls with shrimp, avocado, rice noodles, and fresh herbs (including island-grown cilantro and fresh mint) wrapped in rice paper and served with Thai peanut sauce. Main courses run the gamut from lemongrass chicken salad with a spicy sweet chile vinaigrette to Pasta Gerry (its namesake is Ellman's sister and chef de cuisine) with fresh tomato sauce, ginger, garlic, shiitake mushrooms, fresh herbs, and goat cheese lau lau. My personal favorite is something that has been referred to by some as "the Jell-o mold of the 90s," the chile seared salmon tiki style. It's Avalon's signature dish—a layered salad of salmon, greens, mashed potatoes, eggplant, and mango and tomato salsa drizzled with a plum vinaigrette. A waiter will tell you how to mix the towering salad when it arrives at your table. Don't miss Avalon's only dessert: the Caramel Miranda. It's a scoop of macadamia nut ice cream surrounded by fresh fruit (raspberries, blueberries, strawberries, mangoes), accented with baby coconuts, all surrounded by a marvelous, light caramel sauce.

Avalon also has an award-winning wine list and a full bar.

BLUE TROPIX, 900 Front St. Tel. 667-5309.
 Cuisine: MEDITERRANEAN. **Reservations:** Recommended.
$ **Prices:** Appetizers $4–$11.50; main courses $9.50–$22. AE, MC, V.
 Open: Daily 6pm–2am.

Whether you're looking for a private dining experience or one in a more social setting, Blue Tropix (located above Chili's Restaurant) will fit the bill, and there's dancing every evening to boot. The brainchild of Mark Dirga, Blue Tropix, with beautiful views and soft gray interior, has helped fill Lahaina's need for a restaurant/nightclub (see Chapter 7 for full nightclub listing). Its varied menu is the creation of Chef Joey Macadang. Specialties include the rolled ahi with grilled asparagus and roasted peppers to start, followed by pan-fried lasagne and sashimi pizza with capers, aioli, and parmesan. Other appetizers featured on the menu are escargots with feta cheese and shiitake mushrooms, and Tropix pot stickers with lemon-ginger sauce. If you're getting tired of fish, try the peppered rack of lamb with port wine and apples or the chicken breast stuffed with baby spinach and goat cheese served with pasta. Other pizza choices are eggplant pizza with smoked mozzarella and roasted peppers. My favorite is the shiitake mushroom pizza with macadamia nut pesto.

COMPADRES MEXICAN BAR & GRILL, 1221 Honoapiilani Hwy. (at Lahaina Cannery). Tel. 661-7189.
 Cuisine: MEXICAN. **Reservations:** Not necessary.
$ **Prices:** Appetizers $3.75–$8.50; main courses $9.50–$21.65. AE, DC, MC, V.
 Open: Daily 11am–10pm.

When Compadres first opened in Honolulu in 1984 it was so well received and became so popular that owners Richard J. Bradley and Richard M. Enos decided to expand their business. Since then they have opened restaurants in San Francisco, the Napa Valley, Sacramento, Palo Alto, Brisbane, and Lahaina. Indoor and outdoor dining is available, and the furnishings are casual and comfortable. Rattan and weathered pine furniture, Mexican artifacts, a fountain, an aviary, and lots of greenery are charmingly accented by the wall paintings of Peggy Chun.

Lovers of authentic Mexican cuisine will find traditional favorites on the menu, as well as some variations. The seafood tacos are filled with deep-fried calamari, shredded cabbage, and guacamole tartar sauce and are served with a basket of Compadres fries. Carnitas—lean pork that is fried, slow roasted, shredded, and served with soft flour tortillas and salsa Navarro—originated in Jalisco and are a favorite here. The nachos are good, and so is the taco salad, which is served on refried beans in a flour tortilla boat. There are always several fresh fish entrees

FROMMER'S SMART TRAVELER: RESTAURANTS

1. If you want to sample the food at one of the island's nicer restaurants, go at lunch when the prices are a little lower.
2. Stay in an apartment with a full kitchenette and cook breakfast or lunch so you can save money for a nice dinner.
3. If your hotel offers a buffet breakfast, indulge yourself and then skip lunch.
4. Dine early. Some restaurants offer an early-bird special that is significantly cheaper than it would be during the later hours.
5. Go to the local supermarket and pick up supplies for a picnic lunch that you can take with you to the beach.
6. Ask some of the locals where they eat—they know where the bargains are.

offered, and if you're watching your caloric intake, look for the Compadres 400 menu items—all of which have 400 calories or less. Sandwiches and burgers are also available. The bar, which remains open until about 1am, has a full selection of Mexican beers and the bartender mixes a fantastic margarita. The complete menu and appetizers are also available at the bar.

DAVID PAUL'S LAHAINA GRILL, 127 Lahainaluna Rd. Tel. 667-5117.
   Cuisine: NEW AMERICAN. **Reservations:** Recommended.
$ **Prices:** Appetizers $6.50–$12; main courses $13.95–$24.95. AE, MC, V.
   Open: Wine and cheese Mon–Fri at 5pm; dinner daily 6–11pm.
Chef/co-owner David Paul Johnson has a gold mine in this restaurant. Located just off Front Street next door to the Lahaina Hotel, David Paul's is one of the island's most popular eateries. Casually elegant with black and white tiled floors, plain black chairs, green marble-topped tables, changing artwork, and a beautiful pressed tin ceiling, David Paul's offers a constantly changing selection of innovative dishes, the likes of which you'll be hard-pressed to find anywhere else. An absolutely spectacular appetizer that was offered on one of the recent menus was fried maki sushi. It's impossible to impart its flavor here on paper, but its main ingredients include tiger prawns and Okinawan shoestring potatoes. Wrapped in nori and quickly deep fried, the fried maki sushi gets much of its zip from a sesame plum sauce and some extraordinary ginger chips. Another incredible dish, this time an entree, is the Seafood Painted Desert. It is so beautifully presented that you might experience a pang of guilt as you raise your fork and dig in. Not to worry—the wonderful flavors of local seafood served on a chardonnay and gorgonzola sauce with three pepper-flavored butters, vanilla-bean rice, and fresh vegetables will leave you with little conscience for the aesthetics of food presentation. If you're in the mood for something more substantial, try the Kona-coffee-roasted lamb (lamb chops marinated in Kona coffee and herbs, lightly roasted and then grilled over kiawe wood); forget the mint sauce, this lamb is served with a very unique, rich Kona-coffee sauce. Desserts change daily, but a favorite is the sweet chile carrot cake, made with red chiles and covered with a cream cheese frosting and chopped pistachios. Don't be afraid to try something new here—I guarantee you, you won't be disappointed. David Paul's has also begun serving a Mediterranean bistro lunch weekdays from noon to 2:30pm. Platters of Mediterranean-style dishes are beautifully presented at the restaurant's bar. You serve yourself and it's all you can eat for only $13.95. Budget-minded travelers might use this as their opportunity to sample the food here without breaking the bank.

KOBE JAPANESE STEAK HOUSE, 136 Dickenson St. Tel. 667-5555.
   Cuisine: JAPANESE. **Reservations:** Accepted.

$ Prices: Appetizers $6.90–$16.50; full dinners $13.90–$32.90. AE, JCB Card, MC, V.

Open: Dinner 5:30–closing.

You might be surprised to find an authentic Japanese steak house just off Front Street. The moment you enter Kobe you'll be carried right out of the hustle and bustle of Lahaina into a traditional Japanese country inn setting. Heavy wood tables are surrounded by beautiful Japanese wall hangings and other rare artifacts and antiques like a 300-year-old kimono, porcelain hibachis, and emperor dolls. Begin your meal here with a warm sake. If you're in the mood for some sushi (Kobe boasts "Hawaii's most beautiful sushi bar"), the sashimi is excellent here. If you opt for a teppanyaki dinner you'll get teppan shrimp and shabu-shabu soup to start. The chef will prepare your choice of meat or fish with a variety of vegetables on the teppanyaki-hibachi grill right at your private table (or a communal one). Some of the choices might be teriyaki chicken, hibachi steak, sukiyaki steak, a lobster and steak combo, filet mignon, Kobe emperor steak, or chicken and shrimp. Also included in your dinner are rice and hot tea. All the beef served here has been prepared and raised in traditional Japanese fashion (the cows are even given massages). Try the green tea ice cream for dessert. There is a children's menu available.

LA TASCA NOUVEAU BISTRO, 900 Front St. (in Lahaina Center). Tel. 661-5700.

Cuisine: INTERNATIONAL. **Reservations:** Recommended.

$ Prices: Appetizers $3.95–$7.95; main courses $14.95–$17.95. Early-bird special $11.95. AE, DISC, MC, V.

Open: Lunch Mon–Fri 11:30am–2:30pm; dinner daily 5:30–10pm.

Located at the back of Lahaina Center, La Tasca offers specialty items from around the globe. The cuisines of France and Italy to those of Greece and Spain are all represented. The setting is intimate with blue- and white-curtained French windows, and bottles of wine and olive oil unobtrusively but charmingly displayed on countertops. The occasional backdrop of classical or Spanish guitar sets the scene for a romantic dinner, and the fresh flowers at each table add a special touch. You'll recognize most of the items offered on the menu because they are traditional Mediterranean dishes. Start with the Spanish potato salad or stuffed grape leaves (the stuffing changes daily according to the whims of the chef), or if you're in the mood for a hot appetizer, try marinated back ribs in a diablo sauce with pimentos, olives, and cornichons. Follow your appetizer with a rack of lamb sautéed with shallots, garlic, brandy, and rosemary, the crispy confit of duck, or the hot *gamberone* (giant prawns) sautéed with garlic, shallots, chervil, and marsala. From the eclectic tapas menu you may sample small portions of entree offerings, like mussels maison or ratatouille. Save room for La Tasca's selection of fine desserts.

LONGHI'S, 888 Front St. Tel. 667-2288.

Cuisine: ITALIAN. **Reservations:** Accepted, but not required.

$ Prices: Appetizers $4–$8; main courses $7–$14 at lunch, $13–$26 at dinner. AE, DISC, MC, V.

Open: Daily breakfast 7:30–11:30am; lunch 11:45am–4:45pm; dinner 5–10pm.

Proprietor Bob Longhi has been in business here for over 15 years, and his restaurant, Longhi's, is still going strong. People from all walks of life seem to enjoy the way the waitstaff recites the constantly changing menu from memory (be careful—the bill might mount up without warning since it's difficult to keep track of the prices as your waiter announces them). The open-air first floor dining room with tile floors and koa wood tables is a pleasant and welcoming spot for breakfast or lunch, and it's great for people watching as there's a constant flow of tourists passing by. The slightly more elegant upstairs dining room is available for evening dining. Breakfast choices include fresh-squeezed juice, an assortment of fresh fruit, various types of pastry, and more substantial items like frittatas, quiches, eggs Benedict, pancakes, omelets, and bagels and lox. At lunch imported Italian cold cuts make great (huge) deli sandwiches, and fresh pasta or seafood are big sellers. The dinner menu, most of which has an Italian twist, offers a variety of meat and poultry, seafood, and of course, pasta. The fettuccini Lombardi and porcini is excellent, as is the shrimp Longhi. Desserts here are divine. Longhi's employs a full-time pastry chef to create everything from cakes and tortes to cold soufflés and eclairs. In fact, in the history of the restaurant over 1,000 different desserts have been served (and enjoyed) at Longhi's. Live entertainment is offered every Friday and Saturday evening, and complimentary valet parking is available every night.

PACIFIC'O, 505 Front St. Tel. 667-4341.
   Cuisine: CONTEMPORARY PACIFIC. **Reservations:** Recommended.
$ Prices: Appetizers $7–$12; main courses $15–$22. MC, V.
   Open: Lunch 11am–3pm, dinner 5:30–10:30pm, pupus 11am–midnight.
Pacific'O, located right on the beach, is a relatively new addition to the Lahaina restaurant scene. Those who dine here enjoy their meals at floral-clothed tables in the shade of white canvas umbrellas against a backdrop of sea and sand. I would call the cuisine here Hawaiian regional, but the chef prefers "contemporary Pacific." What it's called matters less than how it tastes, and so far, Pacific'O seems to be faring rather well. The shrimp pot stickers with fresh coriander Tobiko sauce are a tasty way to start your meal, and so is the lobster and papaya salad. One of my favorite appetizers is the pizza pupu with a smoked shrimp, goat cheese, and eggplant caviar topping. If all you want is a snack, pupus are served all day until midnight. However, if you want something more, Pacific'O offers some delicious entrees as well. Try the fish grilled in a banana leaf and smothered with a lemongrass pesto and vanilla-bean sauce. The sesame-crust lamb is also an excellent choice. It's covered with a blackened sesame crust, drizzled with a roasted macadamia-nut sauce, and complemented by a mango/pineapple chutney. Vegetarians will be pleased with the Asian mushroom ravioli (steamed ravioli stuffed with a duxelle of mixed Asian mushrooms) served with a light beet-root sauce and goat cheese. Sunsets here are spectacular, and there's live jazz on the beach every Friday and Saturday evening from 10pm to 1am.

SCAROLES RISTORANTE, 930 Wainee St. Tel. 661-4466.
   Cuisine: ITALIAN. **Reservations:** Recommended.
$ Prices: Appetizers $4–$12.95; main courses $14.95–$24. AE, MC, V.
   Open: Lunch Mon–Fri 11:30am–2pm; dinner daily 5:30–9:30pm.
Billing itself as "the New York side of Lahaina," Scaroles Ristorante is tucked away in an inconspicuous corner on the mauka side of Wainee Street. You'll know it by the awnings and black trellis fence with white trim outside. There are also some outdoor tables with black-and-white-checked cloths and fresh flowers in black bud vases. The interior decor mirrors the exterior with the addition of an abundance of hanging plants and a number of prints hanging on the walls. The large windows on the front and side of the restaurant can be opened to give diners the open-air feeling that is so prevalent in the beachside restaurants.

Begin your meal with Scaroles' cold antipasto or mozzarella marinara. The baked, stuffed clams are excellent, as is the homemade pizza bread. If you love pasta, give the pasta Scarole a try; it's served in a cream and gorgonzola sauce with sun-dried tomatoes, pine nuts, and mushrooms. The chicken saltimbocca, with prosciutto and fontina cheese, is one of several chicken dishes offered on the menu. Of course, there's veal parmigiana, but my recommendation for veal would be the veal calvados, which is sautéed in apple brandy with cream, shallots, and apples. There are several traditional seafood offerings as well. For dessert try the tiramisù, cannoli or ricotta cheesecake, and a nice dark cup of espresso.

INEXPENSIVE

CAFE MAESTRO, 608 Front St. Tel. 661-8001.
   Cuisine: ITALIAN. **Reservations:** Recommended.
$ Prices: Appetizers $2.95–$7; main courses $7–$15. AE, DISC, MC, V.
   Open: Mon–Sat 5–10:30pm. Bar and pizza until 2am.

If you've got a craving for Italian food in a casual setting, head for Cafe Maestro where you'll find modern furnishings, lots of tropical greenery, and terra-cotta–tiled floors. The red chairs and white-tiled tabletops are sleek, fresh, and inviting. On the menu you'll find some of the standard offerings like *escargots a l'aioli* (snails in a garlic butter sauce) and calamari *posillipo* (fried calamari with a spicy marinara sauce and feta cheese) to start. It wouldn't be an Italian restaurant if the menu didn't offer a variety of pizzas. Among those on Cafe Maestro's menu are the pizza calabria topped with pepperoni, mushrooms, and black olives; and a seafood pizza with shrimp, zucchini, bell peppers, tomatoes, and herbs. Spaghetti Bolognese, pasta pesto, and lasagne are standard pasta offerings. Some of the more interesting dishes include veal gypsi (top veal cutlet stuffed with spinach, mushrooms, prosciutto, and mozzarella) served on a bed of pasta, and rainbow tortellini carbonara (tortellini filled with cheese, cream, bacon, and parmesan and accented with spinach and carrots). Entree plates come with soup or salad. Don't miss dessert—the selection of fresh pastries changes daily. Wines and champagne are offered.

KIMO'S, 845 Front St. Tel. 661-4811.
   Cuisine: SEAFOOD/STEAKS. **Reservations:** Recommended.
   $ Prices: Main courses $7.95–$19.95. AE, MC, V.
   Open: Lunch (downstairs) daily 11:30am–2:30pm; dinner (upstairs) daily 5–10:30pm. Bar daily 11:30am–midnight.

Located on Front Street in the center of Lahaina and right on the waterfront, Kimo's is something of a Lahaina landmark. Tired of exotic foods? Kimo's offers a simple surf-and-turf menu in a congenial atmosphere. The oceanfront view is the biggest draw, however. Like many of the other restaurants on Maui, Kimo's offers a variety of fresh fish prepared in several different ways. Fish options for the day might include ono, ahi, onaga, *a'u* (broadbill swordfish), mahi mahi, opakapaka, *ulua* (pompano), or lehi, depending on what the day's catch brings in. Once you decide on the fish you'll have a choice of preparation. Fish baked in the restaurant's orange-ginger sauce (fresh ginger, orange zest, and macadamia nuts) is tasty, or you can simply have it sautéed in seasoned bread crumbs and parmesan cheese and topped with lemon butter. If you're on a health kick you can also have it broiled without oil or butter and served with tropical salsa. If shellfish is more your speed, try spiny lobster served with drawn butter or shrimp Tahitian (sautéed in butter and wine with garlic and cheese). Steak and prime rib are other popular dishes, and the menu also offers some island favorites, such as kalua pork ribs and Polynesian chicken. Dessert options are limited; however, Kimo's original hula pie is delicious. There is a children's menu.

LAHAINA COOLERS RESTAURANT & BAR, 180 Dickenson St. Tel. 661-7082.
   Cuisine: INTERNATIONAL. **Reservations:** Not necessary.
   $ Prices: Appetizers $2.50–$6.90; main courses $6.75–$14.50. AE, DC, MC, V.
   Open: Breakfast Mon–Sat 7–11:15am, Sun 7am–noon; lunch and dinner 11:30am–midnight.

With a motto like, ". . . because life is too short to eat boring food," how could anyone pass up a stop at Lahaina Coolers? The atmosphere is casual and inviting. Small Formica-topped tables are surrounded by white plastic chairs, and surfboards hang from the ceiling. The largest female marlin ever caught in Hawaii hangs (stuffed, of course) inside the restaurant as well. The breakfast menu includes eggs Benedict, bagels and lox, various kinds of omelets, and pancakes. The varied lunch and dinner menu is offered all day. On the pupu list, the crispy wontons with peanut and plum sauce are excellent. A familiar dish with a twist is the baked brie in puff pastry, served with a raspberry sauce. The spinach and feta cheese quesadilla is excellent. Favorite menu items are the Evil Jungle Pasta and the Evil Jungle Pizza. Both are topped with grilled chicken and a spicy Thai peanut sauce. There's also a smoked salmon pizza with herbed gorgonzola sauce, basil, and red onion. An excellent salad choice would be the ginger calamari salad with fresh papaya spears or the

Coolers' Thai salad with a peanut-coconut-mint dressing (served with shrimp or chicken). Items that fall under the category of "More Stuff" include a bistro burger with bacon, mushrooms, and gorgonzola cheese and the standard cheeseburger and french fries. For dessert give the Baked Lahaina (a mini baked Alaska with raspberry sorbet) or the Mousse That Roared (the flavor changes daily) a whirl.

OLD LAHAINA CAFE, 505 Front St. Tel. 661-3303.
   Cuisine: HAWAIIAN/AMERICAN. **Reservations:** Not accepted.
$ **Prices:** Appetizers $3.50; main courses $5.95–$21.95. AE, MC, V.
   Open: Breakfast Mon–Sat 7:30–11:30am; Sun brunch 8am–3:30pm; Lunch Mon–Sat noon–3:30pm; dinner daily 5:30–10pm.
The Old Lahaina Cafe is located on the beach side of the 505 Front Street complex, and is a delightful spot for a low-key breakfast, lunch, or sunset dinner. The spacious dining room is dotted with blue-and-white-clothed tables and overlooks the beach and the grounds of the Old Lahaina Luau (see Chapter 7 for full listing). Breakfasts are substantial but inexpensive. My favorites include the Molokai French toast, which is Molokai sweetbread grilled in an egg batter and drizzled with maple syrup, and the macadamia nut pancakes. The paniolo breakfast includes two eggs, a choice of sausage, bacon, or a papaya wedge, Molokai sweetbread toast, and rice or home fries. Lunch offerings include standard sandwiches and burgers and some more interesting alternatives, like the kalua pig sandwich or kiawe-broiled mahi mahi. Dinner is heavy on seafood with some beef, chicken, and vegetarian selections as well. You may also have the Old Lahaina Luau dinner of kalua pork (baked in the beachside imu), kalbi ribs, chicken long rice, lomi lomi salmon, sweet potato, rice, and poi. Dive into a Chocolate Suicide for dessert.

BUDGET

JUICY'S HEALTHY FOOD DELI, 505 Front St., #142. Tel. 667-5727.
   Cuisine: VEGETARIAN. **Reservations:** Not accepted.
$ **Prices:** Menu items $2.75–$6.25. No credit cards.
   Open: Mon–Sat 8:30am–9pm, Sun 11am–6pm.
One of the many establishments located at 505 Front Street, Juicy's Healthy Food Deli is a great spot for breakfast, lunch, or a light dinner. Not much more than a hole in the wall, the interior of Juicy's is jam-packed with goodies, a deli counter, and a few tables (there are more tables with umbrellas outside). For breakfast try the muffins or the fruit with granola, cinnamon, yogurt, and raisins. A good "healthy food" lunch or dinner item here is the vegetarian chili made with fresh vegetables, tomatoes, beans, tofu, and some serious spices served over brown rice and topped with melted cheese. Other choices might include the hummus platter or the ultimate Bogie Burrito (an enormous flour tortilla stuffed with beans, melted cheese, avocado, tomato, lettuce, salsa, and sour cream). Try the garden burger, a vegetarian cheese patty served warm with tomato, onions, lettuce, sprouts, and mayonnaise. There are also salads and "mile-high" sandwiches, as well as daily entrees (in which no meat or meat products are used). The fresh-squeezed juices and fruit smoothies are excellent.

SCAROLES VILLAGE PIZZERIA, 505 Front St. Tel. 661-8112.
   Cuisine: ITALIAN. **Reservations:** Not necessary.
$ **Prices:** Appetizers $4–$9.95; main courses $5.95–$11.95; pizzas $11.50–$24. AE, MC, V.
   Open: Mon–Thurs 11am–10:30pm; Fri–Sat 11am–midnight.
The owners of Scaroles Ristorante have also opened a New York–style pizzeria where you can get thin- or thick-crust pizzas, sandwiches, appetizers, calzones, and pastas. It's a more casual version of the restaurant on Wainee Street, but the food is equally delicious. Pizza toppings run the gamut from homemade sausage to pineapple and pesto. The house special is the clam and garlic pizza, which is, without a doubt, some of the best pizza you'll ever have. You can get whole pizzas (14 or 16 inches), or if you just want a snack, you can pick up a slice or two. If you're not in

the mood for pizza, there's a full selection of appetizers available, including baked stuffed mushrooms, fried calamari, and mozzarella marinara. The sandwich menu includes a sausage and pepper sandwich and a meatball hero, both of which I recommend highly. Calzones of every variety are offered—just choose two of your favorite pizza toppings and the chef will make you a "pizza sandwich" to order. Baked ziti, spaghetti, lasagne, and ravioli are also offered.

There's a selection of desserts, coffees, beer, wine, and cocktails available.

SMOKEHOUSE BBQ, 1307 Front St. Tel. 667-7005.
Cuisine: BARBECUE. **Reservations:** Not accepted.
$ Prices: Appetizers $2.95–$9.95; main courses $4.95–$17.95. MC, V.
Open: Daily 11am–closing.

Located just across the street from the backside of the Lahaina Cannery Shopping Center, Smokehouse BBQ is billed by many as the best barbecue on Maui. After more than 10 years in the business, the cooks at Smokehouse BBQ have developed a cooking method that involves smoking meat and then broiling it over kiawe wood (a relative of mesquite). The result is a taste treat of naturally sweet, supremely tender meat coated in Smokehouse BBQ's own sauce. Those who like it hot can opt to try the Dragon BBQ Sauce. You can get kiawe-smoked beef ribs as an appetizer, à la carte, or as a complete dinner with french fries, coleslaw, and baked beans. Pork ribs are also a specialty of the house. Hamburgers and fish sandwiches are offered, and there are several rib and chicken or Louisiana hot-link combinations available. If you're dining with someone who would rather not eat meat, the California style avocado burger and the charbroiled veggie burger are among the vegetarian offerings. There is a short children's menu.

KAANAPALI

EXPENSIVE

LAHAINA PROVISION COMPANY, 200 Nohea Kai Dr. (in the Hyatt Regency). Tel. 661-1234.
Cuisine: STEAK/SEAFOOD. **Reservations:** Not necessary.
$ Prices: Appetizers $4–$17; main courses $17–$26. AE, DC, MC, V.
Open: Daily lunch 11:30am–2pm; dinner 6–11pm.

An open-air garden restaurant and cocktail lounge, Lahaina Provision Company is a less expensive and more casual alternative to the Hyatt's elegant Swan Court restaurant. The lunchtime bill of fare includes some standard sandwich offerings in addition to a few more substantial entrees. The Pacific niçoise with seared ahi, fresh spinach leaves, herb vinaigrette, and anchovies tempura is light but satisfying, and the tropical seafood salad bar offers a variety of seafood and pasta salads, marinated vegetables, and sliced deli meats and cheeses. There are also several burgers on the menu—my favorite is "The Outside in Burger" with the cheese in the middle. At lunch you'll find something on the menu for the whole family. The kids will particularly love the soft ice cream. The dinner menu is more sophisticated. The Shrimp Nokekula, beer-battered coconut shrimp with a delectable orange horseradish sauce, is a delicious way to begin your meal. Sweet Maui onion rings with Hawaiian barbecue sauce are also excellent as an appetizer. My recommendations for entrees would be the sugar-cane skewered grilled shrimp with a pineapple cilantro salsa or the rack of lamb marinated in rosemary and olive oil. There are several steak offerings, including a tasty filet mignon with roasted Maui onions, top sirloin steak, prime rib, and grilled New York steak. All entrees are served with a vegetable and potatoes or rice. A word of advice: Save room for dessert. The Lahaina Provision Company is known for its Chocoholic Bar, loaded with irresistible chocolate desserts.

SOUND OF THE FALLS, 2365 Kaanapali Pkwy. (at the Westin Maui). Tel. 667-2525.
Cuisine: PACIFIC BISTRO. **Reservations:** Recommended.
$ Prices: Appetizers $5.75–$9.25; main courses $23–$38. AE, DC, JCB Card, MC, V.

Open: Dinner Mon–Wed and Fri–Sat 6:30pm–midnight; brunch Sun 10:30am–2pm.

Sound of the Falls, the Westin's signature restaurant, is one of Maui's most romantic dining spots. The open-air dining room, fronted by the ocean, as well as a beautiful paddling pool for the resident swans, is a great venue for watching the spectacular sunset every evening. On Tuesday and Saturday evenings, live piano music adds an extra special touch. All these things, combined with the restaurant's Pacific bistro cuisine, promise an evening you won't soon forget.

As a first course here, I would recommend the smoked salmon with a red onion and caper salad, salmon caviar, and sour cream dressing. Lovers of escargot (and even those of you who have avoided trying these delectable gastropods) will enjoy the provincial snails in a crispy phyllo with boursin cheese and a roasted Kula tomato sauce. If you've come to love ahi sashimi during your stay on the island, the sesame-seared sashimi with straw mushrooms, chiso, and Japanese mustard is terrific. If you'd rather begin your meal with a salad, the three summer tomato salad with marinated Maui onions and crisp Molokai herbs is an excellent choice. Everything on the main-course menu looks so good that you'll probably have a difficult time making a decision. Not to worry—the waiters here are exceptionally friendly and will eagerly recommend their favorite dishes. Seafood dishes include the vegetable-wrapped opakapaka in a shredded phyllo pastry crust with purple garlic flower (which you should make a point to taste) and ginger butter; and the pan roast of Pacific seafoods in a light lobster-lemongrass essence. Other offerings include a marinated and wok-seared duckling with a warm Asian salad and spicy hoisin plum sauce, and braised veal with artichokes and shiitake mushrooms on a crispy sweet potato scallion cake. Desserts change daily, but if you're lucky you might be dining on a night when the Chocolate Kona Bomb is on the menu. It's vanilla and Kona coffee ice cream wrapped in a hard chocolate shell and drizzled with a most incredible sauce. Soufflés are always an option, but be prepared for a 25-minute wait. Sunday brunch ($24.75 per person) at Sound of the Falls is one of the best on the island. Live piano music is featured, and champagne is on the house. Children are welcome diners here, and smaller portions are available for them at half price.

SWAN COURT, 200 Nohea Kai Dr. (in the Hyatt Regency). Tel. 661-1234.
   Cuisine: CONTINENTAL. **Reservations:** Required.
$ Prices: Appetizers $7–$14; main courses $25–$37. AE, DC, MC, V.
   Open: Breakfast Mon–Sat 7–11:30am, Sun 7am–12:30pm; dinner daily 6–10pm.

The setting at Swan Court couldn't be more romantic. In fact, it was named one of the top-ten most romantic restaurants in the world by "Lifestyles of the Rich and Famous." Elegant swans glide through the water only a few feet from your table, and the comforting sounds of rushing waterfalls calm your spirit at any time of the day. Breakfasting here will quietly coax the sleep from your bones without your slightest consciousness, and the food will awaken your senses in a most agreeable fashion. Relax with a glass of fresh-squeezed juice and a bowl of fruit while you wait for your main course. Perhaps you're in the mood for a breakfast classic like eggs Benedict or an omelet with three cheeses (in this case, boursin, mozzarella, and brie). Or, maybe you'd rather try the macadamia nut griddle cakes drizzled with a warm coconut syrup. For those who want a little of everything, the Court Buffet is an excellent choice. You will be able to choose from a variety of fresh island fruits, breakfast pastries, pancakes, French toast, and omelets—all for only $14.95.

Later in the day, Swan Court will affect your senses and those of your partner in a way that is equally pleasurable but quite different than the forenoon hours. By candlelight choose hot or cold appetizers such as smoked salmon or lobster pot stickers (with lilikoi and black-bean sauce), or even a gratinée of Maui onions topped with gruyere and mozzarella cheeses. The bisque of Kauai prawns with cream and cognac is also excellent. Featured entrees include a delectable macadamia-nut rack of lamb with a Kona coffee sauce and Poha mint chutney and a seafood collage of lobster-, snapper-, and salmon-wrapped scallops with a crisp potato cake. The Cuisine Naturelle offering when I last dined at Swan Court was a sautéed filet of Pacific salmon, bulgar wheat salad, and grilled tomato. For dessert try the velvet chocolate pâté with pistachio sauce or the Grand Marnier–flavored caramel custard with marinated orange segments.

MODERATE

LOKELANI, 100 Nohea Kai Dr. (in the Maui Marriott). Tel. 667-1200.
   Cuisine: REGIONAL SEAFOOD. **Reservations:** Recommended.
   Directions: Proceed on Kaanapali Parkway following the signs to the Maui Marriott. Nohea Kai Drive is on your left.
$ Prices: Appetizers $6–$9; main courses $15–$19. Sundowner menu $19. AE, DC, MC, V.
   Open: Wed–Sun 6–9pm.

Named for one of the island's beautiful flowers, Lokelani is the Maui Marriott's fine dining room. Overlooking the hotel's courtyard and gardens, the dining room has a comfortably elegant atmosphere. Before you order, tempt your palate with French bread or Lavosh and seasoned olive oil delivered to your table by your waiter. Every offering is prepared with the freshest of ingredients—so fresh that Chef Scott Sibley often plucks herbs out of his own private garden just outside the restaurant at the near edge of the courtyard. The menu changes frequently, but choices might include the Hawaiian fish and Maui corn chowder with Yukon potatoes and Makawao sweetbread toast or Dungeness crab cakes with a Chinese garlic and black-bean sauce, Lahaina mango coulis, and ginger mayonnaise. For the entree you might have the good fortune of ordering the sesame pepper–crusted char sui rack of lamb or the pan-seared opakapaka marinated in Ponzu lemongrass. I particularly enjoyed the herb-crusted ahi pan-seared with a papaya-basil vinaigrette and Roma tomato. Alongside each menu item the chef has listed his personal recommendation for wine by the glass. Desserts change daily, but anything the pastry chef whips up will be worth the indulgence. You're sure to leave Lokelani feeling contented, relaxed, and supremely satisfied.

NIKKO, 100 Nohea Kai Dr. (in the Maui Marriott). Tel. 667-1200.
   Cuisine: JAPANESE STEAKHOUSE. **Reservations:** Required.
$ Prices: Appetizers $3.25–$7.25; dinner selections $12.95–$25.95. AE, DC, MC, V.
   Open: Daily 6–9pm (last seating at 8:30pm).

In Japanese, *nikko* means "sun's rays," and it is also the name of one of Japan's most well-known and loveliest parks, hence, the word has become synonymous with magnificence. The Maui Marriott strives for magnificence in its own version of Nikko, an authentic Japanese restaurant with teppanyaki-style cooking. Appetizers include breaded scallops, deep-fried and glazed with a teriyaki sauce; Japanese dumplings stuffed with pork and vegetables, served with a spicy sauce; and shrimp and vegetable tempura. Don't forget to order the sake or plum wine, another Japanese favorite. In addition, there's a selection of Japanese beers and wines by the glass. Each dinner selection includes shrimp or scallops, miso soup or *tori* soup (clear broth with chicken, mushrooms, scallions, and daikon), a fresh island salad, steamed rice, teppanyaki vegetables, and green tea. You might opt for the sesame chicken or the sukiyaki steak. Or, if you can't decide, go for the chicken and New York sirloin dinner. Offerings always include a chef's special and a vegetarian stir fry. For dessert try Nikko's fried ice cream (a vanilla ice cream ball rolled in a crunchy coating, deep fried, and topped with honey or chocolate sauce). If you're a fan of green-tea ice cream, you can also get that here. There is a children's menu.

PAVILLION, 200 Nohea Kai Dr. (in the Hyatt Regency). Tel. 661-1234.
   Cuisine: AMERICAN. **Reservations:** Not necessary.
$ Prices: Appetizers $2.75–$6; main courses $4.75–$15. AE, DC, MC, V.
   Open: Breakfast daily 6–11:30am; lunch 11:30am–6pm.

If you've decided to spend the day on Kaanapali Beach but don't feel like dining in bustling Whalers Village, the Pavillion at the Hyatt Regency is an excellent alternative. I recently enjoyed a lovely late breakfast in the poolside, open-air restaurant and was happy to find "Cuisine Naturelle" (low in sodium, cholesterol, calories, and fat) on the first page of the menu. On the lighter side you'll find fresh juices, seasonal fruits, and assorted hot or cold cereals with or without fruit. For the calorie conscious with a heartier appetite there's an egg-white omelet, apple cinnamon oatmeal with dried fruits and cinnamon apples, or chicken hash florentine (sautéed chicken hash on a bed of spinach, served with whole-wheat toast). If you're less concerned with calorie counting, the Leilani waffle with fresh fruit or seasonal berries or the Kaanapali pancakes with macadamia nuts and warm maple syrup are both excellent. There are several alternatives for egg lovers, including the No Ka Oi omelet with cheddar or jack cheese, ham, bacon, mushrooms, and green onions. There's even a Japanese Bento breakfast with all the traditional accompaniments. At lunch, begin with a fruit smoothie (papaya, coconut, banana, pineapple, strawberry, or peach), "rummed up" or virgin. There are several other tropical drink options available as well. Lunch appetizers like sashimi, Cantonese pot stickers, or Philippine Lumpia (thin-skinned egg rolls with plum sauce and hot mustard) are among the offerings. Salad entrees, such as the Kalani with chicken, avocado, egg, tomato, bacon, and greens with blue-cheese dressing, are very filling. The rest of the menu features pizzas, burgers, and sandwiches. An excellent sandwich choice is the Heavenly Hana—macadamia-nut bread spread with cream cheese and topped with sliced banana, papaya, pineapple, and other seasonal fruits. The cheesecake with fresh seasonal berries and the double-fudge kahlua cake are scrumptious.

SPATS, 200 Nohea Kai Dr. (in the Hyatt Regency). Tel. 661-1234.
  Cuisine: ITALIAN. **Reservations:** Recommended.
$ Prices: Appetizers $6–$12; main courses $5–$23. AE, DC, MC, V.
  Open: Dinner Tues–Sat 6:30–10pm.

For Northern Italian cuisine in an intimate setting, try Spats, one of the Hyatt's award-winning restaurants. Traditional appetizers include *prosciutto con melone fresco* (thinly sliced prosciutto with fresh melon) and *calamari fritti* (fried calamari). I enjoyed the *involenti di polenta*, a tasty, light, rolled polenta with mushrooms, chicken, tomatoes, and mozzarella. There's also a good hearty minestrone soup. As is customary at the Hyatt, there are also some "Cuisine Naturelle" offerings on the menu. Try the *capesante e verdure alla griglia* (grilled scallops and vegetables in tomato sauce) or the *insalata d'espinachi* (a salad of spinach, carrots, and mild onions tossed in a horseradish yogurt dressing). To help you out, the Cuisine Naturelle offerings also list the number of calories, carbohydrates, cholesterol, sodium, and fat. The *ravioli d'aragosta* (lobster ravioli in a seafood sauce) and the *fettuccini speciale* (fettuccine, mushrooms, sun-dried tomatoes, garlic, roasted pepper, olive oil, and fresh herbs) are good pasta choices. There are also several meat and fish offerings available. The *tagliato di filetto* (marinated filet of beef with a light herb Chianti sauce) is excellent, as is the *filetto di salmone* (grilled salmon fillet with roasted red peppers in a light balsamic vinaigrette). After dinner try The Spatstick—espresso with Baileys and Tuaca, or the Cocoa Mac Cafe (crème de cacao and macadamia-nut liqueur served with Kona coffee, whipped cream, and sprinkled with macadamia nuts). For dessert (no, the Cocoa Mac Cafe is not the dessert) the white and dark chocolate mousse shouldn't be ignored, but if you must, go for the fresh seasonal fruits and berries with warm port wine zabaglione.

BETWEEN KAANAPALI & KAPALUA

EXPENSIVE

ERIK'S SEAFOOD GROTTO, 4242 L. Honoapiilani Hwy. Tel. 669-4806.
  Cuisine: SEAFOOD. **Reservations:** Accepted.
$ Prices: Appetizers $3.95–$10.95; main courses $13.95–$20.95. AE, MC, V.
  Open: Daily dinner 5–10pm.

Located at the Kahana Villas, Erik's Seafood Grotto might be a little out of the way for some, but if you're a lover of seafood you might consider making the trip

FROMMER'S COOL FOR KIDS: RESTAURANTS

R.J.'s Ranch House *(see p. 122)* is probably the best place on the island for dining with children because the menu offers dishes that are appealing to a child (as well as sophisticated adult items), and there are six televisions scattered throughout the restaurant on which cartoons and westerns play constantly.

Scaroles Village Pizzeria at 505 Front street *(see p. 116)* in Lahaina is another good place to take kids—they'll welcome the change from seafood and hamburgers.

Kimo's *(see p. 115)* in the center of Lahaina is a family-style eatery that has a childrens' menu as well as a pleasant view.

If your kids like Mexican food, take them to the fast-food style **Tito's Tacos** *(see p. 123)* for lunch or an early dinner. The traditional menu offers extremely healthful dishes and the atmosphere is very casual.

because Erik's offers one of the widest selections of fresh seafood on the island. Before you get started on the menu, have one of Erik's cocktails, like the Lava Flow, made with fresh bananas, pineapple juice, coconut syrup, cream, and rum topped with grenadine; or Leslie's Libation, a blend of blackberry brandy and fruit juices. If you can still walk after one of these, check out the menu. Appetizers include clams casino, escargot bourguignon, sashimi, and smoked salmon. All entree selections include a soup or green salad with Erik's macadamia nut dressing, bread, and potatoes or rice. There are up to nine different fishes offered daily (and they're all displayed nightly), including a'u (broadbill swordfish), mahi mahi, ono (a delicious game fish), ahi (yellowfin tuna), ulua (Hawaii's pompano), uku (Hawaii's gray snapper), hapupu'u (Hawaiian sea bass), and onaga (red snapper). Each of the fish selections is prepared according to the way it's listed on the menu, but all can be prepared with Cajun spices. House specialties include a tasty bouillabaisse, scampi Olowalu (shrimp sautéed in garlic butter and drizzled with a creamy caper sauce), and Hawaiian saltwater prawns (sautéed with fresh basil, thyme, and anisette and served on a bed of fettuccine). Shellfish choices include barbecued shrimp, coquilles St.-Jacques, and king crab. Rack of lamb, filet mignon, and New York steak are also offered. There are several dessert offerings and a limited children's menu. Early-bird specials are offered from 5 to 6pm.

ROY'S KAHANA BAR & GRILL, 4405 Honoapiilani Hwy. (at Kahana Gateway Shopping Center). Tel. 669-6909.
Cuisine: HAWAIIAN REGIONAL. **Reservations:** Recommended.
$ Prices: Appetizers $5.50–$8.50; main courses $5.95–$28.50. AE, DC, JCB Card, MC, V.
Open: Dinner daily 5:30–9:30pm.

The original Roy's Kahana Bar & Gill opened in Honolulu in 1988 and proved to be such a success that chef/owner Roy Yamaguchi decided to open a second restaurant on Maui (a third opened in Tokyo in 1992). Today it's one of the island's hottest upscale eateries. The atmosphere in the large dining room is upbeat, vibrant, and convivial. In fact, it can be very noisy at times, but that's all part of the fun. In the center of it all is an open kitchen that rises to the ceiling in a brilliant flash of copper. Local art colors the walls, picture windows treat diners to lovely views, and elegant floral arrangements dot the room. And the food? Well, simply put, it's amazing. Part of the menu is fixed, while the rest changes according to the whims and creative inspiration of Yamaguchi and his protègé David Abella. Some appetizers that might tempt your tastebuds are the island-style pot stickers in a lobster and Thai peanut sauce, the crispy Asian spring rolls served with a Japanese mustard soy, and the polenta and cheese ravioli in a red wine sauce. Individual imu pizzas are an excellent choice if you're not too hungry—especially the spicy Thai chicken pizza with Oriental vegetables. Other excellent main-course choices are the crispy lemongrass chicken with a Thai curry and cabernet sauce, the grilled Mongolian loin of lamb, and the lemongrass-crusted *shutome* (fish) with Thai basil and peanut sauce. Desserts change frequently and all are good, but if the chocolate macadamia nut tart is on the menu, don't skip it. I loved everything I tried at Roy's, and I'm sure you will too.

MODERATE

R.J.'s RANCH HOUSE, 4405 Honoapiilani Hwy. (at Kahana Gateway Shopping Center). Tel. 669-5000.
   Cuisine: INTERNATIONAL/FAMILY STYLE. **Reservations:** Accepted.
$ **Prices:** Appetizers $1.95–$7.95; main courses $6.95–$16.95. AE, DC, JCB Card, MC, V.
   Open: Dinner daily 5:30–9:30pm; bar menu until midnight.
Chef/owner Roy Yamaguchi had great success with Roy's Kahana Bar & Grill (see above); however, he began to realize that many of his customers needed a restaurant that offered excellent food but was also a good place to take the kids. More often than not, places you feel comfortable with your children are not known for the quality of their food. Mr. Yamaguchi has been successful in his endeavor with the opening of R.J.'s Ranch House. Younger kids will love the fried mozzarella to start, and those with advanced tastebuds will enjoy R.J.'s spicy coyote wings with a buttermilk horseradish sauce. Grown-ups might prefer something a little more adventurous for the first course—an excellent selection would be the Mongolian-style lamb riblettes. Between appetizers and entrees kids can entertain themselves by watching cartoons and westerns on one of the six televisions scattered around the restaurant. Selections for main courses are varied. There are burgers and sandwiches (the Caesar and bacon burger with Caesar-dressed lettuce and parmesan will tickle your tastebuds like no other burger). Among the Mexican specialties offered on the menu are the 12-inch beefy beef burrito (with black beans, Southwestern risotto, guacamole, and pico de gallo) and island-style grilled tuna tacos (with caramelized onions and salsa). Offerings of the "down-home" variety include Yankee pot roast "with smashed potatoes-n-gravy," and the Good 'Ole Southern Fish Fry (Louisiana catfish, lightly breaded in cornmeal, deep fried, and served with authentic hushpuppies, french fries, and two sauces). If you're afraid of clogging your arteries Southern style, there are some menu items "On the Healthy Side." There's a kiawegrilled vegetable platter served with seasoned olive oil, and a grilled island fish dinner, marinated in shoyu garlic and served with steamed vegetables. There are nightly specials and a separate children's menu is available.

INEXPENSIVE

DOLLIES PUB & CAFE, 4310 L. Honoapiilani Hwy. (in Kahana Manor). Tel. 669-0266.
   Cuisine: SANDWICHES/PIZZA. **Reservations:** Not necessary.
$ **Prices:** Appetizers $1.75–$6.95; main courses $3.95–$19. MC, V.
   Open: Mon–Sat 10am–midnight, Sun 8am–midnight, Sun brunch 8am–1pm.
A sign outside Dollies Pub & Cafe announces "Dollies, home of the $1 draft." Perhaps best known for the selection of beer and wine, Dollie's Pub & Cafe is a festive spot for a quick bite at lunch. There are 20 varieties of sandwiches—pastrami and provolone, tuna salad on pita bread, teriyaki beef, and meatball and mozzarella in a

marinara sauce, to name a few. Items on the pupu menu include potato skins, chili and rice, hot chicken wings, nachos, and garlic bread. Entrees are more substantial. The vegetarian lasagne with three cheeses, carrots, and spinach is good, and so is the fettuccine Alfredo. Dollies will also make small, medium, and large pizzas to order, and from 10am to 4pm you can order individual 5-inch pizzas. There are 36 different beers on the menu, including international favorites like Red Stripe (Jamaica), Steinlager (New Zealand), Bass Ale (England), and Guinness Stout (Ireland). Every day brings a new drink—for instance, there's Tequila Tuesday and Long Island Iced Tea Day.

BUDGET

TITO'S TACOS, Napili Plaza. Tel. 665-0222.

Cuisine: MEXICAN. **Reservations:** Not accepted.
$ Prices: A la carte $2.50–$6; combination plates $6–$7.50. No credit cards.
Open: Daily 11am–8pm.

Another one of Mark Ellman's (of Avalon fame) exploits, Tito's Tacos promises to have the island's best and most authentic Mexican food. The restaurant is so new that when I was there my menu was still warm off the press. Ellman wanted a restaurant with authentic yet healthy Mexican fast food and it certainly seems as though he's created it. Place your order at the counter and wait in one of the booths that line the walls on the left and right side of the restaurant. You can get everything from chili relleño to tacos, nachos, and burritos. It's also possible to order a combination plate that's served with rice and beans. Try a bean or potato tostada or a fresh fish soft taco. Burritos come stuffed with beans, beans and rice, potatoes and beans, and chili verde. *Platillos de huevos* (egg plates) include *huevos con chorizo* (Mexican sausage with scrambled eggs), *huevos rancheros* (eggs served sunny-side-up with salsa roja), and *nopales y papas con huevos* (cactus and potato with scrambled eggs—don't knock it until you've tried it). Two kinds of breakfast burritos are also served—one with salsa, potatoes, rice, beans, and scrambled eggs, and one with all of the above and chorizo (Mexican sausage).

To make everything as healthful as possible, all dishes are prepared with 100% vegetable oil. Before you leave, try the *orchata* (a rice drink) or the iced Mexican coffee.

KAPALUA

EXPENSIVE

THE BAY CLUB, One Bay Dr. (in the Kapalua Bay Hotel & Villas). Tel. 669-5656 or 669-8008 (after 5pm).

Cuisine: HAWAIIAN REGIONAL. **Reservations:** Recommended.
$ Prices: Appetizers $3.95–$9.50 at lunch, $6–$12.50 at dinner; main courses $5.95–$12.95 at lunch, $6–$12.50 at dinner. AE, DC, MC, V.
Open: Lunch daily 11:30am–2pm; dinner daily 6–9:30pm.

If you choose to dine at The Bay Club you'll be treated to one of the most spectacular dining views on the island. At lunch the atmosphere is nautical, but at dinner the restaurant is full of romance as the lights are dimmed and the sun falls below the horizon. This is a perfect place for a quiet dinner for two on any night of your Maui vacation.

I began my meal here with the sashimi. It comes with wasabi and pickled ginger and is superb. Other appetizers include the smoked salmon and Belgian endive with fresh dill and sour cream, escargot served in puff pastry with a wild mushroom sauce, or a salad of Kula tomatoes, cucumbers, and Maui onions (the walnut oil and raspberry vinaigrette is excellent). For entrees there are meats and poultry, including a filet mignon in port wine sauce and a half roasted duckling with passion fruit and black currant sauce. The shellfish is also excellent—choices include sautéed prawns with pepper flakes, garlic, basil, and lemon on cappellini pasta, or the South Pacific bouillabaisse. My favorites, however, are the fresh island fishes that can be prepared several different ways. You might have yours sautéed, broiled, poached, or blackened, and there are a variety of sauces as well. Try the artichoke and shiitake mushroom sauce or the tropical salsa. If you'd rather have a more Asian touch, request the ginger, cilantro, shiitake mushroom, and sesame sauce or the ginger and leek sauce. Whatever you choose, it will be a taste sensation.

At lunch the selections are less exotic but equally delicious. For starters there's baked onion soup and tropical fruit salad, or marinated scallops with Maui onions and tomatoes. Entrees might include grilled eggplant with Maui onions, Kula tomatoes, and mozzarella cheese, or chicken almond Alfredo. In addition, sandwiches and a salad bar are offered for those preferring a light lunch.

THE GARDEN RESTAURANT, One Bay Dr. (in the Kapalua Bay Hotel). Tel. 669-5656.
Cuisine: MEDITERRANEAN/CONTINENTAL/AMERICAN. **Reservations:** Accepted.
Directions: Follow Honoapiilani Highway past Lahaina town, the Kaanapali Beach Resort, Kahana, and Napili. On your left you'll see the sign for the Kapalua Resort. Go left and follow the signs to the Kapalua Bay Hotel. The restaurant is located within.
$ Prices: Appetizers $6–$12; main courses $19–$29. Prix fixe $37 without wine, $49–$51 with wine. AE, DC, MC, V.
Open: Breakfast Mon–Sat 6:30–11am, Sun 6:30–10am, Sun brunch 10:30am–2:30pm; dinner Tues–Thurs, Sat 6–10pm. Fri seafood buffet 5:30–9:30pm.

Looking for a perfectly charming spot for breakfast? The Garden is a perfect place to start the day. The restaurant, like the rest of the hotel, is about to undergo a major renovation (which might be completed by the time you read this) and perhaps a change in name, but the location and quality of food and service will remain the same or only get better. Enjoying the ocean view and warm breezes, you might choose to start your day with whole wheat pancakes with macadamia nuts and coconut syrup, or maybe a malted Belgian waffle with grilled bananas, or a fresh fruit salad in a honey yogurt dressing might be more your speed. Naturally, there are cereals, yogurts, and fruits, not to mention a variety of eggs. There is also an extensive breakfast buffet.

At dinner you might choose one of the prix-fixe menus that includes appetizers, salads, entrees, and dessert plus the sommelier's selection of wines. Of course, there's the à la carte menu as well. Start with creamy mussel soup with saffron or a green papaya salad with sesame-seed shrimp and island watercress drizzled with a mango lime vinaigrette. Main courses include steamed ono Oriental style with shiitake mushrooms, cilantro, and ginger, or the delectable charred paillard of Pacific salmon *mi-cuit* served on wilted greens and lightly dressed with a chive beurre blanc. Other choices might include a tenderloin of beef with paillasson potato and a shiitake ragoût or grilled rack of lamb with mixed sweet Kula beans and a rosemary jus. For dessert don't miss the Manjari chocolate cake with a vanilla sauce or the strawberries with almond cream and mint.

THE GRILL, One Ritz-Carlton Dr. (in the Ritz-Carlton Hotel). Tel. 669-6200.
Cuisine: HAWAIIAN REGIONAL. **Reservations:** Recommended.
$ Prices: Appetizers $5.50–$14.50; main courses $21–$38. AE, DC, MC, V.
Open: Dinner Mon–Sat 6–9:30pm; brunch Sun 10:30am–2:30pm.

In keeping with traditional Ritz-Carlton standards, The Grill restaurant offers fine dining in a classically elegant setting. One needn't worry too much about a dress code here—after all, it is Hawaii—but shorts are definitely out of the question. Comfort reigns supreme here, and the beautiful view of the Pacific Ocean and the island of Molokai coupled with the light of a flickering candle will guarantee you a relaxing and romantic dining experience. Start with the ahi kajiki sashimi tempura with a Kona orange mustard sauce or the lehua honey-seared squab served with a lentil salad with Pacific lobster and sweet-and-sour tomato essence. If you'd rather start with a soup, I'd recommend the roast Molokai corn seafood chowder or the smoked duck and green papaya soup—both are superb. As a main course I had the salt-crust Pacific snapper with grilled island vegetables and a black-bean Manilla clam sauce. I've never had a moister fish. The salt crust helps to retain moisture during the cooking process. Don't worry—the waiter will remove the salt crust before serving the fish. For dessert, order a special soufflé.

PINEAPPLE HILL RESTAURANT, 1000 Kapalua Dr. Tel. 669-6129.
   Cuisine: SEAFOOD/STEAK. **Reservations:** Recommended.
$ **Prices:** Full meal $30–$65 per person. AE, DC, MC, V.
   Open: Dinner daily 5pm–closing.
At the end of a mile-long row of exquisite pines you'll find Pineapple Hill Restaurant, once the home of the late David Thomas Fleming, who was one of the first to introduce pineapples, mangoes, lichee, and a variety of other plants and trees to the Maui landscape. He called his home Maka'oi'oi, or "sharp eyes," most likely because of its beautiful views of the Pacific and the rolling landscape that is now home to the Kapalua Golf Courses and the Ritz-Carlton Hotel. Today you can dine on fine seafood and choice-cut meats in this historic building. To begin, treat yourself to a bucket of fresh steamer clams or sautéed Dungeness crab legs. The house specialty on the list of appetizers is Nehms, an "Oriental delight." Continue with New York strip steak and lobster or shrimp. There's also a Hawaiian teriyaki steak. If what you're looking for is strictly seafood, shrimp Tahitian (large prawns seasoned and baked in the shell with wine and cheese) is the house specialty, and the king scallops au gratin are delicious. Of course there are several fresh fishes available to be poached, sautéed, or broiled to your liking. The menu also offers several poultry and pasta dishes, as well as a veggie plate for those who prefer a light meal. All dinners are served with the house soup, a garden salad, fresh vegetables, and bread.

MODERATE

THE GRILL & BAR, 200 Kapalua Dr. (between The Tennis Garden and The Golf Club). Tel. 669-5653.
   Cuisine: AMERICAN/INTERNATIONAL. **Reservations:** Accepted.
$ **Prices:** Appetizers $2.95–$8.95 at lunch, $1.95–$9.95 at dinner; main courses $6.95–$11.95 at lunch, $8.95–$23.95 at dinner. AE, DC, MC, V.
   Open: Lunch daily 11am–2pm, dinner daily 5pm–10pm; bar open until midnight or 1pm.
Part of the Kapalua Resort, The Grill & Bar offers full lunch and dinner menus, as well as cocktails, in an open-air, country-club setting. Small birds fly in and peck around by diners' feet hoping to pick up a crumb or two, but most people don't even notice them because they're too busy taking in the beautiful views of the Kapalua Golf Course, Kapalua Bay, or the West Maui Mountains. I prefer the tables that look out over the ocean. Many people stop in here after their morning tennis matches or a round of golf for a light luncheon. The Thai chicken salad with strips of chicken, carrots, and spicy linguine drizzled with peanut dressing is a regular favorite. The veggie pizza (on the cafe menu) with sliced eggplant, sun-dried tomatoes, roasted peppers, and Puna goat cheese is excellent also. If you're in the mood for something more substantial, there is a menu of burgers, deli sandwiches, and fish sandwiches. Dinner appetizers might include sashimi; Puna goat cheese with roasted peppers, fresh herbs, and garlic croutons; or Thai shrimp summer rolls in rice paper with mint and a spicy dipping sauce. My personal favorite is the Portuguese bean soup. Entrees include a choice of fresh fishes prepared in one of the following ways: grilled with Haiku lemon butter sauce; sesame-crusted and baked with spicy lilikoi sauce; nori-wrapped and sautéed with wasabi and lime sauce; poached in a citrus marinade with an Oriental black-bean sauce; or coriander-dusted and dry sautéed with fresh basil and romano cheese. The Chinatown Ginger Duck (duck breast stir-fried with Maui pineapple and macadamia nuts) and the naturally raised Waianae chicken (herb-roasted with a shiitake-chardonnay sauce) are among the poultry

offerings. If you like lamb, you shouldn't pass up the Australian rack of lamb marinated in garlic, dijon mustard, and herbs and served with a Madeira and mint sauce. The grilled tournedos served in a gorgonzola and Maui red wine (from Tedeschi Vineyards) sauce is also a good choice. A few vegetarian selections are always on the menu, and there is a children's menu available on request. For dessert try the white chocolate cheesecake or the passion fruit and candied ginger sherbet.

THE PLANTATION HOUSE RESTAURANT, 2000 Plantation Club Dr. Tel. 669-6299.
   Cuisine: HAWAIIAN REGIONAL/MEDITERRANEAN. **Reservations:** Recommended.
$ **Prices:** Appetizers $2.95–$7.25 at lunch, $2.95–$9.95 at dinner; main courses $5.95–$9.95 at lunch, $14.95–$23.95 at dinner. AE, DC, MC, V.
   Open: Breakfast daily 8–11am; lunch daily 11am–3pm; dinner daily 5:30pm–closing.
The moment you enter The Plantation House Restaurant you'll fall in love with its casual old-world elegance and you'll be drawn in by the walls of windows that open the restaurant to vistas voted by islanders as the "best and most spectacular dining views." So many restaurants that offer intimate dining experience also force you to be intimate with the people sitting next to you and behind you. In addition, they seem to confuse intimacy with sitting virtually on top of your dining partner. Not so at The Plantation House. The dining room is light and spacious, the heavy wood tables are large, and the dining chairs are roomy and comfortably upholstered. You may dine near the central, double-sided fireplace; down a couple of steps and closer to the windows; or out on the lanai. Owners Michael Hooks and Roy Dunn have had a great deal of experience in the restaurant business, and they have perfectly blended that experience and their innate talents with the expertise and creativity of Chef Alex Stanislaw whose "Kamaaina" (or local) cuisine is known island-wide. Stanislaw has successfully blended the flavors of Mediterranean cuisine with those of the Asia-Pacific islands (using island-grown produce) to create his own personal variety of Hawaiian regional cuisine.

My favorite dinner appetizer is the crab cakes, served with a red pepper pesto and a Pacific Island herb mayonnaise. The honey guava-scallops (Atlantic sea scallops wrapped in guava smoked bacon and broiled in a lehua honey-guava glaze) and the Hawaiian-style sashimi (sliced ahi on a bed of shredded cabbage, pickled ginger rose, daikon, and hot wasabi) are also delicious. House specialties include the incredible shichimi-crusted opakapaka (crusted in black sesame seeds, seared, and sake-glazed) served on a somen kiware sprout salad in black-bean sauce—you won't soon forget the taste. Other fishes can be prepared in a variety of styles. One of my favorite preparations is blackened and seared with mango chutney, beurre blanc, or lime-tequila butter. It's light but packed with flavor. "Specialties from the ranch" include double-cut lamb chops broiled and served with a wild rosemary-shallot bordelaise, and a pepper-crusted New York strip steak that's finished tableside with a green peppercorn brandy sauce. If you've still got room for dessert, try the Da Kine Brownie.

In addition to dinner, The Plantation House serves an excellent breakfast of fresh fruits, omelets, and pancakes. Lunch consists of salads, sandwiches, and pizzas. Both lunch and dinner are reasonably priced.

INEXPENSIVE

THE MARKET CAFE, 115 Bay Dr. (at the Kapalua Shops). Tel. 669-4888.
   Cuisine: CAFE/INTERNATIONAL. **Reservations:** Not accepted.
$ **Prices:** Appetizers $4.95–$7.95; main courses $3.50–$13.95. AE, DC, MC, V.
   Open: Mon–Sat breakfast 8–11am, Sun 8am–1pm; lunch and dinner Mon–Sat 11am–9pm, happy hour 4–7pm.
If you don't feel like hanging out with the tennis and golf set at the Grill & Bar, and you're watching your wallet, The Market Cafe is a nice alternative. Smack in the middle of the posh Kapalua Shops is this charming little restaurant/Italian deli. At breakfast you can get anything from fresh fruit and muffins (priced much more reasonably than what you'll find on hotel breakfast menus) to eggs Benedict.

Omelets, with your choice of fillings, are priced between $5.95 and $6.50 and are very satisfying. Pancakes can be ordered plain, with banana, pineapple, blueberries, or macadamia nuts, and range from $4.95 to $6.50. You can even get a bagel with lox, cream cheese, and capers. Naturally there's a great selection of coffees available all day as well—espresso, cappuccino, caffe latte, cafe mocha, keoke coffee, and Kapalua coffee. At lunch there are deli sandwiches, burgers, soups and salads, and cafe specials such as the beef tenderloin sandwich or fried chicken with cole slaw. One of my favorites is the roasted eggplant with goat cheese. Dinner entrees take a decidely more Italian twist, featuring such regional specialties as linguine coggiola, chicken tetrazzine, chicken marsala, and scampi bianco. Two people can easily dine here for less than $30, which is a wonderful change of pace if you've been on the island long enough to realize that you've been spending close to or more than $30 per person everywhere you go.

2. CENTRAL & SOUTH MAUI

It's most likely that you'll be in Central Maui in the morning or afternoon, and all of the restaurants I've listed for Kahului and Wailuku are good choices for lunch. Some are also nice spots for dinner, but if you don't happen to be in the area at dinner time, there's no reason to make a special trip.

South Maui is another story, however. While Kihei is known for its fast-food establishments, there are also quite a few excellent places for dinner, including Carelli's on the Beach and The Greek Bistro. The Wailea resort area is positively loaded with superb dining establishments.

KAHULUI

EXPENSIVE

WOLFGANG'S BISTRO GARDEN, 33 Lono Ave. Tel. 871-7555.
   Cuisine: CONTINENTAL. **Reservations:** Recommended.
$ Prices: Appetizers $5.25–$12.75; main courses $9.95–$29. AE, DISC, MC, V.
   Open: Lunch Mon–Fri 11am–2:30pm; dinner Tues–Sat 5:30–10pm.
One of the newer restaurants in the Kahului area, Wolfgang's Bistro Garden is a more upscale choice for lunch or dinner than most of the other restaurants in Central Maui. The general quality of the food is good, but it has been known to have its ups and downs. The lunch menu offers a variety of salads and sandwiches, as well as a selection of entrees. Try the warm spinach salad accompanied by a sliced, grilled London steak and topped with fresh mushrooms and chopped egg whites, or the sliced breast of basil chicken grilled and served on a bed of romaine and Boston lettuce with garlic croutons and an orange and Maui honey dressing. The fettuccini with pesto sauce is good. At dinner try some smoked Alaskan king salmon or an order of escargots to start. Follow up with Wolfgang's fresh hand-cut spinach spaetzle served with assorted seafood sautéed in garlic butter with chopped coriander. Another nice dish is the medallions of mahi mahi in chardonnay served on sautéed-butter lettuce with a dill-mustard sauce.

INEXPENSIVE

MING YUEN, 162 Alamaha St. Tel. 871-7787.
   Cuisine: CANTONESE/SZECHUAN. **Reservations:** Recommended.
$ Prices: Appetizers $1.75–$9.95; main courses $3.50–$37. DISC, MC, V.
   Open: Lunch Mon–Sat 11:30am–5pm; dinner daily 5–9pm.

2 2

4 2 2 2

4 2

I am extremely picky when it comes to Chinese food, but I have to admit that Ming Yuen is an excellent choice—some even think it's the best Chinese restaurant on the island. The spacious interior is done in a traditional red-and-black scheme, and the atmosphere is relaxed and comfortable. The well-trained staff is attentive and congenial from the moment you enter, and all the dishes are artfully presented. Appetizers of note are the Crispy Gau Gee and the hot-and-sour soup. One of the more unusual offerings in the soup category is the premium-grade shark's-fin and bird's-nest soup with a choice of crabmeat or chicken. As in most Chinese restaurants, there are a variety of offerings under the categories of duck, chicken, pork, beef, and seafood. A few you should look for are the chicken with sugar snaps, crispy roast chicken, mu shi pork, Mongolian and hunan beef, and the chile shrimp. Grandma's tofu is a spicy, Szechuan-style vegetarian dish (there are about 17 other vegetarian offerings on the menu). Try the Mandarin mousse for dessert.

BUDGET

MAUI COFFEE ROASTERS, 444 Hana Hwy. Tel. 877-2877.
Cuisine: CAFE/BAKERY/DELI. **Reservations:** Not accepted.
$ Prices: Bakery items 96¢–$1.95; other menu items 48¢–$7.95. MC, V.
Open: Mon–Sat 7am–6pm, Sun 9am–3pm.
If you happen to be passing through Kahului at breakfast or lunchtime and you don't feel like stopping at one of the many fast-food places, Maui Coffee Roasters offers a nice alternative. Inside there are several round, cafe-style, handpainted tables for two. Overhead hangs a large inflatable Godzilla-like creature who has apparently swept Barbie off her feet. Superman, also suspended in mid-air, is in hot pursuit. Bright posters and various other artwork adorn the walls, and tall directors' chairs line the front of the coffee bar. Aside from coffee by the pound, there are teas, coffee-making paraphernalia, coffee mugs, T-shirts, and greeting cards for sale. Breakfast items include the veggie egg bagel (eggs, tomato, cream cheese, sprouts, and onions on a choice of bagel) and the turkey egg bagel (same as the veggie egg bagel, with the addition of turkey). At lunch there are various sandwiches, like the basmoto sandwich (basil, mozzarella, and tomato drizzled with a balsamic vinaigrette, served on French bread). The Caesar salad can be ordered with shrimp or without, and the Nicky salad is composed of brown and wild rice, melted cheddar cheese, lettuce, tomatoes, cucumbers, and a balsamic vinaigrette served with French bread. There is always a daily soup offering (always vegan—no dairy, no meat) and several daily specials. There are about 30 different coffees and teas on the menu.

SIR WILFRED'S ESPRESSO CAFFE, Maui Mall, 355 Kamehameha Ave. Tel. 877-3711.
Cuisine: CAFE/DELI **Reservations:** Not accepted.
$ Prices: Breakfast items $1.50–$5.95; deli/cafe items $3.25–$5.95. No credit cards.
Open: Mon–Thurs 9am–6pm, Fri 9am–9pm, Sat 9am–5:30pm, Sun 11am–5pm.
Sir Wilfred's, located in the Maui Mall, is a cozy spot for a light breakfast or lunch. Small wood tables are located on the right side of the restaurant, and the walls are hung with the work of local artists. Have a croissant and a cup of espresso at breakfast. Soups and sandwiches, as well as wines by the glass, are offered on the lunch menu, and coffee is served all day. Vegetarian lunch offerings figure prominently on the menu. The avocado sandwich plate with avocado, lettuce, tomato, sprouts, cucumber, and mayonnaise is a good choice, as is the vegetarian Boboli pizza with garlic, cheese, tomato, onion, and green pepper. There's a daily pasta special, and several salad options, including a three-bean salad, tabbouleh salad, and a pesto pasta salad with roasted red peppers, pesto sauce, artichoke hearts, and parmesan cheese. There's a daily selection of pastries, as well as six different kinds of cheesecake—the white chocolate raspberry and the chocolate macadamia nut cheesecakes are excellent. Try the coconut or vanilla and hazelnut cappuccino, or if you'd like something with a little punch, the cappuccino or mocha frappé royale

with your choice of liquor should do the trick. There is also a selection of iced coffees.

WAILUKU

INEXPENSIVE/BUDGET

CAFE KUP A KUPPA, 79 Church St. Tel. 244-0500.

    Cuisine: INTERNATIONAL CAFE. **Reservations:** Accepted for parties of 7 or more.

$ Prices: All items $2–$17. No credit cards.

    Open: Mon–Fri 7am–4:30pm, Sat 8am–3pm.

Cafe Kup A Kuppa is a popular breakfast and lunch spot with locals and tourists alike. The decor is sparse, and the white walls are hung with the works of local artists. Regular menu items at breakfast include fresh fruit cups, scrambled eggs with potatoes, cheese, and toast, bagel and lox, and the breakfast burrito. Lunch items include 6- or 10-inch pizza fresca. Pizza toppings include fresh herbs, olive oil, and cheese; mushrooms, fresh vegetables, and cheese (my personal favorite); pesto shrimp, tomato topping, and cheese; or spicy sesame chicken, mushroom, and cheese. Other options are the salad niçoise with ahi or P.J.'s Mexicali salad, both of which are scrumptious. Cafe Kup A Kuppa also offers quesadillas, sandwiches, and daily specials. Desserts are made fresh daily and are delicious.

    Cafe Kup A Kuppa also sponsors a monthly gourmet night. Included in the $30 charge per person is a three-course meal, tax, and gratuity. They have no liquor license, so you may bring your own beer or wine (there's a corkage fee of $2.50 per person). Call in advance to see if your visit to Maui coincides with the monthly gourmet night and to find out what the menu will be. Reservations are necessary.

HAMBURGER MARY'S, 2010 Main St. Tel. 244-7776.

    Cuisine: AMERICAN. **Reservations:** Not necessary.

$ Prices: Appetizers $3–$7.25; main courses $3.95–$7.95. MC, V.

    Open: Breakfast Mon–Fri 9–10am, Sat–Sun 8–10am; lunch and dinner 10am–10pm.

Though Hamburger Mary's attracts a large gay following in the evening when the lights go down and the music gets turned up, during the day the crowd is mixed. The decor is eclectic, with, among other things, neon bar signs and celebrity posters. Naturally, most people come here for the hamburgers, like the "Meaty Mushroom" (a charbroiled burger topped with cheddar and cream cheese and smothered with sautéed mushrooms). The "Famous Chili Size" burger is topped with chili, onions, and whatever kind of cheese you like. There's a veggie garden burger for the vegetarians in the crowd, and there's also the "Meatless Mary" with cheese, pineapple, and mushrooms. Breakfast offerings include the Lahaina breakfast (two eggs any style, served with rice and toast). The Hawaiian breakfast is three eggs any style served with charbroiled ham and fresh pineapple slices. However, my favorite is the "Hawaiian Toast." You get a choice of multigrain or Hawaiian sweetbread dipped in an egg batter, spiced with vanilla, nutmeg, and cinnamon. Topped with maple syrup, it's divine. Mary's bar and dance floor are open until 2am.

MAUI BOY RESTAURANT, 2102 Vineyard St. Tel. 244-7243.

    Cuisine: LOCAL FOOD. **Reservations:** Not necessary.

$ Prices: Menu items $3.50–$9.95. MC, V.

    Open: Sun–Thurs 7am–9pm, Fri–Sat 7am–10pm.

Part of the fun in traveling is finding the places that locals frequent. Maui Boy is one of those places. Don't be swayed by the exterior; the interior is immaculate and nicely decorated with floral-print curtains and the walls are hung with interesting paintings. Breakfast here is a treat, especially if you have the Portuguese sweetbread french toast—it's good with either the blueberry or strawberry filling. At lunch time the restaurant is more crowded as local businesspeople gather for the delectable teriyaki chicken, beef, or pork, or saimin. Burgers and sandwiches are also good here. If you're really hungry, lunch plates come with a choice of french fries, rice, mashed potatoes, or potato macaroni salad. Another excellent selection at lunch would be the Korean shortribs. Maui Boy also serves a combination dinner (a choice of two meat or fish options) that comes with the same choice of french fries, rice, mashed potatoes, soup, or salad. Some of the options for the combination dinner include teriyaki chicken, roast pork, breaded shrimp, chicken katsu, and the fish of the day. If you like luau food, go for Maui Boy's Hawaiian Style, which gives you a choice of lau lau, kalua pork, or kalua cabbage served with rice or poi, lomi salmon, onion, rock salt, and chile water.

SAENG'S THAI CUISINE, 2119 Vineyard St. Tel. 244-1567 or 244-1568.
  Cuisine: THAI. **Reservations:** Recommended.
$ Prices: Appetizers $4.95–$8.95; main courses $5.95–$11.95. MC, V.
  Open: Lunch Mon–Fri 11am–2:30pm, dinner daily 5–9:30pm.

Locals flock to Saeng's Thai for the atmosphere as much as the cuisine. The setting is pleasant and garden-like—in direct contrast with Siam Thai (see below), Wailuku's other excellent Thai restaurant. The mildly spicy satay shrimp or broccoli served with a peanut sauce are excellent choices to start, and so are the fresh spring rolls stuffed with shrimp, somen noodles, lettuce, basil, and mint leaves served with bean sauce. If soup is what you're looking for, there's a great chicken coconut soup on the menu, and the tom-yum soup (lemongrass, kaffir lime leaves, green onion, and Thai parsley simmered in a spiced bouillon) with chicken is some of the tastiest I've ever had. Saeng's Thai offers several specialties as well, including Kai Yang (marinated cornish hen with lemongrass and kaffir leaves, grilled to perfection) and shrimp asparagus (stir-fried shrimp with green onion, asparagus, and mushrooms sautéed in a delectable sauce). One of my particular favorites is the honey shrimp, deep-fried shrimp with sesame seeds served on a bed of broccoli. Red, green, and masman curries with beef, chicken, or pork are prepared according to your level of tolerance for spicy food. There are about 20 different vegetarian offerings, as well as fixed-price family dinner selections (including appetizer and dessert) for two, three, or four. Try the Thai tapioca pudding for dessert (there are special desserts on the weekend).

SIAM THAI, 123 N. Market St. Tel. 244-3817 or 242-4132.
  Cuisine: THAI. **Reservations:** Recommended.
$ Prices: Appetizers $4.50–$7.50; main courses $5.95–$13.95. AE, MC, V.
  Open: Lunch Mon–Fri 11am–2:30pm; dinner daily 5–9:30pm.

Siam Thai is another local favorite, and it's no wonder. The food is delicious and surprisingly inexpensive. The black and white exposed brick walls are accented by black booths that line the left side of the restaurant. On the right there are tables next to which is a reclining buddha and a tropical fish tank. There's a bar in the back of the restaurant and piped-in music plays softly in the background. One of my favorite appetizers is mee krob (Thai crispy noodles) with bean sprouts, green onions, and a sweet sauce. Siam Thai also offers boneless chicken wings stuffed with carrots, long rice, mushrooms, green onion, and egg—a tasty treat, especially for those who don't much like spicy dishes. The tom-yum soup (chicken, lemongrass, and kaffir lime leaves simmered in a spiced bouillon) and the chicken coconut soup are also excellent. You can specify the degree of spiciness. The Siam Thai fried chicken is excellent (Cornish game hen deep fried and served with a sauce of garlic and black pepper). Equally delicious is the Evil Prince, your choice of beef, chicken, or pork sautéed in hot spices with fresh basil and served on a bed of cabbage. Of course, you'll find the traditional red, yellow, green, and masman curries on the menu, and my favorite fish dish, *Pla Raad Prig* (deep-fried whole fish topped with the chef's special spicy sauce). There are also a number of vegetarian offerings.

TASTY CRUST RESTAURANT, 1770 Mill St. Tel. 244-0845.
  Cuisine: AMERICAN/HAWAIIAN. **Reservations:** Not accepted.
$ Prices: Breakfast items $1.10–$3.75; lunch and dinner items $1.50–$7.94. No credit cards.
  Open: Breakfast and lunch daily 5:30am–1:30pm; dinner Tues–Sun 5–10pm.

Ask anyone on the island where you should go for hot cakes and the answer is always the same—Tasty Crust. With a reputation like that and some of the lowest prices around it will come as no surprise that Tasty Crust is about as local as they come. The diner-style interior, complete with video games, is a little run-down, but clean, and you'll almost always find the place completely packed. The hot cakes are so popular that they're served all day. Of course, there are other menu items as well, like plate lunches and dinners served with rice and a salad. And you can't go wrong with a grilled cheese or a hamburger deluxe, but I'd put my money on those hot cakes.

KIHEI

EXPENSIVE

CARELLI'S ON THE BEACH, 2980 S. Kihei Rd. Tel. 875-0001.
   Cuisine: ITALIAN/SEAFOOD. **Reservations:** Required.
$ **Prices:** Appetizers $8–$18; main courses $12–$30. AE, MC, V.
   Open: Daily 5:30–10pm.
Carelli's on the Beach is Kihei's most popular restaurant to date, and it boasts a long list of celebrity diners, including Donald Trump and Debra Winger. It's no surprise, really—Carelli's has one of the best locations and most sophisticated atmospheres on the island. Owners Tony Habib and Craig Delaney designed the restaurant in the style of Tony's grandfather, Rocco Carelli. Tiles have been imported from Italy, and beautiful murals grace the restaurant's walls. Even Rocco's original wood-burning pizza oven has been imported for the creation of Carelli's daily specialty pizzas. Antipasti runs the gamut from fresh seared Hawaiian ahi sorrentine (with lime and caper aioli) to the always welcome *calamari fritti* (fried calamari), and the staff will assemble any combination you might request from the seafood bar. The specialty of the house is Carelli's *zuppa di mare cioppino*—clams, mussels, scallops, prawns, lobster, squid, and crab in a spicy tomato sauce. The rest of the menu changes daily, but you can be sure you'll find a variety of pastas, meats, and a fish of the day. Desserts change daily as well. There is a minimum charge in the main dining room, but there isn't one at Rocco's Mangia Bar, where you can have a light meal and a drink.

THE MAALAEA WATERFRONT RESTAURANT, on Maalaea Bay. Tel. 244-9028.
   Cuisine: CONTINENTAL/SEAFOOD. **Reservations:** Required.
$ **Prices:** Appetizers $5.50–$9.75; main courses $16.50–$24.95. AE, MC, V.
   Open: Dinner daily 5pm–closing.
A family-run business located at the Kihei end of the Maalaea Harbor, the Maalaea Waterfront Restaurant was voted by the *Maui News* to have the best seafood and service on Maui in 1992 and 1993. Needless to say, it's one of Maui's most popular dinner spots, so be sure to get a reservation a couple of days in advance—it's unlikely that you'll be able to drop in at the last minute and get a table. Dining here is a lovely experience. The view is marvelous, the service impeccable, and the ambience romantic. Red crescent-shaped booths are comfortable, and fresh flowers grace each table. Begin your meal with chilled colossal shrimp or crab-stuffed mushroom caps au gratinée. The Maine lobster chowder is excellent, as are the sautéed Alaskan king crab cakes. For your entree, choose a cooking method for your favorite fresh fish. Perhaps you're in the mood for something on the Southwestern side—try the timbale of smoked tomato, cilantro, salsa, black beans, white jasmine rice, and fried corn tortilla strips topped with a chile pepper and cumin butter sauce. How about Italian? Go for the Sicilian-style Provençal, a sauté of red and green bell peppers, black olives, artichokes, fresh mushrooms, tomato, garlic, olive oil, rosemary, and nutmeg. If you'd rather have something light, your fish can also be broiled or poached and then topped with steamed straw mushrooms, julienne bell peppers, snow peas, fresh leeks, carrots, and watercress. The Chilean shrimp served with a white wine juslie is also good. Other entrees include scallops au gratinée, live Maine lobster (steamed or stuffed), roasted rack of lamb (served with a delectable Szechuan peppercorn sauce),

and tournedos of beef au poivre in a light cognac cream demi-glace. In addition, Chef Ron offers a "Game du Jour" (wild game prepared in traditional and contemporary styles). The wine list here is extensive.

MODERATE

THE GREEK BISTRO, 2511 S. Kihei Rd. (in Kai Nani Village). Tel. 879-9330.
  Cuisine: CONTINENTAL GREEK. **Reservations:** Recommended.
$ Prices: Appetizers $2.95–$6.95; main courses $9.95–$16.95. AE, MC, V.
  Open: Lunch daily 11am–5pm; dinner daily 5–9:30pm.
Located at the rear of Kai Nani Village, The Greek Bistro is one of Maui's hidden surprises. The restaurant has an authentic Mediterranean feeling—in fact, the place is so charming that a friend of mine drives all the way from Haiku (which is a long way to residents of Maui) just to dine here. Start your meal with a Greek salad, or better yet, the Macedonian salad (a salad of kalamata olives, cucumbers, tomatoes, onions, and feta cheese dressed with a mixture of olive oil and "Grecian spices"). The leg of lamb kabob is excellent, as is the *spanikopita* (layers of filo dough, spinach, onions, and cheese). The moussaka is absolutely authentically prepared with chopped lamb and baked with sliced eggplant, potatoes, onions, herbs, and wine topped with béchamel sauce. There are a few continental specialties on the menu like chicken and mushroom pasta or filet mignon cooked with mushrooms, wine, and Grecian herbs. What's for dessert? Baklava, what else?

INEXPENSIVE

MARGARITA'S BEACH CANTINA, 101 N. Kihei Rd. (in Kealia Beach Plaza). Tel. 879-5275.
  Cuisine: MEXICAN. **Reservations:** Not necessary.
$ Prices: Appetizers $3.95–$6.95; main courses $5.95–$16.95. AE, MC, V.
  Open: Lunch daily 11:30am–5pm; dinner daily 5–10pm. Bar 11:30am–midnight.
Margarita's Beach Cantina is located on the upper level of this commercial complex. Once inside the festive Mexican restaurant you can choose to dine on the large outdoor deck overlooking the ocean, or indoors amidst the strings of chile lights, neon beer signs, and hanging plants. Menu items are fairly standard as far as Mexican restaurants go—nachos, tostadas, tacos, enchiladas, burritos, and chili relleños. To start, try the jalapeño poppers (jalapeño peppers filled with cheddar or cream cheese). The fiesta tostada is a crispy flour tortilla filled with beef, chicken, or tofu, lettuce, tomato, cheese, olives, sour cream, and guacamole. Combination plates of two or three separate menu items are served with rice and beans, and there are several sandwich offerings, including a chicken fajita burger and a Mexican burger with cheese and jalapeños. There are a few house specialties, including tacos al carbon (marinated flank steak grilled and served with flour tortillas, guacamole, and sour cream). Desserts change daily. Happy hour is from 2:30 to 5:30pm, and during that time you can get 96¢ margaritas ($4 per liter). There is live entertainment on some evenings, and there is often a cover charge.

ROYAL THAI CUISINE, 1280 S. Kihei Rd. Tel. 874-0813.
  Cuisine: THAI. **Reservations:** Not necessary.
$ Prices: Appetizers $4.50–$7.50; main courses $5.95–$13.95. AE, MC, V.
  Open: Lunch Mon–Fri 11am–3pm; dinner daily 5–9:30pm.
This little Thai restaurant has a big reputation here on the south shore. The focus here is not on the decor (the green vinyl booths and bent cane chairs around small tables are plain and unadorned)—it's on the food. The menu is simply packed with noodles, curries, seafood, and vegetable dishes. Begin with the marinated shrimp satay or the delicious green papaya salad. For a main course try the Thai red curry with chicken, beef, or shrimp, or the chile shrimp (shrimp marinated with spices and sautéed in a chile sauce with bamboo shoots and green onion). The sweet-and-sour fish (deep-fried mahi mahi with vegetables in a sweet and sour sauce) is tasty, as is

the Thai garlic or the Thai ginger (both with your choice of chicken, beef, or pork). Vegetarian dishes range from satay broccoli and tofu to cashew nut vegetables. Everything at Royal Thai Cuisine is reasonably priced. You get great food that doesn't put a dent in your wallet.

BUDGET

THE SAND WITCH, 145 N. Kihei Rd. Tel. 879-3262.
  Cuisine: SANDWICHES/SALADS. **Reservations:** Not accepted.
$ Prices: Appetizers $5.25; sandwiches $3.95–$6.95. AE, MC, V.
  Open: Daily 11am–11pm.
Located adjacent to the Sugar Beach resort condominium complex near the end of North Kihei Road, The Sand Witch is a cozy spot for a quick, inexpensive lunch or dinner. Pupus include nachos topped with melted cheddar cheese, jalapeño salsa, onions, and guacamole and potato skins filled with ham, chili, salsa, cheddar and parmesean cheese, and guacamole—it tastes much better than it sounds. Under the heading "Sheer Witchery Sandwitches" you'll find the Witch Hoagy with turkey breast, roast beef, baked ham, cheddar cheese, onions, tomatoes, sprouts, and romaine lettuce, all served on french bread. There are more standard offerings as well, like your average ham and cheese, corned beef, or tuna salad. If you're a hot dog lover this is the place for you. There are several varieties of "Warlock Weiners" (¼-pound beef hot dogs). The Wild Dog is topped with beef and bean chili, melted cheddar, onions, and salsa, and the Poor Man's Reuben is smothered with sauerkraut, cheddar, onions, and "the Sorcerer's special dressing." The Sand Witch has a large bar and is well known for its selection of tropical drinks. Takeout is available.

STELLA BLUES CAFE & DELI, 1215 S. Kihei Rd. (in Long's Center). Tel. 874-3779.
  Cuisine: DELI. **Reservations:** Not accepted.
$ Prices: Sandwiches $4.75–$7.50. MC, V.
  Open: Breakfast Mon–Sat 8–11am, Sun 8am–2pm; lunch daily 11am–4pm; dinner Sat–Tues and Thurs 4–8pm, Wed 4–9pm, Fri 4–10pm.
The plain plastic tables and chairs that flank the front window of Stella Blues Cafe & Deli are not indicative of what you'll find on the inside of one of Kihei's trendiest gathering spots. Multicolored zebra-print tablecloths will likely be surrounded by groups of hip Mauians engaged in animated conversation. At the deli counter you'll find specialty items from Bali and Thailand side by side with Club Dead stickers and T-shirts. At breakfast you can get any variety of bagel smothered with anything from cream cheese to peanut butter and jelly. "The Manhattan" with layers of salmon topped with tomato, onion, cream cheese, and capers is available for all-day dining. Choices for full breakfasts include the Quickstart (two eggs any style with homefries and toast), the South of the Border (two eggs scrambled with cheddar cheese, onions, jalapeño peppers, a side of salsa, served with homefries and a warm flour tortilla), pancakes, or homestyle waffles served with coconut or maple syrup and fresh island fruit. Stella's Caffe Latte, a mocha with cinnamon, orange, and whipped cream, is great with anything. At lunch and dinner, salads and sandwiches are standard fare. Try the curried chicken salad or Stella's Special Sandwich (roasted red peppers, feta, grilled eggplant, cucumber, lettuce, roasted garlic, and a pesto mayonnaise served on sourdough bread). Desserts and pastries are ever-changing and are baked fresh daily, so be sure to check the pastry case. Live Blues and Jazz are featured every Wednesday and Friday night (see Chapter 7 for full listing).

WAILEA

EXPENSIVE

GRAND DINING ROOM MAUI, 3850 Wailea Alanui (in the Grand Wailea). Tel. 875-1234.
  Cuisine: HAWAIIAN REGIONAL. **Reservations:** Recommended.

$ Prices: Appetizers $6–$14.50; main courses $27–$35. AE, DC, MC, V.

Open: Breakfast daily 6:30am–11am; dinner daily 6pm–10pm.

The Grand Dining Room in the Grand Wailea Resort, with 40-foot ceilings, a 180-degree view that includes Molokini, Lanai, the West Maui Mountains, Wailea Beach, and scores of fountains, pools, and gardens, lives up to its name. Overlooking the white-clothed tables and French-style, upholstered, cameo-backed chairs is an inspiring portrait of the demigod Maui caught in the act of snaring the sun over Mount Haleakala.

The bright light of morning brings breakfast to the Grand Dining Room where diners might enjoy assorted pastries, eggs Benedict, sliced smoked salmon on a bagel with cream cheese, banana macadamia nut waffles with tropical syrup, or pineapple fritters. An ethereal glow from the setting sun is the backdrop for fine evening dining. Begin with the seared ahi tuna carpaccio with wild thyme, diced peppers, and cucumbers, or the unusual baked crab cake in sea urchin with a saffron coconut sauce. One might also begin with the Hawaiian lobster bisque or the warm jade salad with seared sea scallops. As an entree, the roasted snapper with a stir fry of vegetables and stone crab cake with a Thai opal basil jus will melt in your mouth. Another favorite is the hoisin-crusted lamb loin with an Oriental ratatouille. There is always a "Spa Suggestion." One of the nights I visited, it was Norwegian salmon with a cucumber ginger coulis. As you can imagine, desserts here are not to be missed.

KEA LANI, 4100 Wailea Alanui (in the Kea Lani Resort). Tel. 875-4100.

Cuisine: PACIFIC RIM. **Reservations:** Recommended.

$ Prices: Appetizers $4–$19; main courses $9.50–$32. AE, CB, DC, DISC, JCB Card, MC, V.

Open: Breakfast daily 6–10:30am; lunch daily 11am–3pm; dinner daily 5:30–10pm.

The open-air Kea Lani restaurant is simple, but graciously elegant with its low lighting, white-cloth tables, straight-backed chairs with a carved pineapple motif, and large tropical flower arrangements. Diners may choose a table indoors or outside on the lanai. The menu changes monthly, so there's no telling what delicacies you'll find when you're there, but some of the appetizers included on the menu the last time I visited were the Szechuan-seared ahi with crispy sprouts and hot mustard sauce and a wild mushroom strudel with capers and fresh thyme. Entrees included the day's fresh Hawaiian fish prepared in a variety of ways. I have enjoyed my fish grilled with arugula and sun-dried tomatoes and charbroiled with papaya and a green tomato relish. Black angus New York sirloin steak was prepared teriyaki style and served with steamed rice, or grilled and served with a broiled Hawaiian lobster tail. The teppan-style scallops with Dungeness crab served with baby bok choy and a scallion butter are also delicious.

KINCHA, 3850 Wailea Alanui (in the Grand Wailea). Tel. 875-1234.

Cuisine: JAPANESE. **Reservations:** Necessary.

$ Prices: Appetizers $5–$30; main courses $20–$85; fixed-price meals $58–$500. AE, DC, MC, V.

Open: Dinner daily 6–10pm.

Enter Kincha (meaning "teapot") and you're in another world. Greeted by the sight of a 24-karat-gold Japanese teapot you'll feel as though you're entering a quiet cave. In fact, 800 tons of rock from the base of Mount Fuji have gone into the construction of this restaurant, a brilliant work of art, which only hints at the artistic presentation of its authentic Japanese cuisine. The architectural design for Kincha, conceived along the lines of a teahouse in Kyoto, was actually done in Japan, shipped in pieces to Maui, and finally, reconstructed by a master Japanese craftsman. From the corner pillars to the bridges that cross koi ponds, not one nail is visible. One of the central features of this cultural oasis is a stage, upon which nightly flower arranging and tea ceremonies are performed.

Diners may choose to sit at the sushi or tempura bars, at Koagari or Zashiki table seatings, or in one of the three private tatami rooms. The tatami rooms (which open onto beautiful gardens and waterways) are for those who choose Kaiseki dining, a very expensive but extraordinarily beautiful way to enjoy Japanese cuisine. A Kaiseki dinner consists of at least 14 courses of the freshest and highest-quality foods available. Vegetables are carved into elaborate flowers, and fresh lobster or sashimi might be served in a small ice igloo. Tiny quail eggs are often served with handpainted faces, and everything is served on matching, handcrafted dinnerware. The Miyabi (meaning "elegance") dinner consists of an appetizer, clear broth soup, sashimi, hassun, broiled fish, boiled vegetables, steak, onmono, a vinegar course, shokuji, seasonal fruit, dessert, and green tea. Also included in the Miyabi dinner is a home-made fruit wine. This meal will run you about $300 per person. Advance reservation is required for the tatami rooms. Of course, you can dine à la carte as well. Try the Japanese-style chicken steak with the chef's special sauce, or the hamachi shioyaki, broiled salted yellowtail tuna. You may also order assortments of sashimi, sushi, and tempura. Excellent hot appetizers are the agedashi tofu (fried tofu with sweetened shoyu sauce) and the chawan mushi (bits of shrimp, bamboo shoots, ginkgo nuts, and mushroom in an egg custard). The seaweed salad served with a vinegar-miso dipping sauce, and the cha soba (tea-flavored buckwheat noodles), also served with a dipping sauce, are excellent choices as well. If you order dessert à la carte you'll have a choice of ice creams; among them are green tea, azuki bean, and ginger. Hiyashi zenzai, sweet azuki red beans served with ommatcha ceremonial green tea, is a taste treat.

PACIFIC GRILL, 3900 Wailea Alanui (in the Four Seasons Resort). Tel. 874-8000.
    Cuisine: PACIFIC RIM. **Reservations:** Recommended for dinner.
$ **Prices:** Appetizers $4–$12.75 at lunch and dinner; main courses $9.25–$15.75 at lunch, $9.25–$31.50 at dinner. AE, DC, MC, V.
    Open: Breakfast daily 6–11:30am; lunch daily 11:30am–2:30pm; dinner daily 5:30–9:30pm.

Also located in the elegant Four Seasons Resort, the Pacific Grill is a comfortable breakfast and lunch stop, and a casual yet traditional dinner spot. In the morning two breakfast buffets are available—one with island fruits, cereals, granola, yogurt, fresh pastries, health foods, juice, and coffee, and the other with all of the aforementioned dishes plus omelets, made-to-order eggs, and an assortment of breakfast meats. You may also order from the à la carte menu. For lunch try the island sashimi with soyu sauce and pickled ginger to start. The saimin Wailea with Oriental vegetables, char-sui chicken, and dim sum is also a favorite appetizer. There is a great salad bar with a changing assortment of island greens and vegetables, as well as a daily selection of previously prepared salads, and soup. On the sandwich menu, the grilled swordfish sandwich on a dill kaiser roll with pesto aioli and new potato salad is a good choice. A great specialty item is the poached island fish with a miso-ginger broth and somen noodles (it's good for you too). If you're up for it, after lunch head over to the Pacific Grill dessert buffet.

The dinner menu lists Pacific Rim, as well as North American specialties to start, including Vietnamese spring rolls or a Caesar salad with herb-laced croutons. The selection of main courses is varied and includes such specialties as the wok-fried Pacific salmon with a sesame seed vinaigrette, vegetables, and wonton egg noodles. The Korean beef (thinly sliced sirloin) with hot chile oil and a garlic sesame soy sauce, and the Thai coconut curry with lobster, shrimp, scallops, and stir-fried oriental vegetables served in a crispy lumpia basket are both worth a try. There are several pasta options, and a menu of lighter fare that includes some sandwich choices. There is a fairly extensive children's menu.

SEASONS, 3900 Wailea Alanui (in the Four Seasons Resort). Tel. 874-8000.
    Cuisine: MEDITERRANEAN. **Reservations:** Recommended.
$ **Prices:** Appetizers $7.50–$16.50; main courses $19–$34. AE, DC, JCB Card, MC, V.
    Open: Dinner daily 6–9:30pm.

The view of the ocean from Seasons' orchid-filled terrace is magnificent, especially at night as the sun falls smoothly and swiftly below the horizon. The decor is light and airy, allowing the diner full appreciation of the view and the food. Seasons is fine dining at its best. Begin with the consommé of duck with a porcini spaetzle or the sauté of foie gras and wild mushroom layer cake with a Madeira sauce. The grilled vine-ripened tomatoes and marinated onions dressed with a warm balsamic vinaigrette is a more healthy alternative. Main courses include a selection of pastas, such as the tagliatelle with rare seared ahi and a lemon caper sauce, and a variety of meats and fishes. The sautéed opakapaka with a saffron-celeriac purée and fennel essence is flavorful, as is the peppered beef tenderloin with garlic bread pudding and an oven-dried tomato relish. For dessert, chocoholics will be intrigued with the Chocolate Enchantment. Fruit lovers will enjoy seasonal berries with crème fraîche or crème anglaise or the almond crêpes with sautéed bananas and caramel nougat ice cream. There is a short list of dessert wines by the glass.

MODERATE

BISTRO MOLOKINI, 3850 Wailea Alanui (in the Grand Wailea). Tel. 875-1234.
  Cuisine: ITALIAN. **Reservations:** Recommended.
$ **Prices:** Appetizers $4.50–$7.50 at lunch, $5–$9.50 at dinner; main courses $9.50–$17 at lunch, $14.50–$29 at dinner. AE, DC, MC, V.
  Open: Lunch daily 11:30am–4pm (light lunch 4pm–6pm); dinner daily 6pm–10pm.
Even if you're not in the mood for Italian food, you and other would-be diners will be tempted to enter Bistro Molokini—the spectacular dessert presentation at the restaurant's entrance is hard to pass up. While dining here you'll enjoy lovely views and catch a glimpse of the chef (who hails from northern Italy) at work in the restaurant's exhibition kitchen. Lunch antipasti are fairly standard—*insalata caprese* (tomato and fresh mozzarella cheese salad) and fried calamari. *Carpaccio malatesta*, thin slices of raw beef with vegetables in a light lemon dressing, is an interesting addition. The *fusilli alla plinio* (pasta spirals with chicken, wild mushrooms, and sun-dried tomatoes) is a good choice for an entree, and pizzas with a variety of toppings are available. The *straccetti alla romana* (sliced, marinated, grilled beef served on a warm garlic bruschetta) is excellent. The dinner menu offers many of the same appetizers, pastas, and pizzas, but the meat and fish dishes are a bit different. Try the *galletto alla diavola*, a mustard-marinated baby chicken that's clay-baked and served with fresh tomatoes. The grilled lamb chops in balsamic vinegar and basil sauce *(costolette d'agnello)* and the sautéed veal chops with porcini mushrooms and fontina cheese *(nodino di vitello alla piemontese)* are both excellent choices. For those who are watching their weight, the lunch and dinner menus also offer several spa suggestions. And those spectacular desserts? Well, if you're lucky, you might get to try the *torta di mele alla milanese* (thin, apple tart with vanilla gelato and an amaretto sauce), or the *torta al cioccolato amaro* (a flourless chocolate tart with fruit sorbet and a raspberry coulis). If either of those will make you feel too guilty, you can always have the *caffè semi freddo*, espresso with white chocolate gelato and chocolate truffle liqueur.

CAFE KULA, 3850 Wailea Alanui (in the Grand Wailea). Tel. 875-1234.
  Cuisine: SPA. **Reservations:** Not necessary.
$ **Prices:** Appetizers $4.50–$7.50; main courses $8.50–$13. AE, DC, MC, V.
  Open: Daily 6am–3pm.
Recently featured in *Vegetarian Times* magazine, Cafe Kula is one of my favorite restaurants on the island. Even if you're not a guest at the Grand, you should make a trip to Cafe Kula. The open-air setting couldn't be more pleasant. Some of the tables are located under a covered portico, while others stand, cabana-covered, outside on the lanai. Ceiling fans whir silently overhead, cooling guests as they dine at marble-topped tables. The coral-and-turquoise-colored floor tiles are complemented by brightly striped seat cushion covers. The goal of Chef Kathleen

Daelemans "is to offer food for better living." She has daily contact with Upcountry farmers who tell her which organically grown fruits, vegetables, and herbs are ready to be harvested so she can plan her menus. Produce is picked at about 6:30am and arrives in the kitchen by 10:30am. All fishes are local, meat and poultry are the freshest available, and each dish has low sodium, fat, and cholesterol.

When I dined at Cafe Kula I began with crostini spread with Maui sun-dried tomato paste and a light but tasty homemade herbed ricotta cheese. The Kula and toybox tomato salad with fresh island herbs, topped with thinly sliced reggiano parmesan cheese and drizzled with a delicate but flavorful balsamic vinaigrette, is also a superb way to begin a meal here. Follow either of those appetizers with the spicy black-bean chili served with a mango salsa and a delectable sweet Maui corn bread (all breads are homemade). The Hawaiian ahi tuna sandwich served with a tasting of homemade pickles is prepared on the kiawe wood-fired grill, as is the Cafe Kula grilled vegetable sandwich with slow baked tomatoes, caramelized Maui onions, roasted peppers, and that delicious herbed ricotta cheese. While desserts are also prepared in the ways of spa cuisine, they are not lacking in flavor. Try the Hawaiian blueberry almond torte with orange coulis or the tropical fruit tart. The chocolate raspberry crêpes with mango yogurt are also excellent. There's also a nice fruit plate.

Cafe Kula also offers breakfast items, such as fresh fruit smoothies, the Spa Power drink (a combination of tropical fruit juices and protein); muesli with fresh and island-dried fruit; homemade granola with fresh fruit; Haiku apple-banana pancakes with pecans; eggs; muffins; and pumpkin bread. It's a great way to start the day.

CAFFE CIAO, 4100 Wailea Alanui (in the Kea Lani Resort). Tel. 875-4100.
Cuisine: GOURMET ITALIAN DELI. **Reservations:** Not accepted.
$ Prices: Main courses $17–$29. AE, CB, DC, DISC, JCB Card, MC, V.
Open: Daily 6:30am–8pm.

You can't help but fall in love with Caffe Ciao, a charming little authentic Italian gourmet deli. The tiled floors and black and white tiled walls (up to the chair rail) are lined with small metal tables and chairs where you can grab a quick bite or linger over a cup of cappuccino while reading one of the many available newspapers. In addition to the pasta salads and deli items you can also select from the menu that includes a fresh fish of the day prepared to order. You might like to have it grilled with arugula and sun-dried tomatoes or pan-seared with grilled shrimp and chow mein vegetables. Other entrees include cappellini with grilled scallops in a basil broth, grilled boneless lamb chops in a wild cherry ginger sauce, crispy crab pancit with seared scallops, or barbecue shrimp and New York steak in a spicy peanut sauce. Desserts here are spectacular—from tortes and tarts to cakes and cookies. The menu changes monthly, and on sale are various specialty food items (oils, vinegars, and sauces among them).

SANDCASTLE AT WAILEA, 3750 Wailea Alanui (in Wailea Shopping Village). Tel. 879-0606.
Cuisine: INTERNATIONAL. **Reservations:** Accepted.
$ Prices: Appetizers $1.95–$8.95; main courses $4.95–$22.95. AE, MC, V.
Open: Daily 11:30am–9pm.

Located at the center of the Wailea Shopping Village, the Sandcastle at Wailea is a large, open-air, family-style eatery. Tables are clothed with floral-print fabrics, and the high-backed cane chairs are extremely comfortable. Because it's tucked away in the shopping village, Sandcastle isn't nearly as crowded as many of the restaurants on the Kihei strip and dining can be a much more pleasant experience. It's a great place to take a break from a little shopping before you head back to the beach. The lunch menu is served all day and consists mainly of sandwiches and appetizers. There are hamburgers (a meatless version as well), hot dogs, deli meat sandwiches, and a vegetarian sandwich of the day. Pupus include buffalo wings, Maui onion rings, teriyaki chicken strips, mozzarella marinara, and stuffed mushrooms. There are a few plate lunches served with sticky rice and Hawaiian potato salad. Plate lunches are served from 11:30am to 3pm. The dinner menu includes favorites like spaghetti with meatballs, Boboli pizzas, teriyaki chicken breast, grilled mahi mahi, filet mignon (with a cognac and green peppercorn sauce), and even roasted rack of lamb (in a garlic cream sauce with roasted garlic and fresh vegetables). The Wednesday night special is barbecued baby back ribs, and on Friday and Saturday nights Alaskan king crab legs and New York steak or prime rib are offered as a special. The dessert menu is short, but the mud pie and the cheesecake are good choices.

3. UPCOUNTRY

Dining choices Upcountry are more limited than those in West Maui, and the drive can take up to an hour and a half depending on where you're staying (unless it's Hana, in which case it will take you a lot longer), but you won't be disappointed with any of the restaurants I've listed below. All of them are local favorites, and while some are more upscale than others, all serve excellent, high-quality food.

MAKAWAO

EXPENSIVE

CASANOVA ITALIAN RESTAURANT AND DELI, 1188 Makawao Ave. (P.O. Box 1166). Tel. 572-0220.
Cuisine: ITALIAN. **Reservations:** Recommended.
$ **Prices:** Appetizers $3.95–$12; main courses $7.50–$23. CB, DC, DISC, MC, V.
Open: Deli daily 8:30am–7:30pm. Restaurant, lunch Mon–Sat 11am–2pm; dinner Mon–Sat 5–9pm. Bar stays open until 1am.

At some point when you're exploring Upcountry Maui you'll probably find yourself in the old paniolo town of Makawao, and you simply must make a stop at Casanova. You might be surprised to find an authentic Italian restaurant (owned by Stefano Segre, Francesca LaRue, and Steven Burgelin who hail from Milan) in this cowboy town where you'll still find hitching posts and men in 10-gallon hats, but don't let that stop you from heading inside for a bite to eat.

All meals in the restaurant begin with warm focaccia baked fresh in the central kiawe-wood-fired pizza oven (direct from Italy) at a temperature of 700 degrees. It practically melts in your mouth. Couple the focaccia with an antipasto of *spinaci saltati al burro e parmigiano* (fresh Kula spinach sautéed with garlic, butter, and parmesan cheese) or the antipasto *misto all'Italiana* (a selection of fine deli meats, marinated seafood, roasted peppers, and a variety of cheeses), and you'll think you've died and gone to heaven. It only gets better when the entrees arrive. You might choose a pasta dish. Casanova is known island-wide for having the best homemade pasta on the island (they even supply their pasta to some of the island's finest hotels and other restaurants). Try the *gnocchi strozzapreti* (ricotta and spinach dumplings in a tomato and gorgonzola sauce) or the *paglia e fieno aii funghi* (linguine with a variety of mushrooms in a creamy garlic sauce). There is always a fresh fish (and veal chop) of the day, and if you've got a half-hour to spare (this dish takes a while to prepare), I'd recommend trying the *pesce intero al forno,* a whole fish oven-baked with white wine, fresh herbs, and garlic. Bread isn't the only thing they cook to perfection in that enormous pizza oven, so if you've got a craving for a really fine pizza, now's the time to satisfy it. The pizza Greca with tomato sauce, feta cheese, Greek olives, and oregano is always a good choice, and so is the Vulcano with baked eggplant, smoked mozzarella, and fresh tomato. You can also create your own pizza by choosing from a list of toppings. Desserts are baked fresh daily, so be sure to take a look at the dessert tray. Homemade gelato is a standard daily offering. Stay on after dinner and enjoy an evening of dancing and live entertainment—your cover charge will be waived if you're dining.

The original deli next door to the restaurant serves an excellent breakfast, sandwiches at lunch, coffees, and mouth-watering pastries any time of the day.

HALI'IMAILE GENERAL STORE, Hali'imaile. Tel. 572-2666.
Cuisine: HAWAII REGIONAL/AMERICAN/INTERNATIONAL. **Reservations:** Recommended. **Directions:** Five miles up Highway 37 (Haleakala Highway) turn left at the Hali'imaile cut-off sign. Continue 1½ miles to Hali'imaile General Store.
$ Prices: Appetizers $4–$7; main courses $13–$24. MC, V.
Open: Tues–Sun lunch 11am–3pm; dinner 6–10pm. Sunday brunch 10am–3pm.

First of all, you're probably wondering how to pronounce the name of this wonderful restaurant, right? Well, it goes something like this: hi-lee-ee-meye-lee, and roughly translated, it is "a covering of the fragrant maile twining shrub." This whole area was once overgrown with the aromatic maile plant, and it was often used in the making of redolent leis. Today the restaurant is surrounded by about 1,000 acres of pineapple fields. Owners Bev and Joe Gannon have transformed the General Store, which originally opened in 1929, into one of Maui's best restaurants. They planned originally to open a gourmet deli/catering business, but on opening day when scores of people showed up looking for a place to sit down and have a good meal, the Gannons decided they'd better turn the place into a restaurant. With the presence of lofty pine shelves that hold ceramics, glassware, gourmet foods, and basketry, you'll still feel like you're in a general store. There are two dining rooms here—one for more casual dining up front, and an intimate room in the back. Local artwork, including the bartop and the bas-relief next to the bar (both by Tom Faught, whose work is also on display in the Ritz-Carlton Kapalua), is present throughout the restaurant. I love this restaurant for several reasons, not the least of which is that you get some of the finest food Maui has to offer in a casual setting.

Begin your meal with the incredible leek and goat cheese tart, served with crispy pancetta and smoked tomato coulis; or the unique brie and grape quesadilla served hot with a sweet pea guacamole. Their "Famous House Salad" is reminiscent of something my mother used to make with fresh mixed greens, onions, mandarin oranges, and walnuts in a balsamic vinaigrette topped with crumbled blue cheese. For a main course, try the Italasian shrimp and scallops—they're sautéed with shiitake mushrooms and served in a cilantro pesto cream sauce over angel hair pasta. The Szechuan barbecued salmon, topped with a sauce of caramelized onions, garlic, orange zest, Szechuan peppercorns, and fresh herbs, is absolutely out of this world. You might also like to try the Australian rack of lamb Hunan style. It's marinated in hoisin sauce, sesame, and Oriental black beans and then grilled to perfection. The wine list here is extensive, and Joe Gannon will help you find a bottle that goes perfectly with your meal. Desserts change daily, but Hali'imaile General Store's own signature dessert (which appeared on the cover of *Food & Wine* in March 1992), piña colada cheesecake, is superb.

MAKAWAO STEAK HOUSE, 3612 Baldwin Ave. Tel. 572-8711.
Cuisine: AMERICAN. **Reservations:** Recommended.
$ Prices: Appetizers $2.95–$11.95; main courses $15.50–$24.95. MC, V.
Open: Dinner daily 5pm–closing.

Opened since 1990 and located right in the center of Old Makawao Town, the Makawao Steak House is exactly what you might picture it to be—it is, after all, right in the heart of paniolo country. Wood-paneled walls, a working fireplace, and comfortable wood chairs have all been carefully considered by owner Dickie Furtado, who designed his restaurant specifically with the diner's comfort in mind. It is exactly as cozy as you might expect, and there's even a blue-plate special. Start with a seafood sampler or the appetizer they call "Dynamite" (scallops and fresh vegetables baked in a firecracker sauce). The Portuguese bean soup is good, and there are several salad offerings. Entrees include fresh seafood (there's even a calamari steak), as well as items from the kiawe broiler and from the barnyard. On the seafood side, there's a bouillabaisse, baked scallops, crab legs, and shrimp scampi. Most come for the steak, though, and there are several options here. Try the filet mignon or the porterhouse steak. There's a nice teriyaki steak as well, and lamb lovers will be happy to find rack of lamb on the menu. The Greek chicken is boneless chicken breast filled with spinach, feta cheese, and black olives, served with a lemon sauce. Something with a more Hawaiian twist might be the chicken in phyllo (boneless chicken breast filled with a macadamia nut herb dressing, butter, and encased in phyllo pastry) or the boneless breast basted in a ginger and teriyaki sauce. Oh, and that blue-plate special—it's a 16-ounce porterhouse steak, kiawe-broiled and served with a caper-and-garlic-flavored olive oil sauce. It comes with rice and sautéed spinach. Try the white chocolate mousse or the mud pie for dessert.

BUDGET

THE COURTYARD DELI, 3620 Baldwin Ave. Tel. 572-3456.

Cuisine: DELI. **Reservations:** Not accepted.
$ Prices: Sandwiches $4.95–$5.50.
Open: Daily 8am–4pm.

The first thing you'll notice about this place is that it smells divine. The menu quotes literary greats like George Bernard Shaw who believed that, "There is no love sincerer than the love of food"; and James Beard, who once said, "Too few people understand a really good sandwich." The people at the Courtyard Deli seem to be in agreement with Mr. Shaw and Mr. Beard. Offerings here include the king of deli sandwiches, the pastrami melt; a weekly variation on the chicken salad sandwich; and everyone's favorite, the tuna melt. More unusual items include the "Garden Burger with Da Works," a blend of mushrooms, herbs, and oatmeal topped with mozzarella cheese served on a whole-wheat bun; or the "Fakin' Bacon BLT," slices of "fakin' bacon" topped with tempeh, avocado, mayonnaise, and Maui onion. You can also have a sandwich made to order, and there's always a soup of the day. Desserts are made fresh daily and are constantly changing, so don't forget to ask what they are. If you're in Makawao in the morning, stop in for breakfast. Try Claire's cinnamon custard French toast (croissants baked in custard and served with syrup) or the Belgian waffles (served with maple syrup and fresh fruit). There are several variations on scrambled eggs, and the Mauka Morning Burrito (scrambled eggs, cheese, and salsa wrapped in a whole-wheat chapati) will satisfy even those with the healthiest of appetites.

CROSSROADS CAFFE, 3682 Baldwin Ave. Tel. 572-1101.

Cuisine: CAFE/DELI. **Reservations:** Not accepted.
$ Prices: Menu items $1.50–$5.50. No credit cards.
Open: Breakfast Mon–Sat 8–10:30am; lunch Mon–Sat 11am–4pm.

Located right across the street from Casanova (see above), the Crossroads Caffe is a great place for you to stop for refreshment between shops and art galleries. Small marble-topped tables surrounded by metal versions of the more traditional cane-back chairs flank the walls of this tiny cafe. There are a few tables outdoors as well. Breakfast choices range from bagels and English muffins to Belgian waffles and breakfast burritos. Lunch options include the popular Boboli pizza of the pesto and veggie varieties, a turkey melt, "dolphin-safe" tuna sandwiches, grilled cheese, and a veggie burger with cheese. Lunch specials are offered daily. Beverages include natural juices and sodas, as well as many different kinds of coffee. Check the pastry case for the day's bakery selections, which might include muffins, croissants, and more elaborate choices, like the delicious Kona mocha cheesecake. If nothing on the menu strikes your fancy, maybe the frozen yogurt will.

KULA

MODERATE

KULA LODGE & RESTAURANT, Rte. 377 (RR1, Box 475), Kula. Tel. 878-1535.

Cuisine: HAWAII REGIONAL/CONTEMPORARY. **Reservations:** Recommended.

$ Prices: Appetizers $2.75–$9.50; main courses $7.25–$22. MC, V.
Open: Breakfast daily 7–11:30am; lunch daily 11:30am–5:30pm; dinner daily 5:30–
9pm.
While sea and sand is probably why you came to Maui in the first place, you might
get a little homesick for a cooler climate and that fireplace you left behind. If that's
the case, head Upcountry to the Kula Lodge & Restaurant. The views are spectacular. Lunchtime brings a mixed crowd of local businesspeople and early-rising tourists
who made the journey to Haleakala Crater to watch the sun rise. At dinner the
lights are dimmed and a fire in the hearth sets the scene for an intimate, candlelit,
moderately inexpensive dinner for two. An excellent lunch or dinnertime appetizer is
the sizzling escargot bourguignon. If you love onion soup, you've come to the right
place. The Kula onion soup is prepared with sweet onions sautéed in a rich broth
with just a touch of sherry and a topping of garlic croutons and Swiss cheese. Sandwiches of note are the mahi mahi sandwich with tartar sauce or the macadamia nut
meatless garden burger with cheese. Naturally, there is a large selection of fresh fish
and shellfish, and true to the Upcountry theme, several varieties of steak, and a delicious New Zealand rack of lamb marinated in Worcestershire sauce and garlic,
lightly breaded and then baked, are also offered. One of my favorites in the pasta
section of the menu is the Thai noodle stir-fry, a combination of celery, sprouts, carrots, and green onions in a black-bean sauce; served over Soba noodles, it can be ordered with or without shrimp. Breakfasts, from the whole-grain cereals to buttermilk
griddle cakes, are hearty and delicious. There's a children's breakfast menu also.

BUDGET
GRANDMA'S COFFEE SHOP, Hwy. 37, Keokea. Tel. 878-2140.
Cuisine: AMERICAN. **Reservations:** Not accepted.
$ Prices: Menu items $1.75–$6.95. No credit cards.
Open: Mon–Sat 7am–5pm.
Grandma's Coffee Shop is an excellent place to stop for coffee and pastry on your
way up to Haleakala Crater. That is, if you're not headed up there for the sunrise.
If you are, you're going to have to stop on the way back down. Several years back
Alfred Franco began learning the fine art of coffee roasting. His teacher? You
guessed it—his grandmother. His family has actually been roasting coffee on Maui
for almost 80 years now (the cafe is only about 8 years old, however), and today
you can buy the coffee by the pound right here in Grandma's Coffee Shop. Alfred
says that people often ask him why his coffee is so expensive, and he simply ex-
plains that it's of a much higher quality. If you know your java, you'll know that
you're getting your money's worth at Grandma's. There are cafe tables available for
eating in, but you can order items to go (it's great if you're planning a picnic on the
crater). In the morning you can order any number of freshly baked, homemade pastries from coffee cake to cinnamon rolls or even banana bread. At lunch there are
several sandwich offerings available, and maybe the day will bring a piping-hot chili.
If you can get a table and you're not in a hurry, eat in the coffee shop—you'll get a
wonderful idea of just what it's like to live on Maui. Local patrons come and go
greeting their friends and talking story. You'll envy them and their island lifestyle. In
case you're wondering, the artwork displayed on the walls of Grandma's is local.

PAIA
EXPENSIVE
MAMA'S FISH HOUSE, 799 Poho Place (on Rte. 36). Tel. 579-8488.
Cuisine: SEAFOOD. **Reservations:** Recommended at dinner.
$ Prices: Appetizers $5.25–$12.50; main courses $16.95–$28.50. AE, DISC, MC, V.
Open: Daily 11am–9:30pm.
One of the oldest restaurants on the island, Mama's is located just 1½ miles from
Paia. You'll have no trouble finding it because the entrance is marked by a ship's

flagpole and a couple of vintage vans. On one of Maui's prettiest beaches, Mama's is actually a converted beach house that belongs to the restaurant's namesake, "Mama" Doris Christiansen, who decided to open her home as a fresh fish house in 1973. Everybody, locals and tourists alike, enjoy dining in this beachfront establishment. The interior, plastered with items that are reminiscent of Old Hawaii, like kapa cloth, grass skirts, and old photos, is inviting and comfortable. All the fish served at Mama's is brought in on Mama's own fishing boats, and fresh herbs are grown in the Christiansens' backyard. At dinner, the house salad topped with smoked fish is delicious. Try one of the day's fresh catches sautéed in white wine and sprinkled with macadamia nuts. You can't leave here without having Mama's famous macadamia nut cheesecake.

WUNDERBAR, 89 Hana Hwy. Tel. 579-8808.

    Cuisine: GERMAN. **Reservations:** Recommended.

$ **Prices:** Appetizers $2.50–$10; main courses $4–$16 at lunch, $5.95–$25 at dinner. AE, MC, V.

    Open: Breakfast daily 7:30–11:30am; lunch daily 11:30am–2pm; appetizers daily 2:30–6pm; dinner daily 5–10pm. Bar stays open until about 1am.

Though Wunderbar is only furnished with plain wood tables and chairs, it's an upbeat and friendly spot. A piano in the center of the restaurant and an abundance of beer signs hanging on the walls liven the place up. The bar is almost always hopping, and the TV above it is always on. Though the breakfast specials have intriguing names, like Sunset Beach, Olympic, Bijorka, and Berlin, what they include is fairly standard—eggs, breakfast meats, cereal, and fresh fruit. The lunch menu offers a soup of the day, sandwiches, and several pasta dishes. You may order a regular ground-beef burger, or go for something a little more interesting, like the Nürnburger with three Nürnberg bratwursts in a bun topped with lettuce, sauerkraut, and mustard, or the Schnitzelburger made with turkey-breast schnitzel in a bun with lettuce, tomato, onion, pickles, and a special sauce. At dinner the menu is much more extensive, including pastas, several seafood specialties (including *gambas à la plancha,* four tiger prawns sautéed in lemon garlic butter), several hearty entrees (including wiener schnitzel and Hungarian goulash), and the catch of the day (prepared Mediterranean style with tomatoes, garlic, red wine, and sliced Sicilian olives; or Norwegian style with a white wine and shallot cream sauce among others). Desserts include *schwartzwalder kirchtorte* (black forest cake), *schoggimousse* (chocolate mousse from Switzerland), and *apfelkuechle* (baked apple slices in a cinammon sugar served with a homemade vanilla-bean sauce). Most people, however, come for the large selection of beers and nightlife, which typically begins at 10pm.

MODERATE

CAFFE PARADISO, 120 Hana Hwy. Tel. 579-8819.

    Cuisine: ITALIAN. **Reservations:** Recommended.

$ **Prices:** Appetizers $6.95–$13.95; main courses $7.95–$20.95. AE, MC, V.

    Open: Dinner Tues–Sun 6–10pm.

How does dining under palm trees and a bougainvillea sound to you? Well, you might be surprised to find just such a place in Paia in the form of Caffè Paradiso, a wonderful little Italian restaurant located just across the street from the Paia General Store. Try the *crostini al prosciutto* (homemade bread topped with Parma prosciutto and melted fresh mozzarella) or the Saint Tropez (a mix of fancy young lettuce topped with a brie cheese and dijon mustard vinaigrette) to start. As a main course you might like to try one of the freshly made pasta dishes. The *penne alla puttanesca* with tomato sauce, garlic, capers, anchovies, black olives, and red wine, and the *gnocchi del giorno* served with a choice of Napoli, pesto, bolognese, or gorgonzola sauce, are both excellent choices. Meat and fish dishes, including the *sopa de pescado* (seafood cioppino prepared in a Mediterranean style) and the *saltimbocca Paradiso* (a breast of chicken sautéed in a white wine and butter sauce and topped with prosciutto), are served with vegetables and potatoes, or the pasta of the day. Desserts change daily and are generally excellent. Caffè Paradiso also has a fine espresso bar.

PAIA FISH MARKET RESTAURANT, 100 Hana Hwy. Tel. 579-8030.
Cuisine: SEAFOOD. **Reservations:** Not accepted.
$ Prices: Appetizers $2–$8.95; main courses $3–$13.95. No credit cards.
Open: Daily 11am–9:30pm.

Paia is known for its offbeat restaurants, and the Paia Fish Market is no exception. You can eat in and sit at one of a few heavy wood picnic tables, or you can take it away, whichever suits your fancy. No matter what you do, you'll get to meet some locals, many of whom rave about the fish market. Menu offerings include all varieties of charbroiled seafood—snapper, mahi mahi, swordfish, ahi, opah, salmon, and ono to name a few. Fish and chips (cooked in cholesterol-free oil and lightly coated in a beer batter) is served at lunch and dinner. In addition, you can choose from scallops and chips, shrimp and chips, and calamari and chips. There are several pasta options, as well as some Mexican dishes, like fajitas and quesadillas. The Fish Market also offers steak (filet mignon or New York steak) served with home fries or Cajun rice and cole slaw. A decent selection of beers and wines is also available.

BUDGET

PIC-NICS, 30 Baldwin Ave. Tel. 579-8021.
Cuisine: SANDWICHES. **Reservations:** Not accepted.
$ Prices: Menu items $1.25–$15.95. No credit cards.
Open: Daily 7:30am–7pm.

If you stay on Maui long enough, you'll get curious about Pic-nics' spinach nut burgers because everyone on the island is singing their praises. The decor is nothing special, but the orange and yellow Formica-topped tables are cheerful and inviting and the food is delectable. The spinach nut burger is made of spinach, chopped nuts, sesame seeds, and spices and is served topped with cheddar cheese on a whole-wheat bun. It is so well known that it has been featured in major magazines and newspapers all over the country. Other popular sandwiches include the picnic burger supreme, organically grown lean ground beef topped with cheddar and Swiss cheeses, two strips of bacon, tomato, lettuce, sweet Maui onion, and mayonnaise. The Windsurfer is a variation on the spinach nut burger—it's topped with bacon, Swiss and cheddar cheeses, lettuce, tomato, sprouts, and dressing on a whole-wheat bun. There are other sandwiches—ham and Swiss, turkey, roast beef, and BLTs. At breakfast try the Paia Plantation Breakfast, which is scrambled eggs topped with cheddar cheese on buttered toast served with papaya-pineapple jam and Kona coffee (all for only $3.75!). There's also an assortment of fresh-baked pastries and muffins, and a variety of coffees and frozen yogurt treats (shakes and sundaes).

If you're headed out on an excursion and know you'll be passing Pic-nics (on your way to Hana or something), give them a call in advance and order a picnic lunch so you can pick it up on your way by.

HANA

HANA GARDENLAND CAFE, Kalo Rd. Tel. 248-8975.
Cuisine: SANDWICHES/REGIONAL SPECIALTIES. **Reservations:** Not accepted.
$ Prices: Breakfast items $2.25–$4.75; lunch and snack items $2.75–$6.95. MC, V.
Open: Daily 9am–5pm.

The Hana Gardenland Cafe is the best place in Hana to stop for breakfast or lunch (in fact, Hillary Clinton stopped here three mornings in a row on her recent visit to Maui). Order your food at the window and enjoy your surroundings in the palm frond-covered patio, or wander through the art gallery and gift shop located adjacent to the restaurant (or to your right as you entered). The art gallery displays the work of local and regional artists, and the gift shop is full of wonderful local souvenirs (none of which are trashy or plastic).

4. SPECIALTY DINING

BREAKFAST

If you're an early riser in need of a light breakfast, try the **Sunrise Cafe** at 693A Front St., right on the corner of Market Street (tel. 661-3326), where you can get coffee and great pastries starting at 5:30am. **Marie Callendar's** in the Lahaina Cannery Mall (tel. 667-7437) also opens early (7am) and serves full breakfasts; try the macadamia nut and banana waffles. If you're Upcountry in Paia, the **Peaches and Crumble Cafe and Bakery** (2 Baldwin Ave., tel. 579-8612) is an excellent choice for baked goods. Looking to try something new? Head for the **Komoda Store and Bakery** (tel. 572-7261) in Makawao. It opens at 6:30am, and people line up to get their masaladas and cream buns. If you simply can't live without your morning bagel, **Maui Bakery Bagelry & Deli,** at 201 Dairy Rd. (tel 871-4825) in Kahului, will satisfy you.

CASUAL & FAST FOOD

Ever had a guava shake? Well, **Bullock's of Hawaii** (3494 Haleakala Hwy., tel. 572-7220), in Pukalani, is famous island-wide for their guava shakes. They also make a mean "moonburger." Go for lunch, but be sure to get there before late afternoon—they close at 3pm. **Azeka's Market Snack Shop** (tel. 879-0078) in Kihei's Azeka Place also serves hamburgers in addition to inexpensive plate lunches.

If you like Japanese food, take a trip to **Sam Sato's** at 318 N. Market (tel. 244-7124) in the Happy Valley, just outside of Wailuku. Locals flock to Sam Sato's for their *manju* (a pastry filled with meats, fruits, or beans)—give it a try.

Used to be that when you visited Maui you couldn't get fast food of any sort, shape, or variety, but these days you'll find representatives from almost every fast-food franchise on the island. The best places to look for fast-food establishments are Kihei and Kahului. Lahaina has a McDonald's, but that's about it.

CHAPTER 7

WHAT TO SEE & DO ON MAUI

Most people who come to Maui have only a few things in mind—salt, sand, sun, and tropical drinks. While all of those are perfectly legitimate vacation expectations, Maui has much more to offer its visitors. From the slopes of Haleakala to the Iao Valley and all the way to Hana, the vistas and varieties of plant and animal life are unequaled anywhere else in the United States. There are art galleries and museums, and a brand-new cultural center is under construction as this book goes to press. This chapter will cover all the attractions listed above, with a little shopping and nightlife thrown in for good measure.

SUGGESTED ITINERARIES

IF YOU HAVE ONE DAY

What a horrifying prospect! First and foremost, get an early start. Before you head to the beach you might consider making a reservation to attend an evening luau. Most hotels hold their own luaus, so check with the concierge at your hotel. If the hotel doesn't have a luau, you might consider trying the Old Lahaina Luau. If you've been traveling the islands for some time now and have had your share of luaus, try a sunset sail instead (most of the hotels offer their own).

Since it generally takes a long time to get from one town to another, a major excursion (like a trip to Haleakala or Upcountry) probably wouldn't be worth the effort. Instead, I'd recommend that you spend the morning and early afternoon on the beach near your hotel. For lunch, head to Lahaina. Try dining at Avalon or David Paul's Lahaina Grill. Work off your lunch with a walk along Front Street where you can visit some interesting shops and art galleries. You also might like to follow the walking tour that has been put together by the Lahaina Historical Foundation. It will take you to all the historically significant sites in Lahaina, and later in this chapter you can read more information about some of the stops on the tour.

After exploring Lahaina, you'll probably be ready to give your weary feet a rest. Head back to the hotel and get ready for that luau!

IF YOU HAVE TWO DAYS

If you've only got two days on Maui you'll still have to hustle, but you should be able to fit in a major excursion.

Day 1   Spend Day 1 as described above, but try to get to bed early because you'll need to get up early on your second day in order to take an excursion.

Day 2   Most of the island's major excursions will take you a full day, so plan carefully. If you want to see the sun rise atop Haleakala, you'll have to get a very early start because it could take up to 3 hours to get to the summit. If you simply can't get up early enough, try taking a trip to the Iao Valley in the morning. Save some time by asking your hotel to prepare a picnic lunch—you'll be able to take a short hike through the valley without having to head back to town when you get hungry.

Later in the day, if you still want to take the trip up Haleakala, you can try to catch the sunset (which is spectacular). Be sure to take a sweater or jacket because it will get cold when the sun goes down.

If you're not interested in driving up Haleakala and you finish your hike fairly early in the afternoon, take a trip Upcountry instead. On the way you might like to make a quick detour to the Alexander & Baldwin Sugar Museum. After that, head for Hana Highway and drive up to Paia where you'll find some unique boutiques and excellent restaurants. If you want to see some incredible windsurfing (or do some of your own), go just beyond Paia town on Hana Highway to Ho'okipa Beach Park. When you're finished there, turn around and go back to Paia town and go left on Baldwin Avenue through Paia into the town of Makawao. Here you'll find some more shopping, some wonderful art galleries, and some more of the island's finest restaurants (which you should keep in mind for dinner—you might even consider making a reservation while you're in town).

If you find that you haven't run out of time (or energy) after you're finished in Makawao, there's one more stop you should make before you make the drive back to your hotel. Check to see if Tedeschi Vineyards is still open. If it is, drive up there and have a taste of Maui blanc (the famous pineapple wine) or even the passion fruit wine they just started making.

By the time you've done all, or most, of the above you should be ready for a substantial dinner. Try the Kula Lodge if you're in the mood for Hawaiian regional/contemporary cuisine and excellent views. If you'd rather have Italian food, go back to Makawao and see if you can get a table at Casanova. Or, if seafood is what you crave, go back to Paia and give Mama's Fish House a try.

IF YOU HAVE THREE DAYS

Days 1 and 2   If you came to Maui to relax, then I'd recommend spending your first day on the beach. Go snorkeling, take a scuba-diving or surfing lesson, and if you're feeling particularly adventurous, go parasailing or take a helicopter ride. If you came to Maui to explore, then you should start your trip by following the itinerary listed under Day 2.

On your second day, follow the itinerary for Day 1 or Day 2 depending on what strikes your fancy. If you've already done the Upcountry Tour (or Haleakala), take the other trip suggested on Day 2.

Day 3   If you're still energized, now's the time to take a trip to Hana. Begin early: It will take you at least three hours to get there and three hours to get back, and if you're not a confident driver, you should make every effort to leave Hana well before dark because the road is very curvy and can be dangerous. You'll probably want to spend several hours exploring the waterfalls and blue pools in the area, and if you're a hiker, you'll find much to do in Hana. There are no restaurants along the way, but if you leave early you won't be ready for lunch until after you get to Hana. The Hana Gardenland Cafe is an excellent spot for lunch. Otherwise, pack a picnic.

If you want to spend your last night in Hana, there is an airport that will get you to Kahului for your flight off Maui with time to spare. If you've never made the drive before, don't be tempted to fly to Hana—the drive is most of the fun.

IF YOU HAVE FIVE DAYS OR MORE

If you've got at least 5 days, you can take it easy.

Days 1-3   Spend a couple of mornings on the beach and do only one activity a day. Take one afternoon to explore Lahaina and another to hike in the Iao Valley or visit Paia, Makawao, and the winery. On the third day, try to make it to the top of Haleakala for the sunrise and then spend the afternoon relaxing on the beach.

Days 4-5   On Day 4, go to Hana and spend the night. On Day 5, either continue exploring Hana or head back down and take the trip you didn't get to on Days 1 through 3 (it should probably be the trip to the Iao Valley since the trip Upcountry will be another long one).

1. WEST MAUI

West Maui is the island's playground: Great restaurants and interesting shops stand side by side, and beautiful resorts stand majestically along the coastline. If there's an activity in which you would like to participate during your stay on Maui, it very likely originates somewhere in West Maui. Many locals refer to Maui's western shore as the "New York City" of Maui.

LAHAINA

Lahaina means "merciless sun" and it is one of the hottest spots on the island, and not just because of its temperature. From the founding of this small town, Lahaina has been one of the centers of activity on Maui. Maui's King Kahekili called Lahaina home until King Kamehameha's troops defeated him in the Iao Valley in the late 1700s. Then it was Kamehameha I who set up his power base in Lahaina. Today, during your stay in Lahaina, you can still visit the ruins of Kamehameha I's brick palace. It remained the seat of Hawaiian power until Kamehameha III moved it to Honolulu in the mid-1800s.

In 1819 the whaling men arrived in search of humpback whales, and they found much more than they could have hoped for—Hawaiian women, grog shops, and plenty of hospitality. They turned Lahaina on its ear for about 5 years before the missionaries arrived and began to put an end to their lawless ways. The missionaries prohibited the sale of alcohol and helped build a jail to hold unruly sailors (see later in this chapter for details). Reverend William Richards built his home in Lahaina (which the sailors, angered by the meddlesome missionaries, tried to destroy with cannonball fire), and more missionaries, like the Reverend Dwight Baldwin, followed. The Lahainaluna School was built in the West Maui Mountains, overlooking Lahaina town, and the island's first printing press was delivered to Lahaina, making it the point of origin for the very first newspaper in the Hawaiian islands. When Lahaina's days as the whaling capital of the Pacific came to an end, Mauians turned their attention away from the ocean and back to the land to boost the economy. It was at that time that the island's abundant growth of wild sugarcane became important. It wasn't long before the sugar industry came to Maui in full force, but it didn't do much in the way of reviving Lahaina's economy. Lahaina reverted to its sleepy ways, and remained that way until the mid-1960s when tourism became the town's major draw.

HISTORIC LAHAINA ATTRACTIONS

In the pamphlet "Lahaina Historical Guide," obtainable at virtually any hotel or at the Maui Visitors Bureau, you will find a walking tour of the town of Lahaina.

FROMMER'S FAVORITE MAUI EXPERIENCES

Sunrise at Haleakala Crater Get to bed early and set your alarm for 3 or 4am so you can make the 2- or 2½-hour drive to the summit of Haleakala before the sun rises. It's an experience you'll never forget.

An Arts Crawl Along Front Street There are many wonderful galleries along Front Street—try to see them all.

Driving the Road to Hana You'd think that 3 hours on a road of switchbacks and one-lane bridges would deter people from making the trip to Hana, but the scenery and the wonderful waterfalls along the way make it all worthwhile.

Wine Tasting at Tedeschi Vineyards A day spent Upcountry simply must include a stop at the Tedeschi Vineyards for a taste of pineapple and/or passion fruit wine.

Snorkeling Molokini There's nothing better than swimming with the extraordinary tropical fish of Maui, and there's no better place to do it than Molokini.

Each of the stops on the tour is marked with a signposted number so you will find your way around easily. I have elaborated on some of the information you will find in the guide to give you an even greater understanding of the various sites. Though I have left out several sites covered in the pamphlet, the ones I have written about here appear in order by number following the walking tour provided by the Restoration Foundation.

MASTERS' READING ROOM, corner of Front and Dickenson Sts. Tel. 661-3262.

When ships first began landing at Lahaina Wharf in the early 1800s, sailors had virtually unlimited access to anything they might need or want—fresh water, grog, hogs, and fresh produce; and women would swim out to the ships as they arrived. Seamen looked forward to stopping in Lahaina, but all that changed shortly after the arrival of the missionaries in 1823. By 1825 the 23 grog shops that once lined the streets were shut down due to the prohibition of prostitution and the distribution, production, and sale of alcohol. Sailors who made return visits to their own private piece of paradise were shocked to find that all of their pleasures/vices had been banned. It was at this time that the Masters' Reading Room was conceived as a "shore retreat for both officers and seamen." Many of the town residents and the seamen themselves donated funds and building materials to the reading room. The lower floor served as a storage area, while the upstairs, with its observation deck, was purely for the comfort of the masters and officers. For about 10 years the Masters' Reading Room was an extremely popular onshore gathering spot for the men who docked their ships in Lahaina harbor, but by 1844, with the increase of traffic on the waterway, hotels and bars began reopening and the reading room lost its appeal. It was in 1846 that Dr. Dwight Baldwin (who occupied the building next door) bought the reading room at an auction for $70 to accommodate his growing family. In 1855 he divided the room in two and took tenants.

BALDWIN HOME, Front St. Tel. 661-3262.

In 1830 Reverend Dwight Baldwin and his young bride Charlotte left their New England home and sailed for the Hawaiian islands where Reverend Baldwin was to serve as a doctor at a "medical station" in Waimea on the

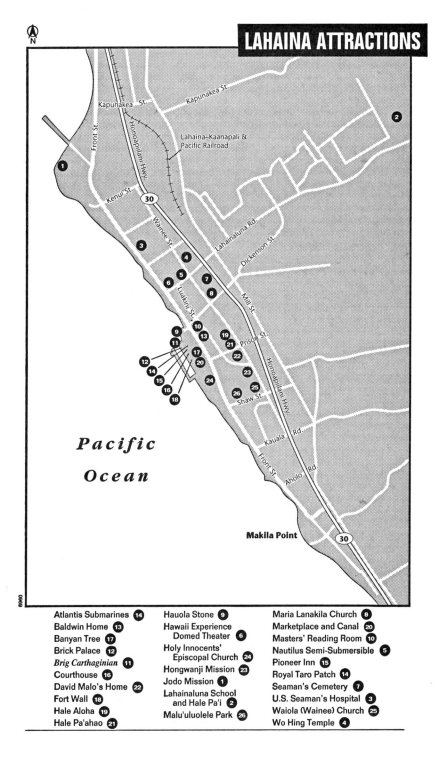

Kapunakea St.

Kapunakea St.

Front St.

Honoapiilani Hwy.

Lahaina–Kaanapali &
Pacific Railroad

Kenui St.

30

Wainee St.

Lahainaluna Rd.

Dickenson St.

Luakini St.

Mill St.

Prison St.

Honoapiilani Hwy.

Shaw St.

Kauala Rd.

Front St.

Aholo Rd.

Pacific

Ocean

Makila Point

30

Atlantis Submarines **14**
Baldwin Home **13**
Banyan Tree **17**
Brick Palace **12**
Brig Carthaginian **11**
Courthouse **16**
David Malo's Home **22**
Fort Wall **18**
Hale Aloha **19**
Hale Pa'ahao **21**

Hauola Stone **9**
Hawaii Experience
  Domed Theater **6**
Holy Innocents'
  Episcopal Church **24**
Hongwanji Mission **23**
Jodo Mission **1**
Lahainaluna School
  and Hale Pa'i **2**
Malu'uluolele Park **26**

Maria Lanakila Church **8**
Marketplace and Canal **20**
Masters' Reading Room **10**
Nautilus Semi-Submersible **5**
Pioneer Inn **15**
Royal Taro Patch **14**
Seaman's Cemetery **7**
U.S. Seaman's Hospital **3**
Waiola (Wainee) Church **25**
Wo Hing Temple **4**

Big Island. In 1835 he was transferred to Lahaina's Wainee Church where he hoped to continue full time in his missionary pursuits. It soon became clear that he was the only missionary in Maui County qualified to practice medicine, and thus continued his work as a doctor in Lahaina.

The oldest building standing in Lahaina today, the Baldwin Home was built in 1834. The walls were constructed of coral, stone, and timber. Today visitors may view the original construction through a cut-out section of the inner wall in the back room. Though the house was built in 1834, the Baldwins did not move into it until 1838, but there the family remained in residence until 1871. The original building only consisted of one floor, but as the family grew, a bedroom and study were attached, and finally a second story was added. At one time a total of six children were housed within the coral walls of this modest home, and as you tour the inside, you'll get a glimpse of what their lives were like. You'll also be able to view some of Reverend Baldwin's medical tools, old photos, furnishings, books, and kitchen implements.

Admission: $3 adults; $2.50 seniors; $1 children.

Open: Daily 9am–4:30pm.

ROYAL TARO PATCH.

From the Baldwin Home, cross Front Street and head between the buildings on Market Street (which dead ends rather quickly) and the Lahaina Library. On the *makai* side of the library is where the Royal Taro Patch used to be. Taro, which is used to make poi, is a staple of the Hawaiian diet and also plays an important role in Hawaiian mythology. It is said that Wakea's first-born son (Wakea being the god, "the sky father," from which Hawaii's ali'i were said to have been descended), Haloanaka, was born somewhat prematurely and died shortly after birth. He was buried at one end of Wakea's house, and from his body grew a taro plant. The leaf of the taro was given the name *laukapalili*, or "quivering leaf," while the stem was called *haloa*. The second child born to Wakea was named Haloa, and it is believed that Haloa was the father of humankind.

The making of a taro patch was quite an undertaking. Taro was best grown on land that could be easily irrigated (some of the land was considered *malo'o* or "dry"). Once a a good patch of land was found, banks of earth were formed and packed down (trampled by the farmer's own feet) around it. Water was then allowed to flow freely into the patch. After a period of time, when the patch became dry, the earthen dams that surrounded the patch were strengthened with stones, palm leaves, and sugarcane plants until the banks were watertight. The soil was then turned, wetted, and packed down. Rows were marked and taro tops were planted in each row. From that point forward the taro patch would be constantly watered. About a year from planting the taro would be ready for picking.

There are many varieties of taro ranging from *kai* (said to yield the most excellent poi) to the *haokea* (which has a more bland flavor than kai when mashed into poi). Both of the aforementioned types are in the "blue" taro family, and they represent the top and bottom of the scale—there are, in fact, scores of other varieties in the same family that fall between kai and haokea. One very special taro, the *pi'iali'i* (or "king's choice"), was known by its pink-purple coloring and is believed to produce the best poi. In addition to poi, taro was also used in the manufacture of a medicinal drink.

Several historical accounts that include references to this particular taro patch state that King Kamehameha himself could often be seen working in the taro patch in an effort to teach his people that there is dignity to be found in heavy physical labor. One account that documents these activities says that, "The king and his wife, the queen, his trusted friend and official John Young, and his wife, and several others in the party . . . were without shoes and stockings and hats . . . and no more clothes than necessary. They were as happy as any children playing in summer showers."

HAUOLA STONE.

From the taro patch, head toward the water, then proceed to your right, and soon you will see the Hauola Stone (Healing Stone), located in the water on your left (look for the Hawaii Visitors Bureau marker). Stones played a large role in the life of early Hawaiians. They were fashioned into tools such as axes, poi pounders, and squid-fishing implements and were even used in the polishing of wooden bowls and canoes. Some stones (more likely, boulders) were worshiped for their healing properties.

It was believed by ancient Hawaiians that an ill person need only sit on this Healing Stone, with legs in the water being washed by the waves, to be cured.

The Hauola Stone was also used as a hiding place for *piko*, or the umbilical cords of newborns. It was traditional in Hawaiian families that umbilical cords be hidden, and if they were left completely undisturbed, the child whose piko had been hidden would one day become a chief. The Hauola Stone was a logical place to hide these precious items because it was a sacred place, and it was unlikely that anyone would make any effort to violate the stone's secret crevices.

BRICK PALACE.

Just across Wharf Street from the Pioneer Inn, near the library, is a historical site that is extremely important in the history of Maui. In 1802, when King Kamehameha came to Maui on his way to conquer Kauai, he decided to remain in Lahaina for over a year. A brick house had been constructed for the king in Lahaina by two Australian bricklayers a couple of years earlier, and it was during his stay on Maui while he was busy consecrating temples, collecting taxes from other islands, and planning his attack on Kauai that he made the brick building his headquarters. The palace is no longer standing, but it did manage to survive for about 70 years after it was built—quite a feat for the first brick structure the islands had ever seen.

BRIG CARTHAGINIAN, Lahaina Wharf. Tel. 661-8527.

Moored at the old Lahaina Wharf, just across from the Pioneer Inn, the *Brig Carthaginian* is an authentic replica of a 19th-century whaling vessel. The original *Carthaginian* was built under the direction of Captain Allan Villers, an expert on square-rigged ships, for the filming of a movie and was later docked and used as a museum. During a trip to Honolulu for drydock in 1972, the ship was unfortunately lost at sea. Luckily, a new brig (the one you see today) was found in Europe and a crew from Lahaina sailed the ship from Europe to its new home port at the Lahaina Wharf. During the recent hurricane that devastated Kauai, residents feared that the *Carthaginian* would once again be lost at sea, but as you can see, the brig was spared.

Currently operated by the Lahaina Restoration Foundation, the *Carthaginian* museum features audiovisual displays and is an excellent way for visitors to learn about whales and 19th-century whaling life. Though the ship looks large from the outside, the spaces within are rather small and cramped. Don't let that deter you, however; going into the ship is the best way for you to gain an understanding of how the whaling men lived while they were at sea.

Admission: $3.
Open: Daily 9am–4:30pm.

PIONEER INN, 658 Wharf St. Tel. 661-3636.

On October 9, 1901, the Pioneer Hotel Company, Ltd., came to Lahaina to open a hotel and a liquor business. Within a year the Pioneer Hotel was open and operating and began what was to be a very prosperous enterprise. When prohibition was enforced by the missionaries almost two decades after the hotel's opening, business slacked off because a large part of the hotel's business was in the trade of alcohol, especially in the hotel's saloon. At that time, George Freeland, the hotel's general manager, bought out the stockholders and became sole owner of the establishment. The main building of the hotel served the residents of and visitors to Lahaina in its original form up until the mid-1960s when tourism to the island began to grow in leaps. In 1966 a new wing was added to accommodate these new guests, and with the new wing the hotel formed a "C" shape around a lovely courtyard. Most casual observers won't even be able to tell which part of the building is the addition because the architectural details were so closely duplicated.

Today the Pioneer Inn still stands in its original location and is one of the island's least expensive options for accommodations. For decades the Pioneer Inn's saloon has been one of Lahaina's favorite watering holes (which often created problems for those who wished to sleep in the rooms on the upper floors), and I sincerely hope that in spite of the renovation the owners will try to maintain the saloon's festive atmosphere.

BANYAN TREE.

The first time I visited Lahaina I was very young, and my first memories of my experiences on Maui were clouded, but one memory has always remained perfectly clear. It is my vision of this wonderful banyan tree (*Ficus benghalensis*). With branches that cover almost an acre of land and rise to a height of about 50 feet, and about 12 trunks, it's not easy to forget.

A member of the fig family, the tree came all the way from India and was presented as a gift to Lahaina's Smith family in the early 1870s. William Owen Smith was the sheriff of Lahaina, and he planted the tree here in this central location on April 24, 1873. The banyan tree got its name from Hindu traders (banyans) who used to hawk their wares in the shade of the tree's canopy. Throughout history banyans have been gathering places for townspeople and visitors, and the tradition continues in Lahaina. Everything from luaus to children's festivals have taken place here, and the benches scattered among the aerial roots are almost always filled with tired tourists or residents on a lunch break. In the evening, hundreds of mynah birds perch on the tree's branches and serenade visitors with a cacophonous and unrelenting tune.

The banyan tree produces a small red fruit that is edible but not very tasty.

Note: If you have children with you, please try to keep them from swinging on the tree's aerial roots because repeated stress weakens the roots and, eventually, the tree itself.

COURTHOUSE.

On the other side of the banyan tree on Wharf Street is the old courthouse. Like his predecessor, Kamehameha I, Kamehameha III built himself a palace on Maui. It was called *Hale Piula* (or "House with the Tin Roof"), and like the Baldwin Home, it was built of coral bricks. Though the two-story palace was said to be under constant repair, it was reputed to have been very comfortable for guests who were given the "royal" treatment. One visitor's account states that after a long and satisfying lunch, Kamehameha's servants brought an enormous bed into the "dining room," and they all laid down together for an afternoon nap.

In January 1848 the dilapidated palace was restored and converted into a courthouse. It stood in that form for 10 years, serving Maui's judges; in 1858 a meteorological event, known as the Kauaula wind, blew through town and toppled the courthouse. What remained of the courthouse was razed. Rebuilt in 1859, the courthouse building contained a jail (now used by the Lahaina Art Society as a gallery and museum), a post office (in operation since the opening of the new courthouse), and a police station.

FORT WALL.

Adjacent to the courthouse, you'll see the "ruins" of the old Fort Wall. Built between 1831 and 1832 by order of Maui's Governor Hoapili as a show of force against the antics of the wild and woolly whaling men who wintered in Lahaina, the old fort reportedly had 20-foot walls and covered an area of one acre. Every evening a soldier would march upon the ramparts beating a drum as a warning to the sailors. They were to return to their ships or be jailed. The fort housed about 60 fighting men and was well equipped with rifles, bayonets, and swords. The government ordered the destruction of the coral block fort in 1854, and the coral bricks were moved to Prison Street and used in the building of the prison, Hale Pa'ahao. Today, the ruin you'll see is not a real ruin; it is a modern, partial reconstruction. Had the entire fort been rebuilt, considerable damage would have been done to the banyan tree, so restoration authorities opted to reconstruct only a small section of the fort.

MARKETPLACE AND CANAL.

On the other side of Canal Street from Banyan Tree Square there was once an interesting marketplace and canal that breathed life into the daily comings and goings of Old Lahaina. During Lahaina's whaling days there was a canal that ran between the waterfront and Front Street. Whaling men would board their ships' boats, which were loaded with supplies that they used for bartering in the government-regulated canal marketplace. The market, which was probably established before 1833, was covered by a "large straw house" that ran the entire length of the canal. Along each side of the canal, stalls were set up and were rented by the governor to merchants who bid the highest price. Whalers would steer their boats through the canal, bartering for provisions along the way. True to the prohibition of native women from visiting men on the whaling ships, women were not allowed anywhere near or inside the marketplace, in order to ensure that they would not hitch a ride back with the sailors to the whaling ships. If any women were caught in the vicinity of the marketplace, they were fined $1. There were also strict rules of conduct for the merchants. They were not allowed to "overcharge, undersell, wrangle, break bargains, entice, or pursue" a purchaser. If they participated in one or all of these activities, their merchandise was taken from them.

HOLY INNOCENTS' EPISCOPAL CHURCH, 561 Front St. Tel. 661-4202.

Located off Front Street, not far from Prison Street, you'll find a quaint little Episcopal Church. It is particularly important in Hawaii's history because it marked the beginning of the organized Anglican Church in the islands.

In 1861, Reverend Thomas Nettleship Staley was consecrated as the first bishop of Hawaii. The next year, Reverend Staley, along with King Kamehameha IV and a Reverend William R. Scott, arrived in Lahaina and began leading services in a schoolroom on December 14 (12 days after their arrival). Kamehameha had translated the first part of the *Book of Common Prayer*, and Reverend Scott found a residence. Scott remained in residence for one year and was replaced by Archdeacon George Mason. He and his wife headed up a school for boys and a school for girls, respectively.

Much later, in 1874, money for the procurement of the plot of land on the corner of Front and Prison streets was raised, and in 1909 the building of the Church of the Holy Innocents began. (Incidentally, the land upon which the church you see today is built was originally the site of the home of Kamehameha I's daughter.) Today you can visit the church and get a look at some very interesting artwork, done in 1940 by DeLos Blackmar.

The Episcopal Cemetery, where a number of early Mauians are interred, is located on Wainee Street.

WAIOLA (WAINEE) CHURCH, 535 Wainee St. Tel. 661-4349.

The church you see today was built on the original site of the first Hawaiian Christian services, which took place in 1823. The first house of worship was built here in 1832, but it lost its steeple and half of the roof in a windstorm on February 20, 1858. Eventually, with the help of fund-raising Hawaiians, the sale of the old timber, and other donations, the church was rededicated on March 31, 1859. After the reconstruction, the stone church survived until June 28, 1894, when a group of Hawaiians, angered by the overthrow of the monarchy, set fire to it. It was reported by S. E. Bishop that the pastor of the church at the time, Reverend A. Pali, was openly in favor of the overthrow of the monarchy and "had become obnoxious to a majority of his people on account of politics."

It was three years before the church was rebuilt, and though it remained intact for many years, it was once again damaged by fire on October 20, 1947. This time the fire was not deliberately set, and again, the church was reconstructed. Only a few short years later, in January 1951, after termites had made sawdust of the church's foundation, a Kauaula wind blew through town at 80 miles an hour. It literally picked the church up off the ground and tossed it back to earth, where it landed in a heap of rubble and splintered timber. The church you see today was rebuilt and rededicated in April 1953, and it was then that the name was changed from Wainee Church to Waiola Church.

The church's cemetery is probably the most important burial site on the island, for it holds the remains of many of Maui's most prominent leaders. King Kaumuali'i, once the monarch of Kauai, is buried here. Queen Keopuolani and her daughter, Princess Nahi'ena'ena, and Governor Hoapili are all buried near each other. High Chiefess Liliha, granddaughter of King Kahekili, who led a rebellion with 1,000 soldiers while she was governor of Oahu, found her final resting place here. Finally, the Wainee Cemetery is also the burial site of Reverend Richards and some of his young family members.

Note: This cemetery is considered sacred by Hawaiians, so please be respectful while visiting.

MALU'ULUOLELE PARK.

To me, Malu'uluolele Park is one of the most fascinating places in Lahaina—not because of the parking lot, baseball diamond, and tennis and basketball courts, but because of what used to be here. Instead of these sports facilities, try to imagine a pond, and just at the edge of the pond, connected to Front Street by a small bridge, Mokuula, the residence of King Kamehameha III. The royal residence was nothing more than a hut, but it sat on an island surrounded by waters protected by the great dragon/lizard, Kihawahine. The royal family believed that Kihawahine had special powers, so when Kamehameha I took Maui into his kingdom, he claimed the island and the water around it as a sacred spot for Hawaiian royalty. Mokuula was separate from the king's palace, and served as his own private sanctuary. Very few outsiders were allowed the pleasure of visiting the king here.

It is reported that Mokuula was home to many Maui chiefs and three kings, and served as the final resting place for several members of the royal family. Unfortunately, in 1918, the pond was filled in and the island was razed.

DAVID MALO'S HOME.

Born to a man by the name of Aoao and his wife, Heone, in North Kona, Hawaii, David Malo is a prominent figure in the history of Maui. It is thought that he was born around 1793 (a fixed date was never recorded), and as a young man he came to know the high chief Kuakini, brother of Queen Ka'ahumanu. Because of his connection to the royalty of the islands, Malo found himself to be in a position to learn a great deal about the history, traditions, and legends that played such a large role in Hawaiian life. He observed and recorded everything he could learn about Hawaiian lore, and it is thanks to him that we have knowledge of Old Hawaiian traditions. Compiled under the title *Hawaiian Antiquities* (translated from Hawaiian in 1898), his notes have aided in the resurrection of some Hawaiian traditions, like the hula and the art of making kapa cloth. David Malo's home used to stand not far from the corner of Prison Road and Wainee Street.

HALE PA'AHAO (Lahaina Prison), Prison Rd. Tel. 667-1985.

From the early 1830s, prisoners of Lahaina were kept at the old fort (see earlier in this chapter). However, in 1851 the fort doctor reported that the prisoners were increasingly the victims of avoidable illnesses. The inmates were sleeping on the ground, and the doctor believed that if they had a dry place to sleep, they would be less susceptible to illness. No one is absolutely certain if this request was the reason for the building of Hale Pa'ahao, but the construction of the new prison was underway by the end of the year. The land upon which the prison was to be built (which, today, is near the corner of Prison and Wainee streets) was wrested under duress from the Hawaiian who owned it. The superintendent of public works in Honolulu requested that authorities in Lahaina make every effort to "depreciate [the land's] value . . . letting [the owner] know at the same time that if the price is too high the Government will take it anyhow and pay him what they please."

The construction of a wooden prison house was underway in 1852, but it wasn't until 1853 that funds were appropriated for the building of a brick prison wall. When the old fort was demolished in 1854, some of the bricks were used in the wall's construction. The old prison cells were restored in 1959; the rest of the structure was reconstructed in 1988.

HALE ALOHA.

When the Protestants arrived on Maui, they also built churches and meeting houses. The Hale Lai, one of the original Protestant meeting houses, was constructed in the early 1800s for prayer groups, church meetings, and religious schooling. However, by 1855 it was in a state of disrepair. Its most obvious problem was a leaky thatched roof, but when plans were laid to reconstruct the roof using shingles, it was discovered that the roof wasn't Hale Lai's only problem. The walls were structurally unsound, so plans were made to tear down the old meeting house and build a new one.

Protestant leaders decided that the new house should be built in "commemoration of God's causing Lahaina to escape the small pox, while it desolated Oahu in 1853, carrying off some 5,000 or 6,000 of its population." The new meeting house was to be called *Hale Aloha*, or "House of Love." The construction of Hale Aloha was completed in May 1858, almost exactly three years from the date the decision was made to rebuild. By 1860 the government declared Hale Aloha fit to be used as an English school, and it had about 140 students. Two years later it was rented to the Anglican Church to hold the first Anglican services ever in Lahaina. In 1908 the building underwent repairs and became the parish house for Wainee (now Waiola) Church.

MARIA LANAKILA CHURCH, 712 Wainee St. Tel. 661-0552.

The Maria Lanakila Church is significant in that it was built on the same site as Maui's very first Catholic church. The original church was built in 1856. The one you see today is a replica of a larger building that was constructed in 1858.

HONGWANJI MISSION, 551 Wainee St. Tel. 661-0640.

Since 1910, the Hongwanji, members of Lahaina's largest Buddhist sect, have been meeting here on the grounds of the current Hongwanji Mission (erected in 1927). Originally, the Hongwanji built a small temple and started a language school. Today various Buddhist celebrations are held at the Hongwanji Mission.

SEAMEN'S CEMETERY.

The original Seamen's Cemetery was located just adjacent to the one you see today at Wainee Street, between Dickenson and Paneawa streets. In it were buried "the wandering sons of the ocean." Most of the headstones have long since disappeared, but the area is now maintained by the Lahaina Restoration Foundation, so further damage should be prevented.

LAHAINALUNA SCHOOL AND HALE PA'I, 980 Lahainaluna Rd. Tel. 661-8384.

When the Lahainaluna School was formed in the early 1830s, there weren't many books around for the students to read, so an old Ramage printing press was sent to Lahaina from Honolulu in 1833. Not only did it print translations of school texts, but it also produced Hawaii's first newspaper, *Kalama Hawaii* ("Torch of Hawaii"), in 1834. When the school grew, a permanent structure, now known as Hale Pa'i, was constructed to house the printing press. It wasn't long after that the *Grammar of the Hawaiian Language and Dictionary of the Hawaiian Language* was printed.

Whaling men with printing experience originally operated the press. Around 1842, after the school's enrollment had more than quadrupled, students were instructed in the art of bookmaking.

Today, visitors can go inside Hale Pa'i by appointment. Call the above number for information.

WO HING TEMPLE, Front St. Tel. 661-5553.

The Chinese came to Maui by the hundreds to work in the fields of sugarcane and on the pineapple plantations, and in the early 1900s some of them formed what we know as the Wo Hing Society. The Chinese, however, know it as the Chee

Kung Tong, which originated as a secret society hundreds of years ago during the Manchu Dynasty. The Chee Kung Tong was originally founded as a fraternal order in which all members were considered equal and were sworn to protect and aid each other according to need. Eventually, a chapter of the society would be founded everywhere the Chinese congregated in large numbers. The original group that attended the Wo Hing Temple numbered only about 100.

If you're interested in the history of the Chinese as it pertains to Lahaina, head inside and have a look at the display that has been set up by the Lahaina Restoration Foundation. Be sure also to visit the cookhouse, which shows old Thomas Edison movies of Hawaii that he shot in 1898 and 1903, and aptly features cooking displays.

Admission: $2.

Open: Mon–Sat 9am–4pm, Sun 10am–4pm.

U.S. SEAMEN'S HOSPITAL, 1024 Front St. Tel. 661-3262 for information.

No one knows exactly when the U.S. Seamen's Hospital came to be, but there is an early recording by Herman Melville that one of his shipmates on the *Acushnet* died at the hospital in 1843. Built of coral blocks, much like the Baldwin House, the Seamen's Hospital is a two-story building with lanais that run the length of each floor. Some accounts say that the hospital was leased by the United States from King Kamehameha III in an effort to get thousands of ailing American sailors off the streets and beaches. It was common practice at that time for ship captains to simply dump unwanted crew members off in the Hawaiian islands before sailing onward to the Far East where they would do their trading.

In 1865 the Sisters of the Society of the Holy Trinity bought the old hospital for less than $1,000 and opened the St. Cross School for Girls. The school later moved to Honolulu, and it was at that time that the Episcopal minister took up a 30-year residence with his family. In 1908 the old Seamen's Hospital was in horrible shape, and not long after that it became part of the Bishop estate. The Lahaina Restoration Foundation bought the building in 1974 and has restored it to its former glory. Visitors are most welcome.

JODO MISSION.

Heading out of Lahaina in the direction of Kaanapali, you'll pass a sign that reads JESUS COMING SOON. Right after you pass the sign, turn left down Ala Moana Street. As soon as you make the turn, you'll see the pagoda. As you approach the pagoda you'll also see a giant, 3½-ton bronze Buddha. It was placed here in 1968 to commemorate the 100th anniversary of Japanese immigration to Hawaii, and it has the distinct honor of being the largest Buddha in existence outside Japan. This is a perfect spot to get away from hectic Front Street and meditate away from the crowds of sunbathers.

OTHER LAHAINA ATTRACTIONS

HAWAII EXPERIENCE DOMED THEATER, 824 Front St. Tel. 661-8314.

A relatively new addition to the Front Street scene is the Hawaii Experience Domed Theater, where visitors can view a 45-minute film on a 180-degree, 60-foot-long screen. The film, *Hawaii: Islands of the Gods*, is literally a journey around the islands. You'll feel as though you're piloting the helicopter that shot the footage that takes you over the volcano on the Big Island, into canyons, and along the Maui coastline. A bicycle ride down the curvy road from Haleakala gives you the feeling that you're on the bike but have absolutely no control over which way you're turning. You'll go on an underwater scuba-diving expedition, and you'll see a sunset hula show. Basically, the Hawaii Experience Domed Theater is a great place for everyone to explore the hidden wonders of the islands without having to pay the high prices.

Note: If you're prone to motion sickness, you might want to skip this experience. If you want to give it a try anyway, and you begin to feel nauseated during the movie, looking away from the screen momentarily will help. Otherwise, motion sickness bags are provided at every seat in the theater.

Admission: Adults $6.95, children $3.95.

Open: Daily, with hourly showings 10am–10pm.

ATLANTIS SUBMARINES, 665 Front St. Tel. 667-2224.

Don't feel like snorkeling or scuba diving, but you want to see Maui's tropical fish up close? Maybe you've always wanted to take a trip on a working submarine. Well, on Maui, those things are possible. Atlantis Submarines offers the island's only fully submersible submarine rides. A small boat, departing from Lahaina Harbor, takes visitors out to sea where the 65-foot, 80-ton submarine will submerge to a depth of over 100 feet. The vessel will then glide above reef formations, out of which colorful fish and other sea creatures will swim to meet the submarine. Most of the dives are made during the daylight hours, but there is also a twilight trip, which would give those who prefer to snorkel or scuba dive during the day the opportunity to view sea life at a time when most snorkelers and scuba divers are heading out of the water. There are two options for dive packages. The first, and more expensive one, the full Odyssey tour, includes a free whale-watch pass and scuba divers swimming outside the submarine pointing out various sea life. The second tour is without the whale-watch pass and the scuba divers.

To make your reservations, call ahead, or head over to the Atlantis office in the Pioneer Inn Arcade during your visit to Lahaina town. The line is almost always long, and the trip takes about 2 hours, so you should be prepared to give this excursion a morning or an afternoon.

Admission: Full Odyssey tour $79 adults, $39 children 12 and under (must be at least 3 feet tall); regular tour $59 adults, $29 children.

Open: Two dives daily between 9am and 6pm.

NAUTILUS SEMI-SUBMERSIBLE, 129 Lahainaluna Rd. Tel. 667-2133.

If you're a little nervous about diving 150 feet in a submarine, but still want to feel like you're swimming with the fish, perhaps Nautilus Semi-Submersible is more your speed. Though the Nautilus vessels don't submerge entirely, they do have underwater viewing cabins. The hour-long tours of reef areas are narrated, and a professional diver spends time outside the vessel searching for interesting marine life. Nautilus is also a good choice if your budget is tight—it's less expensive than a trip with Atlantis.

Admission: $39.95 adults; $19.95 children 6–12; 5 and under free.

NEAR LAHAINA

About 5 miles outside Lahaina, heading toward Central Maui, is Olowalu, a small town with a big history. It's so small, in fact, that if you blink while you're driving by you might miss it. Your first indication that you're approaching the site of the famed Olowalu Massacre will be a slight drop in the speed limit. Captain Metcalf was responsible for the clash that resulted in the massacre here, and though it was a short-lived incident, the effect it had on the history of the Hawaiian islands was profound (for more information, see "History" in Chapter 1).

To view the petroglyphs, park in the lot in front of Chez Paul and the general store, and head around the back of the restaurant where you'll find a dirt pathway leading to an old wooden stairway. It's quite a hike, so be prepared. Before you make the hike you should try to find someone who knows the way because there are two paths that you can take, but only one leads to the petroglyphs.

LAHAINA SHOPPING

Shopping on Maui is not exactly haute couture—it's mainly limited to malls and shopping centers—but some island towns do have interesting little boutiques and art galleries. Lahaina is one of those towns.

Malls and Shopping Centers

The **Lahaina Cannery Mall** (tel. 661-5304; open 9am–9pm) is located just outside of Lahaina, in the direction of Kaanapali. There you'll find everything from sundries to shoes and sunglasses. ABC Discount Stores (tel. 661-5370) and Longs Drug Stores (tel. 661-4384) are where you'll find all your necessities, plus a few more unexpected items, like Kona coffee and chocolate-covered macadamia nuts to take (or send) home. Alexia Natural Fashions (tel. 661-4110) and Blue Ginger Designs (tel. 667-5433) are where you'll find exclusively designed, 100% cotton batik fashions. There's a branch of Superwhale Children's Boutiques (tel. 661-3424) here. Superwhale specializes in aloha wear and outrageous sportswear for children of all ages. Speaking of kids, they'll love Kite Fantasy (tel. 661-4766). Hobie Hawaii (tel. 661-5777) has beach and sportswear for the whole family. Lahaina Printsellers Ltd. (tel. 667-7843) and Lahaina Scrimshaw (tel. 661-3971) are also represented at the Cannery Mall.

Lahaina Center, at 900 Front Street, on the western edge of Lahaina, is home to the famous Hilo Hattie's (tel. 661-8457), where you can get aloha print shirts, dresses, sportswear, "funwear," and much more. If you're staying in one of the resorts and don't have a car, never fear—Hilo Hattie's will pick you up and shuttle you to the store. And when you get there, you'll get a shell lei and a glass of pineapple juice. If you're a collector of Swatch watches, you'll love Watch-N-See (tel. 661-1776). Here you'll find Swatches in every imaginable shape, size, and variety, and the shopkeeper will be happy to take you on a grand tour of them all.

The **Wharf Cinema Center** (658 Front St.; open 9am to 10pm) is, as its name suggests, where you'll find many of Maui's first-run movies, but it's also a great place to do some shopping, snacking, and people watching. Earth and Company (tel. 667-9342), a sponsor of Greenpeace Hawaii, is an "environmentally aware" gift shop selling posters, jewelry, and T-shirts. Seegerpeople (tel. 661-1084) offers an interesting way to document your Hawaiian vacation. They'll make three-dimensional photographs of you and your family (it's not cheap, however) that are like nothing you've ever seen before. Even if you don't feel like having your picture made, you should stop in and admire their work. I love the Whaler's Book Shoppe (tel. 667-9544). Tucked away in a back corner of the Wharf Cinema Center, it's a combination bookstore/cafe where you can shop for books, then buy a cup of coffee and sit quietly outside the shop perusing your purchases. Whaler's Book Shoppe has a good collection of Hawaiiana. Tropical Artware (tel. 667-7100) is a great place to pick up some unique jewelry (including, but not limited to, ear cuffs and toe rings). They also carry basketware and ceramics.

Not far down Front Street (heading in the direction of Maalaea) you'll also find the **Lahaina Marketplace,** open from 9am to 9pm daily. Mauians sell their wares from outdoor carts while tourists browse and snack. It's a good place to pick up an inexpensive souvenir for someone back home.

Still farther down Front Street is a shopping complex known as **505 Front Street.** There aren't nearly as many shops at 505 as there are in the Wharf Cinema Center, but there are a couple worth stopping in before or after lunch at the Old Lahaina Cafe or Juicy's Healthy Food Deli (for more information on both restaurants, see Chapter 6). At Suite #107, you'll find Foreign Intrigue (tel. 667-4004), a new shop that features unique furniture (folding teak chairs, painted cat benches), clothing (batik silk sarongs), gift items, and artwork. Most of the items are imported from Indonesia, but some are imported from Thailand and Hong Kong. Posters Unlimited (tel. 667-7720) carries a huge variety of posters, and Lei Spa (tel. 661-1178), just across the way from Posters Unlimited, has a wide variety of fragrant soaps and a nice selection of women's clothing. Most of the shops at 505 Front Street are open Monday through Saturday from 9am to 9pm, and from 10am to 5pm on Sunday.

Front Street Shopping

Front Street in Lahaina is a shopper's wonderland. It's not a particularly long street, but on it you'll find everything from tourist T-shirt shops to exquisite art galleries.

In addition to the galleries listed here, try the following shops: Crazy Shirts (865 Front St., tel. 661-4775), with its original design T-shirts, is a step above your average tourist T-shirt shop and so are the prices. Tropical Blues at 754 Front Street (tel. 667-4008) is another good place to find unique T-shirts. The ones you'll find here have been designed by the owners. They also carry some interesting pieces of costume jewelry made by artists from all over the country. Whalers Locker at 780 Front Street (tel. 661-3775) is a "museum of a shop" with collectors' items, including netsuke figurines and Ni'ihau shell leis. One of Lahaina's oldest shops is The Whaler Ltd., at 866 Front Street (tel. 661-4592). Everything in The Whaler has a nautical theme—from jewelry and glasswork to sculpture and scrimshaw.

DAVID LEE GALLERIES, 712 Front Street. Tel. 667-7740.

David Lee Galleries features the stunning works of David Lee, a Chinese artist who has mastered the art of painting with natural powder colors on silk. His unique work has a luminescent quality. Even if you're not shopping, you should stop in and have a look.

DYANSEN GALLERY, 844 Front St. Tel. 661-2055.

Dyansen features the work of LeRoya Neiman, Billy D. Williams, and the Erte sculpture collection. High wall relief sculptures by Bill Mack are also displayed.

GALERIE LASSEN, 844 Front St., Suite 101. Tel. 667-7707.

Here you'll find the work of local artist Christian Riese Lassen as well as works by Richard Stiers, Red Skelton, Ting and Lu Hong, and Sassone.

HANSON GALLERIES, 839 Front St. Tel. 661-0764.

You've probably seen a branch of Hanson Galleries somewhere in your travels around the country. Hanson is the largest privately owned art gallery in the United States, and they feature the work of Claude Pissaro, Mark Kostabi, Peter Max, and Maui artist Pierre Resta.

LAHAINA GALLERIES, 728 Front St. Tel. 667-2152.

Here you'll get an up-close look at the work of Robert Lyn Nelson, who originated two- and three-worlds imagery (you'll understand what I mean when you see it), as well as paintings by (among others) the very talented Andrea Smith and Guy Buffet. Many of the artists represented at Lahaina Galleries are world renowned.

MADALINE MICHAELS GALLERY, 713 Front St. Tel. 661-4198.

Specializing in three-dimensional artwork, Madaline Michaels Gallery shows the work of notables such as Mexican sculptor Sergio Bustamente. His work is so bright and colorful that you won't soon forget it. Others represented are Todd Warner, Reinhart, Michael Amman, Jack Dowd, Roark Garley, and Steven Smeltzer. You simply must stop at Madaline Michaels.

MARTIN LAWRENCE GALLERY, 126 Lahainaluna Rd. Tel. 661-1788.

At Martin Lawrence you'll see the modern works of Mark King, Michele Delacroix, Linnea Pergola, Andy Warhol, Keith Haring, Hiro Yamagata, and Susan Rios.

OLD JAIL GALLERY, 649 Wharf St. Tel. 661-0111.

Located adjacent to the banyan tree is the gallery that many of Maui's undiscovered artists call home. There you'll find works in a variety of media—some are even displayed behind bars.

THE ROYAL ART GALLERY, 752 Front St. Tel. 667-1982.

The Royal Art Gallery features original sculpture and painting by international artists such as Wai Ming, Michael David Ward, Richard Stiers, and Carolyn Young.

SOUTH SEAS TRADING POST, 851 Front St. Tel. 661-3168.

South Seas Trading Post is, in my opinion, more of a gallery than a "shop." It's also one of my favorites. Here you'll find all sorts of treasures from the South Pacific, including masks, jewelry, wall hangings, and puppets. Much of the work is imported from Borneo, Papua New Guinea, Thailand, and Kashmir.

VILLAGE GALLERIES, 120 Dickenson St. Tel. 661-4402.

Just off Front Street you'll find Village Galleries, my favorite art gallery in Lahaina. It displays the work of Hawaii's finest artists. Names you'll learn to recognize are George Allan, Macario Pascual, and Richard Nelson.

WYLAND GALLERIES, 711 Front St. Tel. 667-2285.

At Wyland Galleries you'll find the work of "America's leading environmental artists," as well as bronze sculptures by Dale Evers. Wyland has two other galleries in Lahaina, one at 697 Front Street, and the other at 136 Dickenson Street. They all feature the works of different artists.

LAHAINA EVENING ENTERTAINMENT

OLD LAHAINA LUAU, 505 Front St. Tel. 667-1998.

Unanimously the best luau on Maui's west side (perhaps on the whole island), the Old Lahaina Luau takes place right on the beach behind the shopping complex at 505 Front Street.

When you arrive you'll be given a shell lei greeting, a tropical drink, and you'll be escorted to your seat. You may choose in advance whether to sit on mats in the more traditional fashion or to be seated at a table. Photographers mingle during the Hawaiian crafts and lei-making demonstrations, so if you forget your camera you won't have to worry—just enjoy yourself. The feast is served buffet style, and you'll be treated to a traditional imu (in-ground oven) ceremony and a taste of kalua pig. Poke, lomi lomi, and haupia cake are among the traditional Hawaiian offerings for dinner, but if those menu items don't strike your fancy, you can always have teriyaki beef, fried rice, salad, and fresh fruit. There is an open bar all evening, and after dinner authentically attired Hawaiian men and women perform traditional hulas, accompanied by chanting and music performed with ancient-style instruments. The price of admission includes open bar, all-you-can-eat buffet, flower lei, and the hula performance.

Tickets: $56 for adults, $28 for children ages 2 to 12.

FRIDAY NIGHT IS ART NIGHT.

Every Friday night from 7 to 9pm, several of Lahaina's art galleries stay open late, so visitors and locals alike can gather to admire the works of local and international artists. Refreshments may be provided by individual galleries, and there is often live entertainment. Check the paper or call the Lahaina Town Action Committee (tel. 808/667-9175) for more information on what's happening while you're in town.

BLUE TROPIX, 900 Front St., Bldg. A202. Tel. 667-5309.

Blue Tropix features dance music with a deejay weeknights, and frequently hosts live entertainment like The Cosmetics, men in drag who pass themselves off as celebrity look-alikes. There's usually a $5 cover after 9pm. (See Chapter 6 for full restaurant listing.) Open Monday through Saturday from 6pm to 2am.

MOOSE MCGILLYCUDDY'S, 844 Front St. Tel. 667-7758.

Moose McGillycuddy's regularly features live rock bands and attracts a young crowd. Cover charge varies according to performers but is usually only $2 or $3. Open nightly from 9:30pm to 1:30am.

STUDIO 505, 505 Front St. Tel. 661-1505.
Thursday nights Studio 505 comes alive with salsa music. Friday and Saturday you'll find them spinning disco tunes, and Sunday and Monday nights might feature reggae. Sometimes there's a Teen Disco on Saturday nights from 6:30 to 9:30pm. Cover charges range from $2 to $5 or more. Open daily from 10pm to 2am.

EN ROUTE FROM LAHAINA TO KAANAPALI

As a point of interest, along Honoapiilani Highway as you drive from Lahaina to Kaanapali, you'll pass the old site of the Royal Coconut Grove of Mala. Flanking both sides of the highway, the coconut grove was originally planted in 1827 by Hoapili Wahine, the wife of Governor Hoapili. Reverend William Richards suggested that she plant the coconut grove on her empty plot of land, but Hoapili didn't see the point—she knew she wouldn't live to see the trees grow to full maturity. He pointed out that her grandchildren would be able to enjoy them when they became adults. Hoapili Wahine was convinced and immediately sent one of her men to the Big Island for a load of coconuts. When he returned, they proceeded to plant what was to become the Royal Coconut Grove of Maui.

KAANAPALI

Located only a few miles west of Lahaina, just off Honoapiilani Highway, is the Kaanapali Resort area. It's hard to believe that this area, with its glitzy, high-class resorts and beautiful white-sand beaches offering unparalleled views of neighboring Molokai and Lanai islands, was once a sugar plantation owned and operated by the Pioneer Mill Company. At Black Rock, nearby the Sheraton-Maui, was a wharf from which sugar, molasses, canned pineapple, fuel, and various other products were shipped. Nearby there were two enormous storage tanks, one for molasses, the other for fuel, a sugar warehouse, a small grouping of homes for the wharf employees, and a plant whose purpose was to turn pineapple cores and skins into cattle feed. Just mauka of the wharf and the sugar plantations was an old racetrack, used only on weekends and holidays. It was also Maui's first commercial airport.

Today, the warehouses, fuel and molasses tanks, and the wharf are gone, and in their places stand some of the island's most beautiful hotels and golf courses.

To get around the Kaanapali Resort, you can hitch a ride on the Free Kaanapali Resort Trolley. It services all hotels and runs all day. Pickup points are the Kaanapali Villas, the Royal Lahaina, the Sheraton/Kaanapali Beach Hotel, the Marriott/the Hyatt, and the Kaanapali Golf Course.

If you'd rather leave your car parked in Lahaina Center, there are other ways for you to get to Kaanapali from Front Street. If you're on a budget, you should probably opt for the **Lahaina Express,** which shuttles visitors from its stop at the Wharf Cinema Center to hotels in the Kaanapali Resort beginning at 9:34am. It runs approximately every 45 minutes and makes its last trip from Whalers Village in the Kaanapali Resort area at 9:47pm, arriving at the Wharf Cinema Center at about 10pm.

If you'd like a bit of history as you're making the trip and are willing to spend a little money to get it, I'd recommend that you take the **Lahaina–Kaanapali & Pacific Railroad** (tel. 661-0089), otherwise known as the Sugar Cane Train. Children especially love the songs and stories of the conductor as they take the 12-mile journey on a fully reconstructed turn-of-the-century train. The original locomotive was used to transport sugarcane from sugar plantations to the ships anchored off Kaanapali Beach. The one-way trip is approximately 25 minutes. Prices are $8 for adults, $4 for children, one way; $12 for adults, and $6 for children, round-trip. If you want to combine your round-trip train ride with a visit to the Hawaii Experience Domed Theater, you can buy a combination ticket for $16 adults, $8.25 children. A combination ticket that allows admission to the Baldwin House, the Wo Hing Temple, and the *Carthaginian,* is $13.50 for adults, $6 for children.

KAANAPALI ATTRACTIONS

Other than the beaches and golf courses (see later in this chapter for details), there are very few real attractions in the Kaanapali Resort area. One interesting place to visit is the **Whale Center of the Pacific** (tel. 661-5992), located in Whalers Village at the center of the Kaanapali Resort. It's a great place to stop during a shopping spree in Whalers Village, and if you're traveling with children, they'll love it. Admission is by donation, and it's open daily from 9:30am to 10pm. Don't skip this museum just because you might already have been to the *Brig Carthaginian*—the two museums are very different. Though the Whale Center, like the *Brig Carthaginian,* focuses on the whaling industry and whaling life, it takes a different approach by displaying exhibits about the life and plight of the whale.

Special Hotel Attractions

Even if you're not a guest at the ✪ **Hyatt Regency Maui** (200 Nohea Kai Dr.), you should stop in during the day to have a look at this beautiful $80-million resort complex. When you walk through the hotel's entrance you might think that you've entered an unusual, open-air museum. That's because the Hyatt is home to an incredible Asian and Pacific art collection. The hotel's lush tropical gardens cover 18 beautifully maintained acres dotted with waterfalls and tropical fish pools. The grounds also function as a wildlife preserve and home to some extraordinary exotic birds—there are even some penguins. A half-acre swimming pool winds through streams, rock formations, and waterfalls, and is crossed by a rope bridge. In addition, there are 19 different shops on the hotel's lobby level.

If you have an interest in astronomy and know you're going to be near Kaanapali in the evening, make a reservation for the Hyatt's "Tour of the Stars," at which you will get to use the hotel's new computerized telescope that has the capacity to chart and identify over 1,000 different celestial objects. As the viewer focuses on a particular object or star, a recorded message describes its attributes. The program is offered six nights a week, and costs $10.40. Call 661-1234 for viewing times and more information.

The **Westin Maui** (2365 Kaanapali Pkwy.) is another must-see hotel. Like the Hyatt, the Westin also has an exquisite art collection, glorious gardens, and brilliantly colored birds. You can walk through the gardens on well-maintained pathways, and even stand behind a waterfall. The pool here is double the size of the one at the Hyatt, and instead of stargazing, here you can take a wildlife tour led by the hotel's wildlife ranger. Call 667-2525 for more information.

If you're interested in a little bit of history, head over to the **Sheraton Maui Hotel.** There you'll find a lava promontory known as Black Rock. It is believed to be the jumping-off place for the souls of Hawaii's dead, and it also has been a place from which an ancient Hawaiian king or chief would jump to prove himself to his army. Every evening, a young man employed by the Sheraton Maui Hotel makes the jump. It begins with the blowing of a conch shell, is followed by the lighting of the torches along the path, and culminates in a spectacular dive. If the Sheraton has completed renovations by the time you visit, you should head over to Black Rock to watch the jump.

KAANAPALI SHOPPING

Though there are scores of shops in hotel lobbies in the Kaanapali Resort, the most popular shopping area is **Whalers Village,** located between the Westin and the Whaler Condominium complex. It can be reached via the Kaanapali Parkway, or by way of the pathway that runs the length of the beach in front of the hotels. There are all kinds of shops located here—you'll find everything from books and sundries to scrimshaw and silks. A free hula show is staged in Whalers Village every Wednesday and Sunday at 1pm.

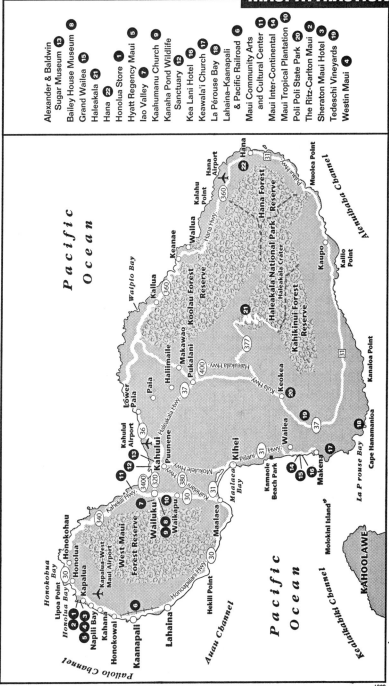

MAUI ATTRACTIONS

Alexander & Baldwin Sugar Museum **13**
Bailey House Museum **8**
Grand Wailea **15**
Haleakala **21**
Hana **22**
Honolua Store **1**
Hyatt Regency Maui **5**
Iao Valley **7**
Kaahumanu Church **9**
Kanaha Pond Wildlife Sanctuary **12**
Kea Lani Hotel **16**
Keawala'i Church **17**
La Pérouse Bay **18**
Lahaina-Kaanapali & Pacific Railroad **6**
Maui Community Arts and Cultural Center **11**
Maui Inter-Continental **14**
Maui Tropical Plantation **10**
Poli Poli State Park **20**
The Ritz-Carlton Maui **2**
Sheraton Maui Hotel **3**
Tedeschi Vineyards **19**
Westin Maui **4**

1969

Airport ✈

There's a small branch of Waldenbooks on the lower level, and there is also an ABC store where you can get everything from tacky souvenirs to sodas and snacks. Next door to ABC is Whalers Fine Wines & Spirits in case you want to surprise someone with a nice bottle of wine or champagne one evening.

One of my favorite shops here is Silks Kaanapali, where you can get beautiful, unique, handpainted silk clothing and accessories. The Dolphin Gallery showcases some fine jewelry, and so do Jessica's Gems, the Pearl Factory, Maui Divers, and Classique Designs of Maui.

If you are in the market for a unique (and expensive) T-shirt or beachwear for yourself or the kids, try Crazy Shirts. Hobie Sports and Sgt. Leisure also carry men's and women's apparel, and a special shop for children is the Superwhale Children's Boutique (parents will go wild in Superwhale).

Designer items more your speed? Well, Benetton, Esprit, and Louis Vuitton are all represented here. Sea & Shell Gallery has some wonderful, locally handcrafted jewelry, as well as some interesting paintings. Ka Honu Gift Gallery features Hawaiian arts and crafts (here you can get koa-wood bowls, pottery, and Hawaiian dolls and jewelry), and so does the Nohea Gallery. Lahaina Printsellers is popular island-wide for their antique maps and prints.

A unique addition to Whalers Village is the popular Endangered Species Store, where you can buy all kinds of things related to the world's endangered species. T-shirts are big sellers, but there are also beautiful animal figurines, as well as posters, crystals, tote bags, and books.

Note: You can ride the Kaanapali Resort Trolley to Whalers Village beginning around 7:30am and ending at 11pm.

KAANAPALI EVENING ENTERTAINMENT

Nightlife in Kaanapali is alive and well. If you're a bar fly, all of the major hotels have good bars, and several offer traditional luaus several evenings during the week. Remember that you must make reservations in advance to attend one of the following luaus.

THE MAUI MARRIOTT LUAU, 100 Nohea Kai Dr. Tel. 667-1200.

At the Marriott's beachside luau you'll receive a shell lei greeting when you arrive, and from that point on you'll have access to the open bar. If you've got the stamina, you can drink Mai Tais all night long. Before dinner you'll be able to participate (or just watch others participate) in a variety of traditional Hawaiian crafts and games. The menu consists of kalua pig (baked in the traditional imu), teriyaki beef steak, Polynesian sweet and sour chicken, fresh mahi mahi in lemon butter, fried rice, Hawaiian baked sweet potatoes, stir-fry vegetables, poi, papaya, pineapple, lomi lomi salmon, fresh baked poi rolls, haupia, and more. The after-dinner show is one of the island's most authentic and features Hawaiian fire dancers and traditional hula dancing. The luau begins at 5pm and ends at 8pm. Nationally recognized, the Marriott's luau is one of the island's best.

Prices: $45 adults; $20 children 5–12; under 5 free.

DRUMS OF THE PACIFIC, in the Hyatt Regency Maui, 200 Nohea Kai Dr. Tel. 661-1234.

The Hyatt Regency offers its own version of the traditional Hawaiian luau. Like the others, the Hyatt offers an open bar and an all-you-can-eat traditional luau buffet, featuring Hawaiian specialties and an imu ceremony. After dinner you'll be taken on a tour of the Polynesian islands as dancers perform authentic dances to the music of Samoa, New Zealand, Fiji, Tahiti, and Hawaii. The luau seating is Monday through Wednesday, Friday, and Saturday at 5:30pm; the cocktail seating is at 6:45pm. The show begins at 7pm.

Prices: Luau seating $44 adults; $36 children 6–12; 5 and under free. Cocktail seating (does not include dinner) $26 adults; $23 persons 20 and under.

SHERATON MAUI HOTEL LUAU, 2605 Kaanapali Pkwy. Tel. 661-0031.
The Sheraton Maui has an excellent luau. Included in the cost of your ticket is a traditional lei greeting, open bar, and an all-you-can-eat buffet of Polynesian cuisine, including poi, pineapple chicken, kalua pig, island fish, and teriyaki steak. The after-dinner show features a fire-knife dance and the songs and dances of Hawaii, Tahiti, New Zealand, and Samoa. The three-hour luau takes place every Monday through Saturday and begins at 5pm.
Prices: $42 adults, $19 children 6–12.

ROYAL LAHAINA LUAU, 2780 Kekaa Dr. Tel. 661-3611.
Second only to the Marriott Luau, the Royal Lahaina Luau is offered seven nights a week in the hotel's luau gardens. The festivities begin with sunset cocktails. The entertainment begins with the traditional imu ceremony and a Hawaiian menu class (among other things). The feast is presented buffet style, and tables are laid with salads, teriyaki beef, pineapple chicken, island fish, and kalua pig. The live show tells the history of the Hawaiian islands through traditional hula song and dance. September through April the seating is at 5:30pm; May through August it's at 6pm.
Prices: $42 adults; $21 children 12 and under.

Hotel Entertainment

My personal favorite nightspot is the **Makai Bar** in the Maui Marriott. Here you can sit and watch the sun fall below the horizon (and catch a glimpse of the Marriott's Luau) while sipping a tropical drink, munching on pupus, and listening to live entertainment. The Marriott's **Lobby Bar** features karaoke singing several nights a week and a comedy club ($12 cover) on Sunday evenings. At the **Royal Terrace Lounge** in the Royal Lahaina Resort, various entertainers perform several evenings a week from 7 to 10pm (call 661-3611 for current schedules). The **Garden Bar** at the Westin also frequently offers live entertainment throughout the week; call 667-2525 for details.

KAPALUA

Today, Kapalua is a beautiful oceanfront resort area with spectacular hotels, chal-lenging golf courses, and well-maintained gardens, but it wasn't always so. In fact, the Kapalua area has an interesting history. It began as a Honolua Ranch with Henry P. Baldwin as its owner. By the late 1800s he had purchased most of the ranch, which was being managed by Richard Searle and used for cattle grazing and coffee growing. In 1911, Baldwin hired D. T. Fleming to run the ranch, and since Fleming had previously been cultivating pineapple in Haiku, he began planting pine-apple at Honolua Ranch. H. P. Baldwin died that same year, and his son, Alexander Baldwin, took over. In 1924 Alexander Baldwin renamed his father's company Baldwin Packers, Ltd.; by 1929 pineapple production had grown to more than eight times that of cattle farming—2,500 acres were planted with pineapple while only 300 were being used for cattle raising. By 1946 cattle ranching had come to a standstill. Pineapple was cultivated at Honolua and then transported by truck to waiting trains that would take the pineapple to the Lahaina Cannery to be canned. Later it was sent to Honolulu and then to the U.S. mainland. In 1962 Baldwin Packers merged with the Maui Pineapple Company and the Lahaina Cannery shut down as the canning operation was moved to Kahului.
While pineapple was the major industry in Kapalua, coffee cultivation continued (without much success) until the late 1920s or early 1930s. Fleming also recognized the medicinal potential of aloe and planted 10 acres for the purpose of making a skin cream. Unfortunately, he never lived to see the product gain in popularity. Of course aloe is used today in every manner and form—from soaps to lotions to shampoos. Fleming didn't stop with coffee beans and aloe; he also planted

watermelon and mango, avocado, citrus, lychee, and macadamia-nut trees between 1938 and 1940. Since the orchards didn't yield much profit compared to the pineapple plantation, they were eventually removed.

Filipino, Hawaiian, and Japanese plantation workers lived in camps along the shoreline (and a bit farther inland), and within each camp a tremendous sense of community developed. Together, they fished, swam, raised their own produce, and played on sports teams. Since the company provided them with all the provisions they needed, there was no need to leave the plantation.

In 1971 Maui Land & Pineapple Company announced plans to begin building the Kapalua Resort. Today, it is home to the Kapalua Bay Hotel & Villas and the Ritz-Carlton Hotel, but pineapple production continues. The resort covers less than 1,000 of the 23,000 acres owned by Maui Land & Pineapple Company.

Other than sporting activities and exceptional beaches, there aren't many tourist attractions in the Kapalua Resort. You can visit the old **Honolua Store** (Honokahua Road) where plantation workers used to go for supplies—today its gift shop and small grocery store attract resort guests. **The Ritz-Carlton** (One Ritz-Carlton Drive) displays a wonderful collection of local art in its public spaces, and it's worth going inside for a look if you're in the area. The **Kapalua Bay Hotel** (One Bay Drive) also has the work of some local artists, including Andrea Smith, and displays some feather leis in the lobby.

The Kapalua Shops on Kapalua Drive are within walking distance of the Kapalua Bay, and they include (among others) a branch of the South Seas Trading Post (tel. 669-1249); Cardin's (tel. 669-6331) and Haimoff & Haimoff (tel. 669-5213), both fine jewelry stores; a branch of the Lahaina Gallery (tel. 669-0202); and Mandalay (tel. 669-6170), which sells designer silks and cottons. The Market Cafe (see Chapter 6 for full listing), also in the Kapalua Shops, is a nice place for a light lunch.

2. CENTRAL & SOUTH MAUI

KAHULUI

Of all Maui's towns, Kahului is the one that has been most beaten and ravaged by the progress of time. It witnessed the early battles of Ka'ahumanu, the arrival of the Europeans, the development of the sugar and pineapple industries, and the coming of America's favorite fast-food restaurants. Today Kahului is home to over one-third of all Mauians, the airport, and most of the island's shopping malls.

KAHULUI ATTRACTIONS

It might be something of a miracle that, in spite of all its shortcomings, within this small city exists **Kanaha Pond Wildlife Sanctuary,** home to the Hawaiian stilt (ae'o). Located at the junction of Route 36 and Route 37, the pond and wildlife sanctuary are open to the public daily, and there is no admission charge. It's just you and the birds out there. You might see some ducks and geese, but what you're really looking for is a glimpse of the ae'o, a medium-sized bird with a black back, white underside, and long, thin, hot-pink legs. There is an observation deck off Route 37.

The only other tourist attraction near Kahului (actually in Puunene) is the **Alexander & Baldwin Sugar Museum** at 3957 Hansen Rd. (tel. 871-8058), next door to a still-operational mill. The museum is small but interesting, and it documents some of the history of the sugar industry on Maui. The building that currently houses the museum was once the home of the mill's superintendent. You'l hear the recorded sounds of sugar production as you walk through, and you'll see photo murals of the early plantation workers and machinery. Some museum artifacts date all the way back to the late 1870s. There are scale models and a working model of factory machinery. Children love this place. When you've finished going through the exhibits, have a look around the museum shop, which sells items relating to sugar production and plantation life. Admission is $3 for adults, $1.50 for children ages 6 to 17, free for children under 6. The museum is open Monday through Saturday from 9:30am to 4:30pm.

KAHULUI SHOPPING

Kahului's **Kaahumanu Center** (275 Kaahumanu Ave.), slated to be Maui's largest shopping mall, was under expansion and renovation at the time of publication, but it should be completed by the time you read this. Currently it's just a small mall with only a few interesting shops, but I've been told that it will feature a six-plex theater, a two-level department store, a food court with 10 restaurants, and about 50 new specialty stores. The **Maui Mall** at 52 Kaahumanu Ave. is an open-air shopping center with frequent outdoor entertainment and a variety of interesting shops.

KAHULUI EVENING ENTERTAINMENT

If you happen to be in Kahului in the late afternoon or early evening and are looking for a place to relax, try checking with **Maui Coffee Roasters** at 444 Hana Hwy. (tel. 877-2877) to see what they've got scheduled for the evening. They sponsor a British High Tea with an accompanying harpist from 3:30 to 5:30pm on Thursdays, and they also frequently have live entertainment on Fridays and Saturdays from 4 to 6pm. **Sir Wilfred's** (tel. 877-3711) in the Maui Mall, usually has some live entertainment on Friday evenings and on Sunday afternoons. For specifics on these and other nightlife options, check *Maui Scene*, the Thursday supplement to the *Maui News*.

MAUI COMMUNITY ARTS & CULTURAL CENTER, Kahului Beach Rd. Tel. 871-8422.
Until now, Maui has been without a performing arts venue. Performing arts groups have used shopping malls and school gyms as their stages. Artists and the people of Maui alike had to endure uncomfortable facilities with no rehearsal studios, poor lighting, and poor acoustics. They won't have to suffer any longer. The Maui Community Arts & Cultural Center opened as we go to press, and it promises to be a very fine arts and cultural events center. The $24-million cultural center houses a 1,200 seat tri-level theater, 30-seat studio theater, exhibition gallery, community rehearsal hall, the Maui Academy of Performing Arts building, the Maui Community Theater building, and classrooms. There is also an outdoor amphitheater. Since it is a nonprofit organization, the whole community came together to raise money for its completion. Individuals purchased theater seats for $1,000, and others who couldn't afford such a large gift raised money with bake sales and other fund-raising activities. Even the children of Maui were instrumental in securing funds for the project. The County of Maui donated the 12 acres upon which the center was constructed.
The center's main theater is capable of hosting major performing arts groups and theater companies from around the world. Its stage, lighting, and sound systems are advanced enough to accommodate the likes of the San Francisco Ballet or a major Broadway production. Equally important, the theater is not so large that small groups will be lost on the stage. No seat is more than 100 feet from the stage. The open-air amphitheater is a versatile facility, capable of hosting outdoor concerts with audiences as large as 4,000 people. In addition to musical and theatrical performances, the center will provide Maui with a 4,000-square-foot noncommercial exhibition space with climate-control and security systems, which means that traveling

exhibitions that could once only be seen on Oahu can now be seen on Maui as well.

Local groups that will have use of the center are the Maui Philharmonic Society, Maui Community College, Maui Academy of Performing Arts, Maui Symphony Orchestra, Maui Community Theater, Hui No'eau Visual Arts Center, hula halaus, and other various cultural organizations.

Later additions to the center will include a 250-seat support theater known as "The Black Box" for experimental theater, a gift shop, and a cafe. The Maui Community Arts & Cultural Center is a welcome addition to island life. Call to see what is scheduled while you're on Maui.

WAILUKU & ENVIRONS

Even though today Wailuku is a bit run-down and ramshackle, it remains one of Maui's most historic towns. For one thing, it was, as its name suggests (*wai* meaning "blood," *luku* meaning "massacre") the site of one of the bloodiest battles ever fought on Maui.

You'll probably be tempted to drive right by Wailuku on your way to the Bailey House Museum or the Iao Needle, but don't. Stop at Ka'ahumanu Church and try to imagine what Wailuku was like in the 1800s, then head over to Main Street for some shopping in the antique stores. There are also some great lunch spots here (see Chapter 6 for listings).

WAILUKU ATTRACTIONS

KA'AHUMANU CHURCH, High St. Tel. 244-5189.

Named for Queen Ka'ahumanu, one of Hawaii's most powerful and influential queens, Ka'ahumanu Church is the oldest stone church on Maui. The first structure that was built on this site was temporary, and when Ka'ahumanu attended services in that temporary church (she was at the forefront of the Hawaiian conversion to Christianity), she asked that when a new church was built, it be named for her. Her wish was granted with the building of a more permanent adobe structure on this site. The adobe church was replaced in 1837 by a large stone church. The one you see today is only part of the original stone church, and it was restored in 1975. You probably won't be able to go inside during the week, but it's worth stopping to have a look around.

BAILEY HOUSE MUSEUM, 2375-A Main St. Tel. 244-3326.

In the early 1820s American Protestant missionaries began settling in the Hawaiian islands so that they might begin to "civilize" the native Hawaiian population by teaching them to read and write. They wanted to save the souls of the Hawaiian people with Christian values, and the only way to do that was to educate them so they could learn to read the Bible. They established schools for adults and children, and created an alphabet for the Hawaiian language, so they could translate the Bible into Hawaiian.

In 1837 the Wailuku Female Seminary was established on Maui so that Hawaiian women would learn the virtue of a good Christian home and family. The seminary founders, Reverend Jonathan and Theodosia Green and Miss Maria Ogden, were replaced at some point by Edward and Caroline Green, but due to lack of funding, the seminary was forced to close its doors in 1849. After it closed, the Baileys purchased the seminary and made it their home for 40 years. Edward Bailey's contribution to Maui was enormous. He helped vaccinate Mauians against smallpox (there was an epidemic on Oahu that devastated the population), built roads, surveyed land, designed churches, defined water rights for the sugar industry, grew his own cane, built sugar mills, and helped found Maunaolu Seminary for women in Makawao. Bailey was also an accomplished artist whose paintings and engravings on copper are an invaluable source of information about 19th-century Maui. Many of his works can be seen on the first floor of the Bailey House

Museum today. Visitors will also be able to view the museum's large collection of "precontact" Hawaiian artifacts, such as stone and shell implements, kapa cloth, and wood and feather work. Upstairs is the Bailey family parlor and a bedroom where you can see period furnishings, clothing, quilts, children's toys, and more. There are also outdoor displays of some of the original varieties of sugarcane brought to Maui, stone artifacts, a koa-wood outrigger canoe, and a redwood surf board.

Admission: $3 adults; $2.50 seniors; $1 children.
Open: Mon–Fri 10am–4pm.

MAUI TROPICAL PLANTATION, Hwy. 30 at Waikapu (RR1, Box 600, Wailuku). Tel. 244-7643, or toll free 800/451-6805.

Situated in the Waikapu Valley and covering 112 acres, Maui Tropical Plantation is a working plantation. Commercial crops here include sugarcane, pineapple, coffee, bananas, mangos, papayas, and macadamia nuts. Visitors may take a leisurely stroll through the Agricultural Village, stopping to view slide shows about Maui agriculture and admire the Southern Cross Windmill, which captures the rainwater that flows from the West Maui Mountains to irrigate sections of the plantation. After that, guests might opt to take a ride on the Tropical Express to see up close how the crops are harvested. The 45-minute Tropical Express tour is narrated, and the tram makes stops along the way for photo opportunities. A trip to the Tropical Nursery where visitors can see hibiscus, orchids, and gingers is worthwhile. The Tropical Market is stocked with breads, jams and jellies, T-shirts, posters, Maui crafts, and books. A luncheon buffet is available, but many people visit the Tropical Plantation in the evenings for the Hawaiian Country Barbecue on Tuesday, Wednesday, and Thursday evenings. Included in the price of admission to the barbecue is an "all-you-can-drink" open bar, sunset tram ride, lei-making demonstration, pineapple-cutting demonstration, Hawaiian crafts, dinner, and the Hawaiian Country Show featuring "Buddy Fo." It's something like a luau with a paniolo/Upcountry twist.

Admission: Admission to the market, nursery, restaurant, and Plantation Village is free; Tropical Express Tour $8 adults, $3 children 5–17, under 5 free; country barbecue $46.95 adults, $19.95 children 5–17, children 1–4 free.
Open: Maui Tropical Plantation daily 9am–5pm; country barbecue Tues–Thurs 4:45–7:30pm (reservations required).

IAO VALLEY.

Follow the signs from Wailuku toward the Iao Valley, and just a short distance from town you'll come to **Kepaniwai Park and Heritage Gardens** (on the left side of the road). The beautifully landscaped gardens are dotted with structures dedicated to the people of Hawaii. The park is the brainchild of architect Richard C. Tongg. Here you'll find a Chinese pagoda, New England salt box, Japanese teahouse and garden, bamboo house, and Hawaiian grass shack. There is no admission charge, and next door is the Hawaii Nature Center at Iao Valley where children and adults can participate in nature activities. Call 244-6500 in advance to sign up for their special programs.

If you leave the gardens and continue up toward the Iao Valley, you'll soon come to a sign that reads, "Black Gorge President Kennedy Profile." Pull over and have a look at the rock formation. I didn't believe it either until I stopped and looked for myself. You'll be amazed.

Continue on up, and after about another mile you'll arrive at the Iao Valley, at the center of which is the **Iao Needle,** a 2,250-foot lava rock that is covered in a layer of beautiful green foliage. This is where Kamehameha won the island of Maui by driving local warriors and chiefs into the valley and "outgunning" them (they were only equipped with spears) with his English cannons. It is said that the carnage was so great that the waters of this stream (Kepaniwai) ran red with blood. Fortunately, you'll find no trace of that today. Instead, you can park your car and follow one of the many well-maintained paths through the valley, along which you'll find a couple of nice swimming holes.

WAILUKU SHOPPING

Shopping options in Wailuku seemed to be dwindling during my last trip to Maui, but there are still some interesting antique shops on North Market Street in an area known as Antique Row. Take a walk along North Market and poke your head into some of the shops. One of the more interesting stops for shopping is **Gima Designs** at 21 Market St. (tel. 242-1839), where you'll find the original silk designs of Elaine Gima. Her work is exquisite, and she makes items to suit everyone's budget (call to see if her shop is still in Wailuku because she had plans to move but hadn't done so at press time).

KIHEI, WAILEA & MAKENA

Maui's south shore isn't known for its sights and attractions, but if you're in the area for the day, there are a few stops worth making.

ATTRACTIONS

Head through Kihei into the planned Wailea Resort where you'll find some of the island's most beautiful hotels. The ✪ **Grand Wailea** off Wailea Alanui has the most incredible art collection of all the hotels on the island, and it also has a fantastic 20,000-foot-long action pool. You simply must take a trip in the hotel's elevator to Kincha, the Grand Wailea's Japanese restaurant. The **Maui Inter-Continental** has recently been refurbished, and the changes include some exquisite Pacific Rim artifacts. Finally, even if you don't go into any of the hotels, you've got to drive by the strange and wonderful **Kea Lani Hotel** for a look at its distinctive architectural design.

Just a bit farther down the road from Wailea is Makena. Continue on until you see a sign indicating Makena Landing. Turn right and you'll be on Honoiki Street. Follow it to the end, and then go left. Here you will find **Keawala'i Church** which is built of coral and lava rocks. If you go back out to Makena Alanui Road (the main road that you were on before you turned right at the Makena Landing sign) and turn right and follow the road until it ends, you'll be at **La Perouse Bay** where you'll find Maui's last lava flow, which occurred at the end of the 18th century. There's a trail here that you can follow. You'll discover some beautiful coves and evidence of ancient Hawaiian villages. *Note:* Please don't stray from the trail because you might damage some of the ancient sites.

SHOPPING

Azeka Place and **Azeka Place II,** just off South Kihei Road, are loaded with tourist shops where you can purchase swimwear, alohawear, handcrafted Maui jewelry, postcards, and water-sports gear. If you're ready for a snack, stop at **Azeka's Market Snack Shop** where you can get Azeka's famous ribs or other tasty treats at the snack bar. Other shopping areas in Kihei include **Long's Center,** the **Dolphin Shopping Plaza, Rainbow Mall,** and **Kukui Center.** All are located just off South Kihei Road. One place worth a stop is the **Kihei International Marketplace,** also off South Kihei Road, next door to McDonald's.

The **Wailea Shopping Village** has more upscale shopping, but it's more of the same as what you found in Lahaina and Kapalua. Most of the Wailea hotels also have shopping arcades.

EVENING ENTERTAINMENT

The Maui Inter-Continental offers **Wailea's Finest Luau** (tel. 879-1922) on Tuesday, Thursday, and Friday evenings from 5:30 to 8pm. It takes place in an oceanfront setting and includes a lei greeting, open bar, imu ceremony, authentic Hawaiian hula show, and a full luau buffet. The cost is $48 for adults and $24 for children. Parking is complimentary.

Stouffer Wailea Resort (tel. 879-4900) presents the **Wailea Sunset Luau** every Monday and Thursday beginning at 5:30pm. Set in the hotel's luau gardens, the Stouffer's luau offers an extensive luau menu and a Polynesian show featuring traditional hula, Tahitian drums and dancing, and a spectacular fire-knife dance finale.

If you're not up for a luau, you might like to try Kihei's **Stella Blues Cafe and Deli** at 1215 South Kihei Rd. (tel. 874-3779), which features jazz and/or blues on Wednesday from 6 to 9pm, Friday from 7 to 9:30pm, and Saturday from 6 to 8pm. There's a $5 minimum purchase required.

Another option would be to head for the hotel bars. **Tsunami** in the Grand Wailea has a deejay from 9pm to 2am on Tuesday and Thursday (no cover charge), as well as on Friday and Saturday (open 9pm to 4am, $10 cover). Sunday and Monday are karaoke nights from 9pm to 2am (no cover charge). For a more relaxing evening you might try the Grand Wailea's **Volcano Bar,** which features "strolling Hawaiian entertainment" nightly beginning at 5:30pm. Jazz musicians perform nightly at the Kea Lani Hotel in the lounge area of the restaurant.

3. UPCOUNTRY

Most people know about Haleakala, but very few people know about the area on Haleakala's western slope known as Upcountry. A trip to Maui simply wouldn't be complete without at least a one-day excursion to Upcountry. Passing through on the way to the crater to see the sunrise or sunset isn't enough. You should plan on spending a day exploring the area's lush countryside, parks, botanical gardens, shops, and even a winery. While you're in Upcountry you'll see where the paniolos ride the range on Haleakala and Ulupalakua ranches and you'll visit the old cowboy town of Makawao where hitching posts are as common as the beautiful boutiques and fine restaurants that line the town's main street. A trip to Kula reveals the things that make Maui unique. There you'll find an abundance of flowers (including unusual protea, jacaranda, and even carnations), Tedeschi Vineyards, and Polipoli State Park.

MAKAWAO

To get to Makawao from Kahului, take the Hana Highway (Route 36) to Haleakala Highway (Route 37). Follow Haleakala Highway to the junction of Route 40 (Makawao Road) and turn left. Follow Makawao Road into Makawao.

When you arrive in Makawao, you'll feel a noticeable change in temperature. For every 1,000 feet above sea level, the temperature on Haleakala drops about three degrees. If you're in the area on a winter evening you won't be surprised to find out that many Upcountry homes have well-used fireplaces. Rather than tropical, the scenes you'll find in Makawao are pastoral, with rolling fields, pine trees, fuchsias, and proteas.

In the late 1700s, Captain George Vancouver presented King Kamehameha with several head of cattle. He then convinced the king to place a kapu on the cattle so they would have time to reproduce and become a food source for the Hawaiian people. In the beginning of the 19th century, Kamehameha imported three *españoles* (Mexican cowboys) to domesticate the cattle, which had grown into a wild herd. Over time, Hawaiian cowboys joined the españoles, and they became known as paniolos. Paniolos still ride the range up here and are responsible for providing Maui with much of its milk and beef. Of course, you can't have cowboys without a rodeo, and there are, in fact, several rodeo events in Makawao every year.

Makawao celebrates the Fourth of July every year with a western twist; among other things, the town's parade includes covered horse-drawn wagons.

Makawao's main street, **Baldwin Avenue,** was once home to simple barbershops, saloons, and general stores, but today it is lined with upscale boutiques, art galleries, and restaurants. Collections (tel. 572-0781) and the Gecko Trading Co. & Boutique (tel. 572-0249) sell women's clothing and accessories; for men's fashions try Tropo; Holiday & Co. (tel. 572-1470) also has clothing and gifts; Goodie's (tel. 572-0288), with tie-dye clothing and crystals, is for the hippie in all of us. The Mercantile (tel. 572-1407) is fittingly filled with country home furnishings and accessories; Kamoda Store and Bakery (tel. 572-7261) is where the locals line up every morning for fresh-baked cream puffs and malasadas on a stick; locals also like to stop at Kitada's Kau Kau Korner (tel. 572-7241) in the morning for saimin and coffee; the Rodeo General Store (tel. 572-7841) stocks a little bit of everything.

Some of the more interesting local **art galleries** here include the David Warren Gallery (tel. 572-0344), which features the work of David Warren; the Arthur Dennis Williams Sculpture Gallery (tel. 572-0344); and Maui Hands (tel. 572-5194), which sells and displays beautiful raku pots, jewelry, drums, rainsticks, baskets, watercolor paintings, and ceramics. View Points Gallery (tel. 572-5979) is an artists' cooperative for local artists. Everyone who has gallery space has to spend time tending the shop. Hot Island Glass (tel. 572-4527) is a glassblowing studio and gallery in "The Courtyard" where you might be able to watch the incredibly talented mother, father, and son team at work. Incidentally, the temperature of molten glass is 2,000 degrees Fahrenheit, the same as lava. The Dragon's Den (tel. 572-2424) is the town's New Age health-care center where you can get massages and healing herbs.

A bit farther down Baldwin Avenue (you'll have to drive to get there) is the **Hui No'eau Visual Arts Center** (tel. 572-6560). The Hui No'eau was founded in 1934 by Ethel Baldwin and some other Maui residents who sought to stimulate an interest in art among the people of Maui. The goals of the Hui were simply to support artistic talent among the local people and to educate the general public. Today the Hui sponsors educational programs in ceramics, painting, drawing, sculpture, printmaking, and jewelry making, just to name a few. There are art studios, and works by distinguished Hawaiian artists are always on display. There is also a gift shop.

If you're passing through Makawao in the evening, stop by **Casanova** (tel. 572-0220) for a night of dinner and dancing (see Chapter 6 for a full restaurant listing). From disco to blues to mambo and swing, there's always something going on at Casanova. There is usually a $5 cover charge (unless you're dining).

KULA

Kula means "plain, field, or open country," and Kula is just that. Today Kula is home to the famous sweet Maui onion and most of the island's herb and flower farms, but its land was once covered with beautiful koa trees. Once the koa tree forests were cleared, Hawaiians began farming the land for vegetables, which they took down to the coastal towns to trade and sell. During the years of the whaling industry, Kula land was cultivated primarily for the production of Irish potatoes.

To get to Kula from Makawao, head back to Haleakala Highway (Route 37) and go left. Haleakala Highway turns into Kula Highway.

Not long after you turn onto Kula Highway, you can make a stop at **Enchanting Floral Gardens of Kula Maui** (just off Route 37 at the 10-mile marker). The gardens display a broad range of native Hawaiian flora, as well as some species from around the world. You'll see the spectacular coral tree, shell ginger, and the sunburst pincushion, among others, and if you call in advance, the owners of Enchanting Floral Gardens (tel. 878-2531) will prepare you a continental breakfast or a light lunch. A small admission fee is charged at the door.

If you're hungry and didn't make advance reservations at the Enchanting Floral Gardens, visit **Grandma's Coffee Shop** (see Chapter 6 for full listing). Continue along Route 37. It's a bit of a drive, so don't think I've sent you in the wrong direction. It will be on your right. There's no parking lot, so just park on the roadside wherever you can find a space.

When you've satisfied your cravings at Grandma's, go back onto Route 37 and continue in the same direction you were going before you stopped. Just past Keokea you'll come to Ulupalakua Ranch (on your right) and then you'll see **Tedeschi Vineyards** (P.O. Box 935, Ulupalakua, Maui, HI 96790; tel. 808/878-1266) on your left. In the mid-19th century, the area that is today known as Ulupalakua Ranch was a sugar plantation. It didn't last more than 10 years as a sugar plantation and was bought by whaling captain James Makee, who turned it into a working cattle ranch called Rose Ranch in honor of his wife's favorite flower. The cattle ranch was a great success for Makee, and as a result, it attracted many notable visitors, including King David Kalakaua, for whom Makee built a cottage on his ranch (which you can still see today). In 1963 when C. Pardee Erdman bought the ranch, it had already been renamed Ulupalakua Ranch. In 1973, Erdman met Emil and JoAnn Tedeschi, Napa Valley wine makers who visited the ranch and decided to test different varieties of grapes here for wine making. One hundred and fifty grapes later, they discovered that the Carnelian grape adapted well to the climate on Maui, and they began making wine in a small winery on the ranch. It's the only working commercial winery in the Hawaiian islands, and currently four wines are being produced from the Carnelian grape: Maui Brut Champagne, Rose Ranch Cuvee, Maui Blush, and Maui Nouveau. In addition to the grape wines, Tedeschi is famous for Maui Blanc, its pineapple wine, which has a light but distinctive flavor. Last time I visited they were also producing an interesting passion fruit wine. There's a tasting room and gift shop on the premises, and it's open daily from 9am to 5pm. If you find something you like, they'll be happy to ship it back to the mainland for you.

When you leave Tedeschi Vineyards, turn around and go back toward Makawao on Route 37. When you get to the junction of Route 377, take Route 377 (Kekaulike Avenue) to Waipoli Road, where you will take a right to get to **Polipoli State Park.** A long series of switchbacks (in preparation for your drive to Hana) will lead you right into the park. You'll be awed by the park's incredible stands of redwood trees. If you'd like to get out and walk around, you can take the Redwood Trail, a 1.7-mile hike through the redwood forest. The trail stays among the trees. From the Redwood Trail you might veer off onto the Plum Trail which will take you through sugi, cedar, and ash groves. There are many other trails in the park.

When you've finished poking around the park, go back out to Kekaulike Road (Route 377) and go right, following it until you get to the **Kula Botanical Gardens** (on your right). The gardens opened to the public in 1971 after 2½ years of planting and nurturing. Today you can take a nice, leisurely stroll here while viewing tropical and local Hawaiian plants of all varieties. The park is open daily from 9am to 4pm; admission is $3 for adults and 50¢ for children ages 6 to 12.

If you still haven't stopped for a bite to eat, now is your chance. Go right out of the Kula Botanical Gardens and continue in the direction of Makawao. Soon you'll come to the **Kula Lodge & Restaurant** (tel. 878-1535) where you can dine on Hawaiian regional and contemporary cuisine while enjoying the dining room's spectacular vistas. After you're done with your meal, you might like to make a stop in the **Protea Gift Shoppe** next door to Kula Lodge. It's open weekdays from 9am to 5pm.

4. HALEAKALA

Haleakala (pronounced "ha-lay-ah-ka-lah"), meaning "House of the Sun," is the world's largest dormant volcano, and it's like nothing you've ever seen before. To me, Haleakala seems omnipotent. The sheer force it must have had to climb 30,000 feet from the ocean floor is mind-boggling. It is easy to understand why ancient Hawaiians feared and respected this mountain. Only the kahuna were brave enough to live on the volcano. Others hoped only to appease the goddess Pele by making sacrifices to her at the crater's edge.

Today, visitors to Maui have much less to fear of the volcano than the Hawaiians of old. Haleakala hasn't erupted for over 200 years, and although it is not extinct, geologists believe that the volcano will not erupt any time in the near future. Maui has shifted away from the "plume" that lies under the ocean and was the cause for Haleakala's eruptions, and chances that the volcano will become active again are slim. Maui should continue to shift away from the plume and the volcano will eventually become extinct. Since Haleakala's last eruption, the main activity seen on the mountain has been erosion. It is believed that over time, rainwater and flowing streams (combined with a slow collapse and sinking of the volcano) have eroded over 3,000 feet off the mountain.

The 7-mile-long crater, big enough to hold the entire island of Manhattan, attracts visitors from all over the world, and it is protected as a national park. Its summit reaches a height of 10,000 feet and the mountain stands 24 miles wide, covering most of the island's width and half of its length. Hundreds of thousands of island visitors trek to the summit of Haleakala every year to see the sun rise or set. Some enjoy hiking on its lush lower slopes or simply marveling at the beauty of its multihued cinder cones. Others come to see the much-talked-about silversword and unusual animal life.

A word of caution: As you are driving up to the summit, you'll probably see a number of bicyclists riding down the mountain. Chances are that none of them are experienced bikers, so be on your guard.

THE DRIVE TO THE SUMMIT

Before you get started there are a few things you should know. From wherever you are on Maui it will take you between 1½ and 3 hours to get to the summit, so plan accordingly. It is also typically much colder at the crater than it is near Maui's beaches, so take a jacket or sweater with you. The air at the top is very thin, so it is advisable that anyone with a heart problem check with their doctor before setting out (it's probably not a good idea for heart patients to make the trip at all).

Most people make the trip in the early morning or early evening because during the afternoon cloud cover around the top of Haleakala obstructs the beautiful views. You should also make sure the weather is good before you make the drive (it would be a shame to get there and find out that you can't see or do anything); call 572-7749 for a weather report. Finally, there are no restaurants at the top, so if you're going to see the sun rise, it would be advisable to pack a picnic breakfast, or plan on visiting one of the restaurants or bakeries at the base of the mountain (Grandma's Coffee Shop, Kula Lodge, or Komoda's Store; see Chapter 6 for full listings).

You'll begin the drive, no matter where your point of origin, on Route 37 (Haleakala Highway), which you will follow until you get to Pukalani, where you will go right onto Route 377 (Upper Kula Road). Follow Route 377 to Haleakala Crater Road (Route 378)—the road is well marked. Your starting elevation is about 3,700 feet above sea level, and 22 miles and 32 switchbacks later you'll reach the summit. There are several stops you should make along the way, the first of which is a lookout a little under 5 miles from the beginning of the trail. It will be on the right side of the road, and stopping here will afford you beautiful views of neighboring islands, Kahoolawe and Molokini. On your right you'll see West Maui Volcano, which was actually the first active volcano on Maui. Eruptions of hot lava from both volcanos joined together to form what you see today as the island of Maui. At one time all of the islands in Maui County, including Molokai, Lanai, and Kahoolawe were joined above sea level.

When you've finished taking pictures and admiring the view, hop back in the car and continue up the mountain. Shortly after you reach the park entrance (where you'll have to pay a fee of $3 for a car or $1 for a bicycle), you'll see a turnoff on your left. Don't take it here—it's easier and safer to make the turn on your way back down.

Park Headquarters will be your next stop (unless you're here for the sunrise, in which case you should stop on the way back down because it only opens at sunrise). Here you'll find a wide variety of books and general information (including the day's schedule for ranger-guided hikes and camping permit information). Outside Park Headquarters you might be able to see a nene or two.

After you leave Park Headquarters, keep an eye out for Leleiwi Overlook, at mile marker 17. The parking lot is about half a mile beyond mile marker 17 on your right. Park there and cross the street to the short trail that leads to the overlook where you'll be treated to an incredible panoramic view of Haleakala Crater which is reminiscent of a moonscape. You're now at an elevation of 8,800 feet. Notice how the colors of the cinder cones change as the clouds move across the sky. Aside from the view, the thing that really brings visitors to this spot is a phenomenon known as the Specter of the Brocken. Sometimes, if conditions are just right (usually in the afternoon when it's very cloudy and the view from here is obstructed), you can see your shadow, ringed by a rainbow, in the clouds below. Were I a scientist I would surely know how to explain this phenomenon to you, but I'm not, so for the purposes of this book, it will have to remain a mystery. (If you're dying to know, I'm sure one of the park rangers can explain it to you better than I can.) While you're at Leleiwi Overlook, notice the drastic change in vegetation from the rolling meadows of Kula and the other towns at the base of the mountain.

Continue up the volcano, and soon you will arrive at the Haleakala Observatory Visitor Center (a little over 3 miles from Leleiwi Overlook), where the views are unsurpassed. In clear weather you'll be able to see for over 100 miles, and you really will feel as though you're at the very edge of the earth. If you're here for the sunrise, you'll understand why ancient Hawaiians named this place Haleakala, "House of the Sun," for the sun appears to rise directly out of the crater. As the sun rises and moves across the sky throughout the day, the giant cinder cones you see below seem to change colors. There are ecological, geological, and archaeological exhibits here that describe the volcano's history. In addition to the informational exhibits, you can buy books, gifts, and film here. There are also restrooms.

The actual summit of Haleakala is a little over a half mile from the visitors' center, so don't turn around at the visitors' center thinking you've seen all you've come to see. Continue on until you get to Pu'u'ula'ula Summit (also known as Red Hill). At 10,023 feet, this is the volcano's highest point. Here you'll also see a cluster of buildings known as Science City. Much of the research that is done here can be performed nowhere else in the world.

DESCENT FROM THE SUMMIT

Now it's time to head down Haleakala. *Put your car in low gear to descend;* if you do that, you won't be one of those tourists who suddenly sees smoke coming from the car and doesn't know why. If you sit on the brake the whole way down, you probably won't have any by the time you reach the base of the mountain.

Along the way, you'll have two more stops, the first of which is Kalahaku Overlook (look for the sign on your right). It's the best place to see silversword, a plant that is unique to Hawaii. Over the centuries, it evolved from the ordinary common daisy and is thought to live for 50 years before it blooms and then dies. (See Chapter 1 for more about silversword.) At one time this unusual plant virtually covered the area, but feral goats and curious visitors have seen to it that it is near extinction. Haleakala National Park has now fenced off many areas where silversword still grows in an effort to protect one of Hawaii's rarest plants.

The second, and last, stop is at Hosmer Grove. There will be a sign on your right. The parking area is about a half mile from the turnoff, and just off the parking lot there is a half-mile-long trail that will take you through a forest of trees introduced and planted by Ralph Hosmer in 1910. Here you will see eucalyptus, sugi pine (from Japan), deodar (from India), and a variety of pine trees. The park provides a brochure at the beginning of the trail that will help you to locate and identify the various trees. There's also a picnic ground here.

HIKING HALEAKALA

There are several hiking trails that vary in length and difficulty. The Halemauu Trail, which begins at an elevation of 8,000 feet, about 4 miles beyond the park headquarters, is a 10-mile hike that takes you from the west side of the crater down to the crater floor and into the east end of Haleakala. During the hike, which follows a series of switchbacks, you'll pass Holua cabin and the Bottomless Pit. The trail won't take you back to the parking lot where you began, so be prepared either to walk back up from the trail's end, or hitch a ride with someone who's going up. Sliding Sands trail begins at 10,000 feet near the visitors' center and follows the south rim of the crater. This trail is also 10 miles long, and as you walk you'll pass Kapalaoa cabin, Paliku cabin, and loose cinder slides. As with the Halemauu Trail, you'll have to rely on the goodwill of others to get you back to your car. The third trail, known as the Kaupo Gap Trail, crosses the most difficult terrain. The area is covered with vegetation and rough lava. It is also extremely difficult to get back to the main road from the end of the Kaupo Gap Trail, so if you're planning to take the hike, you should also plan on camping somewhere in the area so you can walk back the next day. For information about camping in the park, write to Superintendent, P.O. Box 369, Makawao, Maui, HI 96768.

If you'd rather not take the self-guided hikes, ranger-guided hikes are usually scheduled during the summer months and take between ½ and 2 hours. Check at park headquarters for a schedule. Other ways to see Haleakala are on horseback or by bike. See above for more information.

A few words of advice: Never hike alone. Always carry enough water so you won't become dehydrated. Wear the proper shoes. Carry a sweater or jacket because the temperature drops here in the evening. Do not stray from established trails—you might damage the native flora without knowing it. Finally, do not remove anything, other than your trash, from Haleakala. Every year people take pieces of lava from the island, and every year, they send them back with notes begging someone to return the lava to its rightful place. The reason? Well, some say that if you take lava from the island you will have bad luck, and all the people who have sent lava back to Maui have reported unusual bouts of bad luck.

5. HANA

Hana and its environs is a lush tropical rainforest dotted with waterfalls and blue pools (it's famous for its Seven Sacred Pools, or Ohe'o Gulch). It's where you'll find red- and black-sand beaches, and it's where you'll find Hamoa Beach, a favorite of Mark Twain. In short, Hana is paradise. It's what you came to Maui looking for, and it will take you at least 3 hours to get there. The first time I made the trip to Hana I had no idea that I'd find myself confronted with 30 miles of bumpy, unpaved switchbacks and one-car bridges. Today the road is paved (and is currently being repaved), so the drive is a bit easier, but no freak of nature will ever straighten it, so if you have a tendency to get carsick, you should fly. Otherwise, drive: It's a trip you'll never forget—both for the challenge it presents and its beauty.

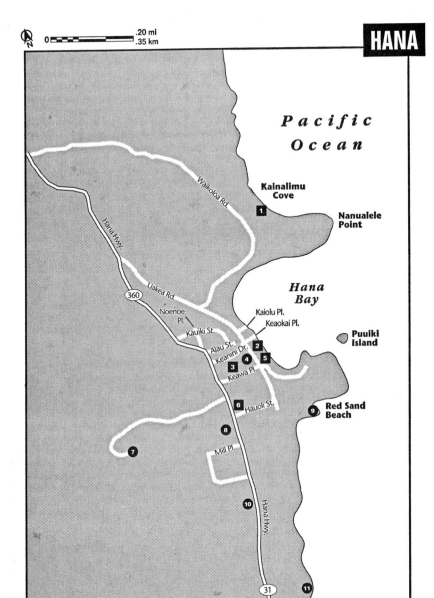

Pacific Ocean

Kainalimu Cove

1

Nanualele Point

Hana Bay

Waikoloa Rd

Hana Hwy

360

Uakea Rd

Noenoe Pl.

Kauiki St.

Kaiolu Pl.

Keaokai Pl.

Alau St.

Keanini Dr.

2

4

5

3

Puuiki Island

Keawa Pl.

6 Hauoli St.

9 Red Sand Beach

8

7

Mill Pl.

10 Hana Hwy

31

11

0   .20 mi   .35 km

6662

ACCOMMODATIONS:
Aloha Cottages **3**
Hana Kai–Maui Resort **5**
Hana Plantation Houses (offices) **2**
Hotel Hana Maui **6**
Waianapanapa State Park cabins **1**

ATTRACTIONS:
Hamoa Beach **11**
Hana Cultural Center **4**
Hassegawa General Store **10**
Memorial to Paul Fagan **7**
Red Sand Beach **9**
Wananalua Church **8**

THE ROAD TO HANA

Before you begin the drive, there are a few things you should know. First, the road to Hana is always crowded, and it isn't unusual to find yourself driving in bumper-to-bumper traffic throughout the drive. Because of the winding (there are 617 curves) road, and the one-lane bridges (there are 56), it will take you about 3 hours to get from Kahului to Hana town. There are no gas stations or places to eat along the way, so you should fill your car before you leave and pack a picnic lunch. I would advise you to begin the drive in the morning if you're planning on making it back from Hana before it gets dark (the road is more dangerous at night). Otherwise, try to get a hotel room in Hana (see Chapter 5 for Hana accommodations) for at least one night. I've actually found the trip to be much more enjoyable if I stay overnight in Hana. If you're planning on hiking, carry water with you—it's not a good idea to drink from most of the streams in the area. Do not make the drive if heavy rainstorms are predicted because mudslides are frequent and often block the road. Finally, don't forget to take your bathing suit; there are some wonderful pools fed by beautiful waterfalls in which to swim throughout the drive.

Now we can begin. From Kahului, take Hana Highway (Route 36) in the direction of Upcountry. Your first stop along the way will be Paia. If you didn't already fill your gas tank, you can do so here. Paia is also a good place to buy things for that picnic lunch. You can get supplies at the **Paia General Store,** which will be on your left after the gas station, or you can go right on Baldwin Avenue to **Picnics, Peaches and Crumble Cafe and Bakery,** or the **Paia Fish Market** (see Chapter 6 for full listings). There are some great little shops here as well, including the **Maui Crafts Guild,** which is on your left just before you get to the center of Paia. The Guild is owned and operated by local Maui artists who are required to use only items found on Hawaii in their works. It's open daily and is a great place to pick up an authentic souvenir. There are plenty of other shops on Baldwin Avenue and the Hana Highway that sell everything from women's fashions to swimwear and aromatherapy oils. With its unusual assortment of shops and its resident artists, Paia has gained a reputation of being a sort of Greenwich Village. After you've shopped around and stocked up on provisions, continue your drive.

The first point of interest after Paia is **Ho'okipa Beach Park,** where scores of windsurfers take advantage of Maui's best windsurfing beaches. Beyond Ho'okipa Beach Park is **Haiku,** known for its pineapple plantations. Many of Maui's permanent residents call Haiku home. Rents aren't so steep, the weather is good, and the beaches are nearby, which makes it one of Maui's more attractive residential areas. It is after you pass through Haiku that civilization thins, and it is about this time that you'll begin to think that I was lying about the curvy roads and one-lane bridges, but enjoy the straight and spacious road while you can. You'll soon see a sign indicating the miles of curvy, bumpy road ahead. That's when the traffic will begin to look like the streets of Manhattan when the president is in town. It doesn't matter, though—you're in no hurry, and you'll be making lots of stops along the way.

By the time you reach **Kailua** (kye-loo-ah), your surroundings will have changed dramatically. Instead of scrub grass and sand you'll begin to see guava trees (guavas are the yellow lemon-like fruits you'll see along the side of the road), heliconias, African tulip trees, gingers, and even bamboo (see Chapter 1 for more information on the flora). Strangely enough, in the early part of this century, Kailua is where the island's criminals were sent, and beyond this town (which still has no grocery store) was only a dirt path leading up to Hana.

As you round the bends to **Waikamoi,** the forest grows more dense. You'll pass through a bamboo forest, and not long afterward (a half-mile after mile marker 9), you'll arrive at a maintained hiking trail. Stop here and take the 1-mile hike along the **Waikamoi Ridge Nature Trail** that will lead you through groves of eucalyptus, ginger, heliconia, ti, and giant philodendron. Be on the lookout for lobster claw heliconia and the beautiful maidenhair ferns.

A couple of miles beyond Waikamoi you'll come to **Puohokamoa Stream.** If you're lucky, there will be space for you to park here so you can get out and take the short trail that leads to a double waterfall and a swimming hole, which can be seen from the bridge near where you'll park the car. Just over one mile from Waikamoi is **Kaumahina State Wayside,** where the dramatic coastal vistas are beyond your wildest imaginings. The bay, edged by a gorgeous black-sand beach, is known as **Honomanu Bay.**

Between 5 and 7 miles farther along the twisting, turning, increasingly beautiful road are the villages of **Keanae** and **Wailua,** which can be seen from the road. They're the last of the true old Hawaiian villages, in which taro farming and poi making are still done in the traditional fashion. When you get to mile marker 18 (actually Wailua) you'll be able to pull off the road and follow the signs to the **Coral Church** and the **Miracle of Fatima Shrine.** In the 1860s, an unusually violent storm visited itself upon the island, and when it was all over, the people of Wailua emerged to find that the storm had washed enough coral up onto the beach so that they would be able to construct the church. They believed it to be a miracle, and then constructed the Miracle of Fatima Shrine.

Drive back out to Hana Highway and continue toward Hana. Soon you will come to **Pua'a Ka'a State Wayside,** which is a great place to stop for that picnic if you haven't already had lunch. There are also two pools, each with a lovely waterfall where you can have a quick swim before lunch. I know that at this point some of you might be thinking that you're never going to reach Hana, but I assure you, it won't be long now. Get back in that winding train of cars, steel yourself for the hairpin turns, and keep going.

You've got to make the next side trip into **Waianapanapa State Park,** where you can visit 120 acres of land that has been preserved by the State of Hawaii. You can camp here, but you should get a permit in advance of your arrival (see "Hiking & Camping" in Chapter 8 for more information on camping, or Chapter 5 for information on the Waianapanapa cabins). Waianapanapa is dotted with the foundations of Old Hawaiian houses and temples, gravesites, and stone walls. There are also several freshwater caves in Waianapanapa that can be reached via a well-marked trail from the parking lot. One of the caves is said to turn red every year at the same time because of a deadly battle between a Hawaiian chief and his adulterous wife.

There's one more stop before you get to Hana. **Hana Gardenland,** on the right side of the road, is a tropical garden with a little cafe and a superb art gallery and gift shop attached. Many local artists are represented in the gallery, including Piero Resta, Kathy Jenson, and Karen Jennings. There are plans to expand the 3-acre botanical gardens to include large aviaries for tropical birds. The cafe is excellent; in fact, when Hillary Rodham Clinton visited Hana, she had breakfast at the Hana Gardenland Cafe three mornings in a row.

HANA

Most people are disappointed when they arrive in Hana because it's just a sleepy little town that happens to be between the rest of the island and Ohe'o Gulch, which is really what people come to Hana looking for. Hana might not be much to look at, but that's not important. Hana is a state of mind, a way of life. Things are slow and simple, and the people who have lived here for decades like it that way. For centuries, Hana was cut off from the rest of the island, but by the middle of the 19th century, civilization made its way to the small town in the form of a sugar plantation, owned by George Wilfong. As with the sugar plantations on the rest of the island, Wilfong's plantation drew immigrants from Portugal, Japan, China, and the Philippines. Sugar production became the lifeblood of the Hana community and lasted until about the middle of this century.

It was then that a man by the name of Paul Fagan bought several thousand acres of land right in the middle of Hana town. He brought in some cattle and began what would eventually become Hana Ranch. Fagan loved "Heavenly Hana" so much that he decided to live out the rest of his life here. It was then that he built the **Hotel Hana-Maui** with the idea that it would be used primarily for the spring training of his baseball team (the San Francisco Seals) and as a place for his friends to stay when they visited, but the first year the Seals came to train, scores of sportswriters and reporters came along with them, and the word was out about this island paradise. From that point on, tourists have come to Hana in force. Today, the Hotel Hana-Maui is still operating, and there's a **memorial to Paul Fagan** (he died in 1960) across the street from the hotel. It's a large, lava-stone cross set atop a hill.

Besides visiting the hotel and memorial, make a stop at the **Hana Cultural Center** (tel. 248-8622) on Uakea Road. It's a quick stop (not a major museum), but it holds some real treasures. There are Hawaiian quilts on display, poi boards (used for the pounding of taro into poi), brooms made of coconut fronds, old fish hooks, a coconut grater, stone lamps, and even some kapa cloth. It's open daily from 10am to 4pm, and admission is by donation. Next door is the tiny old Hana courthouse. Your admission fee to the Cultural Center entitles you to explore the courthouse and jail.

Hana Bay might be your next stop—there's excellent snorkeling and swimming here, and there's also Tutu's, a hamburger/snack shop. In addition to Hana Bay, Hana is home to a **red-sand beach,** and the famous **Hamoa Beach** (located just outside the center of town). The **Hotel Hana-Maui** isn't far inland from Hana Bay, and on its far side is **Wananalua Church,** a beautiful coral stone church that was constructed in 1838. Before you leave Hana, make a stop at **Hasegawa General Store,** which sells absolutely everything: bread, butter, soup, candy, books, clothing, fruits, vegetables, bumper stickers, meats, hammers—the list goes on and on. Hasegawa's has established itself as something of a legend on Maui.

BEYOND HANA

The final stop on your trip to East Maui is **Ohe'o Gulch.** Although commonly referred to as the Seven Sacred Pools, they are neither sacred nor are there seven of them. Before you get there, however, you'll come to **Wailua Gulch,** a spectacular double falls. Ohe'o Gulch is located about 10 miles from Hana in Kipahulu. You'll know when you're there by the number of cars and the rather unattractive parking lot. The pools are like stepping stones, each one flowing down into the next, and finally into the ocean. These are the lower falls, and you can frolic in them with the rest of the tourists who made the drive, or you can venture uphill from the parking lot (don't stop: the uphill trek is tough but short—it levels off after about a half-mile) through a field and a singing bamboo forest to Waimoku Falls. Don't quit at the first falls you see—take a break there if you need one, but then continue on to Waimoku. The total hike is a couple of miles, but I guarantee you won't be sorry you made the trip.

6. COOL FOR KIDS

When your kids tire of the beach or hotel pool, consider the following attractions, all of which will amuse adults as well.

The **banyan tree** (see p. 152) in the center of Lahaina town is a kids' favorite. They love to spend time running around under the tree's enormous branches.

The **Brig Carthaginian** (see p. 151), at the Lahaina Wharf, is also an amusing stop for kids. There are audiovisual displays, and while the interior spaces on the ship are small for adults, they're exactly the right size for children.

The **Hawaii Experience Domed Theater** (see p. 156), on Front Street in Lahaina, with its 180° movie screen, is perfect for kids. The scenery in the movie changes quickly enough to hold a child's attention, and they love feeling like they're piloting the helicopter or riding the bike down Haleakala.

What kid wouldn't love **Atlantis Submarines** *(see p. 157)*? The ride in a full submersible submarine is a real thrill for children. Boats depart from the Lahaina Harbor, and children must be at least 3 feet tall.

As an educational stop try the **Whale Center** in Whalers Village in the Kaanapali Resort *(see p. 162)*. It is constantly filled with children who want to learn more about whales and their preservation.

The **Lahaina–Kaanapali & Pacific Railroad** (a.k.a. the Sugar Cane Train) *(see p. 161)* is sure to please even the crankiest of children. The conductor amuses passengers with songs and stories throughout the 12-mile ride in this reconstructed turn-of-the-century train.

7. ORGANIZED TOURS

See also Chapter 8, "Maui Sports & Recreation," for information on inter-island cruises, horseback tours, bike tours, and other guided sports options.

DRIVING TOURS

Driving around Maui, while time-consuming, can be very interesting, especially if you've got someone (or something) to guide your travels.

GUIDED TOURS When most people travel they want to know the local favorites, but never have the opportunity to travel with a local. On Maui you can **Rent-A-Local** (tel. 877-4042) who will take you on personalized tours of Hana, Haleakala, and Upcountry. Your local will take you to his or her favorite waterfalls and swimming holes, secluded beaches, snorkel spots, hiking areas, and restaurants. All you have to do is provide the rental car. Renting a local is one of the most entertaining and educational ways to see the island.

Rates for 6-hour tours are $135 for one person, $180 for two people ($26 per additional person); 8-hour tours are $156 for one person, $218 for two people ($26 per additional person).

SELF-GUIDED TOURS If your driving travels are going to take you specifically to Hana, you should stop by **Hana Cassette Guide** (at the Shell Service Station on Route 380; tel. 572-0550 for directions) and pick up one of their audiocassettes. They actually provide the tape player, the tape, a flower photo book, and a Hana road map. You can drive at your own pace and along the way the cassette guide will provide all sorts of information about what you'll be seeing. The rental for the full day costs $20.

Another way to see the island is to pick up a copy of Elaine and Tom Clements' *Be Your Own Tour Guide on Maui*. They've put together eight comprehensive, self-guided tours (along with a keyed map) that will take you Upcountry, to the Iao Valley, to and around Lahaina, to Polipoli State Park, along the road to Hana, and along Maui's southeast coast. They tell you where to start your tour, how long the tour will take, and where to stop during the drive. They'll even give you helpful hints along the way. Best of all, they've neatly packaged all this information in pocket-sized folders so they're easy to carry around with you. You'll find the *Be Your Own Tour Guide on Maui* packets at the Maui Visitors Bureau and many of the area's hotels. Last I spoke with Elaine Clements, plans were underway to create the tours for various island hotels. The starting points for each tour would be at a specific hotel, with directions to the first stop beginning at that hotel. Check with your hotel to see if they have the driving tours.

HELICOPTER TOURS

Many people believe the best way to see Maui in a short period of time is to take a helicopter tour. The only reason for not taking a helicopter tour is that they're typically very expensive—you'll be lucky to book a ride for under $100 per person. However, if you can somehow get the money together, you won't be disappointed— it's truly thrilling. Most Maui helicopter-tour operators will take you to Hana, Haleakala, and Molokai in one combination or another. You might be able to book a tour that encompasses all three (that'll probably cost you closer to $200 per person), or one that takes you to both Haleakala and Hana (between $115 and $165 per person). Flight times vary according to the tour you've chosen, but generally last between 45 minutes and one hour. You'll even get to make touchdowns in remote areas where you'll see things (like the spectacular waterfalls of Hana) you'd never be able to see any other way. An hour doesn't seem like much time to see the whole island, but these choppers move fast, and the pilots are exceedingly experienced, so you'll get your money's worth. Many of the tour operators will offer a videotape of your tour, and while you're flying, you'll hear pilot narration as well as prerecorded music. Some aircraft interiors are soundproof, and a couple of operators offer seating with 180-degree views.

All helicopter-tour companies operate out of Kahului Airport, and you should know that you'll be weighed when you arrive at the airport before takeoff so they can evenly distribute the weight in the helicopter. Some people find being weighed while on vacation (without advance warning) stressful, so if it'll ruin your vacation, skip the helicopter tour. Otherwise, consider yourself warned.

۞ Blue Hawaiian (tel. 871-8844, or toll free 800/247-5444) is the Cadillac of helicopter tour companies. The business is family owned and operated, and you'll get to fly on one of their new jet helicopters. Blue Hawaiian touches down in some remote locations and features recorded music and narration on its Helicam system. Interiors are soundproof, and wherever you sit, you'll have 180-degree views. Your tour will be videotaped. The first tape is free; additional tapes cost $5.

Sunshine Helicopters (tcl. 871-0722) also has an excellent reputation on Maui. Sunshine offers some less expensive, shorter flights. They offer four 20- to 40-minute tours for $100 or less. Video is free.

Hawaii Helicopters (tel. 877-3900), **Alexair** (tel. 871-0792), **Cardinal Helicopters** (tel. 877-2400), and **Papillon Helicopters** (tel. 877-0022) all offer similar tours.

CHAPTER 8

MAUI SPORTS & RECREATION

1. WATER SPORTS
2. LAND SPORTS

Maui has scores of sports and recreation activities available for island visitors. Snorkeling is popular, and for the more adventurous there's scuba; hiking and biking are great ways to explore the inland areas; you can take surfing or windsurfing lessons, go hunting, play golf or tennis, and even learn to kayak. No matter what your interests are, you'll find something to do on Maui. Many visitors planning a trip to Maui aren't thinking much about physical activity, but after they've spent good days in the sun and exhausted the sightseeing possibilities on the island, most will be looking for something else to do. That's where this chapter comes in.

A WORD ABOUT ACTIVITIES DESKS Particularly in Lahaina, you'll be regularly solicited by activities desk staff members to buy heavily discounted tickets to island activities. Be aware, however, that in return you may be asked to listen to several hours of hard-sell promotion for time-share condominiums or other products. There are a couple of activities desks that are actually legitimate and will get you slightly discounted rates without this hassle. Try the **Tours and Visitor Information** desk in Lahaina's Wharf Cinema Center (tel. 667-2112) or **Barefoot's Cashback Tours,** located at 834 Front St. (tel. 667-5501).

In addition to all the independent activities owners listed in this chapter, **Ocean Activities Center,** which offers activities ranging from snorkeling to sportfishing, has offices in many Maui hotels. If you're staying in a hotel with an Ocean Activities Center office, it might be easier for you to try and book an activity directly through them. If you're interested in participating in something they don't offer, check what's listed in this chapter—you'll probably find what you need. For Ocean Activities main reservations office, call 879-4485. Hotel and condominium locations include the Aston Maui Vista (tel. 879-1779), Embassy Suites Hotel (tel. 667-7116), Kea Lani Hotel (tel. 879-8804), Kihei Akahi (tel. 879-8998), Mana Kai Maui Resort (tel. 879-6704), Maui Hill resort (tel. 879-0180), Maui Lu Resort (tel. 879-2977), Maui Marriott (tel. 661-3631), and Stouffer Wailea Beach Resort (tel. 879-0181). They are also located in the Lahaina Cannery Mall (tel. 661-5309) and Whalers Village (tel. 661-4444).

1. WATER SPORTS

MAUI'S BEST BEACHES

On the island's west side, ✪ **Kapalua** (Fleming) and ✪ **Kaanapali** ("Dig Me") beaches are both beautiful white-sand beaches. Kapalua Beach is slightly less crowded and a bit more peaceful than Kaanapali, but Kaanapali Beach is where everybody goes to see and be seen.

There are some small white-sand beaches **(Papalaua State Wayside)** between Lahaina and Maalaea just off Honoapiilani Highway (Route 30). They are dotted with kiawe trees and are usually fairly well populated, but sometimes you can find a nice secluded patch of sand for yourself.

Kamaole Beach Parks #1, #2, and **#3** are all good beaches, but they tend to be crowded, especially on the weekends when local families spread out their blankets and picnic lunches (sometimes dinner too) and spend the whole day relaxing in the sun. Watch out for kiawe here (see note below).

Wailea, like Kapalua and Kaanapali, also has some great white-sand beaches— **☉ Ulua, Wailea, Mokapu,** and **Polo** beaches make up the Wailea coastline, while a little farther south, in Makena, you'll find two more wonderful beaches. **☉ Makena Beach** is right at the top of the list as far as Maui's beaches go. For a long time it was known as a hippie haven, and others stayed away. Today there are still a few hippie holdouts left, but the rest of the world has discovered Makena Beach. The section of beach beyond the cinder cone on the main beach (known as Big Beach) is Little Beach (you'll have to climb over the cinder cone to get to it), which attracts nude sunbathers. For the most part no one bothers the men and women who choose to bare it all, but in case you were wondering, nude sunbathing is illegal and there's always a chance you'll get arrested.

Beaches in Central Maui (Wailuku and Kahului) are, simply put, wretched. **Kanaha Beach,** outside Kahului, near the airport, is decent, but I wouldn't drive all the way there just to spend the day on the beach. If you're headed toward Paia to watch the windsurfers strut their stuff at Ho'okipa Beach Park, **Baldwin Beach Park,** just before you get to Paia, is a good place to relax for a few hours and have a picnic lunch. **Ho'okipa Beach Park** just outside of Paia (in the direction of Hana) is the island's premier windsurfing beach. People come from all over the world to windsurf there.

If you have time to make the trip to Hana, you're in for some real treats. Hana Bay has a nice beach that is popular with the locals. There's a snack shop and some picnic tables available. My favorite beach, and the favorite of Mark Twain, is the famous salt-and-pepper **☉ Hamoa Beach.** Unbelievably, in spite of its notoriety, Hamoa Beach remains relatively unspoiled and private. It is utilized primarily by guests of the Hotel Hana-Maui. If you go down to Waianapanapa State Park (before you get to Hana town coming from Kahului), you'll get to see a **black-sand beach,** which also happens to be a good swimming spot. There are freshwater caves here as well. There's an incredible **☉ red-sand beach** in Hana as well. It's difficult to describe exactly how to get there, but ask someone local (the woman at Hana Cultural Center is particularly helpful if you're unassuming and show a genuine interest in the beauty of Hana). The red-sand beach is good for swimming also.

Note: One thing to be aware of, especially on Kihei beaches, is the presence of kiawe trees. They drop needles into the sand that hurt terribly if they get stuck in your feet. Always wear footwear on the beach until you can determine whether or not it's safe.

FISHING

If you like deep-sea fishing and want the chance to go after mahi mahi, ono, tuna, shark, and marlin, call **Luckey Strike Charters** (tel. 661-4606). They offer deep-sea trolling or light-tackle bottom fishing in either a 31-foot or 45-foot, fully equipped vessel. **Hinatea Sportfishing** (tel. 667-7548) will take you out in a custom 41-foot Hatteras Sportfisher. They take honors for the most marlin caught and the most marlin tagged and released. Their motto is "No boat rides here; we go catch fish!" Boats depart from Lahaina Wharf.

INTERISLAND CRUISES

Club Lanai (tel. 871-1144) is one of the most popular interisland cruises (or "adventures") on Maui today. You'll sail over to Lanai, where you'll get to snorkel at a turtle reef, go bicycling, boating, wave skiing, take part in beach sporting activities (like volleyball), explore marine life in touch tanks, take historical wagon rides, lounge in hammocks, and you'll visit the beautiful, pristine, white- and dark-sand beaches of Lanai. It's an all-day affair that includes an outdoor buffet and a fully stocked bar, and access to a beach reserved specifically for guests of Club Lanai. All-inclusive prices are $79 for adults, $39 for children. The Club Lanai boat departs from Lahaina Harbor (pier 4) at 8am and makes the return trip from Lanai at 3pm.

Trilogy Excursions (tel. 661-4743) has a cruise to Lanai as well. The Coon family's *Discover Lanai* charter is the only one with access to Lanai's Hulopo'e Marine Preserve and Beach Park.

Maui Classic Charters (tel. 879-8188) will also take you to Lanai to explore the turtle reef.

KAYAKING

Kayaks were once the fishing vehicle of choice for ancient Hawaiians. Today you too can have a kayak adventure. **Kelii's Kayak Tours** (tel. 874-7652) will supply you with a form-fitting kayak loaded with snorkeling and fishing gear, and they'll take you on a tour along Maui's dramatic sea coast.

South Pacific Kayaks (tel. 875-4848) was Maui's first kayak tour company, and its owners, Michael and Melissa McCoy, have lots of kayak experience (both locally and internationally). They'll provide you with single, double, or triple kayaks equipped with rudder systems for added safety. You'll be able to paddle at your own pace, and South Pacific Kayaks will work with people of virtually any age. You can rent kayaks for the day, the week, or take one of their snorkel/kayak tours ($39 to $125). Tours depart in the morning and last for 2½ to 5 hours. If you go during whale season, you might get closer to a whale than you ever thought was possible.

SCUBA DIVING

If you've never been scuba diving before, many of the hotels in the resort areas offer free first-time lessons. If you're staying in one of those hotels, you should take advantage of the free lesson to decide whether you enjoy the sport. Additional lessons can be expensive.

Beach Activities of Maui is located at several island hotels, including the Embassy Suites Resort (tel. 661-2000), Four Seasons Resort (tel. 874-8000), Grand Wailea (tel. 875-1234), Kea Lani Resort (tel. 874-4100), and Royal Lahaina Resort (tel. 661-3611). They're also in Whalers Village (tel. 661-5552). **Capt. Nemo's Ocean Emporium** (150 Dickenson St., tel. 661-5555) offers lessons and certification to everyone from the beginner to the expert. **Lahaina Divers** (tel. 667-7496) has put together a variety of classes and dives for divers of all levels of experience. Lahaina Divers will complete your open-water training with you; take you on your first dive (you and the instructor use the same air tank); give certified divers a day-long refresher course; and for more experienced divers, they offer one-, two-, and three-tank dives to Molokini or Lanai, or even a night dive. **Scorpion Scuba Safaris** (tel. 669-7427) offers free pool lessons, daily beach dives (one or two tanks), and a dive package that includes all equipment and lasts for three days (three dives). They also offer night dives and certification classes. **Maui Sun Divers** (tel. 879-3337) specializes in instruction for beginners. Prices vary according to dive package, so call for rates.

SNORKELING

Sunbathing aside, snorkeling is one of the island's most popular activities. You can rent snorkeling equipment from most of the hotels (particularly the resort hotels), or from independent agencies. **Snorkel Bob's Inc.** is probably the island's most popular and well-known rental agency. For $15 a week, Snorkel Bob's will provide you with a mask, fins, snorkel, bag, map, fish food, "no-fog goop" for your mask, fish

I.D. book, and the extra bonus—"The Legend of Snorkel Bob." Snorkel Bob's is located in Kihei (tel. 879-7449), Napili (tel. 669-9603), and Lahaina (161 Lahainaluna Rd., tel. 661-4421). **Snorkel Mania** (represented by an octopus named Swami Pau Hana) also rents snorkel gear for either $9.95 or $15.95 a week. The regular snorkel package includes a snorkel, mask, fins, and bag. The deluxe package includes a mask, fins, snorkel, bag, and fish food. The **Maui Dive Shop** sells and rents snorkel equipment. It is also represented island-wide. There are two shops in Kihei (Azeka Place II, tel. 879-3388; and Kihei Town Center, tel. 879-1919); one in the Lahaina Cannery Mall (tel. 661-5388); and another in the Wailea Shopping Village (tel. 879-3166). Check the phone book for other locations.

GREAT SNORKELING OFF MAUI BEACHES Before you even rent that snorkeling gear, you should note that you'll always be able to find a good place to snorkel somewhere on the island, but it might not always be right out your front door. Winter months near Kaanapali, Lahaina, and Olowalu can be very calm, but not far down the coast in Kapalua, the winter months can bring heavy, dangerous surf. In the Kapalua area, the summer is the best time to snorkel. The island's south side, near Wailea and Kihei, is ideal virtually year-round, except when there's heavy surf.

For safety reasons, you should always snorkel with someone else. Swim side by side so you'll always be able to see each other. When you're snorkeling, you might have to swim out a little way in order to see much of a particular reef. If you do, always be on the lookout for boats. If the water is not completely calm and you have a tendency toward motion sickness, you should pick your face up out of the water every once in a while and focus in on the horizon so you won't get seasick. Sounds rather incredible, I realize, but this actually does happen to people sometimes. Always keep the ocean floor in view. If you suddenly lose sight of it, you've gone too far and should turn back—you're not scuba diving. Don't poke your fingers into holes or crevices, and definitely don't swim into caves. Finally, always check the weather and the level of safety of a particular snorkeling site before you head out. Local dive shops should be able to provide you with the information you need. You might also check with your hotel. For more water safety tips see "Health & Insurance" in Chapter 2.

Black Rock, at the Sheraton-Maui Hotel, just off Kaanapali Beach, is a great place (especially in the winter) for beginners to snorkel. The lava formation is a favorite gathering spot for some colorful Hawaiian fish, and if you arrive on Kaanapali Beach early enough in the morning, you might have the added pleasure of seeing a green sea turtle that likes to spend the morning on the beach near Black Rock. If the surf is at all rough, don't venture out here. Also, try to keep an eye out for cliff divers.

Not only is **Kapalua Beach** one of the best sunbathing and swimming beaches in the world, but it fronts a reef, which makes it an excellent place for beginning snorkelers. All you have to do is swim out to the reef and then go left or right along the coastline looking for tropical beauties. Be careful how far you go to the right, because the water suddenly gets deep. If the surf is low, you can venture out on the north side of the bay.

Honolua Bay, just beyond the Kapalua Resort (heading away from Lahaina), is a marine sanctuary. Fish, coral, shells, seaweed, and even the sand are protected, so don't make an attempt to remove anything from the area. Winter months are not good for snorkeling; however, the spring, summer, and early fall are excellent times for snorkelers of all experience levels to explore the area around Honolua Bay. The entrance to Honolua Bay is located just beyond Mokuleia Beach. A dirt pathway leads to the water from the parking area.

Between Kapalua and Honolua bays is **Mokuleia Bay** (also part of the marine sanctuary), a challenge for the more advanced snorkeler. The winter months here, as at Kapalua and Honolua bays, are not good for snorkeling because the surf is too high. If the weather is good, you can follow one of two paths—head out along the reef, or follow the shoreline to the left.

On your way to South or Central Maui, keep an eye out for the small town of **Olowalu.** You'll see a general store and Chez Paul Restaurant. Not far from that small grouping of stores you'll see Olowalu Beach. If you swim out away from shore, you'll come to a reef that is replete with marine life.

Two beaches in Kihei, **Kamaole #2** and **Kamaole #3,** are both good for the beginner and are best snorkeled before noon. A great spot to view fish is around the rock formation that separates the two beaches. Not far along the coast from Kamaole #2 and #3 is **Ulua Beach.** Like the Kamaole beaches, Ulua Beach is separated from a neighboring beach by rock formations where snorkeling is usually good.

Continuing along the coastline in the direction of Makena, **Wailea Beach** is another fine snorkeling spot. Here you'll want to follow the shoreline as you swim.

There is also some snorkeling at **Hana Beach Park,** but if you're not sure of yourself in the ocean, you'd do well to simply avoid snorkeling there because if you go too far out, you might get caught in a strong current. It's easy to lose track of where you are when you've got your face in the water.

OFF-ISLAND SNORKELING The best and most well-known off-island snorkeling site near Maui is ✪ **Molokini Island,** a small, crescent-shaped islet that rises approximately 130 feet above the ocean's surface and, in some areas, drops below the surface to a depth of 300 feet. Molokini is one of the cinder cones (*pu'u*) in a long chain that originates along the slopes of Haleakala. Molokini and a large hill on the Wailea/Makena coastline (known as Pu'u Ola'i) are both the result of one of Haleakala's most recent volcanic eruptions. Ancient Hawaiian mythologies tell that Molokini and Pu'u Ola'i are the head and tail of a mythological lizard who dared cross the romantic path of the omnipotent Pele. You see, Pele had fallen in love with Lohiau, but Lohiau had eyes for the lizard, and when Pele learned of their marriage, she chopped said lizard in half.

In the 1900s, for some unknown reason, rabbits were introduced to Molokini. They not only survived but thrived for over 70 years, until the islet vegetation was killed off during a drought. You can't climb around on Molokini—one reason is it has been declared a Marine Life Conservation District and a State Seabird Sanctuary; the other is that during World War II the U.S. Navy used Molokini for target practice, and there may still be some unexploded bullets and bombs on the islet.

The waters here are usually calm in the morning, but when the tradewinds pick up in the afternoon, the water often becomes choppy. For that reason, excursion boats that make trips to Molokini depart in the morning hours and return to Maui by early afternoon.

Maui Classic Charters, located in Long's Center in Kihei (tel. 879-8188), offers snorkeling and snuba (see later in this chapter for more information) cruises on *Four Winds,* their glass-bottom catamaran. They'll take you to Molokini or to various coral gardens just off Maui shores. Barbecue lunch is optional, and there's an on-board waterslide. This is a good trip for the whole family. The *Lavengro,* also operated by Maui Classic Charters, is a 1926 Biloxi Schooner (the oldest on Maui), and it will also sail to Molokini for snorkeling. They have yet another ship, *Teragram,* that offers morning snorkel excursions. Maui Classic Charters sails from Lahaina and Maalaea.

Trilogy Excursions (tel. 661-4743) is by far one of Maui's best charter companies. Tours depart out of Maalaea Harbor, and on the way to Molokini, your captain will explain, in detail, the history of the island. While you're exploring the marine life around Molokini, the catamaran's crew will be laying out cheese, crackers, and beverages as a pre-lunch snack. For lunch you'll get a delicious hot meal (with real silverware, not the plastic variety). Trilogy service is truly first class.

Friendly Charters (tel. 871-0985) also makes trips to Molokini on a large catamaran. They depart from Maalaea Harbor (slip #78) and provide continental breakfast, deli lunch, beverages, snorkeling gear and instruction, as well as free use of underwater cameras.

Gemini Charters (tel. 661-2591) sets sail out of Kaanapali and Lahaina for half-day snorkel/sail excursions with hot buffet luncheons.

Other snorkel charter companies include the **Lahaina Princess** (tel. 661-8397), which in addition to Molokini, offers trips to Lanai's Turtle Reef. **Prince Kuhio** (tel. 242-8777) also departs out of Maalaea in the early morning and provides breakfast, lunch, and equipment. **PWF (Pacific Whale Foundation) Cruises** (tel. 879-8811) specializes in beginning snorkelers and departs out of Maalaea Harbor. All profits of PWF Cruises benefit marine conservation.

Prices for most snorkel cruises will run somewhere in the neighborhood of $45 to $55 without a discount, but you can often find discount coupons in magazines such as *Guide to Maui* or *Maui Gold* (which you can pick up at any brochure rack or at the Maui Visitors Bureau).

FISH (I'A) TO WATCH FOR   One of Hawaii's most commonly seen reef fish is the **saddle wrasse** (known to Hawaiians as *hinalea lauwili*). It has a purple head and a wide orange stripe around its green body. There are many members of the wrasse family, and though they are not considered good eating fish, early Hawaiians often enjoyed them for dessert. It is also known that these types of fish were frequently offered as sacrifices to the gods in a plea for fertility. A particular variety, known as the *hinalea'aki lolo*, was thought to cure mental instability if eaten. Literally translated, *'aki lolo* means "to heal brains."

The **raccoon butterfly fish** (*kikakapu kapuhili*) is also frequently seen by Maui snorkelers. There are actually 20 different varieties of the butterfly fish, and their predominant coloring is yellow. The raccoon butterfly fish has a black band over the eye, followed by a white band, with several more wide black bands swirling outward and upward toward the fish's back. When viewed at a distance, they do bear a striking resemblance to a raccoon. The **rainbow butterfly** is also common; it can be differentiated by its squarish body, single black stripe through the eye, and teardrop black spot at the center of its back that looks like another eye (to fool predators).

The **convict tang** (or *manini*) gets its name from the evenly spaced black stripes that run the width of its body. You're almost certainly guaranteed to see a school of manini during one of your snorkeling adventures. They typically stay in schools that range from 6 to more than 100 fish. If you see a larger school swimming along a reef, you'll be hooked on this sport for life.

SNUBA

Snuba is a relatively new addition to the water-sports scene. Basically, it combines the freedom and ease of snorkeling with the diving capacity of scuba. The real difference between snuba and scuba is that you won't be carrying your air tanks on your back. They'll be sitting on a "sea sled," to which your breathing apparatus and, consequently you are attached. As you swim, the sled follows you along. Snuba is a good interim step for people who love snorkeling but are afraid to try scuba diving. Most snuba gear allows you to dive to approximately 20 feet.

Maui Classic Charters (tel. 879-8188) runs snuba expeditions. Children under 12 will not be permitted to participate. **UFO Parasail** (tel. 661-7UFO) also offers snuba. Call for details.

SURFING

If you've never surfed before, but you think it looks easy when you watch the locals do it, don't get the idea that you can get out there with them and hang ten. They *do* make it look easy, but in reality, surfing is extremely difficult and requires a lot of practice. No matter what your experience level, you should make arrangements to take some lessons while you're on Maui. The waves are very different here, so it couldn't hurt to get a few pointers.

Try setting up an appointment to take lessons with **Nancy Emerson** (tel. 244-7873). She's a professional surfer who has been winning competitions since she was just a teenager. She's also been in several movies, including *Joe Versus the Volcano.* In her lessons, Emerson places a great deal of emphasis on "water safety and ocean awareness." Soft surfboards, just in case you get hit in the head, are just one of the precautionary measures she employs. Sign up for one-, two-, five-hour, all day, or three- or five-day classes.

Andrea Thomas' Maui Surfing School (tel. 875-0625) guarantees that you'll be standing on your board (in the water, of course) in one lesson, or they'll refund your money. Classes are small, and they specialize in "beginners and cowards." Reservations for advanced instruction and adventure (Thomas calls them Surf-aris) can be arranged.

SWIMMING

Before you go swimming anywhere, be sure to read the ocean safety information in "Health & Insurance," in Chapter 2. If you like freshwater swimming, just about every hotel or condominium complex has a swimming pool. Many of them have more than one, like the **Grand Wailea,** which has a 20,000-foot action pool in addition to its others. The **Hyatt** and the **Westin Hotel** in Kaanapali both also have action pools. The beaches on Maui are almost all excellent for swimming. You should, however, be aware of the fact that surf is high on one side of the island at one time of the year and not another. If you don't want to have to drive to a different hotel to swim at the beach, you should plan accordingly.

In the winter, surf on the Lahaina side of the island is low. However, just a few miles down the road at Kapalua, the surf will be high and not ideal for swimming. Surf at Kapalua is low in the summer months, but the beaches are generally swimmable from April to October. Kihei, Wailea, and Makena are generally good year-round, except for short periods of heavy surf and during Kona storms. Beach swimming in Hana is best during the summer months also. All the beaches on Maui are public, so you shouldn't feel any qualms about going down a dirt road somewhere to get to the beach, or about parking your car in one of the resorts and dragging your family through the hotel to get to one of the nicer beaches.

WHALE WATCHING

Every year humpback whales make the journey from Alaska to Hawaii to mate and give birth. Whale calves may gain up to 100 pounds a day from the nutrients in their mothers' milk, even though the adult whales don't eat at all during their stay in Hawaiian waters. Since the devastation wreaked on the whale population by the whaling industry (which began in the early 1800s), whales have been struggling to increase their numbers, but little progress is being made. Today there are all sorts of regulations in place to protect the whales that winter off Maui's shores, and they are strictly enforced. The use of jet skis and motorboats close to shore has been prohibited during whale season, and the impact has been enormous. The humpbacks now come even closer to shore than ever, and are part of the Maui seascape every year between mid-December and mid-May. You really don't need to go on a tour to watch whales during Maui's whale season because they swim so close to shore, but if you want to get that much closer, you can make a reservation on a whale-watching excursion vessel. Try to make reservations well in advance because space is limited.

The **Pacific Whale Foundation** (tel. 879-8811 or toll free 800/WHALE-1-1) is an environmental organization that has been at the forefront of whale research since the mid-1970s. If you take one of their tours (all proceeds go to benefit marine life conservation), you'll be guaranteed whale sightings, and you'll get to hear the song of the humpbacks on PWF's hydrophones. The cost for whale-watch cruises is $27.50 for adults, $15 for children ages 3 to 12.

Other whale-watching excursions are offered by **Windjammer Cruises** (tel. 661-8600), **UFO Whale Express** (tel. 661-7836), and **Island Marine Activities, Inc.** (tel. 661-8397). Prices vary from one company to the next, but average about $30 for adults and $16 for children.

WINDSURFING

Your best bet for windsurfing lessons is **Hawaiian Island Windsurfing** (460 Dairy Rd., Kahului, tel. 871-4981, or toll free 800/231-6958). They've been renting boards to Maui windsurfers of all levels for over 10 years. If you're a beginner, you can sign up for lessons with Hawaiian Island Windsurfing. There is also instruction available for more advanced sailors, which may include (for an extra $5 per lesson) a videotape and instant replay critique. Classes are small. Three hours of instruction (including equipment) runs about $60. If you want to book a full Hawaiian windsurfing vacation, Hawaiian Island Windsurfing also offers a seven-night package that includes a room, rental car with A/C and unlimited mileage, and a board and rig. Prices for two start at $470 a week and run up to over $650 a week.

The **Maui Windsurf Company** (520 Keolani Place [Airport Rd.], Kahului, HI 96732, tel. 877-4816 or toll free 800/872-0999) also offers semiprivate (maximum four people) lessons to sailors of all experience levels. The cost for 2½ hours is about $60. Three- and five-day lesson packages will run you about $165 and $265. Private lessons are available.

2. LAND SPORTS

BIKING

It's easy to get around Maui by bicycle. You can either rent your own (see Chapter 4, "Getting Around," for information on where to rent bikes) or take a bicycle tour. There are several options.

Chris' Bike Adventures (tel. 871-BIKE) offers tours all over Maui, through eucalyptus forests, down Haleakala, and Upcountry to Tedeschi Vineyards. Chris' will even customize tours on Maui as well as Lanai or Molokai. You'll be picked up in the morning, served breakfast (and lunch later in the day), and you needn't worry about being too slow or too fast—you can bike at your own pace.

Mountain Riders (tel. 242-9739) also offers a variety of tours. You can take guided, self-guided, or custom tours. You might choose to bike down the slopes of Haleakala, or perhaps you'd rather try riding from Lahaina to Wailea, stopping to snorkel and sunbathe along the way. All accessories, including helmets, gloves, and windbreakers (for the cold air on the crater), are provided by Mountain Riders.

Maui Downhill (tel. 871-2155) specializes in tours that take you down the slopes of Haleakala. It's 38 miles of downhill riding with only 400 yards of pedaling, so even the laziest among us will have a pleasurable experience. Maui Downhill requests that bikers be of novice or expert level—they don't supply bikes with training wheels. All bikers must be 12 years or older, and no one under 5 feet will be allowed to ride.

Cruiser Bob's (tel. 579-8444) also specializes in downhill tours of Haleakala and claims to have "spent big bucks developing MegaBRAKES," which you will be using most of the way down the volcano. You'll be supplied with full face helmets, windbreakers, pants, and gloves, and Cruiser Bob's also offers hotel and condo pickups and dining at Kula Lodge (see Chapter 6 for full listing).

GOLF

If you've come to Maui to golf, you won't be disappointed. In fact, the number of golf courses on Maui is almost inconceivable. Each of the resort areas (Kapalua, Kaanapali, Wailea, and Makena) has at least two courses of its own, and there are a few other courses scattered around the island. Greens fees for most of the resort golf courses will run you about $110.

Kaanapali's **North Course,** designed by Robert Trent Jones Sr., has hosted numerous golf events, including the Canada Cup, the Women's Kemper Open, and the Kaanapali Senior Classic. Bing Crosby played in the course's first foursome when it opened in 1962. The course is par 72. The **South Course,** par 72, was designed by Arthur Jack Snyder, and with narrower fairways and smaller greens, it's a challenge to a golfer of any experience level. For information on the Kaanapali courses, write or call, Royal Kaanapali Golf Courses, Kaanapali Beach Resort, Kaanapali Parkway, Lahaina, Maui, HI 96761, tel. 808/661-3691.

The **Kapalua Golf Club** has three courses from which to choose. The Bay Course is a par-72 Arnold Palmer design. They call the greens on this one "forgiving," but if you lose a ball to the water on holes 4 and 5, you'll be watching it drop off a black lava peninsula. Ocean vistas can be enjoyed from virtually every hole on the course. The **Village Course,** a mountain course, was also designed by Arnold Palmer (par 71), and it has six uphill and nine downhill holes. It's a challenge to players of all levels, and in addition to panoramic views of Molokai and Lanai, golfers will be surrounded by eucalyptus trees and Cook pines (planted in the 1920s). The **Plantation Course,** designed by Bill Coore and Ben Crenshaw (par 73), is yet another distinctive Kapalua course. The vegetation is low here, but the valleys are deep and challenging. For more information, write or call The Golf Club, 300 Kapalua Dr., Lahaina, Maui, HI 96761, tel. 808/669-8044.

There are now three unique golf courses in the Wailea Resort. Opened in the 1970s, the **Blue Course** was Wailea's first. Designed by Arthur Jack Snyder, it's a par-72 course that stretches over 6,700 yards of mountain slopes and is dotted with fragrant plumeria and colorful bougainvillea and hibiscus. One of the Blue Course's predominant features is long, wide fairways, ideal for the golfer who hits long, straight shots. Don't be fooled, however; the Blue Course offers challenges in the form of four lakes and 74 bunkers. Wailea's **Orange Course** is being redesigned as this book goes to press, but by publication all renovations should be complete. Plans are that the Orange Course will have fewer trees so no holes will be blind. A large volcanic cinder cone (Pu'u O Lai) along with neighboring islands is the view that will greet players on the course's last hole. The newest addition to the Wailea golf scene is the spectacular **Gold Course.** Opened in late 1994, the Gold Course is located adjacent to the Orange Course—36 holes of uninterrupted golf. Robert Trent Jones Jr. designed this course with its 200-foot elevation change from top to bottom and gorgeous ocean views. For more information, write or call the Wailea Resort Co., 161 Wailea Ike Place, Wailea, Maui, HI 96753, tel. 879-4465.

Wailea's neighbor, **Makena Resort,** offers two golf courses. Together the courses cover 1,800 acres. Both challenging par-72 courses were designed by Robert Trent Jones Jr. and offer ocean views. For more information, call or write the resort (5415 Makena Alanui, Kihei, HI 96753, tel. 879-3344).

Other island golf courses include **Pukalani Country Club Golf Course,** 360 Pukalani St., Pukalani, HI 96768 (tel. 572-1314); and **Silversword Golf Course,** 1345 Piilani Hwy., Kihei, HI 96753 (tel. 874-0777). These courses are not associated with the resorts, so greens fees might be slightly lower. You might not be able to golf on certain days of the week and at certain times, so call ahead for details.

HIKING & CAMPING

Maui is a hikers' paradise. There are marked hiking trails all over the island, and you can either opt to hike on your own, or take guided tours. If guided tours are more your speed, call or write Ken Schmitt of **Hike Maui,** P.O. Box 330969, Kahului, Maui, HI 96733 (tel. 879-5270). He's a longtime Maui resident who specializes in the natural history and geology of Maui. He leads group tours (small) on a variety of different hikes, ranging in difficulty from very leisurely to veritable treks. Prices vary ($70 to $110) according to the tour, but you'll definitely get your money's worth. Ken will even give you helpful hints for camping on Maui.

If you are planning on camping during your stay on Maui, you should know that camping is permitted in two state parks, two county parks, and two federal parks. For state parks you are required to obtain a permit from the Division of State Parks (no charge) before you arrive. For information on obtaining a state park permit, call or write, **Division of State Parks,** 54 South High St., Wailuku, Maui, HI 96793, tel. 243-5354. When you write, you must specify the park where you intend to camp (either **Polipoli** or **Waianapanapa**) and the length of your stay (maximum of five nights). You also have to supply identification numbers of all the people in your camping party (passport number, Social Security number, or driver's license number).

If you want to camp in **H. A. Baldwin Park** or **Rainbow Park** (both in Paia), you should write the **Department of Parks and Recreation,** County of Maui, 1580 Kaahumanu Ave., Wailuku, Maui, HI 96793 (tel. 243-7389). Maximum length of stay in any one campground is three nights.

It is not necessary to obtain a permit for camping in **Hosmer Grove** and **Kipahulu Campground.** Both are federal parks on the slopes of Haleakala. The maximum length of stay is three nights. If you want to camp within **Haleakala Crater,** call or write in advance for details to Haleakala Camping Information, P.O. Box 369, Makawao, HI 96768 (tel. 572-9306).

Note: For Haleakala weather information, call 572-7749 before heading out.

HORSEBACK RIDING

A great way to see Maui is on horseback. You're able to cover more ground in a shorter period of time than you would if you were hiking, and educated, experienced tour guides will take you to remote locations where you'll be able to swim, picnic, or ride off into the sunset. Several companies on Maui offer a variety of horseback adventures to Maui visitors.

Rainbow Ranch, P.O. Box 10066, Lahaina, Maui, HI 96761 (tel. 669-4991 or 669-4702), located not far from Kaanapali and Kapalua, works primarily with small groups of people, all with similar ability levels, so you won't ever feel like you're being left in the dust. The Introductory Ride ($30/person) is a one-hour ride designed specifically for beginners. Before you ride, your guide will give you some quick pointers on horseback riding, and then you're off to see beautiful views of Molokai and Lanai from the lush tropical greenery of the West Maui Mountains. The Pineapple Ride ($50/person) takes riders through a pineapple plantation and includes pineapple tasting, tropical fruit drink refreshments, and other taste sensations. The ride lasts approximately 2½ hours. Advanced riders will be challenged here as well—there are three 2- to 3½-hour rides from which experienced riders may choose.

Adventures on Horseback, P.O. Box 1771, Makawao, Maui, HI 96768 (tel. 242-7445 or 572-6211) will take groups of no more than six to some of Maui's unspoiled areas. Each of the rides is different, but you're guaranteed to see a different side of Maui than most tourists do, and you'll no doubt get the chance to swim beneath a waterfall. Morning refreshments and lunch (sandwiches, fruits, vegetables, and beverages) are provided on all excursions. Each ride takes approximately 5 hours, and the rate per person is $130.

Pony Express Tours, P.O. Box 535, Kula, Maui, HI 96790 (tel. 667-2200) takes riders on tours through Haleakala Ranch and to Haleakala Crater. You'll "go places only horses can go," and you'll see things you might not have seen otherwise. There's a one-hour ride available for those who have made the drive up Haleakala to see the sun rise and would like to see a little more but want to be back to the hotel in time for lunch. It begins at 9am and costs only $30. The longer Paniolo Ride takes 3 hours ($50) and allows riders to explore much more of Haleakala Ranch. If you're more interested in taking a ride into the volcano, Pony Express can take you there as well. The cost is $110 per person, and it's a 3½- to 4-hour, 7½-mile, round-trip ride. Riders of all experience levels are welcome. Only 10 riders go into the volcano at a time, and throughout the trip, experienced guides narrate about flora, fauna, and Hawaiian mythology and legend. A 7½-hour ride takes adventurous (and hardy) souls right to the crater floor. Along the way, riders will see, among other things, the nene goose and Pele's Paint Pot. Lunch at Kapalaoa Cabin, a cabin located 6 miles into the crater, is included in the $130 fee.

Makena Stables, Old Makena Rd., Makena, Maui, HI (tel. 879-0244) offers a 3- to 4-hour ride during which you'll get to see a 200-year-old lava flow, the Ahihi-Kinau Nature Reserve, and scores of island plants and animals. Only one ride a day is scheduled at Makena Stables, so you can be sure the horses are well rested. Makena Stables also organizes a ride to the Tedeschi Vineyards where riders will be treated to a personalized tour of the winery.

All of these companies have a weight limit (somewhere in the neighborhood of 220 to 250 pounds), and all require that you wear long pants (jeans are probably best) and closed-toe shoes. I would recommend that you also carry a sweater—mountain temperatures are often significantly lower than beach temperatures. Horseback riding companies also have age limits for children. Some don't want any younger than 16; others will take children age 12 and up. Call ahead for information.

HUNTING

Believe it or not, you can hunt on Maui. You must apply for a nonresident hunting license ($20) from the **Division of Conservation and Resources Enforcement.** Call the Maui office at 808/243-5414 for information on obtaining licenses. In order to get that license, you must apply for a "Letter of Exemption" or complete an approved hunter education/safety course before applying for the license. If you write (or call) the **Division of Conservation and Resources Enforcement, Hunter Education Program,** 1130 N. Nimitz Hwy., Suite A-230, Honolulu, HI 96816 (tel. 808/543-2710), they will give you information regarding the education program or exemption qualifications. Maui Sporting Goods (92 N. Market St., Wailuku, Maui, HI 96793, tel. 808/244-0011) is qualified to issue hunting licenses, and they also have a good selection of equipment available.

Hunting rules are constantly changing, so if you plan to hunt, I would recommend that when you call the above agencies, you ask for Forestry & Wildlife Title 13, Chapter 122, if you're interested in game-bird hunting, Forestry & Wildlife Title 13, Chapter 123, for big-game hunting.

GAME ANIMALS None of the game animals you'll find on Maui today are native to the islands—they were all introduced at one time or another. You've got to have a strong will and a strong spirit (not to mention fast feet) to hunt Maui's feral pigs. I've been told that they're hunted using dogs and spears. Feral pigs have contributed to the annihilation of many species of plant life and often muddy the waters of Hana's lovely pools. If you're planning on hunting feral pigs, make sure you know what you're doing—they're extremely dangerous.

There are axis deer (introduced from India) on Maui, as well as Molokai and Lanai, but you can't hunt them on Maui. Hunting axis deer on Molokai and Lanai is permitted, however. Axis deer are light brown and have beautiful white spots on their backs.

If you're a game-bird hunter, Maui has its share of pheasants (both ring-necked and green), quail, and doves. For a list of birds you can hunt, contact the Department of Parks & Recreation, District Office & Permits (tel. 243-7389).

PARASAILING

Always wanted to parasail? Well, now's your chance, and I guarantee it's an experience you'll never forget. How could anyone forget being suspended hundreds of feet above the earth? By the time you're on the boat, you'll probably wonder why on earth you signed up to do this in the first place. But after you've been harnessed into the chute and it's too late to say no, you'll forget your fear. These days they launch you right off the boat. In one quick roar of the motorboat's engine you're off and flying, legs dangling, and then suddenly everything becomes quiet, and you feel like you can see into forever. It's over before you want it to be, and when the motorboat cuts its engine, you drift slowly toward the earth and land in the water.

There are several reputable parasail companies on Maui. If this sounds like something you want to do, try calling **Kaanapali Parasail** (tel. 669-6555) or **UFO Parasail** (tel. 661-7UFO). Rides typically last for approximately 15 minutes, give or take a couple of minutes. Both companies operate out of Kaanapali and will pick you up right on the beach.

TENNIS

There are tennis facilities all over Maui. As with the golf courses, if you're staying in one of the resorts, you'll have access to any number of tennis courts. Daily and hourly fees vary from place to place, but you can be sure that if you're a resort guest, rates on those courts will be lower.

In addition to the facilities listed above, all of which have six or more courts, many of the other hotels and condominium properties have their own courts. Some of them may not even charge for court time.

Here's a list of the major island resort tennis facilities: **Kapalua Tennis Garden,** Kapalua, Maui, HI 96761, tel. 669-5677; **Village Tennis Center,** Ritz-Carlton, Kapalua, Maui, HI 96761, tel. 665-0112; **Makena Tennis Club,** 5415 Makena Alanui, Kihei, HI 96753, tel. 879-8777; **Royal Lahaina Tennis Ranch,** 2780 Kekaa Dr., Lahaina, Maui, HI 96761, tel. 661-2092; **Wailea Tennis Club,** Wailea Resort, 131 Wailea Ike Place, tel. 879-1958.

Access to public courts is on a first-come/first-serve basis. There are six lighted courts in **Wells Park** (at Wells and Market streets) in Wailuku; four lighted courts at the **War Memorial Gym** off Kaahumanu Avenue in Kahului; **Malu'uluolele Park,** at 520 Front St., also has four lighted courts. **Lahaina Civic Center,** off Honoapiilani Highway (near the main post office across from Wahikuli Beach), has five lighted courts; **Kalama Park,** off South Kihei Road, has four; and **Maui Sunset,** off South Kihei Road, has four courts (none lighted) as well.

APPENDIX

A. HAWAIIAN VOCABULARY

The first thing you're likely to notice about the Hawaiian language is that it seems to use the same letters over and over again in the same word. That's because the Hawaiian alphabet consists of only seven consonants (H, K, L, M, N, P, and W) as well as the five vowels. You'll be confronted by scores of repeating vowels and consonants, and virtually all street names will look the same to you in the beginning. Pronunciation is actually a lot easier than it seems. Just pronounce every letter and you'll be on the right track. If you see two vowels side by side, like o'o or a'a, pronounce them both, like this: "oh-oh" or "ah-ah." Don't worry if you're not pronouncing something correctly at first—it takes a while. Listen to the way the locals say it. You'll get the hang of it!

WORDS

ENGLISH	HAWAIIAN	PRONUNCIATION
rough lava	a'a	*ah*-ah
sharp gravel	a'a' pu'upu'u	*ah*-ah-poo-oo-poo-oo
yes	ae	*ah*-ee
Why?	aha	*ah*-ha
friends	aikane	eye-*kah*-nay
road	ala	*al*-lah
welcome, farewell, love	aloha	ah-*low*-hah
no	aole	ah-*oh*-lay
pineapple	halakahiki	hah-lah-kah-*hee*-kee
school	halau	*hah*-lau
house	hale	*hah*-lay
work	hana	*hah*-nah
Caucasian	haole	*how*-lay
half	hapa	*hah*-pah
happiness	haouli	how-*oh*-lee
ancient temple	heiau	hey-*ee*-au
to walk	hele	*hey*-lay
to run	holo	*ho*-low
to kiss	honi	*ho*-nee
angry	huhu	*hoo*-hoo
to dance	hula	*hoo*-lah
underground luau oven	imu	*ee*-moo
priest	kahuna	kah-*hoo*-nah
sea	kai	kye
old-timer	kama'aina	kah-mah-*eye*-nah
man	kane	*kah*-nay
keep out	kapu	*kah*-poo

ENGLISH	HAWAIIAN	PRONUNCIATION
food	**kaukau**	kow-*kow*
child	**keiki**	kay-*kee*
porch	**lanai**	lah-*nye*
garland/necklace	**lei**	lay
feast	**luau**	*loo*-ow
thank you	**mahalow**	mah-*hah*-low
seaward	**makai**	mah-*kye*
toward the mountains	**mauka**	*mau*-kah
chant	**mele**	*may*-lay
coconut	**niu**	*nee*-oo
delicious	**ono**	*oh*-no
Hawaiian cowboy	**paniolo**	pah-nee-*oh*-low
finished	**pau**	pow
hors d'oeuvre	**pupu**	*poo*-poo
woman	**wahine**	wah-*hee*-nay
hurry, quickly	**wikiwiki**	wee-kee-wee-kee

PHRASES

ENGLISH	HAWAIIAN	PRONUNCIATION
Bottoms up!	**Okole maluna**	oh-*ko*-lay mah-*loo*-nah
Good evening	**Aloha ahiahi**	ah-*low*-ha ah-hee-*ah*-hee
Good morning	**Aloha kakahiaka**	ah-*low*-ha kah-kah-hee-*ah*-kah
Come and eat	**Hele mai ai**	hey-lay-*my*-eye
Many thanks	**Mahalo nui loa**	mah-*hah*-low noo-ee-*low*-ah
What is your name?	**Owai kau inoa?**	*oh*-why *kah*-oo ee-no-ah

B. GLOSSARY OF ISLAND FOODS

Bento Japanese box lunch.

Chicken luau Young taro or spinach leaves cooked with chicken and coconut milk.

Crackseed A popular Chinese confection, akin to dried, candied fruit.

Guava A slightly sour fruit that grows on mountainside trees. On Maui you will see roadside guava trees as you drive up to Hana. In the Hawaiian islands guava is used most frequently in the making of jellies and juices.

Halakahiki You're not likely to encounter anyone using this Hawaiian word to refer to pineapple, but since you'll be visiting the pineapple capital of the world on your trip to Maui, I thought you should know it.

Haupia Coconut pudding that is a traditional luau dish.

Laulau Directly translated, laulau means "wrapping" or "wrapped." As a food item, laulau is individual servings of pork, beef, or salted fish with bananas, sweet potatoes, and taro tops wrapped in a ti or banana leaf and baked in the imu (ground oven) or steamed. The term *laulau* might be used to refer to any sort of netting or wrapping.

Lilikoi Passion fruit. There are several varieties, including the purple water lemon or the purple granadilla; however, the variety that is grown commercially in the islands for the purpose of manufacturing juice (guava/passion fruit juice is very popular) is yellow and has a more pleasant taste than the purple variety.

Macadamia nuts These flavorful nuts are grown primarily on the Big Island and are in abundance on all of the islands. Dry-roasted macadamia nuts are tasty; however, you should also try them raw (you'll need a good hammer to get them open). Macadamia nut honey, made from the flower of the macadamia nut tree, has a very light flavor.

Malasadas Square, deep-fried Portuguese doughnuts, served hot and coated with sugar.

Manapuas A relative of Chinese dim sum, manapuas are steamed dumplings filled with beef, pork, or bean paste.

Maui onions Every restaurant on Maui serves these onions, which are sweeter than most varieties. They are grown Upcountry in Kula and are sometimes referred to as Kula onions.

Niu Coconut.

Papayas At breakfast you'll discover that papayas are the grapefruit of the Hawaiian islands. Most papayas are grown on the Big Island.

Pipikaula Beef jerky.

Poi Often referred to as "the Hawaiian staff of life," poi is made from cooked, mashed taro root. It's pounded until smooth and then thinned with water. There are many varieties of taro, and therefore many different kinds of poi.

Portuguese bean soup A wonderful combination of *linguica* (Portuguese sausage), beans, kale, potatoes, and various other vegetables in a beef/tomato broth.

Portuguese sweet bread A staple of the Portuguese diet, this soft, sweet bread is made with eggs and has a consistency similar to Jewish challah bread (only slightly lighter).

Saimin A very popular island dish, saimin is a soup of noodles in a clear broth with shrimp, pork, chicken, fish, and vegetables.

Sashimi Raw fish. You'll find sashimi offered on just about every Maui restaurant menu. It's a Japanese delicacy. Ahi is the fish most often used in the preparation of sashimi.

FISH

Ahi Yellowfin tuna. This fish is often used for sashimi, but it is equally delicious cut into steaks and broiled or pan seared.

Mahi mahi Dolphin fish (not actual dolphin), mahi mahi is probably one of Hawaii's best-known fish.

Ono A delicious, long, thin, mackerel-like fish. Incidentally, the Hawaiian word *ono* means "delicious."

Ulua You won't often find this fish on the menu, but if you do, you should give it a try. It's a sort of crevalle, jack, or pompano game fish.

Opakapaka Though most people will tell you that opakapaka is pink snapper, I've seen it referred to as blue snapper in many dictionaries.

ACCOMMODATIONS

Key to Abbreviations: B = Budget; E = Expensive; I = Inexpensive;
M = Moderately priced; VE = Very expensive.

Now Save Money on All Your Travels by Joining
FROMMER'S ™ TRAVEL BOOK CLUB
The World's Best Travel Guides at Membership Prices

FROMMER'S TRAVEL BOOK CLUB is your ticket to successful travel! Open up a world of travel information and simplify your travel planning when you join ranks with thousands of value-conscious travelers who are members of the FROMMER'S TRAVEL BOOK CLUB. Join today and you'll be entitled to all the privileges that come from belonging to the club that offers you travel guides for less to more than 100 destinations worldwide. Annual membership is only $25 (U.S.) or $35 (Canada and foreign).

The Advantages of Membership

1. Your choice of *three* free FROMMER'S TRAVEL GUIDES (any *two* FROMMER'S COMPREHENSIVE GUIDES, FROMMER'S $-A-DAY GUIDES, FROMMER'S WALKING TOURS *or* FROMMER'S FAMILY GUIDES—plus *one* FROMMER'S CITY GUIDE, FROMMER'S CITY $-A-DAY GUIDE *or* FROMMER'S TOURING GUIDE).
2. Your own subscription to **TRIPS AND TRAVEL** quarterly newsletter.
3. You're entitled to a **30% discount** on your order of any additional books offered by FROMMER'S TRAVEL BOOK CLUB.
4. You're offered (at a small additional fee) our **Domestic Trip-Routing Kits.**

Our quarterly newsletter **TRIPS AND TRAVEL** offers practical information on the best buys in travel, the "hottest" vacation spots, the latest travel trends, world-class events and much, much more.
Our **Domestic Trip-Routing Kits** are available for any North American destination. We'll send you a detailed map highlighting the best route to take to your destination—you can request direct or scenic routes.

Here's all you have to do to join:

Send in your membership fee of $25 ($35 Canada and foreign) with your name and address on the form below along with your selections as part of your membership package to **FROMMER'S TRAVEL BOOK CLUB, P.O. Box 473, Mt. Morris, IL 61054-0473.** Remember to check off your *three* free books.
If you would like to order additional books, please select the books you would like and send a check for the total amount (please add sales tax in the states noted below), plus $2 per book for shipping and handling ($3 per book for foreign orders) to:

FROMMER'S TRAVEL BOOK CLUB
P.O. Box 473
Mt. Morris, IL 61054-0473
(815) 734-1104

[ ] **YES.** I want to take advantage of this opportunity to join FROMMER'S TRAVEL BOOK CLUB.
[ ] **My check is enclosed.** Dollar amount enclosed_____*
(all payments in U.S. funds only)

Name_____
Address_____
City_____ State_____ Zip_____
All orders must be prepaid.

To ensure that all orders are processed efficiently, please apply sales tax in the following areas: CA, CT, FL, IL, NJ, NY, TN, WA and CANADA.

*With membership, shipping and handling will be paid by FROMMER'S TRAVEL BOOK CLUB for the three free books you select as part of your membership. Please add $2 per book for shipping and handling for any additional books purchased ($3 per book for foreign orders).

Allow 4–6 weeks for delivery. Prices of books, membership fee, and publication dates are subject to change without notice. Prices are subject to acceptance and availability.

AC1

Please Send Me the Books Checked Below:

FROMMER'S COMPREHENSIVE GUIDES
(Guides listing facilities from budget to deluxe,
with emphasis on the medium-priced)

	Retail Price	Code		Retail Price	Code
☐ Acapulco/Ixtapa/Taxco 1993–94	$15.00	C120	☐ Japan 1994–95 (Avail. 3/94)	$19.00	C144
☐ Alaska 1994–95	$17.00	C131	☐ Morocco 1992–93	$18.00	C021
☐ Arizona 1993–94	$18.00	C101	☐ Nepal 1994–95	$18.00	C126
☐ Australia 1992–93	$18.00	C002	☐ New England 1994 (Avail. 1/94)	$16.00	C137
☐ Austria 1993–94	$19.00	C119	☐ New Mexico 1993–94	$15.00	C117
☐ Bahamas 1994–95	$17.00	C121	☐ New York State 1994–95	$19.00	C133
☐ Belgium/Holland/ Luxembourg 1993–94	$18.00	C106	☐ Northwest 1994–95 (Avail. 2/94)	$17.00	C140
☐ Bermuda 1994–95	$15.00	C122	☐ Portugal 1994–95 (Avail. 2/94)	$17.00	C141
☐ Brazil 1993–94	$20.00	C111	☐ Puerto Rico 1993–94	$15.00	C103
☐ California 1994	$15.00	C134	☐ Puerto Vallarta/Manzanillo/ Guadalajara 1994–95 (Avail. 1/94)	$14.00	C028
☐ Canada 1994–95 (Avail. 4/94)	$19.00	C145	☐ Scandinavia 1993–94	$19.00	C135
☐ Caribbean 1994	$18.00	C123	☐ Scotland 1994–95 (Avail. 4/94)	$17.00	C146
☐ Carolinas/Georgia 1994–95	$17.00	C128	☐ South Pacific 1994–95 (Avail. 1/94)	$20.00	C138
☐ Colorado 1994–95 (Avail. 3/94)	$16.00	C143	☐ Spain 1993–94	$19.00	C115
☐ Cruises 1993–94	$19.00	C107	☐ Switzerland/Liechtenstein 1994–95 (Avail. 1/94)	$19.00	C139
☐ Delaware/Maryland 1994–95 (Avail. 1/94)	$15.00	C136	☐ Thailand 1992–93	$20.00	C033
☐ England 1994	$18.00	C129	☐ U.S.A. 1993–94	$19.00	C116
☐ Florida 1994	$18.00	C124	☐ Virgin Islands 1994–95	$13.00	C127
☐ France 1994–95	$20.00	C132	☐ Virginia 1994–95 (Avail. 2/94)	$14.00	C142
☐ Germany 1994	$19.00	C125	☐ Yucatán 1993–94	$18.00	C110
☐ Italy 1994	$19.00	C130			
☐ Jamaica/Barbados 1993–94	$15.00	C105			

FROMMER'S $-A-DAY GUIDES
(Guides to low-cost tourist accommodations and facilities)

	Retail Price	Code		Retail Price	Code
☐ Australia on $45 1993–94	$18.00	D102	☐ Israel on $45 1993–94	$18.00	D101
☐ Costa Rica/Guatemala/ Belize on $35 1993–94	$17.00	D108	☐ Mexico on $45 1994	$19.00	D116
☐ Eastern Europe on $30 1993–94	$18.00	D110	☐ New York on $70 1994–95 (Avail. 4/94)	$16.00	D120
☐ England on $60 1994	$18.00	D112	☐ New Zealand on $45 1993–94	$18.00	D103
☐ Europe on $50 1994	$19.00	D115	☐ Scotland/Wales on $50 1992–93	$18.00	D019
☐ Greece on $45 1993–94	$19.00	D100	☐ South America on $40 1993–94	$19.00	D109
☐ Hawaii on $75 1994	$19.00	D113	☐ Turkey on $40 1992–93	$22.00	D023
☐ India on $40 1992–93	$20.00	D010	☐ Washington, D.C. on $40 1994–95 (Avail. 2/94)	$17.00	D119
☐ Ireland on $45 1994–95 (Avail. 1/94)	$17.00	D117			

FROMMER'S CITY $-A-DAY GUIDES
(Pocket-size guides to low-cost tourist accommodations
and facilities)

	Retail Price	Code		Retail Price	Code
☐ Berlin on $40 1994–95	$12.00	D111	☐ Madrid on $50 1994–95 (Avail. 1/94)	$13.00	D118
☐ Copenhagen on $50 1992–93	$12.00	D003	☐ Paris on $50 1994–95	$12.00	D117
☐ London on $45 1994–95	$12.00	D114	☐ Stockholm on $50 1992–93	$13.00	D022

FROMMER'S WALKING TOURS
(With routes and detailed maps, these companion guides point out the places and pleasures that make a city unique)

	Retail Price	Code		Retail Price	Code
☐ Berlin	$12.00	W100	☐ Paris	$12.00	W103
☐ London	$12.00	W101	☐ San Francisco	$12.00	W104
☐ New York	$12.00	W102	☐ Washington, D.C.	$12.00	W105

FROMMER'S TOURING GUIDES
(Color-illustrated guides that include walking tours, cultural and historic sights, and practical information)

	Retail Price	Code		Retail Price	Code
☐ Amsterdam	$11.00	T001	☐ New York	$11.00	T008
☐ Barcelona	$14.00	T015	☐ Rome	$11.00	T010
☐ Brazil	$11.00	T003	☐ Scotland	$10.00	T011
☐ Florence	$ 9.00	T005	☐ Sicily	$15.00	T017
☐ Hong Kong/Singapore/			☐ Tokyo	$15.00	T016
Macau	$11.00	T006	☐ Turkey	$11.00	T013
☐ Kenya	$14.00	T018	☐ Venice	$ 9.00	T014
☐ London	$13.00	T007			

FROMMER'S FAMILY GUIDES

	Retail Price	Code		Retail Price	Code
☐ California with Kids	$18.00	F100	☐ San Francisco with Kids (Avail. 4/94)	$17.00	F104
☐ Los Angeles with Kids (Avail. 4/94)	$17.00	F103	☐ Washington, D.C. with Kids (Avail. 2/94)	$17.00	F102
☐ New York City with Kids (Avail. 2/94)	$18.00	F101			

FROMMER'S CITY GUIDES
(Pocket-size guides to sightseeing and tourist accommodations and facilities in all price ranges)

	Retail Price	Code		Retail Price	Code
☐ Amsterdam 1993–94	$13.00	S110	☐ Montréal/Québec City 1993–94	$13.00	S125
☐ Athens 1993–94	$13.00	S114	☐ Nashville/Memphis 1994–95 (Avail. 4/94)	$13.00	S141
☐ Atlanta 1993–94	$13.00	S112	☐ New Orleans 1993–94	$13.00	S103
☐ Atlantic City/Cape May 1993–94	$13.00	S130	☐ New York 1994 (Avail. 1/94)	$13.00	S138
☐ Bangkok 1992–93	$13.00	S005	☐ Orlando 1994	$13.00	S135
☐ Barcelona/Majorca/Minorca/ Ibiza 1993–94	$13.00	S115	☐ Paris 1993–94	$13.00	S109
☐ Berlin 1993–94	$13.00	S116	☐ Philadelphia 1993–94	$13.00	S113
☐ Boston 1993–94	$13.00	S117	☐ San Diego 1993–94	$13.00	S107
☐ Budapest 1994–95 (Avail. 2/94)	$13.00	S139	☐ San Francisco 1994	$13.00	S133
☐ Chicago 1993–94	$13.00	S122	☐ Santa Fe/Taos/ Albuquerque 1993–94	$13.00	S108
☐ Denver/Boulder/Colorado Springs 1993–94	$13.00	S131	☐ Seattle/Portland 1994–95	$13.00	S137
☐ Dublin 1993–94	$13.00	S128	☐ St. Louis/Kansas City 1993–94	$13.00	S127
☐ Hong Kong 1994–95 (Avail. 4/94)	$13.00	S140	☐ Sydney 1993–94	$13.00	S129
☐ Honolulu/Oahu 1994	$13.00	S134	☐ Tampa/St. Petersburg 1993–94	$13.00	S105
☐ Las Vegas 1993–94	$13.00	S121	☐ Tokyo 1992–93	$13.00	S039
☐ London 1994	$13.00	S132	☐ Toronto 1993–94	$13.00	S126
☐ Los Angeles 1993–94	$13.00	S123	☐ Vancouver/Victoria 1994–95 (Avail. 1/94)	$13.00	S142
☐ Madrid/Costa del Sol 1993–94	$13.00	S124	☐ Washington, D.C. 1994 (Avail. 1/94)	$13.00	S136
☐ Miami 1993–94	$13.00	S118			
☐ Minneapolis/St. Paul 1993–94	$13.00	S119			

SPECIAL EDITIONS

	Retail Price	Code		Retail Price	Code
☐ Bed & Breakfast Southwest	$16.00	P100	☐ Caribbean Hideaways	$16.00	P103
☐ Bed & Breakfast Great American Cities (Avail. 1/94)	$16.00	P104	☐ National Park Guide 1994 (avail. 3/94)	$16.00	P105
			☐ Where to Stay U.S.A.	$15.00	P102

Please note: if the availability of a book is several months away, we may have back issues of guides to that particular destination. Call customer service at (815) 734-1104.